ARCHAEOLOGIES OF THE BRITISH

The One World Archaeology (OWA) series stems from conferences organized by the World Archaeological Congress (WAC), an international non-profit making organization, which provides a forum of debate for anyone who is genuinely interested in or has a concern for the past. All editors and contributors to the OWA series waive any fees they might normally receive from a publisher. Instead all royalties from the series are received by WAC Charitable Company to help the wider work of the World Archaeological Congress. The sale of OWA volumes provides the means for less advantaged colleagues to attend World Archaeological Congress conferences, thereby enabling them to contribute to the development of the academic debate surrounding the study of the past.

The World Archaeological Congress would like to take this opportunity to thank all editors and contributors for helping the development of world archaeology in this way.

D1566476

ONE WORLD ARCHAEOLOGY

Series Editor: (Volumes 1–37): Peter J. Ucko
Academic Series Editors (Volume 38 onwards): Martin Hall and Julian Thomas
Executive Series Editor (Volume 38 onwards): Peter Stone

ARCHAEOLOGIES OF THE BRITISH

Explorations of identity in Great Britain
and its colonies 1600–1945

Edited by

Susan Lawrence

LONDON AND NEW YORK

First published 2003 by Routledge
2 Park Square, Milton Park, Abingdon, Oxon, OX14 4RN

Simultaneously published in the USA and Canada
by Routledge
270 Madison Ave, New York NY 10016

Routledge is an imprint of the Taylor & Francis Group

Transferred to Digital Printing 2010

Typeset in Bembo by
Florence Production Ltd, Stoodleigh, Devon

British Library Cataloguing in Publication Data
A catalogue record for this book is available from the
British Library

Library of Congress Cataloging in Publication Data
Archaeologies of the British : explorations of identity in the
United Kingdom and its colonies, 1600–1945 / edited by
Susan Lawrence.
    p. cm. – (One world archaeology ; 46)
    Includes bibliographical references and index.
    1. Great Britain–Antiquities. 2. Archaeology and history–Great
Britain. 3. Excavations (Archaeology)–Great Britain. 4. Group
identity–Great Britain–Historiography. 5. National characteris-
tics, British–Historiography. 6. Excavations (Archaeology)–Great
Britain–Colonies. 7. Archaeology and history–Great Britain–
Colonies. 8. British–Foreign countries–Historiography.
9. Great Britain–Colonies–Antiquities. I. Lawrence, Susan,
1966– II. Series.

DA90 .A67 2003
930.1'07'2041–dc21   2002031941

ISBN10: 0–415–21700–8 (hbk)
ISBN10: 0–415–58905–3 (pbk)

ISBN13: 978–0–415–21700–2 (hbk)
ISBN13: 978–0–415–58905–5 (pbk)

Contents

Part II
The Second Empire: 1800–1945

Figures

Tables

Contributors

Mary C. Beaudry, Department of Archaeology, Boston University, Boston USA

Alasdair Brooks, Archaeology, La Trobe University, Melbourne, Australia

C. Pamela Graves, Department of Archaeology, University of Durham, UK

Adrian Green, Department of History, University of Durham, UK

Matthew Johnson, Department of Archaeology, University of Cambridge, UK

Eric Klingelhofer, Department of History, Mercer University, Macon, Georgia USA

Jane Klose, Historical Archaeology Research Group, Department of Archaeology, University of Cape Town, Cape Town, South Africa

Claude Lafleur, CELAT, University Laval, Québec, QC Canada

Susan Lawrence, Archaeology, La Trobe University, Melbourne, Australia

Roger Leech, Department of Archaeology, University of Southampton, UK

Jane Lydon, Centre for Australian Indigenous Studies, Monash University, Melbourne, Australia

Antonia Malan, Historical Archaeology Research Group, Department of Archaeology, University of Cape Town, Cape Town, South Africa

Peter Merrington, English University of the Western Cape, Bellville, South Africa

Harold Mytum, Department of Archaeology, University of York, UK

Kylie Seretis, Deparmtne of Archaeology, University of Glasgow, UK

Ron Southern, Ballarat, Victoria Australia

James Symonds, ARCUS, Research School of Archaeology, University of Sheffield, Sheffield, UK

Gamini Wijesuriya, Conservation/Heritage Management Specialist, Hamilton, New Zealand

Foreword

One World Archaeology is dedicated to exploring new themes, theories and applications in archaeology from around the world. The series of edited volumes began with contributions that were either part of the inaugural meeting of the World Archaeological Congress in Southampton, UK in 1986 or were commissioned specifically immediately after the meeting – frequently from participants who were inspired to make the own contributions. Since then WAC has held three further major international Congresses in Barquisimeto, Venezuela (1990), New Delhi, India (1994), and Cape Town, South Africa (1999). Other, more specialized, 'Inter-Congresses' have focused on *Archaeological ethics and the treatment of the dead* (Vermillion, USA, 1989), *Urban origins in Africa* (Mombasa, Kenya, 1993), *The destruction and restoration of cultural property* (Brač, Croatia, 1998), *Theory in Latin American archaeology* (Olavaria, Argentina, 2000) and *The African Diaspora* (Curaçao, Dutch West Indies, 2001). In each case these meetings have attracted a wealth of original and often inspiring work from many countries.

The result has been a set of richly varied volumes that are at the cutting edge of frequently multi-disciplinary new work. The series provides a breadth of perspective that charts the many and varied directions that contemporary archaeology is taking.

As series editors we should like to thank all editors and contributors for their hard work in producing these books. We should also like to express our thanks to Peter Ucko, inspiration behind both the World Archaeological Congress and the One World Archaeology series. Without him none of this would have happened.

Martin Hall, Cape Town, South Africa
Peter Stone, Newcastle, UK
Julian Thomas, Manchester, UK
November 2001

Introduction: archaeological perspectives on the British and their empire

SUSAN LAWRENCE

INTRODUCTION

Who are the British, and why should a whole volume in a series like One World Archaeology be devoted to them? The answer to the first question is that in fact there is no single monolithic group readily identifiable as 'the British'. At home in the United Kingdom, the British are a highly variable and complex amalgam of people of English, Scottish, Irish, Welsh and Cornish descent, as well as those of Huegenot, Flemish, Jewish, South Asian, West Indian and African ancestry, to name but a few. Abroad the British are even more varied. People who were once part of the British Empire are descendants of all the above groups as well as the indigenous people of places as disparate as Canada and the United States, Belize and Jamaica, Gibraltar and Cyprus, Sri Lanka, Pakistan, Namibia, Kenya, South Africa, Fiji and Australia. In short, the British in many ways are, or at one time have been, many peoples of the world.

That they are so diverse is also the answer to the second question – because of their ubiquity, the British have been an unproblematised category that is frequently the silent 'other' in archaeological studies that encompass identity, ethnicity, gender, race, domination and resistance, culture contact, post-colonialism, and the myriad other issues regularly addressed by the One World Archaeology Series and the World Archaeological Congresses. These publications have done much to demonstrate the complexities and poly-vocalities of archaeology within a post-colonial world. They have extended archaeological discourse to include the perspectives of people, places and periods heretofore considered marginal. It is appropriate within that context that new understandings and perspectives also be employed to re-examine the material culture of one of the modern world's most dominant cultures.

The contributors to this volume all believe that the category of 'British' is one which requires critical evaluation. British is historically contingent, constructed differently with each addition, and later loss, of territory, from the English plantation of Ireland in the sixteenth century through the unification with Scotland in the eighteenth century to Queen Victoria's claim to the title of 'Empress of India' in 1867, and the subsequent twentieth-century fragmentation of empire. British is also situationally defined – what is British in the British Isles may be muted and contested by regional and ethnic affiliations to stronger Gaelic or provincial identities. In settler contexts, English-speaking, colonial-born people of mixed Irish, English, Scottish and Welsh ancestry might claim a British identity that distinguished them from Dutch, French or indigenous residents of the same colony. At the same time, colonials not of Anglo-Celtic origin fought wars as part of British military units, joined in the celebration of the Diamond Jubilee of Queen Victoria in 1897 and were (when convenient) considered loyal British subjects. When indigenous and settler groups resisted the cultural, political and economic hegemony of the United Kingdom, it was this hydra called the British that they struggled against.

Existing historiography on the British and their empire is enormous, but archaeologists have been slower to take up the British as a subject for analysis. While there is a large and growing literature of archaeological studies of British people in the United Kingdom and abroad, particularly in North America, few of these studies are consciously or explicitly about 'the British' and few archaeologists consider their work on these sites as part of a global cultural system. Within historical archaeology in North America, South Africa and Australasia, and post-medieval and industrial archaeology in the United Kingdom, the British colonial context is generally either taken for granted or used as the basis for comparison with other empires such as the Spanish or the Dutch (South 1977; Leone and Potter 1988; Thomas 1988; Falk 1991; Hall 1992). Far less common are the studies that have considered colonial dynamics specifically within the British system (but see Birmingham 1988; Winer and Deetz 1990; Delle 1999; Symonds 1999). In other areas, such as Roman studies, Mesoamerican studies and Islamic studies, colonialism and empire have taken more central roles in archaeological inquiry (Grabar 1978; Dyson 1985; Hingley 1999; Baram and Carroll 2000). The processes of colonialism and the organisation of imperial states have been productive subjects of analysis, while empires have provided a broader context for comparison and interpretation of sites and material culture (Sinopoli 1994, 1995; Alcock et al. 2001).

Two problems which have held back any more systematic archaeological study of the British have been the lack of detailed work on recent periods in Britain itself and of comparable work from a wide range of its former provinces (Dyson 1985: 2). However, that has begun to change. In the last decade there has been an increasing awareness among archaeologists of the global scales at which historical processes have operated over the last 500 years (Deetz 1993; Schrire 1995; Johnson 1996; Orser 1996; Leone and Potter 1999). Communication between archaeologists working in different parts of the modern world has also increased markedly over this period, as evidenced by a variety of international conferences and their resultant publications, the World Archaeology Congress among them (Falk 1991; Redknap 1997; Egan and

Michael 1999; Funari *et al.* 1999; Tarlow and West 1999). The burgeoning interest in world-wide networks and the availability of new data suggests that it should now be possible to begin to consider archaeologies of the British in a more comprehensive and sophisticated manner as archaeologies of empire. Such an approach ought to contribute to general debates about imperial processes, and at the same time it has merit as providing a logical historical context for studies of areas of British settlement in which the Empire was a dominant framework of experience for much of the English-speaking world until relatively recently.

Greater communication has brought together disciplines with overlapping interests but differing histories, and in this environment discussions about fundamental principles and mutually meaningful vocabularies are perhaps inevitable. Associated with the rise in interest in the archaeology of the last 500 years has been renewed debate about the scope of archaeological inquiry and definitions of key terms such as historical archaeology, post-medieval archaeology and industrial archaeology (Clark 1987; Palmer 1990; Gaimster and Stamper 1997; Courtney 1999; Schuyler 1999; West 1999). While some have advocated unified approaches to a 'modern-world archaeology' (Deetz 1991; Orser 1996; Johnson 1999; Leone 1999; Orser 1999), there has also been criticism of the Euro-centric and presentist bias inherent in the capitalist approach and the narrowly exclusive appropriation of the term 'historical archaeology' by American scholars to mean the study of this period (Funari *et al.* 1999; Tarlow 1999; Carman 2000). To argue that there can or should be a single-world archaeology of the recent period implies that anything which does not conform to that agenda is misguided and illegitimate. It also seeks to deny the pluralism and poly-vocality which is one of the characteristics of the period. So far the lack of programatic unity has not impeded the development of valuable and thought-provoking research. Instead, it has offered room for alternative perspectives and for fluid and flexible approaches to analysis. It may be that in 'deliberately trying to resist classification' (Tarlow 1999: 264) the contributors to *The Familiar Past* might be on a more productive track.

The essays included here are global in scope and multi-scalar in approach, but they are not universalising. Rather than seeking to apply a single explanatory framework, they emphasise the variety of experience in some way touched upon by 'British'. The British Empire provides the broader scale within which the detailed local studies presented here are situated. Following Sinopoli (1994: 169) and Baram and Carroll (2000: 12), the studies explore the interplay between social developments at the scale of empire with material consequences at the local level. Within the framework of empire the authors consider a variety of themes, including status, race, ethnicity, gender, domination and resistance, consumption and trade. The themes provide new insights on archaeologies of the British Empire, while the imperial context provides a different way of thinking about the operation of these processes.

IDENTITY AND ETHNICITY

As the thread connecting all of the essays here is 'Britishness', of necessity one of the most central themes is that of identity. British is an ethnic identity which includes elements of politics and geography, citizenship and race, legal and administrative structures, moral values and cultural habits, language and tradition. At the same time, it is an identity which is not satisfactorily defined by any of these attributes (Hassam 2000: 12–16). No ethnic group can be conceived of as a bounded, static or homogenous entity, and this is certainly true of the British. Ethnicity consists of traits believed to be shared with others, but the constellation of those traits is fluid and actively negotiated according to circumstance. The stimulus for the social construction of identity is the perception and acknowledgment of difference in others. Jones (1999) uses Bourdieu's theory of habitus as a way of defining ethnic identity through praxis, and this conceptualisation may be useful for understanding Britishness. Individuals are socialised within particular cultural systems that shape and are shaped by individual practice, and these practices and beliefs, or habitus, are shared with others within the same cultural system. This shared habitus is the source from which distinctive elements are selected to form an ethnic identity that will be relevant within a given situation (Jones 1999: 225–7). As ethnicity is relationally defined against the otherness of someone else, how that 'other' is constituted will help to determine which of the available elements of habitus will be incorporated in an ethnic identity within a particular context. As the relationships to 'others' change, different elements can be deployed and the sense of ethnicity maintained.

This enacted ethnicity helps to explain the variability of Britishness which is so historically and geographically contingent. Within the British Isles and in the Empire those who might wish to be called British encountered a wide variety of 'others'. Historian Linda Colley argues that 'being British in the eighteenth century was primarily a case of being not French' (1996: 5–6). At a time when political unification was still under way in the British Isles, the almost continuous wars with France provided a valuable foil against which a new national identity could be constructed. As the French were also white and European, the elements selected as markers of difference included language, politics and religion. These identifiers were not unproblematic at home, as the Irish and the Scots were also potentially Catholic, and the Gaels did not speak English, but the external threat nevertheless provided the beginnings of some sense of common purpose. Imperial expansion overseas provided new and even more obviously different 'others'. Race, citizenship and perceived degree of 'civilisation' now had their contrasts and were added to the elements that defined Britishness (Hassam 2000: 13). The peoples of the newly defined Orient provided yet more sources of difference against which the British, as part of the Occident, could be situated (Said 1978). Race, citizenship, civilisation and even sex could be and were used to divide and exclude within the Empire as British ethnicity shifted and changed. Indigenous people and women could be legally defined as 'non-persons' and denied legal and property rights, but indigenous men remained eligible for military service. White Australians remained officially British citizens until 1949, while Aboriginal people were not legally included in the Australian census until 1967. At the same time, Indians from the sub-continent who travelled to England in the nineteenth century found themselves to be as much at 'home' as did other colonial travellers (Burton 1998: 19–20).

Changing national circumstances that produced such complex dynamics of self and other were worked out in smaller and more immediate ways for individuals. Essays here illustrate some of the ways in which Britons living in the British Isles negotiated identity. Graves explores civic ritual in seventeenth-century Newcastle, where for the merchants engaged in the North Sea trade, a Britishness that emphasised difference from their Germanic trading partners was frequently less important than the political manipulation of a regional identity that was sometimes narrowly defined as English, but at other times expanded to include the Scots labourers resident in Newcastle. Likewise, as Brooks indicates, the Welsh labourers of nineteenth-century Pembrokeshire may have had access to the broader Britishness of empire, but their own daily ethnicity was enacted in relations with English landlords. Symonds, Green and Leech also point to meaningful local identities that have corresponding expression in material culture. In these cases 'Welshness', 'Scottishness' or regional 'Englishness' may have been more meaningful than the more generic and distant 'British', but for the colonials engaged in creating the pageants described by Merrington, empire and Britishness had more immediate significance. Mytum's study of burial practises also demonstrates the geographic spread of shared cultural practices with roots in Great Britain. As Southern's essay on the Moravians reminds us, Britain has always been home to 'foreigners' as well, who had to negotiate quite different meanings of Britishness with their English neighbours.

British is an identity that is composite, consisting of the juxtaposition of English, Irish, Welsh and Scottish, rather than blending them to create something new and distinctive. There is little that could be considered 'British' that is not one of its constituent elements (Colley 1996: 5–6; Hassam 2000: 2). The most powerful symbols of the British, rather than the English, or the Scottish, or the Welsh, are the invented traditions surrounding the monarchy and the military (Hobsbawm and Ranger 1983). They are effective because they consciously draw on distinctive regional elements that have been re-contextualised to serve pan-national purposes. Thus the Prince of Wales is a member of the English royal family and the British monarchy, and the Highland regiments fight imperial wars in Africa and Asia. The more distant from the United Kingdom itself, the more generically 'British' and less regional Britishness becomes. In his survey of the history of the British Empire, historian P.J. Marshall (1996: 320) has suggested that 'those who had settled the empire generally experienced a greater sense of undifferentiated Britishness than those who stayed at home'. At times this may have been a Britishness with which they themselves identified, but in other circumstances it may have been a pan-British identity which was projected back onto those in the British Isles. As I argue in my essay here, for Australians engaged in the project of federation, Britishness encompassed all the separate ethnicities in the United Kingdom in order to serve as the other against which a new Australian identity was constructed.

Because ethnicities are not fixed they are also not mutually exclusive. It is possible for people to identify with several different ethnic groups at once and to be able to accommodate all of those ethnicities, whether they are competing or complementary. Australians, Canadians and Indians could all consider themselves to be both colonial and British at the same time (Hassam 2000: 3–4). They could also recognise their ancestry as Welsh, Scottish, Irish or Indian without surrendering either their Australian or their British allegiance. The same was true for residents of the United Kingdom, who could be both Welsh, i.e. not English, and British, i.e. not French. Material culture that was used in the service of these multiple and co-existing ethnicities could also be highly flexible, its meaning dependent on context. Goods might be of English manufacture, Staffordshire pottery, but with Welsh motifs (Brooks, this volume), or used in locally meaningful ways (Symonds, this volume), or they might be English gardens with German plants (Southern, this volume).

In a diverse society the size of the British Empire, material culture provided symbols that helped to draw together its various elements, symbols that Hassam (Hassam 2000: 18) calls 'agreed markers of Britishness'. These included the numerous statues of Queen Victoria and monuments to fallen soldiers that marked the public spaces of Empire, the flags, maps and portraits of monarchs that adorned every school room and government office and, as Merrington demonstrates, the pageants, costumes, displays and tableau, that enabled the physical enactment of Empire. By extension, these markers also defined who was excluded from Empire. Even today there are few monuments to the indigenous people who were killed defending their lands against the British invaders, and just which flags are entitled to official recognition is still hotly contested.[1] Alongside the development of overt symbols there were more subtle physical signs of Britishness. These included the private architecture of landlords and labourers such as those analysed in the essays by Klingelhoffer and Johnson. Seretis provides further evidence that it also included the public architecture of customs house, court, school and legislature and the town plans and institutions laid out to common designs by officials who spent careers in the public service moving between the colonies. In many countries the administrative structures of the public service, including archaeological heritage management, are another legacy of Britishness, as Wijesuriya demonstrates for Sri Lanka, while the manufactured goods carried between colonies by the Empire's vast trade networks, such as those described by Malan and Klose and Lafleur, provide yet further links. The essays here provide numerous examples of the multiple ways in which goods were used to unite, and also, as Southern and Lydon show, how they could be used to divide those who were considered not British.

EMPIRE

It should by now be obvious that it is impossible to discuss British identity without reference to Empire. As Johnson indicates in his essay, debates about British identity have considerable currency within modern Britain, yet in today's debates Britishness is largely confined to the British Isles themselves. This is perhaps a logical consequence of the fragmentation of the British Empire, yet it seems an exercise doomed to failure. Aside from the unavoidable fact that many of today's residents of the British Isles are people of non-Anglo-Celtic descent who have migrated from various parts of the former Empire, the historical roots of Britishness are embedded within imperial history. J. P. Marshall (1996: 319) notes that 'empire did more than reflect the Britishness of the British in Britain; it helped to focus and develop it'. Britishness grew along with the Empire, and in response to the political and social upheavals associated with it. Before the time of Empire there was no united nation which could be British, and the plantation of Ireland was the first act of overseas Empire. Britain and Britishness are themselves just as much creations of Empire as any of the English-speaking settler societies around the world. Britishness and Empire are deeply entangled and no amount of convenient post-colonial amnesia will make it otherwise. Until Britain acknowledges the legacies of Empire on its doorstep, and among its population, discussions of Welsh, Irish or Scottish self-determination and union with Europe will remain arid political debates that do not address the schisms in British society, particularly the alienation of the large non-white segment of the population derived from former colonial populations. Contemporary re-badging as 'the Atlantic Archipelago' removes British, and its associations with Empire, from the label, but it will not return the islands to a pre-imperial white past.

Any archaeological consideration of Britishness must also include the imperial other. This means the settler societies such as Canada, Australia and South Africa, whose English-speaking settlers considered themselves to be, and who were considered, British. It also includes those within the Empire who were more likely to resist Britishness, and whose Britishness was more contested, such as indigenous peoples, indentured Chinese, Indian and Pacific Islander labourers, and African slaves. All of these people, voluntarily or otherwise, were implicated in Empire and all of them, consciously or not, helped to define Britishness (Stoler 1995).

While the Empire was a valuable source of otherness against which Britishness could be defined, elements appropriated from the colonies were also incorporated into British identity, even within Britain itself. Artists and architects found inspiration in the traditions of the conquered lands, and ethnographic and archaeological objects brought back and housed in British museums reinforced notions of savagery and civilisation (Smith 1960; Thomas 1991; Bennett 1995). Experience gained during service in the colonies was drawn on by public servants when shaping policy in Britain (Hall 1994). British manufacturers were dependent on supplies of raw material such as cotton, wool, and timber, and on the markets that settler colonies provided. British expertise and factories built the railways of the world, and in return the profits built the British manufacturing industry (Freeman 1999: 241–2). British consumers relied on the colonies for their daily tea, coffee, sugar and soap (Shammas 1990).

Perspectives derived from archaeologies of empire have much to offer the archaeology of modern Britain and its former colonies. As Dyson (1985: 1) notes in the context of Roman archaeology, comparison with other parts of the empire enriches the understanding of local sites. Increased understanding of material culture and behaviour within the imperial heartland also provides invaluable assistance in interpreting the archaeology of migrants and settler societies. Until recently, the prolific research of historical archaeologists in North America has meant that English-speaking archaeologists in other settler countries have tended to rely on models developed in the United States. However, the divergence of British and American politics and society during the nineteenth century means that for archaeologists in much of the former Empire more appropriate models must be sought in Britain (Lawrence 2003).

Within Britain, considerations of Empire could help to re-invigorate the archaeology of the recent past. One of the great strengths of British archaeology has always been its links with locally based avocational associations. This has produced innumerable studies rich in the detailed local knowledge that are only possible with a lifetime's familiarity. At times however, this approach can also be a weakness because the significance of that studied is defined in the narrowest of local terms (West 1999: 6). In the context of local histories spanning six thousand years, it is easy to dismiss deposits relating to the last four or five hundred years as obstacles in the way of reaching the more interesting story beneath. From a broader perspective, however, the topmost deposits take on greater significance. Local-history approaches overlook the global significance of Britain as a world power in recent times. The deposits that are merely overburden in the search for a deeper local history are integral components of a global archaeology. This is a perspective which has particular significance within rescue archaeology, where both West (1999: 10–11) and Gould (1999) point to considerable difficulty in convincing heritage managers, developers and even rescue archaeologists themselves of the value of deposits less than 500 years old.

Within a context of imperial analysis there are a number of areas in which archaeology in Britain takes on new significance, and a variety of questions are raised. How did ways of life in the colonies differ from those in Britain itself? Were migrants better off than those who remained behind, as settler mythologies frequently assert? How did life in Britain influence the traditions that migrants took with them? To what extent can patterns in the colonies be attributed to regional or ethnic background in Britain? How were experiences of domination and resistance translated to the colonies (where in many cases the dispossessed labourers of the Celtic fringe became the capitalist landowners who in turn dispossessed Indigenous people)?

The interplay of goods and capital is crucial in this analysis. The Empire provided increased access to a range of consumer goods, such as textiles, foodstuffs, exotic plants and tobacco. How were the effects of these imports distributed across the landscape in Britain? Factories in Britain were producing goods for a world market. Making explicit links between colonial artefacts and their places of manufacture may help to refine understandings of marketing and distribution networks and consumer preference. Knowledge and experience also flowed in both directions. Sixteenth-century Ulster plantations have been cited as models for imperial expansion in the New World (Orser 1996). The relationship between frontier experiences in Africa, Australasia and the New World and the imposition of model farms on the British countryside has yet to be traced. The clearances in the Hebrides, for example, made way for methods of farming that are on the face of it very similar to methods employed in Tasmania and New South Wales at the same period (Bairstow 1988; Symonds 1999; Murray 2000).

OVERVIEW

The essays presented here are the product of two conferences, the World Archaeological Congress in Cape Town, South Africa in January 1999 and the Society for Historical Archaeology conference in Québec City, Canada in January 2000. The volume and the conference sessions that have contributed to it reflect the WAC's continued commitment to approaches that are not confined to specific periods, and which are inclusive of the recent past as well as the more ancient. The diversity of papers which is brought together in this volume is the product of a number of emerging and related trends. One trend is the increasing participation of American scholars in the global forum that the WAC provides. This increasing global awareness is also evident within the Society for Historical Archaeology, which has begun to deliberately seek to include archaeology conducted outside of North America. International content is seen more frequently within the pages of its journal, *Historical Archaeology*, and there is also significant representation from outside North America at the annual conferences, as is demonstrated by the session from which some of these essays were drawn. Finally, this volume is also indicative of the renewed dialogue between archaeologists in Britain and North America which has been evident in such events as the two joint conferences of the Society for Historical Archaeology and the Society for Post Medieval Archaeology. It is hoped that this volume, which includes essays by authors from outside both North America and Great Britain, will demonstrate the value of extending that dialogue into a conversation that includes voices from around the world. Regrettably, due to other commitments, several of the North American papers presented at the two conference sessions could not be included here. However, their publication elsewhere (e.g. Delle 1999, Praetzellis and Praetzellis 2001) ensures that the conversation begun then has continued.

The essays take up a number of themes that are current within contemporary archaeological discourse. Brooks, Graves, Green, Lafleur, Leech, and Malan and Klose address issues concerning consumption patterns and trade. Some of these, particularly Graves and Green, also consider issues of status and class, as do Johnson and Klingelhofer, and both of these themes slide into that of modernisation. Gender is not an explicit focus within the essays, but it does inform the analyses of Graves, Lawrence and Southern. The migration of people within the Empire and its consequences is considered by Seretis and Symonds, while Lawrence, Klingelhofer, Malan and Klose, and Mytum explore some of the dimensions of the settler societies that emerged. The British Empire as an institution is directly the subject of the essays by Merrington and Wijesuriya, while race and non-Anglo-Celtic responses to Empire are considered by Wijesuriya, Lydon and Southern. Concern with ethnicity and identity shape all the essays, but are most apparent in those by Brooks, Lawrence, Lydon, Mytum, Seretis, Southern and Symonds.

The essays have been organised by time period, with the first section covering the First British Empire, which ended with the loss of the 13 American colonies in the 1770s, and the second section covering the Second British Empire which arose thereafter and extended to Asia, Africa and the Pacific. This framework enables the effects of chronological change on Britishness to be made more apparent, and also enables differing but contemporary perspectives and experiences to be juxtaposed. As so many of the papers touch on interconnected networks of issues, chronological organisation also avoided the need to artificially force the essays into arbitrary thematic boxes.

CONCLUSION

Matthew Johnson has elsewhere written that 'if an archaeology of the colonial encounter is to be part of a world historical archaeology, let us give historical and cultural depth to all parties in that encounter' (1999: 29). This volume is an attempt to address that challenge. Part of a post-colonial project is to re-evaluate the colonisers as well as the colonised, and to provide more subtle, nuanced analyses of who they were, where they came from and how migration was experienced. The breadth of approaches and peoples represented here demonstrates the vibrancy that can be possible within a global framework. It also demonstrates what an unwieldy construction Britishness is, and mitigates against any simplistic attempts to depict it in stereotypical and normative terms.

Charles Orser (1996) has argued that archaeologists need to 'think globally and dig locally', and this is a strategy that has been implicitly endorsed by the approaches taken here. However, thinking globally does not need to mean thinking the same, or ignoring the small-scale and particular historical contingencies that informed daily life. Britishness has been taken as a unifying theme, but not because it is expected that it would provide analytical or interpretive unity or dictate the questions to be asked. Britishness provides a broad framework for these studies because it is a category with historical relevance to the places and times being investigated, and in some way it shaped and was shaped by the lived experience of those whose material culture we study.

NOTE

1 When Cathy Freeman, an Aboriginal athlete, spontaneously displayed both the Australian flag and the Aboriginal flag following her track and field victories at the Commonwealth Games in 1994, considerable official furor resulted, although she received wide popular support.

REFERENCES

Alcock, S., D'Altroy, T., Morrison K. and Sinopoli, C. (eds) (2001) *Empires: Perspectives from Archaeology and History*. Cambridge: Cambridge University Press.

Bairstow, D. (1988) From Carrington to Goonoo Goonoo. In J. Birmingham, D. Bairstow and A. Wilson, *Archaeology and Colonisation: Australia in the World Context*, 87–98. Sydney: Australian Society for Historical Archaeology.

Baram, U. and Carroll, L. (2000) The future of the Ottoman past. In U. Baram and L. Carroll, *A Historical Archaeology of the Ottoman Empire: Breaking New Ground*, 3–32. New York: Kluwer Academic/Plenum Publishers.

—— (2000) *A Historical Archaeology of the Ottoman Empire: Breaking New Ground*. New York, London: Kluwer Academic/Plenum Publishers.

Bennett, T. (1995) *The Birth of the Museum: History, Theory, Politics*. London: Routledge.

Birmingham, J. (1988) The refuse of empire: international perspectives on urban rubbish. In J. Birmingham, D. Bairstow and A. Wilson, *Archaeology and Colonisation: Australia in the World Context*. Sydney: Australian Society for Historical Archaeology.

Burton, A. (1998) *At the Heart of Empire: Indians and the Colonial Encounter in Late-Victorian Britain*. Berkeley: University of California Press.

Carman, J. (2000) Review, Funari, Hall and Jones: *Historical Archaeology: Back from the Edge*. *Historical Archaeology* 34(4): 122–3.

Clark, C.M. (1987) Trouble at t'mill: industrial archaeology in the 1980s. *Antiquity* 61: 169–79.

Colley, L. (1996) *Britons: Forging the Nation 1707–1837*. London: Vintage.

Courtney, P. (1999) 'Different strokes for different folks': the trans-Atlantic development of historical and post-medieval archaeology. In G. Egan and R. Michael (eds), *Old and New Worlds: Historical/Post-Medieval Archaeology Papers from the Societies' Joint Conferences at Williamsburg and London 1997 to Mark Thirty Years of Work and Achievement*. London: Oxbow Books, in association with the Society for Historical Archaeology and Society for Post-Medieval Archaeology: 1–9.

Deetz, J. (1991) Archaeological evidence of sixteenth and seventeenth century encounters. In L. Falk (ed.), *Historical Archaeology in Global Perspective*, 1–10. Washington: Smithsonian Institution Press.

—— (1993) *Flowerdew Hundred: The Archaeology of a Virginia Plantation, 1619–1864*. Charlottesville: University of Virginia Press.

Delle, J. (1999) 'A good and easy speculation': spatial conflict, collusion, and resistance in late sixteenth-century Munster, Ireland. *International Journal of Historical Archaeology* 3(1): 11–36.

Dyson, S.L. (1985) Introduction, *Comparative Studies in the Archaeology of Colonialism*, 1–7. British Archaeological Report No. 233, Oxford.

Egan, G. and Michael, R. (eds) (1999) *Old and New Worlds: Historical/Post-Medieval Archaeology Papers from the Societies' Joint Conferences at Williamsburg and London 1997 to Mark Thirty Years of Work and Achievement*. London: Oxbow Books, in association with the Society for Historical Archaeology and Society for Post-Medieval Archaeology.

Falk, L. (ed.) (1991) *Historical Archaeology in Global Perspective*. Washington: Smithsonian Institution Press.

Freeman, M. (1999) *Railways and the Victorian Imagination*. New Haven and London: Yale University Press.

Funari, P.P., Hall, M. and Jones, S. (eds) (1999) *Historical Archaeology: Back from the Edge*. One World Archaeology. London: Routledge.

—— (1999) Introduction: archaeology in history. In P.P. Funari, M. Hall and S. Jones, *Historical Archaeology: Back from the Edge*, 1–20. London: Routledge.

Gaimster, D. and Stamper, P. (1997) Introduction, *The Age of Transition: The Archaeology of English Culture 1400–1600* ix–xiii. Oxford: Oxbow Books.

Gould, S. (1999) Planning, development and social archaeology. In S. Tarlow and S. West (eds), *The Familiar Past? Archaeologies of Later Historical Britain*, 140–154. London: Routledge.

Grabar, O. (1978) Islamic archaeology, an introduction. In R. Schuyler (ed.), *Historical Archaeology: A Guide to Substantive and Theoretical Contributions* 57–60. Farmingdale, New York: Baywood.

Hall, C. (1994) Rethinking imperial histories: the Reform Act of 1867. *New Left Review* 208: 3–29.

Hall, M. (1992) Small things and the mobile, conflictual fusion of power, fear and desire. In A. Yentsch and M. Beaudry (eds), *The Art and Mystery of Historical Archaeology: Essays in Honor of James Deetz*. Ann Arbor: CRC Press.

Hassam, A. (2000) *Through Australian Eyes: Colonial Perceptions of Imperial Britain*. Melbourne: Melbourne University Press.

Hingley, R. (1999) The imperial context of Romano-British studies and proposals for a new understanding of social change. In P.P. Funari, M. Hall and S. Jones (eds), *Historical Archaeology: Back from the Edge*, 137–50. London: Routledge.

Hobsbawm, E. and Ranger, T. (eds) (1983) *The Invention of Tradition*. Cambridge: Cambridge University Press.

Johnson, M. (1996) *An Archaeology of Capitalism*. Cambridge: Basil Blackwell.

—— (1999) Historical, archaeology, capitalism. In M. Leone and P.B. Potter (eds), *Historical Archaeologies of Capitalism*, 219–32. New York: Kluwer Academic/Plenum Publishers.

—— (1999) Rethinking historical archaeology. In P.P. Funari, M. Hall and S. Jones (eds), *Historical Archaeology: Back from the Edge*, 23–35. London: Routledge.

Jones, S. (1999) Historical categories and the praxis of identity: the interpretation of ethnicity in historical archaeology. In P.P. Funari, M. Hall and S. Jones (eds), *Historical Archaeology: Back from the Edge*, 219–32. London: Routledge.

Lawrence, S. (2003) Archaeology and the nineteenth century British Empire. In S. Lawrence and G. Karskens, *Recent Archaeology in Australia and New Zealand*. Society for Historical Archaeology.

Leone, M. (1999) Setting some terms for historical archaeologies of capitalism. In M. Leone and P.B. Potter, *Historical Archaeologies of Capitalism*, 3–20. New York: Kluwer Academic/Plenum Publishers.

Leone, M. and Potter, P. (eds) (1999) *Historical Archaeologies of Capitalism*. New York: Kluwer Academic/Plenum Publishers.

—— (1988) *The Recovering of Meaning: Historical Archaeology in the Eastern United States*. Washington: Smithsonian Institution Press.

Marshall, J.P. (1996) *The Cambridge History of the British Empire*. Cambridge: Cambridge University Press.

Murray, T. (2000) Digging with documents: understanding intention and outcome in northwest Tasmania 1825–1835. In A. Anderson and T. Murray (eds), *Australian Archaeologist: Collected Papers in Honour of Jim Allen*, 145–55. Centre for Archaeological Research and the Department of Archaeology and Natural History, Australian National University, with the Department of Archaeology, La Trobe University, Canberra.

Orser, C. (1996) *A Historical Archaeology of the Modern World*. New York: Plenum Press.
—— (1999) Negotiating our 'familiar' pasts. In S. Tarlow and S. West (eds), *The Familiar Past? Archaeologies of Later Historical Britain*, 273–86. London: Routledge.
Palmer, M. (1990) Industrial archaeology: a thematic or a period discipline? *Antiquity* 64: 275–85.
Praetzellis, A. and Praetzellis, M. (2001) Mangling symbols of gentility in the Wild West: case studies in interpretive archaeology. *American Anthropologist* 103(3).
Redknap, M. (1997) *Artefacts from Wrecks*. London: Oxbow Books.
Said, E. (1978) *Orientalism*. New York: Random House.
Schrire, C. (1995) *Digging Through Darkness: Chronicles of an Archaeologist*. Johannesburg: University Press of Virginia and Witwatersrand University Press.
Schuyler, R. (1999) The centrality of post-medieval archaeology to general historical archaeology. In G. Egan and R. Michael (eds), *Old and New Worlds: Historical/Post-Medieval Archaeology Papers from the Societies' Joint Conferences at Williamsburg and London 1997 to Mark Thirty Years of Work and Achievement*, 10–16. London: Oxbow Books, in association with the Society for Historical Archaeology and Society for Post-Medieval Archaeology.
Shammas, C. (1990) *The Pre-Industrial Consumer in England and America*. Oxford: Clarendon Press.
Sinopoli, C. (1994) The archaeology of empires. *Annual Review of Anthropology* 23: 159–80.
—— (1995) The archaeology of empires: a view from South Asia. *Bulletin of the American Schools of Oriental Research* 299/300: 3–12.
Smith, B. (1960) *European Vision and the South Pacific, 1768–1850 : A Study in the History of Art and Ideas*. Oxford: Clarendon Press.
South, S. (1977) *Method and Theory in Historical Archaeology*. New York: Academic Press.
Stoler, A.L. (1995) *Race and the Education of Desire: Foucault's 'History of Sexuality' and the Colonial Order of Things*. Durham and London: Duke University Press.
Symonds, J. (1999) Toiling in the vale of tears: everyday life and resistance in South Uist, Outer Hebridges, 1760–1860. *International Journal of Historical Archaeology* 3(2): 101–22.
Tarlow, S. (1999) Strangely familiar. In S. Tarlow and S. West (eds), *The Familiar Past? Archaeologies of Later Historical Britain*, 263–72. London: Routledge.
Tarlow, S. and West, S. (eds) (1999) *The Familiar Past? Archaeologies of Later Historical Britain*. London: Routledge.
Thomas, D.H. (1988) Saints and soldiers at Santa Catalina: Hispanic designs for colonial America. In M. Leone and P. Potter (eds), *The Recovery of Meaning*, 73–140. Washington: Smithsonian Institution Press.
Thomas, N. (1991) *Entangled Objects: Exchange, Material Culture, and Colonialism in the Pacific*. Cambridge, MA: Harvard University Press.
West, S. (1999) Introduction. In S. Tarlow and S. West, *The Familiar Past? Archaeologies of Later Historical Britain*, 1–16. London: Routledge.
Winer, M. and Deetz, J. (1990) The transformation of British culture in the Eastern Cape, 1820–1860. *Social Dynamics* 16(1): 55–75.

Part I

The First Empire: 1600–1800

1   Muffling inclusiveness: some notes towards an archaeology of the British

MATTHEW JOHNSON

In this chapter, I have put together a set of notes towards an archaeological understanding of some aspects of an archaeology of the British. These notes attempt to move towards a preliminary understanding of how to answer the question 'what have archaeologists got to say about the creation and development of "Britain"?'. I suggest that this very basic and apparently simple question breaks down into a series of more specific, yet more complex and intractable issues. These issues revolve around national identity, the writing of national history, and more broadly the social and political resonances and difficulties of doing archaeology in the present. This social, cultural and political climate in turn acts as a frame for academic questions such as history's relationship to archaeology, and the theoretical basis of much writing in British historical or 'post-medieval' archaeology. Many of these issues are also raised in Adrian Green's chapter in this volume, which deals with much of the detail of the historical development of ideas of region and nation-state within the British Isles; this chapter should be read in conjunction with his.

Ultimately, as an archaeologist living and working in the British Isles, I want to find a way of thinking, researching and writing about 'the British' that challenges conservative and complacent notions of Britishness, and which produces an interesting and challenging historical archaeology of these islands. I want to do this in a manner that on the one hand refuses to sweep under the carpet much of the conflict and contestation in the British past, but on the other hand does not descend into a sterile and impotent, guilt-ridden navel-contemplation. First, I want to ask the question: why a reassessment of the archaeology of the British now?

STORIES ABOUT THE BRITISH

Britishness, or at least the act of writing about Britishness and what it might mean, is a fashionable topic in literary and cultural circles at the moment. Over the last few years, we have had historical reassessments by Colley (1992) and others of the history of the British. As I write, the historian Simon Schama is halfway through his television history of Britain (2000), a history that has managed to be condemned simultaneously for being desperately traditional and also dangerously radical.

To state the obvious, such contemplation by the 'chattering classes' of Britain's past is a statement about the present – a symptom of unease at the contemporary condition of the British nation-state. Over the last few years, the constituent elements of what currently comprises Britain – England, Scotland, Wales and Northern Ireland – have all experienced constitutional change in one form or another. Scotland and Wales now have their own parliaments; the devolved assembly for Northern Ireland faces an uncertain future. In parallel to what many on the political Right argue is the first phase of the internal dissolution and break-up of Britain, there is external 'threat'. Closer integration of Britain with the European Union has brought on further cultural anxieties, whether of the cultural xenophobia of the Right or self-conscious disdain for such xenophobia from the Left.

This unease on the part of academics with the current state of Britishness, then, reflects the anxieties of a wider world. However, I think it also reflects the internal, theoretical failings and contradictions within intellectual under- standings of the nation-state. I suggest that unease about the British nation, and the national past, is based on a failure to adequately think through questions of identity and history. Why have British academics failed in this task? In part, I suggest the reason is partly discursive: that instead of being openly and overtly argued through, questions about the real or assumed identity of the British have been subjected by academics to a muffling inclusiveness.

I borrow the phrase 'muffling inclusiveness' from the work of Stephan Collini (1991). Collini uses this phrase in a quite specific manner, which I will try to broaden and deepen in this paper. For Collini, muffling inclusiveness addresses the way Welsh, Scots and Irish identities are often subsumed within an all-encompassing British identity. The 'Britishness' thus defined and consti- tuted then turns out on any sort of critical analysis to be really English, and frequently south-eastern English at that. This elision of national pasts is an intellectual sleight of hand rather than overtly ideological. It is founded, for Collini, not on an overtly or stridently partisan ideological position, but iron- ically on the formation of a national past through lack of class-based ideological divisions at a particular historical moment in the formation of national identi- ties. Collini writes:

> during the late 19th and early 20th centuries, 'the English' . . . expe- rienced neither the most common promptings to a self-conscious nationalism nor the kind of systematic and repetitive political and ideological divisions which make all aspects of a society's life matter for partisan dispute. As a result, the dominant relation to the English past during this period . . . was conceived along the lines of what might be called the 'National Trust' model, a repository of

treasures which all members can enjoy as part of their uniquely glorious heritage.

(1991: 131–2)

Collini is careful to stress that 'English cultural nationalism has in fact been a vast presence in British history of the last two centuries' (1991: 132); writing from a literary perspective, he illustrates this by reference to the literary canon.

One does not have to engage in sophisticated cultural critique to see muffling inclusiveness in action. There are some fairly blatant examples of it in both popular and scholarly thinking. Prime Minister John Major described 'Britain' in terms of long shadows on country cricket grounds and old maids cycling to communion in the mist, a description which (apart from the mist) would be quite unrecognisable to anyone living north of Yorkshire or west of Glamorgan (cited in Johnson 1999: 113). The Renaissance scholar Sir Roy Strong has described Welsh and Scots history as essentially a footnote to England; for him England and Britain are virtually coterminous (Strong 1998). What is interesting is that both Major and Strong tie the comments to an insistence that the identity of Britain is solid, unchanging, unambiguous. In both cases the identity of Britain is placed beyond contestation by assertion rather than argument. For Major, 'Britain will survive unamendable in all essentials'; for Strong, a key characteristic of Britain has been its island status and hence the continuity of its boundaries (in fact the boundaries of Britain have been changed, on average, less than every twenty years).

It would take some time to fully uncover the various strands of ideology at work here. For the very limited purposes of this chapter, I simply want to note that muffling inclusiveness is an ideological tactic that can be argued to be characteristically British. Other nations, the British feel, deny or repress violent or divisive elements of their past; such (perceived) activity is often implicitly looked down upon by the British as rather vulgar and strident. (I remember a very senior figure asserting in a seminar that Greek denial of Macedonian identity was 'simply hysterical'.) In Britain, the ideological messages are not so much denied or repressed as lose their sharp edges: they become muffled. This muffling is arguably more effective than a more strident approach in that the process, being less easily observed and isolated, more effectively insulates Britishness from critique. Nairn (1994) has noted elements of this process with reference to the British monarchy, where the pomp and ceremony surrounding the monarchy cannot be criticised because 'we all actually know' they are deeply trivial and arbitrary; this means, of course, that such pomp and ceremony is insulated from critique and can never be changed.

Historical events, for example, are not denied, but rather stripped of their overtly political edge. In the seventeenth century, the date of 5 November, the anniversary of the foiled plot by Guy Fawkes and a small group of Catholics to blow up Parliament, was celebrated by the burning of the Pope in effigy and not infrequently the smashing of the windows of local Catholics for good measure (Hutton 1994). Guy Fawkes Night is still celebrated today with as much enthusiasm as ever, but any connection with Protestant bigotry has long been forgotten; a stuffed doll or Guy is burnt in place of the Pope and few schoolchildren are aware of the religious/political 'edge' of the celebrations (with one exception: the Cliffe Bonfire Society still burns a Pope, though the protaginists stress that it is an effigy of the seventeenth century Pope being burnt and not the present incumbent (Fraser 1996: 294)).

How do the British react when muffling inclusiveness is threatened? Frequently, the gloves are taken off without too much ceremony; the bulldog is taken off the leash. The National Maritime Museum was forced to withdraw an exhibit in which a human hand could be seen reaching through the hatch of a slave ship into a Jane Austen parlour; mention of slavery 'introduced politics' into our glorious maritime past. Lisa Jardine recounts how simply raising the issue with reference to the poetry of the racist and misogynist yet 'quintessentially English' Philip Larkin led to a stridently abusive response. Jardine wrote an article asking: 'What are we to do with the realisation that a familiar author assumes *throughout his work* that the values and beliefs he and his readers subscribe to are exclusive to an Anglo-Saxon brotherhood of slightly depressed under-achievers? . . .' (1994: 111). In response to this question, she was deluged with letters of abuse:

> I was genuinely astonished at the discourtesy, the intolerance, the deliberate aggression, and the absolute lack of humaneness of these letters. It was as if each of these correspondents had set out intentionally to confirm for me that if you steeped yourself in poetry of petty patriotism and celebration of low achievement, the values you learned were those of intemperate and embittered resentment.
>
> (Jardine 1994: 111)

Rather than multiply examples (an all too easy task), however, I want to focus on a particular response to external threat because the issues it raises lead directly on to an archaeology of the British: a *Times* editorial (Anonymous 1997).

TRENDY HISTORIANS AND THE THUNDERER

The Times, known traditionally as the Thunderer, thundered in this case against a group of trendy left-wing historians who were out to deconstruct the idea of 'Britishness'. It condemned the writing of those such as Linda Colley, who put together an argument familiar enough to archaeological theorists – that British identity, like all national identities, was a specific and contingent historical construction rather than something normal or natural. Colley (1992) specifically argues that 'Britain' is a cultural and political construction of the eighteenth century, when the Protestant elements of England, Wales, Ireland and Scotland saw themselves as embattled and threatened by continental Europe. In this context, the cultural creation of Britain was a political response to external threat.

Calling this 'bad politics based on worse history', the Thunderer drew attention to the obvious implication – that what had been created politically, as a result of contingent events in the past, could be unravelled politically, as a result of contingent events in the not-too-distant future. It implied, therefore, that such history was a coded attempt by the intellectual middle classes to legitimate constitutional reform, in particular devolution, and deliver the constituent elements of an emasculated and divided British Isles into the hands of the burghers in Brussels.

So far, so banal; but what was interesting about this editorial was its assertion that Britishness was much older than the eighteenth century – and, in particular, the evidence it chose to deploy in support of this assertion. *The Times* cited Shakespeare's *Henry V*, in which Welsh, Irish and Scottish characters (all ordinary footsoldiers, of course) fight together for Henry, 'this star of England'. It is interesting to note in passing that this particular Shakespeare play consistently surfaces in popular discourse at moments of perceived national crisis. (By way of illustration, we might cite Laurence Olivier's famous 1944 film of the play, though it must be added that there is also a sense of triumphalism here – the film was intended to be released around the time of another British military adventure in France, the D-Day invasion of Normandy.)

READING SHAKESPEARE HISTORICALLY

The point that really fascinated me about *The Times*'s use of Shakespeare was that precisely the same passage in *Henry V* had been used recently by the New Historicist Stephen Greenblatt to argue in precisely opposite terms. In his paper 'Invisible Bullets', Greenblatt tackles the problem of subversion in English Renaissance documents, arguing that subversion is always present, but always as the thought of another, never one's own; and thus, in Shakespeare the representation of subversion is deeply ideological, as it represents the necessary obverse of authority, and thus functions ideologically as a means to acknowledge and at the same time endlessly defer the realities of 'hypocrisy, ruthlessness and bad faith' (Greenblatt 1991: 42). He writes of *Henry V*:

> By yoking together diverse peoples – represented in the play by the Welshman Fluellen, the Irishman Macmorris, and the Scotsman Jamy, who fight at Agincourt alongside the loyal Englishmen – Hal symbolically tames the last wild areas of the British Isles, areas that in the 16th century represented, far more powerfully than any New World tribalism, the doomed outposts of a vanishing tribalism.
>
> (1991: 42)

So Fluellen, Macmorris and Jamy are ideological – they are constituent elements in a national (and, of course and at the same time, colonialist) myth. Such a myth, of course was to go through a series of complex changes before the advent of Colley's eighteenth-century Britishness, and it had a long series of antecedents (Green, this volume); but myth it was nevertheless.

So it may be worth asking: what might archaeologists draw from Greenblatt's observation, and how might archaeologists use any insights drawn thereby to reflect back on an archaeology of the British? In a general sense, the late sixteenth century was a critical moment in the genealogy of Britishness. Five years after the first production of Henry V, England and Scotland were ruled by one king; a century earlier, Wales had ceased to exist as any kind of political entity, having been absorbed into England as a series of county shires as an act of political equality following the Tudor accession. And of course the problematic nature of Britain's relationship with Ireland was also reaching a critical moment. The late sixteenth-century was the point at which English strategy might be called truly colonial for the first time – strategy shifted from feudal partitioning toward one of wholesale plantation in many areas, culminating in the 'settlements' of Munster and Ulster.

So Henry V is in fact one of these new ideological weapons, one of Greenblatt's invisible bullets, alongside nascent colonialism, new political structures, new systems of force, new uses of space, new techniques of bodily discipline and new technologies of the self. And these weapons are the very stuff of archaeology; it is here, on this ground that a theoretically informed archaeology of the post-medieval British Isles that is not afraid to frame radically challenging responses to issues of British identity can find its place.

MUFFLING INCLUSIVENESS IN ARCHAEOLOGY

Historical archaeologists have set themselves the task of explaining cultural change. We look for the clash of cultures, the creation and renegotiation of identities, and the way these are mediated and expressed through material culture, architecture and landscape. Yet the theoretical models used by British archaeologists and historians, particularly the implicit ones used by those who pretend that they do not use theory, assume rather than explain identities and processes. Specifically they fall victim to an intellectual form of 'muffling inclusiveness'. I suggest that this muffling inclusiveness has impoverished the thinking of British post-medieval archaeologists and is one of the key reasons why British historical archaeology has until recently been much less exciting than comparable work in colonial situations.

Until recently, when it has ventured into 'social' or interpretive thinking at all, work on the archaeology of the Renaissance and of the British has tended to treat its evidence as reflective of certain cultural 'realities' rather than constitutive of those realities. Let me clarify what I mean by this by giving an example. Élite architecture and material culture, for example, is seen as 'conspicuous consumption', reflecting the great wealth and power of that élite (Girouard 1978; Airs 1995). Again, the urban middle classes are seen as engaging in 'competitive emulation' of their social betters, trying to move up the social scale (Courtney 1997: 15; for an effective critique of these ideas see Campbell 1987).

This work marks a striking advance on previous models, in which social factors were hardly considered at all. But it does run the danger of treating as real and pre-existing precisely those elements of culture that were being created *through* these practices. The ladder of social status, for example, was created through the deployment of material objects; objects were not simply passive reflections of certain intentions or desires. In the process, discordant elements are written out of the picture as aberrations contrary to the general trend, rather than as interesting counterpoints. Such assumptions fit easily into the pre-existing pattern of archaeological and interdisciplinary study of the British that I have described above. It subjects the very different practices that we find in the archaeological record to an archaeological form of muffling inclusiveness.

Let us look at a piece of material culture to illustrate the point. I select a site that resonates with the points made above; it dates from the time of Shakespeare and is itself a Great National Monument, now owned by the National Trust: Montacute House, Somerset. Montacute was built on an H plan at the same time as Shakespeare's writing of *Henry V* (1597–1601); its builder was Sir Edward Phelips, a successful lawyer. Phelips went on to be Speaker of the House of Commons in 1604 and Master of the Rolls in 1611. As such, Montacute has traditionally been interpreted as a 'power house', a piece of conspicuous consumption suited to the upwardly mobile and successful Phelips.

The original front, on the other side from that now approached by the visitor, has large windows and nine worthies in Roman armour. In front of it one approached between two pavilions. Montacute in many narratives is compared with Hardwick Hall in Derbyshire, and classified generally as a house of one of the 'new men' of Elizabethan England. Architecturally, such houses are held to represent a synthesis of late Perpendicular and Renaissance architecture; such a synthesis is often seen by traditional architectural historians in explicitly value-laden terms. Montacute and Hardwick are evidence of the 'peculiar English genius' for compromise and assimilation of the new without abandonment of the old, an aesthetic affirmation of 'the essential moderation' or what Pevsner in *The Englishness of English Art* (1956) calls the 'essential middle-class reasonableness' of the English people.

But when one looks at Montacute in detail, one find that its underlying articulation, or rather lack of articulation, contradicts this easy reading. Montacute can be deconstructed – that is, shown to have meanings quite opposite to those on its surface. I want to draw attention to the elements of the house which directly contradict or at the very least run counter to such a straightforward analysis. In the first place, Montacute is not really Montacute. Its west front is actually that of Clifton House, which was pulled down and the stone transferred to Montacute in 1786. Montacute is a collection of fragments.

One such fragment is the 'Skimmington frieze' (Figure 1.1). In the words of one popular guide, this 'shows a henpecked husband taking a drink while minding the baby and later being paraded around the village astride a pole'.

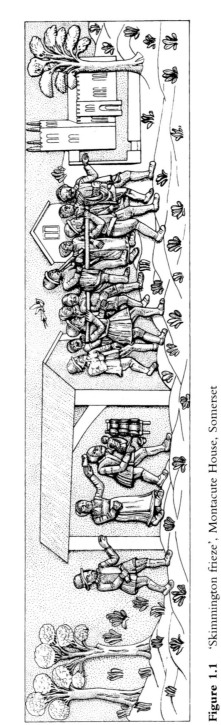

Figure 1.1 'Skimmington frieze', Montacute House, Somerset

In the left-hand scene, an unknown person discovers the husband being beaten by his wife, possibly for indulging in drink while minding the baby. The same person then recurs to the right, apparently informing the community who organise a traditional skimmington ride. The whole was probably originally coloured.

This depiction of community does include women, but they are placed at the back. After all, the ideological message of the skimmington ride is in part that they should stay indoors, just as in the words of the contemporary Puritan moralists Dod and Cleaver they should keep their tongues firmly locked inside their mouths. The ride appears to have a leader with a cloak; they do not have pots and pans but they do have pipe and drum. The person sitting on the pole, with all its sexual innuendo, does not appear to be the husband (traditionally, the husband was carried backwards on the pole).

The social historian Anthony Fletcher writes: 'This community shaming ritual – the rough music of pots, pans, effigies and rhymes – was for centuries the authentic voice of the English people about what is tolerable and what intolerable in marital relations.' For Fletcher, the Montacute frieze represents 'an affirmation by Sir Edward Phillips [sic] . . . that everyone knew about patriarchy having to have its final sanctions' (1995: 201, 273).

My point about this frieze is that it contains multiple meanings. To put it another way, I dispute the claims of authority, the notion of a single voice of 'the English people', a voice that spoke for what 'everyone knew' that Fletcher imputes to it and which again conspires to aid muffling inclusiveness. Such a single voice is also implied in the writing of other social historians: thus Underdown writes of scolds that 'from the 1560s many places began to show an increasing concern about *the problem*' (1985: 119; my italics) as if the problem had a real existence rather than being constructed through the changing anxieties of patriarchy. Such statements of authenticity fall into the trap that I have already noted in this chapter, of replicating accounts of authenticity and continuity in the very act of questioning it.

First, the ritual itself. Skimmington could be threatening of social order as much as reinforcing it. Gentry families could see skimmington as a threat; Kings Bench judgments of 1676 and 1693 decreed that riding skimmington constituted riot. Of course, being carnival, skimmington could also and at the same time be subjected to the process that we have already seen with the modern British monarchy, that is that 'we all know' its customs and rituals are actually deeply unimportant. It was justified to those who objected, such as Puritan clerics, on the basis that it was a harmless pastime (Fletcher 1995: 202).

The portrayal itself is done in uncompromisingly vernacular style, much more so than any other decoration in the house. This does not mean that it is crude; pamphlet illustrations of this kind had a whole series of sophisticated allusions (cf. Williams 1990). The location and context of the frieze also militates against an easy reading. Grotesque figures are well known at the lower end of halls. Panelling in the parlour at Montacute also has grotesque figures in this style. One thinks of the grotesque screens within polite halls, where disorder is simultaneously acknowledged and marginalised. It might be logical then to place such a frieze above the screens at the lower end. But it is in fact above the door to the parlour at the upper end.

This can be explained in part by remembering the changing use of the hall in polite buildings of this kind during this period. There is a separate dining room at Montacute, where Phelips presumably dined on an everyday basis. So the hall would be used for ceremonial, reception of the 'local community' or, in other words, the male heads of household, whether for feasts or other rituals. As they waited to greet and show deference to their master, then, before he appeared at the upper end, his place would be metaphorically taken and reinforced by the frieze itself, alongside the heraldic glass in the windows of the hall. But they would *not* see other artefacts of power, such as the dining room and the long gallery upstairs; these are written out of the picture, just as a few years later Ben Jonson would write out the long gallery and private apartments from his poem 'To Penshurst'.

At the same time, the 'audience' for the frieze is predominantly male. Judith Butler (1991) has commented on the early modern theatre as a whole that it is inherently subversive: the apparently natural order of gender is presented there as staged, as in part artificial. Therefore, the more overtly the early modern theatre paraded the values of patriarchy, the more those very values were shown to be staged. I would extend Butler's comments to other forms of theatricality such as the ceremonial of the hall and its trappings. The frieze presents the values of patriarchy but in so doing opens them up to questioning.

The central point of my analysis of the Montacute frieze is that here is an artefact, a country house, that traditional narratives place right at the centre of narratives of authenticity, continuity and muffling inclusiveness. Even the catalogue of decorative plasterwork for the county as a whole does this – it explains such friezes in terms of social emulation and waves of influence from the Italian Renaissance. For Penoyre and Penoyre (1993), the plasterwork of Somerset is to be explained almost as the early Gordon Childe explained prehistory, as the irradiation of (northern) European barbarism by (in this case Italian) civilisation. As a result, when confronted with this wonderful piece of evidence their discussion has almost nothing to say: the one adjective they use is 'unfeeling'. But I am suggesting that when we look in detail at the frieze itself, we have lots to say – we find instability, rupture, lack of fixity of meaning. We find the anxieties of Shakespeare's England played out in a very direct way.

WRITING ABOUT THE BRITISH

What I have tried to do here is to 'write against the grain', in the sense of the term used by the Shakespeare critic Jonathan Dollimore (1985). Dollimore wants to expose the sharp edges of Shakespeare, against the ahistorical images of placidity and continuity that Shakespeare represents to modern culture. Here, I have tried to expose the sharp edges of one English country house. I have done this not because I am still wedded to the linguistic analogy for archaeological interpretation, but because I think the intellectual work such criticism faces is that which we face in archaeology. In both cases, the task is to take a Great National Monument (Shakespeare or Montacute) and subvert its easy readings.

Such a strategy is one response to Collini's 'muffling inclusiveness'. The most obvious example of this inclusiveness, as we have already noted, is the way England somehow becomes Britain in a variety of discourses. There are other dimensions to this muffling inclusiveness, however. The most obvious is a sense of an assumption of continuity, linked in an untheorised, almost mystical way to an assertion of British/English 'character'. I want to spend the rest of this chapter trying to locate this sense of continuity within various archaeo-logical texts.

FLAYING ENGLISH LANDSCAPES

The classic instance is a notion of the English landscape – and it is usually the *English* landscape – as beyond history, as timeless and unchanging. The work of W.G. Hoskins on the English landscape is interesting in this context. Hoskins's book *The Making of the English Landscape* was published in 1953, ran through scores of editions selling to academic and popular audiences alike, and remains a central text for landscape studies. As Charles Phythian-Adams has pointed out in a characteristically perceptive essay, Hoskins consciously set out to write a history of discontinuity and of moral condemnation of that discontinuity:

> Airfields have flayed [English landscapes] bare . . . Over them drones, day after day, the obscene shape of the atom-bomber, laying a trail like a filthy slug on Constable's and Gainsborough's sky. England of the Nissen hut, the 'pre-fab', and the electric fence, of the high barbed wire around some unmentionable devilment; England of the arterial by-pass, treeless and stinking of diesel-oil, murderous with lories . . . Barbaric England of the scientists, the military men, and the politicians.
> (Hoskins 1953: 231–2, cited in Phythian-Adams 1992: 149)

But of course the basis of Hoskins's passion here is that change is alien; the above quote is wrapped with references to 'the immemorial landscape of the English countryside' and an assertion of what I think to any theoretically informed audience of archaeologists would be an unpalatable antiquarianism: 'let us turn away and contemplate the past before all is lost to the vandals.' There is a tension here between Hoskins's recognition as a scholar, and further as a politically committed scholar (he was a Liberal councillor for Exeter and played a prominent role in post-war conservation debates), that the history of the English countryside has always been one of change, even inequality and exploitation, and his emotional or visceral reaction to the changes of the twen-tieth century. I do not wish to sound deliberately ironic or patronising here, since I think this is a tension that runs through much past and present scholarship, including my own.

Hoskins manages to keep his English landscape a calm and idyllic place by a tight drawing of the boundaries. There is almost no mention in any of his books of the relationship between the landscape changes he delineates and the articulation of England with Scotland, Wales, Ireland and the Empire beyond. For Hoskins and a whole succeeding generation of historians, if Scotland and Wales get drawn in to this muffling inclusiveness, the Empire gets left out, or more accurately Britain's colonies are simultaneously inscribed and erased. We are invited to be proud of the British Museum as an artefact and symbol of the liberal institutions of Britishness, but invited to overlook its nature as a collection of plundered loot by the erasure of those contexts beyond British shores.

Barthes might well call this 'Operation Margarine' – a process by which we all acknowledge the 'imperfections' of an institution in the act of affirming the institution itself (1970: 41). As a result, many of the most appalling events in the history of Britain, occurring outside the bounds of the country, are treated as of marginal relevance; indeed, their very barbarity, taking place as it does outside the bounds of the British Isles, becomes further evidence of the sweetness and reasonableness of life back home. The two most obvious examples are British involvement in the slave trade and the treatment of Ireland. For example, in one popular book published by the British Broadcasting Corporation I have to hand, Cromwell's 'ruthlessness' in Ireland and the conditions of slaves gets half a paragraph and half a page respectively (Billings 1991: 115, 128).

Or to put this reinscription and erasure another way, Britain's history of overseas trade becomes sanitised through this tight drawing of boundaries. One gets the sense from some recent syntheses of British history that the ships left Liverpool and Bristol with trade goods for West Africa, and came back from the West Indies with sugar. By drawing the boundaries of Britain tightly, then, and drawing a veil over the ships as they leave Liverpool, what happened between Africa and the West Indies is left out.

It is tempting to suggest that we write against this by stressing that colonial and post-colonial periphery, and obviously this is a strategy that many of the chapters in this and other volumes are pursuing and is justly a major continuing theme of the WAC and of world historical archaeology. But here, I want to put in a plea that those of us who practise our craft within that exclusive cordon of Britishness recognise that we cannot go on as before.

A final source of the stress on continuity, ironically, are the words of the historical protagonists themselves. The social conflicts and divides that marked much of the post-medieval period were rarely fought out in their own terms, as Marx would put it, but through the use of various ideological codes. I have written before about how conflicts over enclosure, for example, were fought out in part over the meanings of words like husbandry and agriculture (Johnson 1996). One of the key ways in which resistance was expressed during this period was in an appeal to the traditional, to 'time immemorial', to established custom 'since time out of mind'. Such phrases recur over and over again in court records and accounts of community conflict. But just because tradition and custom were some of the few weapons in the armoury of common resistance against élite dispossession and exploitation does not mean that they are not problematic terms, or that they should be taken at face value, any more than the nostalgia of country-house poetry should be taken at face value. We are not fooled when politicians talk of a return to traditional values; we should not abandon our critical faculties when faced with overt affirmation of traditional values in the past.

I have argued in this chapter that we need to write an archaeology of rupture against this. We need to read our material against the grain. I think we have excellent models to inspire us from recent work in cultural history and in literature. We do so within a political context that I think is conducive to such an awakening. Terry Eagleton commented of the 1979–97 Conservative governments that 'Britain has suffered the most ideologically aggressive and explicit regime of living political memory, in a society which traditionally prefers its ruling values to remain implicit and oblique' (1991: xi).

I think that one of archaeology's key failures of the last fifteen years has been in this arena. We have all been very good at tracing the influence of politics on archaeology, but strikingly poor at making our archaeology address contemporary political debates. I started the chapter with Lisa Jardine and Linda Colley; where is the archaeology to go alongside their work?

The potential of our material to write such an archaeology is surely second to none. I suggest that the central task of post-medieval archaeology in the new millennium is that we reconsider material culture and identity. Material culture is central to the constitution of society: a familiar point, but it leads down new paths. It shows how material things are implicated in identity, contrary to so much of the ideology of the aesthetic that continues to pervade Renaissance studies; it posits our material is fragmentary, ruptured, disconnected (and Britain is nothing if not a collection of fragments). Hopefully this will lead not just to a better and more self-critical post-medieval archaeology, but to a better and more self-critical sense of the ideas of Britain and Britishness in the world today.

REFERENCES

Airs, M. (1995) *The Tudor and Jacobean Country House: A Building History*. London: Alan Sutton.

Anonymous (1997) Our island story: history has become a battleground for Britishness. Editorial, *The Times*, 18 December.

Barthes, R. (1970) *Mythologies*. London: Paladin.

Billings, M. (1991) *The English: The Making of a Nation from 430–1700*. London: BBC Books.

Butler, J. (1991) *Gender Trouble: Feminism and the Subversion of Identity*. London: Routledge.

Campbell, C. (1987) *The Romantic Ethic and the Spirit of Modern Consumerism*. Oxford: Basil Blackwell.

Colley, L. (1992) *Britons: Forging the Nation 1707–1837*. New Haven, CN: Yale University Press.

30 MATTHEW JOHNSON

Collini, S. (1991) Genealogies of Englishness: literary history and cultural criticism in modern Britain. In C. Brady (ed.), *Ideology and the Historians*, 128–45. Dublin: Lilliput Press.

Courtney, P. (1997) The tyranny of constructs: some thoughts on periodisation and change. In D. Gaimster and P. Stamper (eds), *The Age of Transition: The Archaeology of English Culture 1400–1600*, 9–24. Oxford: Oxbow.

Dollimore, J. and Sinfield, A. (1985) *Political Shakespeare*. Ithaca, NY: Cornell University Press.

Eagleton, T. (1991) *Ideology: An Introduction*. London: Verso.

Fletcher, A. (1995) *Gender, Sex and Subordination in England 1500–1800*. New Haven, CN: Yale University Press.

Fraser, A. (1996) *The Gunpowder Plot: Terror and Faith in 1605*. London: Mandarin.

Girouard, M. (1978) *Life in the English Country House*. New Haven, CN: Yale University Press.

Greenblatt, S. (1991) Invisible bullets: Renaissance authority and its subversion, Henry IV and Henry V. In J. Dollimore and A. Sinfield (eds), *Political Shakespeare*, 40–55. London: Routledge.

Hoskins, W.G. (1953) *The Making of the English Landscape*. London: Faber.

Hutton, R. (1994) *The Rise and Fall of Merry England: The Ritual Year 1400–1700*. Oxford: Oxford University Press.

Jardine, L. (1994) Canon to left of them, canon to write of them. In S. Dunant (ed.), *The War of the Words: The Political Correctness Debate*, 109–20. London: Virago.

Johnson, M.H. (1996) *An Archaeology of Capitalism*. Oxford: Blackwell.

—— (1999) *Archaeological Theory: An Introduction*. Oxford: Blackwell.

Nairn, T. (1994) *The Enchanted Glass: Britain and Its Monarchy*, 2nd edn. London: Vintage.

Penoyre, J. and Penoyre, J. (1993) *Decorative Plasterwork in the Houses of Somerset 1500–1700*. Taunton: Somerset County Council.

Phythian-Adams, C. (1992) Hoskins' England: a local historian of genius and the realisation of his theme. *Transactions of the Leicestershire Archaeological and Historical Society* LXVI, 143–59.

Schama, S. (2000) *A History of Britain*. London: BBC Books.

Strong, R. (1998) *The Story of Britain*, 2nd edn. London: Pimlico.

Underdown, D.E. (1985) The taming of the scold: the enforcement of patriarchal authority in early modern England. In A. Fletcher and J. Stevenson (eds), *Order and Disorder in Early Modern England*, 111–28. Cambridge: Cambridge University Press.

Williams, T. (1990) 'Magnetic figures': polemical prints of the English revolution. In L. Gent and N. Llewellyn (eds), *Renaissance Bodies: The Human Figure in English Culture c. 1540–1660*, 86–110. London: Reaktion.

2 Civic ritual, townscape and social identity in seventeenth- and eighteenth-century Newcastle upon Tyne

C. PAMELA GRAVES

INTRODUCTION

This chapter examines the inhabited landscape of seventeenth- and early eighteenth-century Newcastle upon Tyne, how the townscape was shaped by, and in turn shaped, social identities and relationships. I attempt to interpret several intertwining strands in the archaeology of one British town. One strand is how the material environment contributed to people's awareness of their position in Newcastle's social and political hierarchy. A second strand is the relationships between the nationalities which constituted the British at that time. A third strand is the ability of people excluded from civic office to challenge or subvert the position of those who did hold power. My emphasis is on social practice as constructive of social identity (Giddens 1985, 1986; Bourdieu 1987; Barrett 1988), and on the material townscape as an environment in which patterns of social life were made possible, understood and lived. I argue that there is a recursive relationship between economic and civic power, the locations of people's livelihoods and the practices by which social identities were reproduced.

Seventeenth-century Newcastle was one of the busiest international ports in Britain. Its wealth was built mostly on coal (Nef 1932; Blake 1967). Coal was shipped to the English east coast ports, and London was dependent upon it. Ellis has described the nature and scale of trade and industry on Tyneside at this time as creating a workforce with the character of an organised proletariat (1984: 193). A complex economy was built on coal, financing 'not only a vast return trade in foodstuffs and commercial goods but also the circulation of capital and credit that supported local industry' (Ellis 1984: 193).

The topography of Newcastle in those times was very different from today's (see Figures 2.1 and 2.2). The Quayside, and its westward extension The Close, was the thriving hub of river-borne commerce, but it was an artificial platform created through piecemeal reclamation from the twelfth century (e.g. O'Brien *et al.* 1988; Ellison *et al.* 1993; Fraser *et al.* 1995). Merchant houses and warehouses were located along the Quayside, and various mercantile and borough

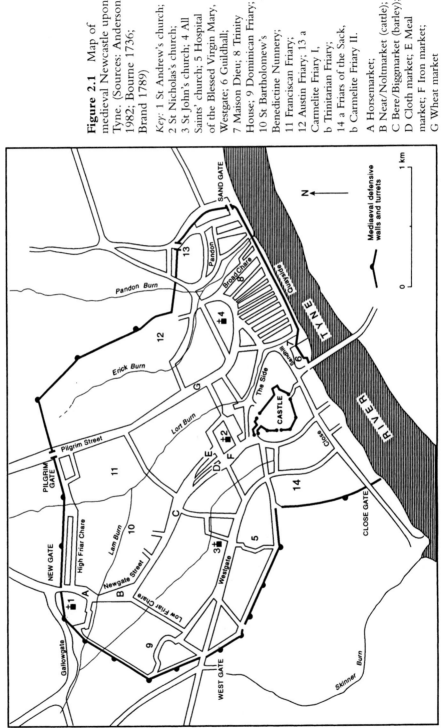

Figure 2.1 Map of medieval Newcastle upon Tyne. (Sources: Anderson 1982; Bourne 1736; Brand 1789)

Key: 1 St Andrew's church; 2 St Nicholas's church; 3 St John's church; 4 All Saints' church; 5 Hospital of the Blessed Virgin Mary, Westgate; 6 Guildhall; 7 Maison Dieu; 8 Trinity House; 9 Dominican Friary; 10 St Bartholomew's Benedictine Nunnery; 11 Franciscan Friary; 12 Austin Friary; 13 a Carmelite Friary I, b Trinitarian Friary; 14 a Friars of the Sack, b Carmelite Friary II.

A Horsemarket; B Neat/Noltmarket (cattle); C Bere/Biggmarket (barley); D Cloth market; E Meal market; F Iron market; G Wheat market

Figure 2.2 Map of post-medieval Newcastle upon Tyne up until *c.* 1736. (Sources: Anderson 1982; Bourne 1736; Corbridge 1723/4)

Key: 1 St Andrew's church; 2 St Nicholas's church; 3 St John's church; 4 All Saints' church; 5 Royal Grammar School; 6 Guildhall & Exchange; 7 Mansion House; 8 Trinity House; 9 Bowling Green and Assembly House on the Forth; 10 Formal walks and gardens on the Forth; 11 Assembly Rooms; 12 Bridewell; 13 Free School; 14 Holy Jesus Hospital; 15 Davison Hospital; 16 Keelmen's Hospital; 17 Blackfriars'/Nine Companies; 18 Nuns' Gardens; 19 Anderson Place; 20 Bessie Surtees's House; 21 Alderman Fenwick's House.

A Horsemarket; B Neat/Noltmarket (cattle); C Bere/Biggmarket (barley); D Poultry market; E Butter market; F Flesh market; G Groat & Wool markets; H Iron market; I Wheat market; J Fish market; K Herb market

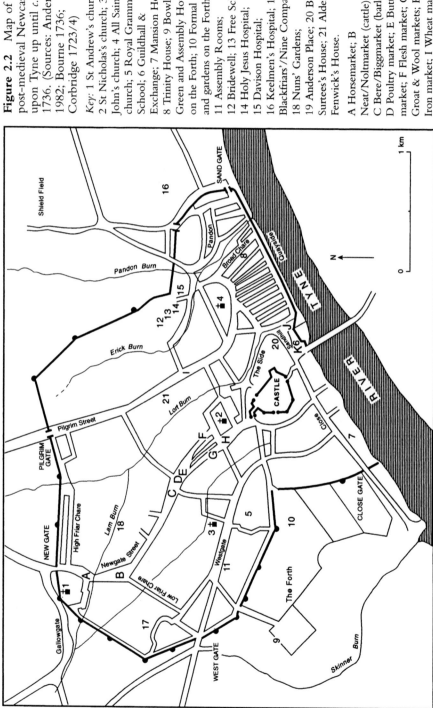

institutions were located on Sandhill, where the Tyne Bridge joined the Quayside. Most significant of these was the Guildhall. This building housed the Town Courts and Court of Assize. There was also a medieval hospital in which the Merchant Adventurers' Company met. The Side was a steep, curving street linking the Quayside to the principal market street, which was long and sinuous and ended in a triangular market place opposite the principal medieval church, St Nicholas's. The medieval castle was located above The Side. The market street was subdivided in name, according to the commodities sold at various points along it (Corbridge 1723/4; Bourne 1736: 53). Other commodities were sold in markets elsewhere in the town, mainly on Sandhill (Gray 1649: 19; Corbridge 1723/4; Bourne 1736; Welford 1916: 14; Heslop *et al.* 1995). Deep water-cut ravines subdivided the town and obstructed east–west movement. The High and Low Bridges formed the east–west connections, principally between the market street and Pilgrim Street. The medieval Hospital of the Blessed Virgin Mary was located on Westgate Road. Sandgate was an eastern extension of the quayside, and formed a large suburb beyond the town wall.

In the history of Newcastle's ruling élite, each broadening of the power base was counteracted by the creation of a new, more narrowly defined élite. This élite grew from three merchant guilds: the Drapers, the Mercers and the Boothmen (corn merchants), who largely controlled Newcastle's trading activities from the fourteenth century, and nine craft guilds or companies. These twelve guilds monopolised the election of civic officers. This did not go unchallenged, and a further group of crafts was grudgingly incorporated by the mid-fifteenth century (Fraser and Emsley 1973: 27). At the same time, the three premier merchant guilds formed the Merchant Adventurers' Company, effectively an oligarchy who held a virtual monopoly of the aldermanic bench (Ellis 1984: 202). The narrow élite further protected their interests by the chartering of the Hostmen's Company in 1601 (Fraser 1984: 169). The Hostmen lodged visiting merchants and conducted their business for them, each visitor being assigned a particular hostman who levied a duty in return (Anderson 1982: xi). The company is first mentioned in 1517, but they rose to power later in the sixteenth century, when they attempted to monopolise the Tyne coal trade (Fraser 1984: 170). Many were owners of coal-pits, and they controlled the extraction and movement of coal. Having established themselves at this pinnacle, the oligarchy allowed by-trades to take part in the election of civic officers in 1604. By the seventeenth century the freemen of Newcastle actually represented a fairly large proportion of the population, but were largely excluded from influence through the monopoly of rights detailed above (Howell 1967: 35–62). By 1600, the town officials were the mayor, ten aldermen, a recorder, sheriff, eight chamberlains, two coroners, the sword-bearer, the common clerk of the chamber, eight sergeants at mace and an electoral college, the 'Twenty-Four', who were representatives of the guilds and who constituted a Common Council (Anderson 1982: ix–x).

CIVIC RITUAL AND THE USE OF THE TOWNSCAPE

In the medieval period the identity and political constitution of Newcastle's governing bodies and guilds was displayed to the public and, to a certain extent, reproduced, through religious celebrations. Thus, the Corpus Christi procession was an occasion on which the mayor, aldermen and guilds walked around the town in order of civic rank (Anderson 1982). Elsewhere in medieval England, the order of precedence amongst the participating guilds often reflected their economic success (James 1983). There are too few references to the marshalling of guilds within the Corpus Christi procession in Newcastle to enable us to make any comment on these changing fortunes. However, the procession and associated mystery plays do give us an indication of the possible routes taken through the town (see Figure 2.3). The Corpus Christi plays are first referred to as an ancient custom in 1427; and last referred to in 1581 (Anderson 1982: xi). The last reference to players' apparel is in 1599. The exact route of the procession is unknown: it is known that it started at St Nicholas's church and marched north through the Meal Market and Bere Market, where the Merchant Adventurers joined, to Newgate. It may have returned the same way, or along High Friar Chare, down Pilgrim Street and along by either of the bridges to the church again (Anderson 1982: xv). It may have gone down to the Quayside, but this is not recorded. This route formed a circuit of the central and upper parts of the town.

Processions reproduced status; they displayed the order of office and power in a ranking of mayor, aldermen, recorder, sheriff, chamberlains and so on. The participation of the guilds accorded with the precedence that the three merchant guilds and nine craft companies claimed over other by-trades. In medieval guild ceremonial, the religious and the secular were indistinguishable (Giles 2000). I believe, however, that significant post-medieval changes to the nature and arena of civic ceremonial in Newcastle were not immediately coincident with the Reformation, nor can they be ascribed to a post-Restoration urban renaissance (Borsay 1989). Instead, they occurred around the beginning of the seventeenth century. This was coincident with the epiphany of the Hostmen as an élite, and tied in with the changing social geography of the town.

The pre-Reformation Corpus Christi procession may be contrasted with ceremonials connected with the election and confirmation of the civic government which continued throughout the seventeenth century and beyond. The most important of these was the election of the mayor, aldermen, bailiffs and other officers on the first Monday after Michaelmas (Brand 1789: 73). This involved processions between the former chapel of the Hospital of the Blessed Virgin Mary, whose east end had been made into an Election-house, St Nicholas's church and the Guildhall (see Figure 2.4; Bourne 1736: 34). In contrast to the route of the medieval Corpus Christi procession, this procession brought the focus of ritual to the lower end of town. According to Borsay (1984), the toing and froing between civic buildings reinforced the movement

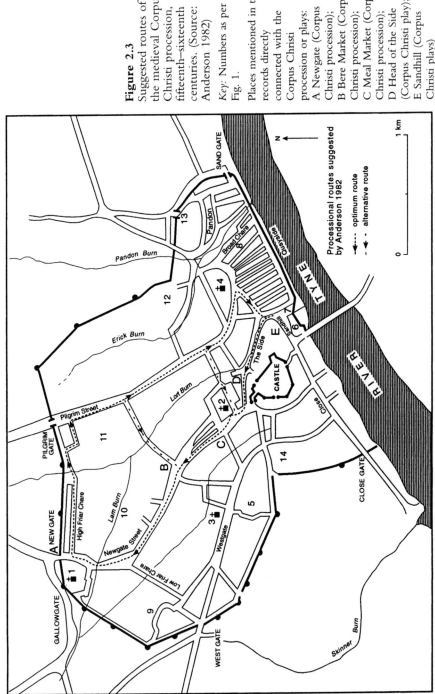

Figure 2.3
Suggested routes of
the medieval Corpus
Christi procession,
fifteenth–sixteenth
centuries. (Source:
Anderson 1982)

Key: Numbers as per
Fig. 1.

Places mentioned in the
records directly
connected with the
Corpus Christi
procession or plays:
A Newgate (Corpus
Christi procession);
B Bere Market (Corpus
Christi procession);
C Meal Market (Corpus
Christi procession);
D Head of the Side
(Corpus Christi play);
E Sandhill (Corpus
Christi plays)

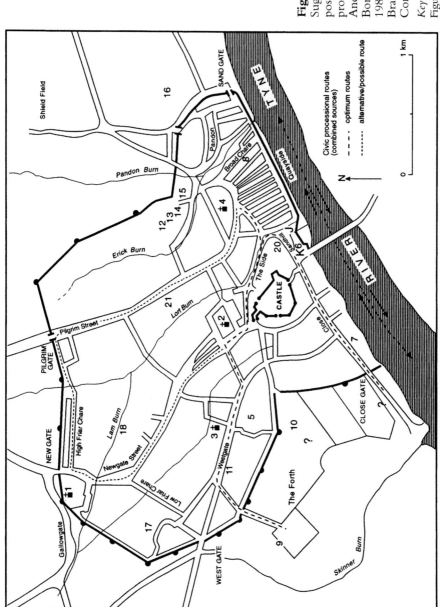

Figure 2.4
Suggested routes of post-medieval civic processions. (Sources: Anderson 1982; Borsay 1984; Borsay 1989; Bourne 1736; Brand 1777/89; Corbridge 1723/4).

Key: Numbers as per Figure 2.2

Civic processional routes (combined sources)
–·–·– optimum routes
········· alternative/possible route

0   1 km

Shield Field

SAND GATE

TYNE

Pandon

Pandon Burn

Broad Chare

Erick Burn

16

Gateshead

The Side

20

K6

CASTLE

Lort Burn

21

Pilgrim Street

12 13 14 15

‡4

‡2

PILGRIM GATE

NEW GATE

High Friar Chare

Lam Burn

18

Newgate Street

Low Friar Chare

17

Gallowgate

‡1

3 ‡

WEST GATE

Westgate

11

5

10

The Forth

9

?

?

Skinner Burn

CLOSE GATE

Close

7

?

RIVER

of office and created the impression that the office and the man were separate. In this way the corporation acquired an immutable identity and authority, impervious to the changing fortunes of those who occupied its offices. By scouring antiquarian sources, it is possible to amass an amount of civic cere-monial subsequent to the election (Bourne 1736: 125, 245; Brand 1777: 252–3; Brand 1789: 517). The routes of these processions and the locus of these festiv-ities bring the focus clearly down to the lower part of town with the Guildhall as a fulcrum, along to the Mansion House, built by the Town corporation in 1691–2 (Fraser *et al.* 1995: 147), up the Side and the lower reaches of Pilgrim Street. I shall return to the Guildhall shortly.

Speed's map of Newcastle in 1610 shows important houses on the Market Street. Grey, in his Chorographia of 1649, states that the 'Burgesses . . . Mayors, Aldermen and richer men of the town of Newcastle in former times built their houses in the upper parts of the town'. 'In after times,' he says, 'the merchants removed lower down towards the river, to the street called the Side, and Sandhill, where it continued [in his day].' In the early eighteenth century, Bourne commented upon the number of notable inhabitants still living along The Close, around the Mansion House and Sandhill (1736: 126). By the mid-eighteenth century, however, the wealthy were moving to the upper parts of the town, or out of town altogether (Ellis 1984: 196). It is my contention that the focus of civic ceremonial changed between the upper part of the town and the lower reaches in accordance with a change in social topography. In the medieval period and up until the end of the sixteenth to early seven-teenth centuries, the wealthy and politically influential of Newcastle lived in these upper reaches or in a pattern of houses well distributed around the town, but in the seventeenth century, they moved towards the lower reaches, and the re-location of civic ceremonial was coincident with this reorientation of the civic élite.

HOUSING, THE SOCIAL TOPOGRAPHY OF THE TOWN AND CIVIC RITUAL

Against this background, there is a project which is currently looking at the distribution of different house types in both the medieval and post-medieval periods (Graves and Heslop forthcoming). Gleaning from antiquarian sources, the distribution of high status, stone-built medieval houses seems to have been widespread across the town, both north and south. The ceremonies that in-volved the merchants most likely to have lived in these houses in the medieval period took place as much in the upper town as on Sandhill. By contrast, seven-teenth-century timber-framed buildings survive on The Close and Sandhill (see Figure 2.5). We can see from these standing buildings and from historical illus-trations that features of the frontages were projecting bay windows, of many storeys, and broad bands of glass along the façade. One of the best examples is that of Bessie Surtees House, 41 Sandhill, dating from between 1657 and the

Figure 2.5 Surviving seventeenth-century houses on Sandhill, including Bessie Surtees House (left) and the Redhouse complex (right)

1660s. The Red House complex further along Sandhill is similar. Combining wills, property conveyances and probate inventories, we can confirm that the people who were building these houses were from the class from which the officers of civic government were elected: Surtees belonged to merchants, a mayor and an owner of coal fields (Heslop *et al.* 1995: 14, 24).

The project is working on the distribution of these houses, based on historical images which have been located topographically. The distribution of documented glass-fronted buildings and projecting bay windows of the seventeenth century is also mostly along the river front: The Close, Sandhill and The Quayside, as well as The Side and the lower reaches of Pilgrim Street, that is the lower part of the town.

The point is that the distribution of these special seventeenth-century buildings is integral to participation in civic ceremonial events, and that these particular building forms provided the flexibility required by, and arising out of, mercantile life in Newcastle, which had its own rhythms. For example, on Ascension Day, the mayor and other civic dignitaries boarded elaborately decorated barges and processed by water to the limits of the town's jurisdiction on the River, to the King's Meadows and Tynemouth (Brand 1777: 270; Brand 1789: 517; Borsay 1984: 231). Projecting towers of bay windows allowed these events to be seen over the Quayside wall, and as far as possible. These events reaffirmed the town's privileges; at the same time they reproduced the élite.

The men who took part in the processions and civic ceremonies, who partook in town government, were of the class who built and occupied these riverfront buildings. The Hearth Tax gives some idea of the location of the wealthiest merchants in 1665, despite associated problems (see Howell 1967: 8–13). The richer wards of Newcastle were all clustered round the castle, the Guildhall and the Quayside. The poorest wards were in the north-east and north-west of the town, and the Sandgate. Of the Common Council of 1662, 27 out of 36 members can be identified. From this we can identify the wards in which they lived. Five out of the six of these aldermen lived in the richest wards; similarly, 13 out of the 21 members of the Twenty Four also lived in those rich wards (Howell 1967: 11). These are the same wards in which the seventeenth-century timber-framed houses with large windows were built. In the riverside Sandgate ward, by contrast, as many as 79 per cent of the population were exempt from Hearth Tax (Ellis 1984: 197).

The windows of the houses of the Sandhill in Newcastle provided views onto the space in front of the Guildhall, and up and down the streets. The distribution of jutting, multi-storey bay windows took advantage of the topography to present almost raked theatre boxes. They could accommodate numerous people. Images of processions in London illustrate the point (Schofield 1995: 150–1, Figures 182–3). It is noticeable that cloths, tapestries, banners and carpets were hung out over the window sills. This is likely to have been the case in Newcastle. As early as 1503, when Henry VII's daughter Margaret was heading to Scotland for marriage to James IV, her entry into Newcastle across the Tyne Bridge was greeted with great ceremony:

> Within the said towne, by ordre, the bourges and habitants war honestly appoynted. The stretys war hanged, and the window loupps, topps, and schipps was so full of people, gentylmen and gentylwomen, in so great nombre, that it was a playsur for to se.
>   (Mackenzie 1827: 18, quoting Leland)

Borsay (1984) has written of passive participation by onlookers in these cere-monials. I shall explore this from two angles: firstly from the point of view of women; secondly from the point of view of other men, notably craft company members who may have been excluded from the civic ceremonials. There were a series of relationships which were created and reproduced in these various forms of inclusion and exclusion. The town élite was constituted by parading in front of others; others were constituted as followers, or even outsiders, by that exclusion. Women were exempt from this government. But where is the agency, the knowledgeable action of women if we stop the analysis here? Extensive windows provided an opportunity for the members and heads of individual households who were participating in the processions to be acknowl-edged by other members of their household at the windows, for example wives, other dependent relatives like children, sisters and elderly parents, and perhaps even servants. The windows also provided a means by which these household members at the windows would be recognised by people in the procession below: peers, subordinates and superiors amongst the civic élite. Those at the window were also on display to those who were crowding the streets in order to watch the ceremonies. In this sense there is an active, constitutive role in appearing at the windows. Households, social and economic rank, even marriage eligibility could be represented, and therefore reproduced, at the windows. The degree to which leading merchant families had intermarried to exclude the lesser merchants evoked complaint in 1714 (Ellis 1984: 204, 206).

Further, visiting merchants and traders, all manner of business and social contacts could be given a favoured viewing place at a window, creating or re-affirming both social and economic relationships and transactions. We should remember that the owner of Bessie Surtees House, for example, was a coal owner (Heslop *et al.* 1995: 24). The interiors of these houses, along with the Exchange, Customs House, cellars and warehouses, were the locales of such transactions, organising cross North Sea and Baltic connections. The windows were a membrane between the arenas in which different identities were created and reproduced. It is significant that so much glass was used. This is not a banal nod to conspicuous consumption. The glass was a major local industry which contributed to Newcastle's dominance as a commercial centre in the North.

I have referred to the rhythms of mercantile life. The summer was the season of greatest commerce on the river. A concomitant of this was that the space in front of the Guildhall was most congested. The windows allow visual access to the scene, without being submerged in the throng: a genteel life above the common crowd. The Sandhill houses look onto the Guildhall, which housed many institutions, amongst them the mayor and sheriff's courts, the Exchange, the weighhouse and town house. The medieval predecessor was rebuilt by the Common Council in 1655. The houses opposite were built either then or shortly after. The only trade or craft company which was allowed to use the Guildhall as its meeting house was that of the Hostmen. The only part of the medieval complex which remained untouched was the Maison Dieu, which had been founded by a fifteenth-century mayor, an example of conti-nuity in institutional identity. The architecture of the new Guildhall building provoked enthusiastic comment from Celia Fiennes in 1698 (Griffiths 1888: 176). The Guildhall also contained a Mayor's Parlour – a further, more private level of definition of room for concourse and discussion amongst the élite. This room is on more or less the same physical level as the first floor of Bessie Surtees House across the way, and it is possible to see into it. I believe that intervisi-bility of parties, both within the merchant's house and the Mayor's Parlour, also denoted a social parity, or at least a presumption of parity. Again, glass acted as the membrane between locations or arenas of discourse.

It has been accepted generally that civic ceremonials were intended· to promote a sense of town identity, of civic pride (Borsay 1984; Ellis 1984). However, if the civic processions were meant to represent the town as a whole, then it was a very partial definition, which excluded the majority of artisans and freemen, industrial workers and coal-labourers, women and children of all

ranks, and others excluded from joining the incorporated crafts, for example.
Moreover, the routes of the civic processions missed out the poorest wards of
the town. Thus the definition of the town could be seen as identical with the
places of wealth creation, consumption and display (the warehouses and shops,
the shops often being incorporated in the merchant housing itself). The
excluded had to physically walk from the place of their own residence (and,
perhaps, work) to those of the élite in order to take part as observers. There is
evidence to contradict the passive acceptance of such ideology, and it has
material and spatial dimensions, which I shall explore below. First, I shall look
at the particular circumstances of the Civil War period in Newcastle when not
only the merchant community was riven, but there was a fluid relationship of
support and antipathy between the English and Scots in the town. Then I shall
look at further expressions of resistance to civic exclusion.

   Civic ceremony may have been intended to display authority and the identity of the corporation as immutable, but in reality, town government was the
focus of bitter opposition from those who were excluded from it, particularly
the freemen or lesser merchants. Increasingly in the seventeenth century this
opposition to the inner ring was formed along Puritan religious lines, that is
those who opposed the reintroduction of ceremonies in the Church of England
and sought a more reformed religion. Reform in religion and reform in both
economic practices and government, nationally and locally, purported to go
hand in hand. This tended to polarize the Mercer/Hostman élite as pro-
Catholic and anti-reform. By the time of the Civil War (1644–49), this was
further caricatured as a Parliamentarian versus Royalist split (Howell 1967).

RELIGIOUS AND NATIONAL IDENTITIES
MANIPULATED WITHIN POLITICS

At the beginning of the seventeenth century the north-east of England was
seen as very conservative, amounting to Roman Catholic by default if not by
devotion (Howell 1967: 72). Puritanism in Newcastle was sustained through
three routes: contacts with the Continent; contacts with London and the south-
east; and contacts with the Scots (Howell 1967: 96–7).

   Trading contacts with the Continent were well established: those with
Antwerp, The Netherlands, Denmark, North Germany and the Baltic had been
formed in the fourteenth century. At least by the seventeenth century, many
of the Newcastle merchants appear to have lived in foreign ports for extensive
periods as a means towards creating links and familiarity with foreign trading
partners and practices (cf. *The Memoirs of Ambrose Barnes*, Longstaffe 1867). On
these visits they learned the customs of different merchant communities and
their rates of exchange. They may also have experienced and taken an interest
in different eating habits and domestic arrangements which required specific
sets of material culture. Within Newcastle, the advent of imported redware
vessels seems to have begun as a slow trickle in the fourteenth century but

steadily increased through the fifteenth and sixteenth centuries, in inverse proportion to the use of locally produced reduced greenwares (Ellison in Harbottle and Ellison 1981: esp. 96, Figure 6). This phenomenon needs to be examined in conjunction with the advent of other imported domestic items and forms of building material, for example Low Countries brick and tile.

I suggest that the chronology and quantity of such imports ran concurrently with the growth in export of coal to the Low Countries from the late four-teenth century (cf. O'Brien 1991). As Newcastle merchants created these contacts, is there enough evidence to suggest that the consumption choices of the merchant élite indicated that they were developing a similar lifestyle (sharing the same material preferences) to their counterparts in other ports around the North Sea rim? Gaimster and Nenk (1997: 172) have argued for a 'Hanseatic' material culture and lifestyle as applicable to London, Norwich and Southampton. Newcastle was a major North Sea port but the same questions have not been asked of the archaeology and social history here. Moreover, I would warn against the kind of analysis that seeks either direct parallels for the patterns found in the south of England, or assigns a 'poor cousin' interpreta-tion to the evidence should it prove that assemblages from Newcastle do not match the full range and quality of imports found in the South. Rather, if the Hanseatic culture is viewed (or theorised) as a range of choices, then the consumption and lifestyle preferences of a north-country urban élite may reflect particular assimilations, selections and innovations through which they created their own distinct regional identity. By the seventeenth century, it is quite clear that there were German and Dutch tableware and other domestic imports to Newcastle, although, thus far, the quantities should not be overstated (e.g. Hurst 1972; Ellison et al. 1979; Heslop et al. 1995). Similarly, although historic photographs and drawings show there to have been many houses in Newcastle with the type of seventeenth-century decoration known as 'Dutch' gables, the extent to which this is indicative of direct North Sea influence or a particular north-eastern English interpretation of prevailing styles is debatable (cf. Louw 1981; Green, this volume).

Newcastle was, equally, a place that attracted foreign merchants and artisans to ply their trade within its walls. Anthony Wells-Cole (1997: 185–200) has identified a carver of exceptional ability based in Newcastle in the first half of the seventeenth century. The artist based his designs on Dutch, German and Flemish prints and engravings and he produced screens and fireplace over-mantels which were unique in England. The majority of traceable works originated in merchant houses, the Guildhall and Mansion House, in The Close, Sandhill and the Quayside. Either the artist, or the taste for such designs on the part of patrons, must have derived from Holland or Germany.

In the seventeenth century many of the men who were to emerge as leaders of the Puritan movement in Newcastle had established trading links with, and stayed in, countries where there were Reformed Churches (Howell 1967: 71–2). Equally, some spent long periods in London, attending Puritan churches. Newcastle families established branches of the families in London to act on behalf of their business interests. They also brought London Puritan ministers to preach in their Newcastle houses (Howell 1967: 81, 89, 93, 101).

The third source of influence was the Scots. The relationship between Newcastle and the Scots was complex. There was a marked hostility to Scots: they were forbidden to become apprenticed to many of the trades, such as masons, plumbers and goldsmiths (Howell 1967: 97). However, of nearly 6,000 people involved in the extraction of coal, the majority were Scots or Borderers (Howell 1967: 98). Similarly, the majority of keelmen who ferried the coal from shore to ship were Scots. Thus the wealth of Newcastle was dependent on them. Moreover, the Scots were very largely Presbyterian Covenanters, opposed to the established Church of England (Ellis 1984: 209). Covenanting preachers were sent to Newcastle from Scotland (Howell 1967: 99). In the seventeenth century Newcastle was flooded with religious and political tracts and pamphlets from Edinburgh (Howell 1967: 104).

If the civic ceremonies in Newcastle reinforced areas of commercial and mercantile use as centres of civic power, the converse is that they created spaces for exclusion and opposition to that power, and marginalisation of certain groups. The majority of the keelmen lived in Sandgate ward, where some 80 per cent of the population lived in poverty. The keelmen often rioted or withdrew their labour. And there were other peripheral parts of the town which were 'Recepticle[s] for Scots and Unfreemen' (Bourne 1736: 50), where 'felons, foreigners, Scots and other undesirables were established'. The disenfranchised freemen often capitalised on social upheavals and riots of those further down the social hierarchy on the grounds of religious conviction or common cause with their grievances. This often masked political ambition. In 1633 the apprentices rioted and held Sandgate and Ballast Hills against the mayor, aided and abetted by the lesser freemen. In 1653, the keelmen stopped their own work and prevented others from working; a similar episode took place in 1660 (Howell 1967: 292).

In the Civil War period, the Newcastle Puritan/Freeman faction welcomed an invading Scots army. Many Puritan merchants had married into Scots families, sought Scots preachers to minister in their houses and became Covenanters. They subsequently supported the Parliamentarian faction against the Crown. During the period of Parliamentarian rule (1649–60) they were able to oust members of the hated Mercer/Hostman élite on the grounds that they condoned the Established Church (Howell 1967). They became aldermen themselves. In all the period of the Commonwealth, however, they did not reform the structure of government itself: they just became the new élite (Howell 1967; Ellis 1984: 203). During this time, they appealed to the Scots and the coal-workers as co-religionists against their political enemies from the former élite of the Mercer/Hostman faction (Howell 1967: 124).

At this point we may return to the houses and architecture, for the Guildhall was commissioned and paid for by the new Puritan government. And many of their members built their houses on the Sandhill and Close, to live cheek-by-jowl with the old enemy élite. From Bessie Surtees House you can almost look straight into the Mayor's Parlour. We do not know the political allegiance of the owner at that time, but the proximity suggests either an ease with the power-brokers of the new regime, or an aggressive intrusion into a space in which the old regime felt it should have resided. Many of the buildings incorporated the fireplaces and screens mentioned earlier. Similarly, a distinctive set of plaster ceiling motifs were used in a number of these buildings. The first must surely have been in the Mayor's Parlour, dated to *c.* 1658 (Heslop and McCombie 1996: 153 for the following). Similar motifs can be found in a room in Bessie Surtees House, overlooking the Guildhall, which was remodelled in *c.* 1658. Another ceiling of this form existed in a timber-framed building called Cosin's House on the Quayside, demolished in 1896. When Alderman Fenwick's brick house was built on Pilgrim Street in the late seventeenth century, the same ceiling moulds were used for the first-floor east room – again a room which overlooked the street. This ceiling must date from between 1660 and 1695. This is traditionally interpreted as an old stock of patterns being reused, 'but may represent a craftsman's lingering fondness for the old style' (Heslop and McCombie 1996: 153). It could, however, have been a conscious reference to the arenas of wealth creation and civic authority (i.e. the Sandhill houses and the Mayor's Parlour), and to a religious/political factional allegiance.

Colley (1992) has argued that religion provided one of the principal means of creating a British identity in the eighteenth and nineteenth centuries. It is clear that ideas of a shared Protestant confession between English and Scots were manipulated from the earliest times in trying to invent a sense of British identity (Williamson 1999). The peculiar attraction of Newcastle's coal-related employment meant that unusual numbers of Scots were resident in the town. The Scots as a political nation at this time, and particularly during the Interregnum (1649–60), also provided a succour to the aspirant lesser merchants normally excluded from Newcastle's civic government. Non-conformity could, seemingly, be used to bridge many differences. The way in which shared religion was manipulated as a means to garner the economically vital support of the Presbyterian keelmen and coalworkers, if and when convenient, only for the same keelmen to be treated as an incalcitrant mob when inconvenient to the Puritan civic government, shows that this religious fellow-feeling was a fleeting thing. We have to appreciate that conviction and political aspiration or expediency might fluctuate within a given situation.

CONTESTING ÉLITE CULTURE AND SPACE

All this has shown a particular form of display, broadcasting the constituent members of civic government for the public to see, integrally bound with the hub of commerce, the Guildhall and the river front. The post-Restoration period has been seen as the era of an urban renaissance when specific spaces were set aside for cultural entertainment and for promenade (Borsay 1984, 1989). Whilst similar trends existed in Newcastle, I am interested in their significance for the creation of identity within the town. It is clear that the space called The Forth (see Figure 2.6) to the west of the town walls, beyond Westgate, had been the resort of the populace of all classes for feast days and festivities, and many processions ended up here (Brand 1777: 252–3, 1789: 418). The space had been leased by the Common Council during the Interregnum in 1657. By the late seventeenth century, however, it had been formalised with a bowling green, associated entertainment house with logia, geometric walkways lined with trees. Celia Fiennes commented at length on The Forth (Griffiths 1888: 177). It is recorded that the trees were brought from Holland in 1680 (Brand 1789: 418 k). This may be an example of Anglo-Dutch garden art, popular at this time, if politically loaded after 1688. Switzer, writing in 1718 for a British audience, 'considered Dutch garden art best suited for town sites' (quoted in Dixon Hunt 1996: 195).

One of the features of Dutch garden planning in towns was that they be established in or around the city wall or other fortifications. The proximity of the town walls to The Forth is notable. Celia Fiennes records that there was a walk all round the walls of the town, and Bourne indicated a walk along the town walls near Pilgrim Street in the 1730s (Griffiths 1888: 177; Bourne 1736). However, this was not merely a place of recourse for an emerging 'polite' town society, a means by which they defined themselves and were seen by others. The town's craft companies had been acquiring the old defensive towers on the medieval walls for their meeting houses since as early as the 1620s, and many were established by the eighteenth century in order to hold business, courts and feasts in them (see Figure 2.7). There was a dynamic here, for the nine ancient companies were given premises in the former Blackfriars priory after the Dissolution (Harbottle and Fraser 1987), but it was largely the by-trades who took up premises on the former defences. This may be thought of as a marginalising of these crafts, but given that the walls became the location for a formal walk, for genteel perambulation, the companies may have found the walls a convenient if not expedient way of advertising and being seen to partake in the expansion of polite culture in the town. Given, also, that it was the by-trades who had such a struggle to gain political recognition and enfranchisement within the town's system of government, the occupation of the town's walls may have been a useful strategy for penetrating at least one of the spatial spheres in which social and political position was reproduced. The walls provided an alternative to the Guildhall/Sandill arena in which to insist on inclusion.

Both Borsay (1984, 1989) and Wilson (1995) have written of the way in which the urban élite withdrew from public spaces for their entertainment and display. We know that in the course of the eighteenth century the élite moved into new housing developments like Charlotte Square and Hanover Square in the west, and gradually moved out from the old town to estates beyond the Leazes in the north-west. Increasingly in the course of that century the urban élite frequented enclosures or buildings especially created for their amusement and promenade: formal gardens, the race course, assembly rooms and coffee

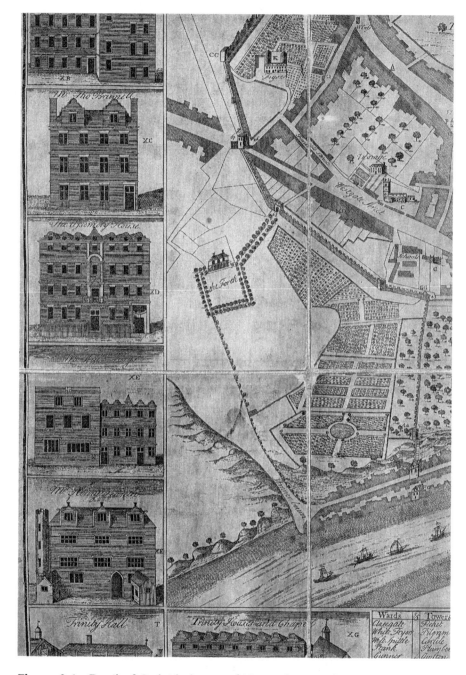

Figure 2.6 Detail of Corbridge's map of Newcastle upon Tyne, 1723/4, showing the Forth, Westgate Road and the Assembly House (marked **XD** on the map, and marginal image). Reproduced by permission of Newcastle Libraries and Information Service

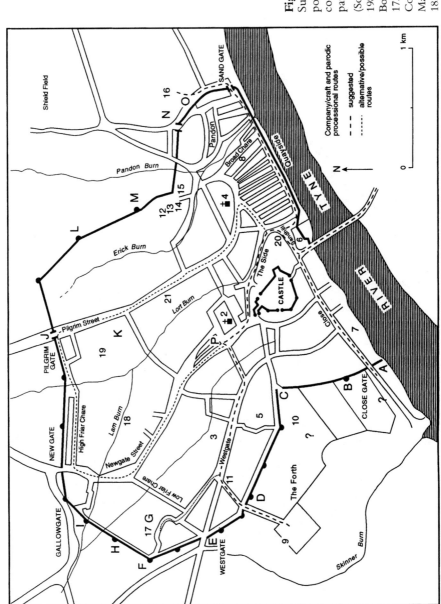

Figure 2.7
Suggested routes of post-medieval company/craft and parodic processions.

(Sources: Anderson 1982; Borsay 1984; Borsay 1989; Bourne 1736; Brand 1777/89; Corbridge 1723/4; Mackenzie 1827; Oliver 1830)

houses. That epitome of seventeenth-century timber-framed merchant housing – Bessie Surtees House on the Sandhill – became a coffee house between 1774 and *c*. 1794 (Heslop *et al*. 1995: 14). The majority of the town's population was excluded from these spaces.

There is, in the provision of leisure facilities in Newcastle, perhaps, a change in landscape focus towards the west and north. The house on The Forth was used for musical events and assemblies in the early eighteenth century. By 1723–4, an assembly house existed on Westgate Road next to Lady Clavering's House (marked 'XD' on Corbridge's map and with an image in the margin: see Figure 2.6). This may have been Mr William Creagh's house, Westgate, referred to in the *Newcastle Courant* on Monday, 28 May 1716 (Hinde 1860: 241). In *c*. 1736 an Assembly House was built in the Groat Market (Hinde 1860: 242); in 1776 new Assembly Rooms were built in the grounds of the vicarage of St John's Church, Westgate Road. The continuing importance of Westgate Road may have remained linked to civic processions. The Assembly House shown on Corbridge's map has a first-floor balcony which implies public address to a crowd congregating below. It is significant that the urban élite of Newcastle raised subscriptions for their new Assembly Rooms at a time when the main river crossing, the Tyne Bridge, lay in ruins after a flood of 1771. The fallen bridge proved little hindrance to the élite, who by this time lived to the west and north of the river, whilst it was a major problem for any workmen trying to cross the river from the south (Wilson 1995: 355). By the time of Brand's map of 1789, the formal gardens of The Forth appear to have gone, and new ones were opened: New Ranelagh Gardens bordering on the Leazes to the north-west of the town. The mayor and town society no longer resorted to The Forth, even after processions (Brand 1777: 252–3), and we have instead the creation of specific buildings to accommodate polite society in its various cultural pursuits – withdrawing from the spaces between – mainly the streets.

At the same time, the civic government supported a prodigious amount of official ceremonial in the eighteenth century, documented by Bourne (1736), Brand (1777, 1789) and Mackenzie (1827). Many of these occasions followed highlights in the Protestant Anglican calendar or celebrated royal events, like coronations and birthdays when particular largesse might be meted out to the crowd, e.g. a fountain in the market place was made to run with wine on the coronation of George II (Brand 1789: 516). Thus ceremony could inculcate a sense of British identity and promote loyalty to authority, which suited the Corporation's aims (cf. Cressy 1990). Some race weeks and assemblies coincided with the assizes, further combining occasions of authoritative control with liberalism. Newcastle had its own Protestant equivalent to carnival on Shrove Tuesday when shops were shut and people released from their work obligations from noon (Brand 1777: 331). Other celebrations were more spontaneous, celebrating occasions like the entry of national military heroes, such as the Duke of Cumberland. It can be argued that officially sanctioned ceremony sought to contain public enthusiasm and exuberance, and reinforce the status quo, both in terms of local power structures and national identities.

Wilson (1995: 296–7), has asserted that

> the most salient feature of the civic and political ceremonial in
> Newcastle, apart from its abundance, was the absence of active popular
> participation, which contrasts sharply with the civic customs of many
> other towns in this period . . . In general . . . ordinary citizens of the
> town, including the members of the guilds and trade companies, were
> relegated to the status of observers on public days or, at best, passive
> recipients of patrician munificence.

I consider that Wilson has failed to recognise the implications of the spatial
aspect of ceremonial which created arenas for opposition to élite culture and
political monopoly; and that she has underestimated the popular, particularly
guild or craft companies', involvement in their own ceremonials.

I have proposed that a particular form of house created spaces, both internal
and external, for the reproduction of the élite; the converse is that they thereby
also created spaces for challenge, subversion and parody of the ruling classes in
the town. It is unclear why Wilson dismisses the evidence for popular ceremonial in Newcastle, as documented by Bourne (1736), Brand (1777, 1789)
and Mackenzie (1827). Moreover, it is by examining the inter-relationship
between space and its occupation that we can counter the accusation of passivity
on the part of Newcastle's politically excluded population. The location of
the craft company houses, described above, may be one particular strategy in
the occupation of space, elbowing into the arenas of polite society, creating a
challenge to its political monopolies. The formalisation of The Forth and The
Shield Field (1738) encroached on and gentrified traditional recreational space.
However, such acts were often opposed, for example when the hedges on The
Shield Field were torn down in 1738 (Brand 1789: 441–2). There were often
riots, in both the seventeenth and eighteenth centuries: for example, in 1701,
1719 and 1738 the keelmen went on strike; in 1705 the shipwrights went on
strike for higher wages; and in 1733 the masons expelled a member of their
company for refusing to join in a strike (Ellis 1984: 207 and *passim*; Wilson
1995: *passim*). In 1740 there were bread riots; in 1772–3 the enclosure of the
Town Moor was opposed. The Guildhall was the spatial focus of violent riots
on numerous occasions. The iconography of the civic élite and of royal government was vulnerable; sometimes there was both a religious and political
dimension to this, as when the statue of James II was torn down in 1688
(Bourne 1736: 126). The food riot of 1740 lasted a week and resulted in one
death, the looting of the Guildhall, the appropriation of £1,200 and the
destruction of the 'Corporation's cherished portraits of Charles II and James II'
(Wilson 1995: 329; Borsay 1984: 238).

The keelmen who conveyed the coals to the larger ships were a formidable
force, but it was often these moments of conflict, these occasions of common
cause, that created them as a recognisable group momentarily making all other
distinctions of nationality or religion of little import. Again, this had its season,

summer being the most effective time to strike. The keelmen lived mostly in Sandgate, in the parish of All Saints' Church, in congested and filthy conditions; it was seen as a den of dissent and the presence of Scots Presbyterians was a source of concern on the grounds of non-conformity as much as a reassurance of British co-religionist loyalty. The response of the civic élite to such riots more often than not exposed the considerable internal political conflict which permeated eighteenth-century Newcastle (Wilson 1995: 316, 329–32). Different political factions amongst the merchants and traders could play on the support or aspirations of those further down the social hierarchy, on grounds of shared economic interests, religious conviction or exasperation at their disenfranchisement, thus moments of shared political identity slashed through the normative picture. When it suited the Corporation, the keelmen were supported as loyal British and pro-Hanoverian. However, in the midst of a particularly intractable keelmen's strike in 1746, the keelmen claimed to support Charles Edward Stuart and this threw the civic authorities into reaction (Wilson 1995: 335, n. 59). This resulted in exaggerated accusations of Jacobitism, as in fact had occurred earlier in 1715, but it was more probably a tag attached to any mob of the time by the élite (Pittock 1997: 25, 120).

The keelmen consolidated their identity in the building and maintaining of their own hospital in 1700, on a prominent ridge in the Sandgate ward, but outside the town walls, in other words in a prominent position in their own part of town. The hospital was funded from voluntary deductions from the keelmen's wages. Moreover, they held their own annual processions. However, by 1723, the Newcastle magistrates 'managed to wrest legal control over the charity from the keelmen ... in order to limit its potential as a strike fund' (Wilson 1995: 62). The location of the first Bridewell or prison is interesting, therefore, as it stood in the easten part of town, above the Sandgate ward, within the town walls (visible on Corbridge's map of 1723/4); and later the proud new symbol of conventional, conformist religion, the Georgian, neo-Classical All Saints' Church, financed from the contributions of Newcastle's polite society, was raised on a hill above the Sandgate between 1786 and 1796, in juxtaposition with the den of dissent at its foot, as if to stamp its authority on the anarchy below. It seems clear that space was consciously articulated within the strategies of both the civic élite and those who were excluded from the heart of political power.

If the fine houses we considered earlier looked onto arenas of civic and economic importance, they themselves were overlooked by the Castle Garth: an area beyond the control of the Common Council, and the only place in the town where one could ply non-incorporated trades and be free of the restrictions and discipline of the craft companies (Nolan 1990). This has been confirmed by archaeological deposits of leather patches from cobbling waste, which represent the residue from shoe repairing, a non-incorporated trade, rather than the residue from shoe-making, a trade which was controlled by a craft company (Vaughan in Harbottle and Ellison 1981: 189). The Castle Garth was also, consequently, a haven for dissenting religion.

The annual processions of the keelmen have been referred to above. In 1789 the glassworkers processed along The Close to the Mansion House, and it was reported to have been initiated as an indignant or ridiculing response to the cordwainers' procession (see Figure 2.7; Mackenzie 1827: 88). Further, a parody of the aldermanic procession on Election Day, Michaelmas Monday, was held by Newcastle's children and seems to have followed the same route as the official procession (Wilson 1995: 297). Thus, there were popular and craft company ceremonies which encroached on the space of official civic ceremonial and challenged both the spheres and activities through which authority and privilege were created and perpetuated in Newcastle.

CONCLUSION

In conclusion, I have shown how the material environment formed, and was formed by, the need to create and assert social relationships, particularly on the part of the ruling élite. Particular house forms found in Newcastle in the seventeenth century were not just the result of fashion, or emulation, but a local response to social and historical circumstances and formative of a landscape of relationships. Equally, this élite landscape created the spaces, the possibility, of radically opposed acts of expression and temporary solidarity. When looking at the landscape of a town, the physical landscape is part and parcel of the dynamic of the *social* landscape; time and the way in which spaces are occupied are necessary considerations in understanding the dynamic in social relationships. I have suggested ways in which we might think of the role of material culture as both constitutive of relationships and strategically deployed.

ACKNOWLEDGEMENTS

I am grateful to David Heslop, County Archaeological Officer for Tyne and Wear, England, an inspiring colleague and companion; to Rebecca King, Department of History, University of Durham, for drawing my attention to Wilson 1995; to Dr Peter Rowley-Conwy, Department of Archaeology, University of Durham, for comments and considerable help with my English; to Yvonne Beadnell for drawing Figures 2.1–4 and 2.6; to Newcastle Libraries and Information Service for Figure 2.6; and to Dr Susan Lawrence, the editor, for her generous patience and support.

REFERENCES

Anderson, J.J. (1982) *Records of Early English Drama: Newcastle upon Tyne*. Toronto: University of Toronto/University of Manchester Press.
Barrett, J.C. (1988) Fields of discourse: reconstituting a social archaeology. *Critique of Anthropology* 7(3): 5–16.

Blake, J.B. (1967) The medieval coal trade of north-east England: some fourteenth-century evidence. In G.C.F. Forster (ed.), *Northern History: A Review of the History of the North of England*, 1–26. Leeds: School of History, University of Leeds.

—— (1984) 'All the town's a stage': urban ritual and ceremony 1660–1800. In P. Clark (ed.), *The Transformation of English Provincial Towns 1600–1800*, 228–58. London: Hutchinson.

—— (1989) *The English Urban Renaissance: Culture and Society in the Provincial Town, 1660–1770.* Oxford: Clarendon Press.

Bourdieu, P. (1987) *Outline of a Theory of Practice.* Cambridge: Cambridge University Press.

Bourne, H. (1736) *The History of Newcastle upon Tyne.* Newcastle: John White.

Brand, J. (1777) *Observations on Popular Antiquities.* Newcastle upon Tyne: T. Saint.

—— (1789) *The History and Antiquities of the Town and County of the Town of Newcastle upon Tyne*, 2 vols. London: B. White and Son.

Colley, L. (1992) *Britons: Forging the Nation 1707–1837.* New Haven, CN: Yale University Press.

Corbridge, J. (1723/4) Map. Newcastle upon Tyne, City Library Service.

Cressy, D. (1990) The Protestant calendar and the vocabulary of celebration in early modern England. *Journal of British Studies* 29: 31–52.

Dixon Hunt, J. (1996) Anglo-Dutch garden art: style and idea. In D. Hoak and M. Feingold (eds), *In The World of William and Mary: Anglo-Dutch Perspectives on the Revolution of 1688–89*, 188–200. Stanford, CA: Stanford University Press.

Ellis, J. (1984) A dynamic society: social relations in Newcastle upon Tyne 1660–1760. In P. Clark (ed.), *The Transformation of English Provincial Towns 1600–1800*, 190–227. London: Hutchinson.

Ellison, M., Finch, M. and Harbottle, B. (1979) The excavation of a 17th-century pit at the Black Gate, Newcastle upon Tyne, 1975. *Post-Medieval Archaeology* 13: 153–81.

Ellison, M., McCombie, G.M., MacElvaney, M., Newman, A., O'Brien, C., Taverner, N. and Williams, A. (1993) Excavations at Newcastle Quayside: waterfront development at the Swirle. *Archaeologia Aeliana*, 5th series, 21: 151–234.

Fraser, C. (1984) The early hostmen of Newcastle upon Tyne. *Archaeologia Aeliana*, 5th series, 12: 169–79.

Fraser, C.M. and Emsley, K. (1973) *Tyneside.* Newton Abbot: David and Charles.

Fraser, R., Jamfrey, C. and Vaughan, J. (1995) Excavation on the site of the Mansion House, Newcastle, 1990. *Archaeologia Aeliana*, 5th series, 23: 145–214.

Gaimster, D.R.M. and Nenk, B. (1997) English households in transition *c.* 1450–1550: the ceramic evidence. In D.R.M. Gaimster and P. Stamper (eds), *The Age of Transition: The Archaeology of English Culture 1400–1600*, 171–95. The Society for Medieval Archaeology Monograph 15, Oxbow Monograph 98.

Giddens, A. (1985) Time, space and regionalisation. In D. Gregory and J. Urry (eds), *Social Relations and Spatial Structures*, 265–95. London: Macmillan Education.

—— (1986) *The Constitution of Society: Outline of a Theory of Structuration.* Cambridge: Polity Press.

Giles, K. (2000) *An Archaeology of Social Identity: Guildhalls in York, c.1350–1630.* British Archaeological Reports British Series 315.

Graves, C.P. and Heslop, D. (forthcoming) Ritual and townscape in Newcastle upon Tyne.

Gray, W. (1649) *Chorographia, or a Survey of Newcastle upon Tyne.* Newcastle: Stephen Buckley.

Griffiths, E.W. (ed.) (1888) *Through England on a Side Saddle in the Time of William and Mary being the Diary of Celia Fiennes.* London: The Leadenhall Press.

Harbottle, B. and Ellison, M. (1981) An excavation in the castle ditch, Newcastle upon Tyne, 1974–6. *Archaeologia Aeliana*, 5th series, 15: 23–149.

Harbottle, B. and Fraser, R. (1987) Black Friars, Newcastle upon Tyne, after the dissolution of the monasteries. *Archaeologia Aeliana*, 5th series, 15: 23–150.

Heslop, D. and McCombie, G. (1996) 'Alderman Fenwick's house', a late seventeenth
century house in Pilgrim Street, Newcastle upon Tyne. *Archaeologia Aeliana*, 5th
series, 24: 129–70.

Heslop, D., McCombie, G. and Thomson, C. (1995) *Bessie Surtees House: Two Merchant
Houses in Sandhill, Newcastle upon Tyne*. Buildings of Newcastle 2. Newcastle: Society
of Antiquaries of Newcastle upon Tyne.

Heslop, D., Truman, L. and Vaughan, J.E. (1995) Excavation of the town wall in the
Milk Market, Newcastle upon Tyne. *Archaeologia Aeliana*, 5th series, 23: 215–34

Hinde, J.H. (1860) Public amusements in Newcastle. *Archaeologia Aeliana*, 2nd series,
4: 229–48.

Howell, R. (1967) *Newcastle upon Tyne and the Puritan Revolution: A Study of the Civil
War in North England*. Oxford: Clarendon Press.

Hurst, J.G. (1972) A Wanfried dish from Newcastle. *Archaeologia Aeliana*, 4th series, 50:
259–62

James, M. (1983) Ritual, drama and social body in the late medieval town. *Past and
Present*, 98: 3–29.

Longstaffe, W.H.D. (ed.) (1867) *Memoirs of the Life of Mr Ambrose Barnes, late Merchant
and Sometime Alderman of Newcastle upon Tyne*. Newcastle: Surtees Society, 50.

Louw, H. (1981) Anglo-Netherlandish architectural interchange *c*. 1600–*c*. 1660.
Architectural History, 24: 1–23.

Mackenzie, E. (1827) *A Descriptive and Historical View of the Town and County of Newcastle
upon Tyne*. Newcastle upon Tyne: Mackenzie and Dent.

Nef, J.U. (1932) *The Rise of the British Coal Industry*. London: G. Routledge and Sons
Ltd.

Nolan, J. (1990) The Castle of Newcastle upon Tyne after *c*. 1600. *Archaeologia Aeliana*,
5th series, 18: 79–126.

O'Brien, C., Bown, L., Dixon, S. and Nicholson, R. (1988) *The Origins of Newcastle
Quayside, Excavations at Queen Street and Dog Bank*. Newcastle: The Society of
Antiquaries of Newcastle upon Tyne Monograph 3.

O'Brien, C. (1991) Newcastle upon Tyne and its North Sea Trade. In G.L. Good,
R.H. Jones and M.W. Ponsford (eds), *Waterfront Archaeology: Proceedings of the Third
International Conference, Bristol, 1988*, 36–42. Council for British Archaeology
Research Report 74.

Pittock, M.G.H. (1997) *Inventing and Resisting Britain: Cultural Identities in Britain and
Ireland, 1685–1789*. London: Macmillan.

Schofield, J. (1995) *Medieval London Houses*. New Haven, CN: Yale University Press.

Welford, R. (1916) Local muniments, 5th Series. *Archaeologia Aeliana*, 3 ser, 13: 17–60.

Wells-Cole, A. (1997) *Art of Decoration in Elizabethan and Jacobean England: The Influence
of Continental Prints 1558–1625*. New Haven, CN: Yale University Press.

Williamson, A. (1999) Patterns of British identity: 'Britain' and its rivals in the sixteenth
and seventeenth centuries. In G. Burgess (ed.), *The New British History: Founding a
Modern State 1603–1715*, 138–73. London: I.B. Tauris.

Wilson, K. (1995) *The Sense of the People: Politics, Culture and Imperialism in England,
1715–1785*. Cambridge: Cambridge University Press.

3 Houses in north-eastern England: regionality and the British beyond, c. 1600–1750

ADRIAN GREEN

The neglected colonial dynamic in British history and historical archaeology has its counterpart in simplified accounts of the British origins of American colonial culture. Deetz (1977) characterised the 'world-view' of seventeenth-century colonists in New England as a quasi-medieval one, rooted in conceptions of the Great Chain of Being and corporate social organisation. For Deetz, this 'Elizabethan' way of making sense of the world was transformed by the reception from England of European Renaissance ideas of order and rationality, between the late seventeenth century and the American Revolution, creating what he labelled the 'Georgian Order'. Johnson (1996) has revised the concept of the 'Georgian Order' in its British context, and argued that England experienced a series of changes in ways of living from the sixteenth century which were crucial antecedents to the changes Deetz detected in the eighteenth-century colonies. Furthermore, changes in the material culture of sixteenth- and early seventeenth-century England, known for houses as the 'Great Rebuilding',[1] were in many ways equivalent to the process of Georgianisation in late seventeenth- and early eighteenth-century Britain and America (Green 2000). The Great Rebuilding involved architectural changes that were ultimately national in scope and employed forms of 'Renaissance' style. Yet both the Great Rebuilding and Georgianisation entailed regionalised practices of building, on both sides of the British Atlantic. Interactions between the inhabitants of the Atlantic Archipelago and America from the sixteenth through to the eighteenth century contributed to shifting conceptions of Britishness while retaining and re-creating regionalised cultural behaviour.

Regionality provides a means to differentiate cultural behaviour (Giddens 1984; Thrift 1994), and ought to be applied to the study of seventeenth- and eighteenth-century material culture on both sides of the British Atlantic. In this chapter I want to address the issue of regional diversity in the external appearance and internal arrangement of houses in north-eastern England. To evaluate their relationship to national identities, I look closely at standing houses in the north-east of England and seek to relate them to scales of cultural variation in housing in England, Britain and beyond. Before doing so, it will be useful to

outline the trajectories of national and regional identities within what is most
neutrally described as the 'Atlantic Archipelago'.

ACCOMMODATING BRITISHNESS

Recent historical research into 'Britishness' has emphasised that the idea of
Britain as a political entity was largely re-created in the sixteenth and seventeenth centuries, as a means to address the tensions entailed by the English
Crown's relationship to the realms of Wales and Ireland, and the kingdom of
Scotland. While the complex and contested process of Protestant Reformation involved pan-European religious identities, and ultimately furnished
England and Wales, and also Scotland, with an enduring source of national self-
definition, the initial political manoeuvre of the English King Henry VIII's
break with Papal authority was legitimated by reviving a concept of British
imperium (Bradshaw and Morrill 1996). This early sixteenth-century idea of
the English Crown's *imperium* over the British Isles was extended in the
late sixteenth and seventeenth centuries to England's newly won overseas
colonies (Armitage 2000). Definitions of Britishness after 1600 were increasingly bound to the formation of a sea-borne empire. Whereas the Union of
the Crowns of Scotland and England in 1603, retaining the two nations, was
largely conducted in a domestic context, the 1707 Act of Union between
England and Scotland that inaugurated the nation-state of 'Great Britain'
occurred in an imperial context. Colley (1992) argues that a sense of Britishness
among the wider populace was inculcated through the experience of imperi-
alist wars with continental European powers, fought by 'British' soldiers and
seamen in the eighteenth century. Britishness between *c.* 1600 and 1750 was
intimately associated with colonialism: in the domestic setting of the Atlantic
Archipelago, in commercial engagement with the East and in settlement in
the New World to the west.

As Bailyn (1988) argues, the peopling of British North America represented
an extension across the Atlantic of the high degree of population mobility
current in Europe for centuries previously. The regionalised origins of European settlers, including those from regions within Britain, fed directly into the
diversity of American colonial culture. Houses in the landscape, as the primary
units of settlement, provide a means of mapping the scales of cultural variation
entailed by patterns of population mobility across Europe, within England and
in the wider British world. Houses, moreover, present an aspect of material
culture that was readily associated with particular social groups and regional
distinctiveness. Studying the houses that accommodated the British enables us
to avoid muffling social difference in our accounts of geographical identities.
Before tracing the relationship of housing cultures to formal geographical units
in north-eastern England and the British beyond, regionality in north-east
England requires contextualisation.

REGIONALITY IN NORTH-EAST ENGLAND

The north-east corner of England always occupied a distinctive place within the trajectories of nation-formation and national identity. Medieval historians have emphasised that the concept of a national people is much older than the modern period of nation-states (Davies 1994), although as Kidd (1999) argues, ethnic identities were subject to reconstruction around regnal territorial units. The early medieval Kingdom of Northumbria occupied territory between the kingdoms of southern England and lowland Scotland, and there were considerable contingencies involved in whether the area ended up in England or Scotland during the eleventh-century Norman Conquest. Through to the occupation of northern England by Scottish troops in the mid-seventeenth century, the River Tees (see Figure 3.1) marked the southern limit of the Anglo-Scottish border zone (Phythian-Adams 2000). From a long way back the inhabitants of north-east England had a very particular perspective on being English, and proximity to Scotland was a fundamental aspect of regionalised identities.

The area defined today as north-east England comprises the historic counties of Northumberland, the 'Town and County' of Newcastle upon Tyne and the 'County Palatine' of Durham (see Figure 3.1). In our period these counties formed the diocese of Durham. Ecclesiastical authority, administered from the cathedral city of Durham, extended across the three counties, but county-based administration of tax collection and law enforcement linked the localities to central government. Until 1536 the 'Regality of the bishops of Durham' entailed the bishop enforcing justice and collecting taxes which elsewhere were the direct prerogative of the Crown (see Lapsley 1900). Although the Bishop of Durham retained extensive secular powers within the County Palatine of Durham, north of the River Trent the King's Council in the North after 1537 was the chief executive authority. (These reforms were part of the same Tudor policy that placed Wales on an equal administrative footing with England after their Union in 1536.) The power of the Church, represented materially by the Bishop's castle and Durham Cathedral's dominance of the cityscape, combined with its extensive landholdings across the Palatinate, contributed to a distinctive county identity into the seventeenth century and after.

The northern counties were not shires since the area's early medieval administrative structure was not part of the shire system of southern England. From the Norman period onwards the north-east was a border zone, at the frontier between England and Scotland. Border service by the populace of the northern counties of England, which exempted people from central taxation in return for military service, was abolished when James VI of Scotland and I of England achieved the Union of the Crowns in 1603. James sought to remove the frontier by declaring the counties on both sides of the border the 'middle shires' of his kingdoms (Watts 1975). This policy of normalising the area conflicted, however, with the beneficial tenurial arrangements of 'tenant right' that had

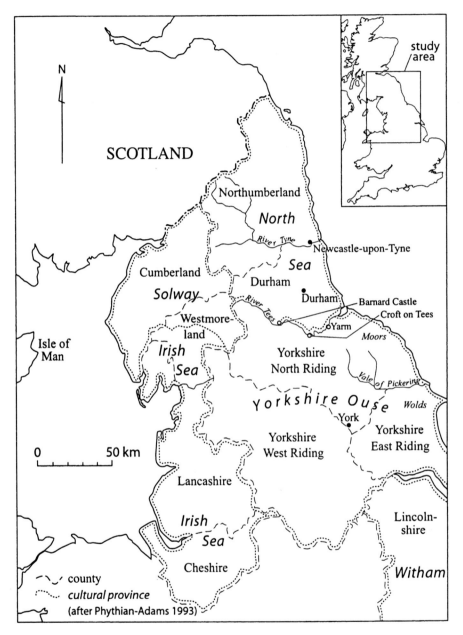

Figure 3.1 Location map and places mentioned in the text. Cultural provinces are taken from Phythian-Adams 1993

developed in association with border service. Following the initiative of the Crown, the Church estates at Durham sought to extract a commercial revenue from their lands, to counter the erosion by inflation of the customary value of fixed rents and renewal fines. The tenants claimed in the courts that their beneficial land-transfer arrangements and low rents retained their customary force despite the abolition of border service (Watts 1971; Drury 1987). These claims, varying in detail from manor to manor, lasted through to the early eighteenth century, testimony to the legacy of the Anglo-Scottish border for the construction of regional solidarities via the tenure of house and lands.

Despite this, regions do not appear to have been the primary spatial units of geographical identity in the seventeenth and early eighteenth centuries. The English county was always a more meaningful geographical unit for both the governing and the governed. No documents for this period refer to 'the north-east', although an awareness of Northumbria was possibly present (Watts 1975: 43). County Durham was known as 'the bishopric' and contemporaries wrote of 'Going into the Bishoprick' when they crossed the rivers of the Tees and Tyne or passed over the high ground of the Pennines (Hughes 1952: 304). The identification of the County Palatine of Durham with the Church entailed its secular powers being regarded as both a blessing and an incumberance. Durham possessed its own Court of Chancery, which saved its residents journeying to London to pursue suits in Westminster (Knight 1990). When the Palatinate of Durham was threatened with abolition around 1688, a petition was launched to defend the courts, submitting that 'at all times, right and justice have, within the same county, been distributed to such of the inhabitants thereof as have sued for the same in any courts of the county palatine' (Hutchinson 1785–94: 1, 561). The county's lack of parliamentary representation, however, had been a constant source of complaint during the seventeenth century. Until the 1670s the county and city of Durham were only represented by the Bishop in the House of Lords, creating considerable tensions with the Bishop who was usually absent in the south (Heesom 1988). North-eastern England's relationship to national politics was clearly focused on the kingdom of England. Following the Act of Union of 1707, creating a single parliament for Scotland and England at Westminster, the main north-east newspaper participated in the textual erasure of Scotland by reporting that 'several of the Representatives for North Britain, as well Lords as Commons, . . . are to be present at the opening of Parliament' (*Newcastle Courant*, 3 November 1711). The early eighteenth-century appellations North and South Britain retained the frictions at the boundary, which the seventeenth-century nomenclature of 'middle shires' had sought to overcome.

The royalist historian Thomas Fuller wrote in the mid-seventeenth century that the Bishopric of Durham 'may be ranked amongst the middling shires of England' (1662: 154). Fuller's recognition of County Durham's ranking, as comparable with the social and economic life of southern England, is more accurate than later historians' emphasis on a backward, inherently 'northern' and predominantly upland region. Recent studies have tended to confirm Fuller's view. Weatherill (1996) has calculated from her national survey of probate inventories that consumption patterns, based on the appearance of 'new goods' in inventories between 1660 and 1760, rank parts of the north-east as 'advanced' as London and ahead of areas in the home counties.[2] Literacy rates across the social range also indicate that the north-east was as 'advanced', and possibly in areas influenced by Scots Presbyterianism 'ahead' of southern England in the seventeenth century (Cressy 1978; Houston 1985). The enclosure of common fields was also very much in advance of southern England: the majority of documented townfield enclosures in County Durham occurred in the seventeenth century, whereas in many areas of southern England this was mostly an eighteenth-century phenomenon (Hodgson 1979). According to Johnson, increasing national homogeneity in literacy levels, along with nationally marketed consumer and agricultural goods, and enclosure, effected a process of centralisation and unification in English culture (1996: 196–8). Yet, the specific ways in which this process operated involved regionalised interactions.

The culture and economy of north-east England was transformed in this period by the expansion of the coal trade between the River Tyne at Newcastle and the Thames at London. As Wrigley (1967) argues, the growth of London exercised a centrifugal force on the English economy, encouraging regional specialisation in products marketed to the capital. From the late sixteenth century, it was north-east coal that literally fuelled the massive growth of London. Industrialisation on Tyneside motivated farmers across the region to maximise their productivity via the enclosure of common fields, to cater for the market for agricultural produce created by the wage-labour workforce needed to mine and move coal or extract salt from seawater (Levine and Wrightson 1991; Morin 1998). While this entailed a substantial degree of social polarisation for those at the coalface, those prospering from industrial and agricultural change increasingly participated in nation-wide patterns of cultural behaviour. The material form of surviving houses indicates that this was the case from c. 1600 in lowland County Durham (Green 1998), and the hearth tax documents that those with equivalent levels of wealth occupied comparable housing in County Durham to those in southern England in the late seventeenth century (Jong forthcoming).

This precocious experience of industrialisation and commercialised agriculture made contemporaries aware that the economic development of the region was of national significance. Coal for London, and feeding the workforce of the coalfield, was crucial to the national interest, as witnessed by the strategic significance of control and defence of Newcastle by English and Scottish forces during the Civil War of the 1640s (Howell 1967). In both the early and late seventeenth century, litigants defending enclosure and the deleterious effects of mining and moving coal in Durham Chancery Court often invoked the importance of the coal industry and agricultural improvement to the 'commonwealth' of England as a whole (Knight 1990: 461–3).

While national identity in its English and British variants was closely associated with political structures and conflicts, regional identities were more closely grounded in the practices of cultural variation. National identity in England and Britain was made explicit in the representation or idealisation of national character; a feature of the late sixteenth-century Elizabethan period as well as the Hanoverian eighteenth century (Johnson, this volume). Regional self-consciousness, by contrast, is relatively muted in documentary sources for this period.[3] It was precisely because it was not perceived to represent a formal political agenda that regional identity was less of a contemporary preoccupation than the nationalism inherent in discourses related to the union of England with Wales, Scotland and potentially Ireland, and the formation of a British Empire. This is not to say that regionalised behaviour did not involve politics: in the eighteenth century, for instance, Newcastle and County Durham elections were advertised in Yorkshire newspapers (Looney 1983: 124). For regional variation was very largely a phenomenon of the precise degree to which people moved around. In the following section I trace some of the ways in which a regionalised identity has left documentary as well as archaeological traces in the north-east, with houses in the landscape representing a primary means of reconstructing scales of regionality.

REGIONALITY IN THE BUILT LANDSCAPE

The material form of houses varied regionally in seventeenth- and early eighteenth-century England, yet the ways in which houses were built and lived in was largely demarcated by social identities current across England as a whole. The houses rebuilt by the middling sort and lesser élite in the towns and countryside of seventeenth- and eighteenth-century north-eastern England, produced housing forms that were generally similar to their counterparts in much of the rest of England. Within this nation-wide housing culture, room arrangements, building materials and construction techniques were regionalised – both for the period of the Great Rebuilding in the sixteenth and earlier seventeenth centuries and Georgianisation in the later seventeenth and early eighteenth centuries. This nexus of social and geographical variation in the architecture of houses is discernible in surviving buildings today. Contemporaries, living in or passing through the landscape, would equally have been able to recognise the social and geographical variation inherent in houses.

The River Tees, marking the boundary between the bishopric of Durham and the county of Yorkshire, provides the location for a series of sites at which to explore these variations. The Tees was no topographical boundary: in both the Pennine uplands of Teesdale and the lowland Tees basin, the river ran through the centre of shared social and economic activity on both banks. This overlap is illustrated in Phythian-Adams's (1993, 2000) map of 'cultural provinces' based on the watersheds of major river catchment areas (see Figure 3.1). Phythian-Adams regards the Tees as a 'frontier valley' between two cultural provinces, which he delineates as county groupings that share cultural characteristics rooted in topography but replicated from at least the early medieval period through to the seventeenth and eighteenth centuries in documented interactions or aspects of material culture such as gravestone styles or buildings.

The Tees was a ceremonial boundary and the bridge and chapel at Croft on Tees, below Darlington, framed the ceremonial entry of new bishops into the bishopric (James 1974: 4–5). The administrative division along the Tees created frictions, and generated county identities where there was otherwise no clear separation in society. Responsibility for repairing the bridge over the Tees at Yarm was disputed in 1621, although statute insisted both Yorkshire and Durham should contribute equally. The 'Yorkshire men' agreed to pay their share to the bridge warden but the 'Durham men' disputed the exemption clause of the statute and claimed that the exaction of a toll on the Yarm side should provide for repairs. The Durham representatives asserted, perhaps with pride in their county's resource, that the bridge had worn out because of Yarm men hauling coals over it from Durham. The legal dispute lasted four years, though Durham offered a levy of £200 in the interim (Campbell 1942: 337–8). Usually relations between the North Riding of Yorkshire and Durham were amicable and close. During the 1640s, a period of social upheaval in many areas as a result of the Civil War, Thomas Smelt kept a school in Danby Wiske, near Northallerton, where 'he taught about three score boys, the greater part of which were gentlemen's sons or sons of the more substantial yeomenry of that part of Yorkshire or the south parts of the bishopric of Durham' (Cliffe 1969: 71). Interactions across the Tees continued into the early eighteenth century, when advertisements for land and houses, for sale or rent, in the North Riding of Yorkshire were advertised in the *Newcastle Courant*, which was printed in Newcastle upon Tyne and distributed as far south as the vale of the Tees (Green 2000).

Houses were central to the experience of geographical variation. Surviving houses in two contrasting towns along the Tees can be used to illustrate the relationship between national house forms by social group and local variations in the experience of the built environment. Figures 3.2a and b illustrate two late seventeenth-century rows of houses, both operated as commercial premises, with shops on the ground floor to the street-frontage, and warehouses to the rear, with living accommodation for merchants or prosperous tradesmen above the shop on the upper floors. This was a housing form built by the commercial upper-middling sort throughout England. The Yarm houses are of brick with pantile roofs, and the plaster rendering is a later addition. The Barnard Castle houses are of stone with stone-slate roofs. Both rows of houses illustrate the concern with symmetrically arranged window and door openings and the prevalence of sash windows, characteristic of Georgianisation. The Barnard Castle houses have greater classical detailing, with rusticated stonework and miniature pilasters to one of the door-cases (refuting notions of upland isolation from Europe-wide patterns of architectural style).

The differences in the built landscape of Barnard Castle and Yarm constituted part of people's sense of place. And yet, Barnard Castle and Yarm were

Figure 3.2a   High Street, Yarm, Yorkshire North Riding

Figure 3.2b   The Bank, Barnard Castle, County Durham

unequivocally part of the same region. Barnard Castle, on the Durham side of the Tees, at the mouth of Teesdale, was a marketing and manufacturing centre, linking the lowlands and Pennine uplands. Yarm, on the Yorkshire side of the Tees, was a port, which exported the agricultural produce of the lowland vale of the Tees and Teesdale, and imported consumer goods which were marketed to the Tees uplands via Barnard Castle. These two towns were interdependent marketing centres, with a linked economy and society, and yet they contained houses with distinctive differences in appearance. Barnard Castle and Yarm's location on the north and south bank of the Tees might associate the built form of each town with its respective county. Yet the existence of similar housing being occupied by the same social groups along either bank was testimony to the mutability of those counties within the commonwealth of England as a whole.

The next major administrative boundary south of the Tees was the division between the North and East Ridings of Yorkshire through the Vale of Pickering. This low-lying area of peat separates the high ground of the limestone edge to the Yorkshire moors and the chalk Yorkshire wolds (see Figure 3.1). This geology contributed to a striking disjuncture in the built landscape of the Vale of Pickering in the seventeenth and early eighteenth centuries. The limestone on the northern side of the vale provided a durable building stone, whereas the softer chalk was used with ashlar stone and later brick on the south (Harrison and Hutton 1984; Hayfield and Wagner 1998). The boundary between the Ridings mainly ran along the River Derwent through the centre of the vale. The availability of building materials re-enacted in the built landscape the divisions entailed by topography. The chalk houses shared their construction format with the Wolds, extending to the south, in the East Riding, while the limestone buildings continue north and west onto the Moors and across to the eastern fringe of the York plain below the western escarpment of the Moors. The contrast between white chalk and yellow limestone is most marked towards the eastern end of the vale, and the quality of light nearer the coast contributes to the contrast. To the west, the limestone geology extends south marking the western limit of the vale and rising to form the northwestern corner of the Wolds. In this area, limestone was the preferred building material, supplemented by brick, in both Ridings. If buildings in the landscape actively contributed to the experience of divisions and affiliations, then an awareness of the broader pattern of building associated with each Riding plausibly contributed to a sense of regional differentiation. For the administrative divisions of Yorkshire, the largest county in England, created sub-county identities akin to those documented above along the Tees.

Regionality in the built landscape operated at varying scales. Across eastern Yorkshire, the stone-slate and thatch roofs of the limestone and chalk buildings were supplemented in the eighteenth century by pantiles. Testimony to the interactions on land and by sea, orange pantile roofs occur along England's east coast, in County Durham and Northumberland to the north, as well as Lincolnshire and East Anglia to the south. In north-eastern England, brick and pantile construction co-existed with the use of local durable forms of stone, whereas in East Anglia brick and pantiles merged with timber-framing. These regionalised forms of construction were themselves linked to wider zones of building. Durham and Northumberland form the northern end of the stone belt running diagonally across England from the south-west to the north-east, and dividing the predominantly timber-framed areas of western and south-eastern England (see Clifton-Taylor 1987). While timber-framed construction was present in north-eastern England (Harrison 1991), more thorough-going rebuilding was done in stone. In south-eastern England, by contrast, the equivalent change in housing among middling and lesser élite groups entailed the introduction of chimneys and ceilings into timber-framed houses (Johnson 1993).

Within the larger pattern of building in England, the specific colouring and texture of materials contributed to a more specific sense of place and localised similarities in the creation and experience of buildings in the landscape. This distinguished the brick and pantile houses of Yarm within the larger east-coast construction format, as it did the stone-built Barnard Castle houses that were linked in outward appearance to the uplands and lowlands of County Durham, serving to reaffirm the towns' respective roles within the region and the wider orientation of their residents and visitors. As the upland location of Barnard Castle and lowland site of Yarm highlights, the greater change in building format across north-eastern England was not from north to south, but from east to west, inland from the coast towards the Pennine uplands.

Whittaker took the Tyne and Tees as boundaries for a study of the *Old Halls and Manor Houses of Durham*, observing a series of changes in architecture between the Scottish border and York. Contrasting 'the cold austere and generally simple architecture of Northumberland' with the 'gentler and more congenial' architecture of the York plain, Whittaker noted that 'Durham lies between these two seeming extremes, an area of change in materials and techniques but more particularly of attitude to building' (1975: 3–4). His aesthetic approach to houses requires modification, with a greater appreciation of the people who occupied them. The agrarian workings of the landscape in south-eastern County Durham continued into the Vales of Mowbray and York; areas of village depopulation in the seventeenth and early eighteenth centuries as fields were enclosed and smaller farmers deprived of access to land. Construction techniques, building materials and resulting house forms were shared across this altered landscape, increasingly characterised by dispersed farmsteads and shrunken villages (Harrison and Hutton 1984; Green 2000). Prospering farmers rebuilt houses that conformed to those current in England as a whole. For instance, the plan-arrangement of accessing the house through a cross-passage behind the hall chimney-stack was common in north and north-eastern England, as it was in south and south-eastern England (Brunskill 1975; Harrison and Hutton 1984; Green 2000). Grange Farm, Monkton, on Tyneside, was successively rebuilt in the seventeenth century, with a cross-passage behind the stack (Fairless 1980). Grange Farm's Middlesex-born occupant provides one instance of the long-range population mobility that helps explain how people in the north could be building and living in similar ways to those in the south.

In northern County Durham, the exploitation of minerals beneath the landscape created a mixed economy of agriculture and industry. Few workers' houses from this period remain above ground but the specific features and form of houses built by prospering farmers and gentry continued into southern Northumberland, up to about the line of Hadrian's Wall. To the north, many farmhouses were constructed in the form of 'bastles', with first-floor living accommodation over a ground-floor byre enabling families to defend themselves from livestock theft by the 'border reivers' of Tynedale and Redesdale (Watts 1975; Ryder 1990). These distinctive bastle houses, found only in the northern counties, were mainly built after the Union of the Crowns in 1603, witness to a feuding culture in the Borders which was not dissolved by the dynastic succession. For whereas southern Northumberland, County Durham and Yorkshire were very much integrated into national cultural trends, northern Northumberland remained part of a distinctive Border society.

To the west of north-eastern England, in the north Pennines, an area of upland farming and lead mining, was a further cohesive zone of building across the high ground of Cumberland, Westmoreland, Durham and northern Yorkshire (Brunskill 1975). The great limitation in discerning geographical variation in the built landscape, however, is by social group. In contrast to the houses of middling and higher social groups rebuilt between 1600 and 1750, the dwellings of the poorer sections of society have largely failed to survive the housing demands of later generations.

NATIONAL AND REGIONAL CULTURE IN HOUSES

The Great Rebuilding entailed both national and regional patterns of housing. In both stone and timber-framed areas of England, sixteenth- and early-seventeenth-century rebuildings entailed the creation of a ceilinged hall with parlour and services to either side, with a proportion of rooms heated by chimneys. For north-eastern England the alteration of open-hall houses was previously not believed to have occurred until after 1660. Barley (1961) and Mercer (1975) suggested that the single-storey longhouse was not replaced by two storey houses with a separate parlour from the ceilinged hall, until after 1660 – the date from which the rest of the country was supposedly going national in architectural style. In fact, middling houses were rebuilt in County Durham from c. 1600, and gentry houses were rebuilt from the late sixteenth century, as these groups rose in social prominence as they prospered from industrialisation and agricultural change. Moreover, each social group rebuilt in a manner broadly comparable to their counterparts in southern England (Green 2000 and 1998).

A yeoman house of c. 1620 at Colly Weston, Northamptonshire (Figure 3.3a), was used to illustrate Hoskins's thesis of a Great Rebuilding (1985: 156).

Figure 3.3a 'A typical yeoman's house' *c.* 1620. Colly Weston, Northamptonshire (F.L. Attenborough photo in Hoskins 1985:156)

This house shares features with Whitfield Cottages (Figure 3.3b), rebuilt (possibly as an inn) in the early seventeenth century on Wolsingham market place in Weardale, County Durham. Both houses were built of locally quarried stone, with stone-slate roofs, and canted bays (to hall and parlour, and chambers over) to either side of a central entrance. At Wolsingham, this arrangement was created through successive rebuilding; the bay windows were probably added in the late seventeenth century and the door-case is perhaps *c.* 1700. The gabled canted bays at Colly Weston are paralleled in a bay window (to parlour and chamber above) on an early seventeenth-century farmhouse (East Oakley House, Figure 3.3c) in West Auckland, central County Durham. The same middling groups were rebuilding in the same style in Northamptonshire as in County Durham, during the seventeenth century. Moreover, this was not simply a rural phenomenon. From at least the early seventeenth century, middling houses represent just as much a national housing style, and way of living, as the typical eighteenth-century Georgian house.

Rebuilding in the sixteenth and early seventeenth centuries was followed by a further alteration in the appearance and use of houses in the late seventeenth and early eighteenth centuries, with Georgianisation marked by a renewed emphasis on external symmetry and the displacement of linear ranges of rooms by more compact house forms. These changes were not uniformly adopted across the country, or by every household among each social group; variations in the proportion of housing rebuilt was accompanied by localised variations in the practice of rebuilding. Craft practices and patron preferences meant

Figure 3.3b   Whitfield Cottages (detail), Wolsingham Market Place, County Durham

that the location of chimney stacks, external entrances and the arrangement of access between rooms produced distinctive differences in the appearance and experience of houses. Yet both seventeenth- and eighteenth-century middling houses were in many ways part of a national housing culture. Middling houses employed the tripartite room arrangements (of hall, parlour and services) and a stylistic repertoire in external and internal detail that was current across England as a whole. Equally, regionalised building materials were used to construct élite as well as middling houses in the seventeenth century, and upper-middling sort houses in the seventeenth century may be regarded as élite architecture writ small. The gabled stair turrets, bay windows and projecting porches of middling houses are stylistically related to the late sixteenth- and early seventeenth-century élite architecture associated with the architect Smythson (see Girouard 1983). Attributing this simply to emulation denies middling householders the wit to manipulate the appearance of their houses in the landscape in an equal fashion to the élite.

The 'vernacular' architecture of wealthier genteel, mercantile, agricultural and commercial households represents versions of building within a stylistic culture shared by both the lesser élite and the upper-middling sort. Such a graded account of housing complements the ways in which contemporaries documented their social standing. Both the upper-middling sort and the lesser élite had very particular ideas of their standing in society, which were articulated in documentary sources as aspects of distinctive social identities within a finely graded hierarchy of social scale (Wrightson 1994). The substantial

Figure 3.3c East Oakley House (detail), West Auckland, County Durham

middling houses rebuilt in seventeenth-century England were invariably occupied by the 'chief inhabitants' of their communities. This strata of the middling sort defined itself both in relation to the grades of society below them and in relation to the upper sort above. Moreover, social and geographical identities were multiple; individual members of households were able to define themselves in relation to their immediate community and in relation to wider social affiliations – on both a regionalised and a national basis (see French 2000). Both the larger national pattern in housing, and regional variation within it, is partly to be explained by the patterns of mobility among people who moved significant distances between their place of birth, upbringing and education or apprenticeship and service, and settlement as householders or housewives (see Wrigley *et al.* 1997). Patterns of population mobility were regionalised, yet also allowed for the complex web of interactions that constructed a national society. The architecture of houses shows that regional variation in style was part of middling and élite culture in both the seventeenth and eighteenth centuries, and that nation-wide stylistic change was hardly new to the eighteenth century.

Regionalised variation persisted in Georgian houses in the eighteenth century (Burton 1996). Pattern books are erroneously credited with creating greater uniformity in eighteenth-century architecture. It is seldom recognised that they too had a regionalised dynamic. In 1747, Daniel Garrett, an established architect practising in the northern counties and a disciple of Lord Burlington's Yorkshire-based Palladianism, published *Designs and Estimates of Farm Houses for the County of York, Northumberland, Cumberland, Westmorland and Bishoprick of Durham*. These northern counties correlate with the regionalised property market in houses and land advertised in the *Newcastle Courant* in the early eighteenth century (Green 2000). Property advertisements before 1730 (when 'pattern books' first appear) already expressed an interest in the tenantable repair of farmhouses, and Garrett's book catered to this landowning clientele rather than farmers directly. Garrett stated that his work answered the 'complaints of gentlemen who have built Farm-Houses, that they are irregular, expensive and frequently too large for the Farms they were intended for'. He proposed applying the 'regularity and proportion' hitherto reserved for grandiose buildings to farm houses, which if placed at a proper distance from the gentleman's houses and artfully masked by trees, would be 'very agreeable objects' to ornament their parks. We should not apply the prejudices of eighteenth-century Palladian taste onto the buildings which preceded it. Pattern books only promoted 'regular' (i.e. Georgian) architecture after it had chrystallised following the period of stylistic change in the late seventeenth and early eighteenth centuries (Green 2000).

Eighteenth-century conceptions of élite architecture entailed transferring the models of the Roman Empire onto British buildings. Colen Campbell's *Vitruvius Britannicus* (1717–25), 'containing the plans, elevations, and sections of the regular buildings, both publick and private, in Great Britain', followed Vitruvius' codification of Roman architecture, while emphasising the modernity of *The British Architect* for a new age of empire. Houses formed a central plank of Deetz's argument for a 'Georgian Order' in America. He claimed that the 'earliest [Georgian] houses show strong ties to the English homeland, and in time become more American and more regionally diverse' (1996: 164). Yet Georgian houses were regionally diverse in England as well as the American colonies. Moreover, the equivalence of regionality and nationality in both the Great Rebuilding and Georgianisation suggests that the whole panoply of material culture that Deetz so admirably drew together as aspects of a unified Georgian Order needs to be recognised as a revolution in ways of living that was preceded by an equally significant set of changes a century earlier in Britain. For lesser élite and upper-middling groups, furnishing and altering houses already entailed in *c.* 1600 participation in 'Renaissance' stylistic practices. Scales of homogeneity and variation in material culture may not so readily signify a coherent world-view, as Deetz argued (with limited attention to social group), as it must indicate the scales of cultural interaction.

Seventeenth- and eighteenth-century housing cultures represent forms of living, specific to certain social groups, that were shared across the British world. The contrast with Hispanic forms of building in the Iberian peninsula and Hispanic America hardly needs stating. Equally well known are the associations between 'British' and 'Dutch' housing. Direct parallels can be drawn between seventeenth-century housing in eastern England and the seventeenth-century Dutch colonies. These styles are commonly associated with a national identity, for instance in the form of 'Dutch gables'. But these forms of building were in fact the outcome of 'Anglo-Netherlandish architectural interchange', and such gable forms developed in eastern England with the same chronology as in The Netherlands (Louw 1981). The origins of the sash-window, that *leitmotiv* of the British Georgian Order, similarly involved Dutch craftsmen working in England (Louw 1983). These interchanges occurred across the Atlantic as well as the North Sea.

In north-eastern England regionalised population mobility seems to have entailed a coherent pattern of movement during the course of individual life-cycles across the northern counties. The Quaker master mason John Langstaffe (1622–94), of Bishop Auckland in central County Durham, is known to us because of his building works for Bishop Cosin. Langstaffe had a son Thomas who followed his father's trade and worked west of the Pennines in Cumberland. Langstaffe's other sons also went into the mason's trade: John went to Whitby on the coast of the North Yorkshire Moors, and Bethwell emigrated to Philadelphia (Colvin 1978: 504–5). Population mobility underpinned the architectural interactions between the north-east and the north-west, as well as Yorkshire and the colonies.

CONCLUSION

The old model of regionalised architectural styles current in the seventeenth century being displaced by a nationalising polite style in the eighteenth century (Barley 1961; Mercer 1975) has been discarded (e.g. Burton 1996). Alterations in housing during the sixteenth and early seventeenth centuries were national in scope, though regionally varied in detail. Equally, the construction and use of houses in the later seventeenth and eighteenth centuries was regionalised within the larger national culture. There were thus considerable continuities running through the Great Rebuilding and Georgianisation. This suggests that we need to re-evaluate the relationship of nation-wide cultural processes to national identity. Clifton-Taylor presented *The Pattern of English Building* (1987) as melting into the landscape, a '*natural*' way of building supposedly ruptured by classical-style élite building from the late seventeenth century. Yet houses must always have stood-out as aspects of a *cultural* landscape, as much as they 'melted' into it. This is all the more convincing when we recognise from documentary social history that the household was the primary social unit for contemporaries: houses were signifiers of social status. The language of polite and vernacular architecture is too firmly entrenched in the study of standing buildings to be easily cast aside, but regional and national cultures need to be recognised as mutualistic rather than antagonistic. American vernacular architecture studies face further interpretative difficulties (see e.g. Upton and Vlach 1986).

The term region was in use in this period as referring to a generic geographical unit and as an administrative sub-division. Contemporary usage also employed the term 'region' to divisions of the atmosphere or body. This notion of the region as an integral sub-division of a fluid whole may be more appropriate to analysing cultural behaviour in this period than sharper concepts of the region as a more discrete entity, developed since the late nineteenth century.[4] The muted nature of regional identity in this period suggests that the ways in which the material form of houses varied is testimony to the social and geographical variation of culture, and presents a means to comprehend the ways in which cultural processes operated. One starting point for such an exploration of cultural process is to recognise that regionalised behaviour was in part sustained by degrees of population mobility, largely dependent upon occupational opportunities, not formal political structures in England and the wider British world between *c.* 1600 and 1750.

Contemporaries were probably far better able to know the regional and social limits of housing than historians or archaeologists who suffer from the myopia of survival. For contemporaries, looking at houses entailed an expectation of the social status of house occupants and an awareness of a regionally differentiated built landscape. The experience of the material world entailed an active awareness of cultural affinity, and difference, which consisted at one scale in regionalised identifications. Yet, the affinities between the housing of certain social groups extended beyond national boundaries, bearing testimony to transnational housing cultures that were not limited to the élite of merchants or the genteel. This social stratigraphy of housing was differentiated by localised building materials, construction techniques and stylistic detail on both sides of the Atlantic. Regional scales of variation in the architecture of houses at all social and geographical levels indicate that it is a mistake to make assumptions about the homogeneity of culture within politically defined units such as nation, county or empire.

ACKNOWLEDGEMENTS

I would like to acknowledge the support of John and Jenny Ruffle during the period of research on which this chapter is based; Paul Lane and Tim Schadla-Hall have discussed buildings in the Vale of Pickering (when we were meant to be looking for the early mesolithic); Matthew Johnson made helpful comments on early drafts; and Charles Phythian-Adams kindly allowed me to reproduce his map.

NOTES

1 Hoskins's (1953) thesis of a Great Rebuilding posited a nationwide alteration in housing in the late sixteenth and early seventeenth centuries. Rebuilding is now recognised to have occurred over a longer chronology and to have varied on a regional basis.
2 'New goods' rare in 1675 are defined as utensils for hot drinks, china, cutlery, window curtains, looking glasses, pictures and clocks; by 1675 books, silver, table linen, pewter and earthenware were more common; basic furniture and cooking utensils ubiquitous.
3 Current research redressing historians' neglect of regionality may modify this view; this recent interest in regional identities is problematic, however, in its rarely disclosed relationship to political debates over regionalism in the present.
4 The term 'regionalism' and its definition as a political movement for self-government within a larger political unit (usually the nation) developed in the nineteenth century. At the same period academic interest in defining regions began, most influentially in Vidal's concept of the *Pays* (see Thrift 1994).

REFERENCES

Armitage, D. (2000) *The Ideological Origins of the British Empire.* Cambridge: Cambridge University Press.
Bailyn, B. (1988) *The Peopling of British North America: An Introduction.* New York: Vintage.
Barley, M.W. (1961) *The English Farmhouse and Cottage.* London: Routledge.
Bradshaw, B. and Morrill, J. (1996) *The British Problem, c. 1534–1707: State Formation in the Atlantic Archipelago.* Basingstoke: Macmillan.
Brunskill, R.W. (1975) The vernacular architecture of the Northern Pennines. *Northern History* XI(2): 107–42.
Burton, N. (ed.) (1996) *Georgian Vernacular,* papers given at a Georgian Group Symposium October 1995. London: Georgian Group.
Campbell, M. (1942) *The English Yeoman Under Elizabeth and the Early Stuarts.* New Haven, CN: Yale University Press.
Cliffe, J.T. (1969) *The Yorkshire Gentry from the Reformation to the Civil War.* London: Athlone Press.
Clifton-Taylor, A. (1987) *The Pattern of English Building,* 4th edn. London: Faber & Faber.
Colley, L. (1992) *Britons: Forging the Nation 1707–1837.* New Haven, CN and London: Yale University Press.
Colvin, H. (1978) *A Biographical Dictionary of British Architects 1600–1840.* London: John Murray.
Cressy, D. (1978) Social status and literacy in north east England 1560–1630. *Local Population Studies* 21: 19–23.
Davies, R.R. (1994) Presidential address: the peoples of Britain and Ireland, 1100–1400: I Identities. *Transactions of the Royal Historical Society,* 6th series, 4: 1–20.
Deetz, J. [1977] (1996) *In Small Things Forgotten: An Archaeology of Early American Life.* New York: Anchor.
Drury, J.L. (1987) More stout than wise: tenant right in Weardale in the Tudor period. In D. Marcombe (ed.), *The Last Principality: Politics, Religion and Society in the Bishopric of Durham, 1494–1660,* 71–100. University of Nottingham, Studies in Regional and Local History No. 1.
Fairless, K. (1980) Grange Farm – a cross passage house in Tyne and Wear. *Transactions of the Durham and Northumberland Architectural and Archaeological Society* 5: 81–90.

French, H.R. (2000) The search for the 'middle sort of people' in England, 1600–1800. *Historical Journal* 43: 277–93.

Fuller, T. [1662] (1952) *The Worthies of England*, ed. J. Freeman. London: George Allen and Unwin.

Giddens, A. (1984) *The Constitution of Society: Outline of the Theory of Structuration*. Cambridge: Polity.

Girouard, M. (1983) *Robert Smythson and the Elizabethan Country House*. London: Yale University Press.

Green, A. (1998) Tudhoe Hall and Byers Green Hall, County Durham: seventeenth and early eighteenth century social change in houses. *Vernacular Architecture* 29: 33–41.

——— (2000) Houses and households in County Durham and Newcastle upon Tyne, *c.* 1570–1730. Unpublished University of Durham PhD.

Harrison, B. (1991) 'Longhouses in the Vale of York'. *Vernacular Architecture* 22: 31–9.

Harrison, B. and Hutton, B. (1984) *Vernacular Houses in North Yorkshire and Cleveland*. Edinburgh: John Donald.

Hayfield, C. and Wagner, P. (1998) The use of chalk as a building material on the Yorkshire Wolds. *Vernacular Architecture* 29: 1–12.

Heesom, A. (1988) The enfranchisement of Durham. *Durham University Journal* 80: 265–85.

Hodgson, R.I. (1979) The progress of enclosure in County Durham 1550–1870. In H.S.A. Fox and R.A. Butlin (eds) *Change in the Countryside: Essays in Rural England*, 83–102. London: Institute of British Geographers.

Houston, R.A. (1985) *Scottish Literacy and the Scottish Identity: Illiteracy and Society in Scotland and Northern England, 1600–1800*. Cambridge: Cambridge University Press.

Hoskins, W.G. (1953) The rebuilding of rural England, 1570–1640. *Past and Present* 4, 44–59.

——— [1955] (1985) *The Making of the English Landscape*. London: Penguin.

Howell, R. (1967) *Newcastle upon Tyne and the Puritan Revolution: A Study of the Civil War in North England*. Oxford: Clarendon Press.

Hughes, E. (1952) *North Country Life in the Eighteenth Century: The North East, 1700–1750*. London: Oxford University Press.

Hutchinson, W. (1785–94) *The History and Antiquities of the County Palatine of Durham*, 3 vols. Newcastle upon Tyne.

James, M. (1974) *Family, Lineage and Civil Society: A Study of Society, Politics and Mentality in the Durham Region, 1500 to 1640*. Oxford: Clarendon Press.

Johnson, M.H. (1993) *Housing Culture: Traditional Architecture in an English Landscape*. London: University College London Press.

——— (1996) *An Archaeology of Capitalism*. Oxford: Blackwell.

Jong, G. de (trans.) (forthcoming) *County Durham Hearth Tax Returns Lady Day 1666*, with an introduction by Adrian Green. Index Library, Hearth Tax series, iii, British Records Society and University of Surrey, Roehampton.

Kidd, C. (1999) *British Identities before Nationalism: Ethnicity and Nationhood in the Atlantic World, 1600–1800*. Cambridge: Cambridge University Press.

Knight, M. (1990) Litigants and litigation in the seventeenth-century palatinate of Durham. Unpublished University of Cambridge PhD.

Lapsley, G.T. (1900) *The County Palatine of Durham: A Study in Constitutional History*. London and New York: Longmans.

Levine, D. and Wrightson, K. (1991) *The Making of an Industrial Society: Whickham 1560–1765*. Oxford: Clarendon Press.

Looney, J. (1983) Advertising and society in England, 1720–1820: a statistical analysis of Yorkshire newspaper advertisements. Unpublished Princeton University PhD.

Louw, H.J. (1981) Anglo-Netherlandish architectural interchange, *c.* 1600–*c.* 1660. *Architectural History* 24: 1–23.

——— (1983) The origin of the sash-window. *Architectural History* 26: 49–72.

Mercer, E. (1975) *English Vernacular Houses: A Study of Traditional Farmhouses and Cottages*. London: HMSO.

Morin, J. (1998) Merrington: land, landlord and tenants 1541–1840: a study of the estate of the Dean and Chapter of Durham. Unpublished University of Durham PhD.

Phythian-Adams, C. (ed.) (1993) *Societies, Cultures and Kinship, 1580–1850: Cultural Provinces and English Local History*. Leicester: Leicester University Press.

—— C. (2000) Frontier valleys. In J. Thirsk (ed.) *The English Rural Landscape*, 236–62. Oxford: Oxford University Press.

Ryder, P. (1990) Fortified medieval and sub-medieval buildings in the north east of England. In B. Vyner (ed.) *Medieval Rural Settlement in North East England*, 127–39. Architectural and Archaeological Society of Durham and Northumberland, Research Report 2.

Thrift, N. (1994) Taking aim at the heart of the region. In D. Gregory, R. Martin and G. Smith (eds) *Human Geography: Society, Space and Social Science*, 200–31. Basingstoke: Macmillan.

Upton, D. and Vlach, J.M. (eds) (1986) *Common Places: Readings in American Vernacular Architecture*. Athens, GA: University of Georgia Press.

Watts, S.J. (1971) Tenant-right in early seventeenth-century Northumberland. *Northern History* 6: 64–87.

—— (1975) *From Border to Middle Shire: Northumberland 1586–1625*. Leicester: Leicester University Press.

Weatherill, L. [1988] (1996) *Consumer Behaviour and Material Culture in Britain 1660–1760*. London: Routledge.

Whittaker, N. (1975) *The Old Halls and Manor Houses of Durham*. Newcastle upon Tyne: Frank Graham.

Wrightson, K. (1994) 'Sorts of people' in Tudor and Stuart England. In C.W. Brooks and J. Barry (eds) *The Middling Sort of People: Culture, Society and Politics in England, 1550–1800*, 28–51. Basingstoke: Macmillan.

Wrigley, E.A. (1967) A simple model of London's importance in changing English society and economy 1650–1750. *Past and Present* 37: 44–70.

Wrigley, E.A., Schofield, R.S., Davis, R.S. and Oeppen, J.E. (1997) *English Population History from Family Reconstitution 1580–1837*. Cambridge: Cambridge University Press.

4 The garden house: merchant culture and identity in the early modern city

ROGER LEECH

Academic interest in élite and urban housing in the early modern period has in recent years been increasingly focused on questions of identity (Yentsch 1994: 97–113; Hall 2000: 83–93; Leech 2000a: 1–10). Historical archaeologists such as Martin Hall and Anne Yentsch have convincingly shown that the building projects of urban élites from the Cape to the Chesapeake were deeply embedded with meaning, the enactment of political dialogue, plays of power and the definition of status. The principal concern of this chapter is the recognition of 'the garden house' as an important but hitherto largely disregarded element of merchant culture and identity in the early modern city in England.

In a view of the mid-eighteenth century (Figure 4.1), we see the quayside of the city of Bristol, England's second seaport for much of the early modern period. Beyond the quaysides we see the hills rising up above the city. Gabled dwellings of the seventeenth century intermixed with later houses. A map of 1673 gives an earlier view of the same landscape – the cartographer James Millerd noted 'comely buildings and pleasant gardens . . . an increase of new building' (Figure 4.2). At least four of these new buildings were individually named – the Red Lodge, the White Lodge, the Royal Fort and Baber's Tower. 'Lodge' and 'tower' might immediately raise questions in the context of domestic space. Why were these houses so named?

Simplistically these houses might be seen to denote the beginnings of suburbia, a facet of emerging modernity, the development of new suburbs ever further beyond the limits of the tightly defined medieval city. Looking more closely at some of the suburban houses on the map of 1673 will reveal a more complex story, centred first on what a 'lodge' signified to the inhabitants of the sixteenth- and seventeenth-century city. In late medieval England the term 'lodge' had come to be applied to either a place of lodging associated with the forest and chase, or to a secondary residence intended as a place for retreat and seclusion, a place to which the gentry or their social superiors might resort for 'recreation and pastime' (Cooper 1999: 110). These two uses were not mutually exclusive, but it is with the latter that this chapter is principally concerned – in a largely unexplored urban context.

Figure 4.1 The quayside of Bristol in the mid eighteenth century, the slopes of St Michael's Hill in the distance (Source: Society of Merchant Venturers)

The dwellings that could be seen in the distance on the slopes beyond the Bristol quaysides were to contemporaries a very visible signifier of merchant wealth. Correlation of the material and documented evidence for many of the houses visible on the 1673 map and the view of 1732 has shown that many were second residences, usually recorded in contemporary documents as lodges, garden houses or summer houses. In the listing made for the Hearth Tax in 1662 the assessors recorded some 19 'garden houses' in the parish of St Michael (Leech 2000b: 22–6). At least 15 of the owners of these houses held a prin-cipal resid-ence not more than 30 minutes walk distant in the centre of the city. For some of these owners, and for others not cited in or immediately contemporary with the 1662 assessment, probate inventories provide critical evidence – listing the contents of both a principal residence and a smaller one, which was clearly distinct.

The correlation of households and probate inventories with identified houses or addresses is a laborious process. Here it is worthwhile and crucial to obtaining a fuller understanding of the material evidence. In 1984 Cary Carson reminded us that probate inventories should 'yield a much greater harvest of informa-tion about a people's style and standards of living' (1984: 5). Matthew Johnson

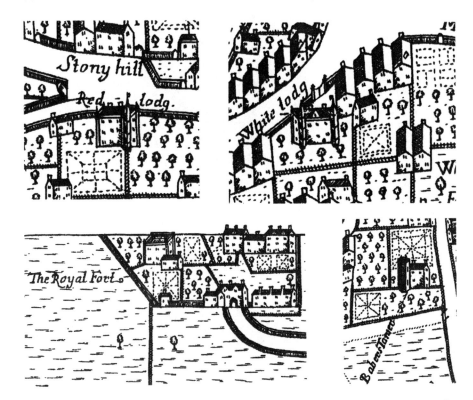

Figure 4.2   Details from James Millerd's map of Bristol in 1673, the Red Lodge, the White Lodge, the Royal Fort and Baber's Tower (Source: Bristol Central Library)

has recently reminded us that the transcription of huge numbers of probate inventories can only be a means to an end (1997: 13). In seeking better to understand life in the early modern city, this end might be found in the conjunction of the material evidence for the form and function of the house and the documented evidence for its use, contents and context at one or more points in time.

All the second residences for which such a correlation has been made were sited so as to be retreats from the city, offering tranquillity and garden space. Such spaces did not exist in the crowded centre of Defoe's 'tightly packed' city, but were to be found on the surrounding hills (Defoe 1971). One of the earliest such houses recorded both in contemporary documents and in later records of its physical appearance was the White Lodge (Figure 4.3). This house was built in 1589 on the lower slope of St Michael's Hill by William Bird, a wealthy draper living at no. 59 Baldwin Street, in the very centre of the city, on a tenement plot almost completely occupied by buildings (Bristol Record Office 04335(10) fol. 2; Bristol City Museum and Art Gllery, Braikenridge Note- book a.32; Leech 1997: 14). Almost 70 years later a smaller house close to St Michael's Church was one of

Figure 4.3   The White Lodge, Bristol, in *c.* 1821 (Source: Bristol City Museum and Art Gallery, M.2574, detail)

19 'garden houses' recorded in 1662 (Figure 4.4). This was the second residence of Gilbert Moore, a wealthy barber surgeon whose principal residence was in Broad Street. Like that of William Bird, Moore's second residence was located on a narrow tenement plot in the centre of the city (Leech 2000b: 98).

Built as second residences, such houses were well finished, but were without exception of only one or two rooms on each floor when first built. The White Lodge was one of the smaller number built with two rooms on each floor. Thomas Wells's lodge, built in 1664 on Stoney Hill, was of the same plan as Gilbert Moore's garden house, one of a number of second residences designed to provide only one room on each floor (Bristol Central Library, Loxton drawings 906L; Bristol City Museum and Art Gallery negatives 1696-7, Braikenridge watercolours M.3596–7). At Wells's death in 1666, this was his house 'new builded' bequeathed together with his city centre house to his wife (Public Record Office, Kew PROB11/325). To judge from the date 1664 and the initials of himself and his wife Elizabeth on the dated chimney piece in the first floor chamber, Wells had been only briefly able to enjoy the pleasures of his new lodge, symbolised above in the plasterwork image of the allegorical figure of Abundance (Figures 4.5–4.6).

Figure 4.4 Gilbert Moore's garden house on St Michael's Hill, Bristol: the further part of the house shown here (Source: Bristol City Museum and Art Gallery, Ma.4023)

In the seventeenth century the term 'garden house' was increasingly used in preference to the term 'lodge' to describe a house secondary to a main residence and standing in its own garden. The siting of these houses in relation to their gardens reveals a relationship between two different open spaces. In theory it would have been possible to place a garden house so as to be totally surrounded by garden. In practice the garden house was most often placed on one side of the garden. Its principal façade faced over the garden, affording a view of the whole plot, the architecture of the house first and foremost for those within the garden. Garden houses were for the most part dwellings that had no direct or principal access to the street. Persons of consequence would generally enter via the garden door, often elaborately finished. To contemporaries the garden house was both garden and house, a single unified space comprising what to us might have appeared as separate spaces.

The garden houses on St Michael's Hill and on other slopes around the city were also signifiers of the wealth and status of their owners. As in Annapolis, Maryland, a century later, such houses provided their owners with 'a panoramic view of the town . . . and provided townfolk in turn with an evocative status-telling imagery' (Yentsch 1994: 127).

Figure 4.5 Thomas Wells's garden house on Stoney Hill, exterior (Source: Bristol City Museum and Art Gallery photographs)

Surrounded by high walls, those of the house rising to three or more stories, those of the garden usually six or more feet in height, these garden houses of wealthy citizens were very distinct from contemporary lodges in the country-side. The high walls surrounding the city lodge formed part of what might be termed a contested landscape. This was a city landscape, where high boundary walls and shutters over windows went hand in hand with laws prohibiting the carrying of weapons and the walking of strangers in the streets after dark. The city lodge or garden house stood within a landscape of fear.

Ralph Oliffe's house in Maudlin Lane was typical of such garden houses (Figure 4.7). Oliffe was responsible in the 1680s for the breaking up and perse-cution of Baptist congregations (Hayden 1974: 300). He would have had good reason to surround his second residence with high walls. Principally resident in

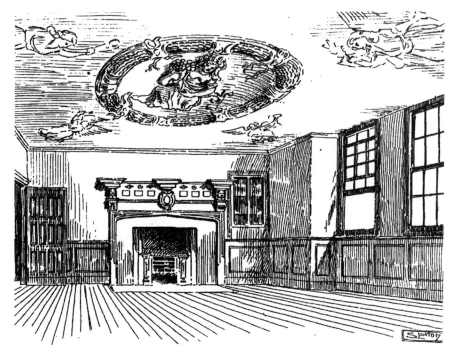

Figure 4.6 Thomas Wells's house, first-floor interior, the figure of Abundance on the plaster ceiling (Source: Bristol Central library, Loxton drawings)

a city centre parish, his second house lay on the edge of the parish in which many of the persecuted lived.

The countryside beyond the fringes of the city was beyond this landscape of fear. Here a small number of the wealthiest citizens were able to build second residences within the parishes surrounding the city. At Stoke Bishop to the west, by the 1660s the merchant Sir Robert Cann possessed a small lodge with one room on each floor. A larger lodge had been built beside the first by 1669 (Figure 4.8). At Ashley the wealthy brewer Robert Hooke built a house of similar plan in the 1650s (Figure 4.9).

Architectural historians have been tempted to see these larger houses as evidence of merchants moving to the countryside, establishing themselves as gentry. Two examples can be considered. Nicholas Kingsley has seen Sir Robert Cann as 'buying land at Stoke Bishop, just outside the city, on which to build a house and establish his family as landed gentry' (1992: 232). Timothy Mowl has read Joseph Beck's early eighteenth-century house at Frenchay as a 'merchant's cheap passport to gentry status' (1991: 53). But, at both Cann's house at Stoke Bishop and Beck's house at Frenchay, the restricted amount of service accommodation contrasted with the amount of space given over to impressive entries and stairs. The houses of both could be seen from a deeper reading of the architectural evidence as occasional residences designed to impress the occasional visitor.

Figure 4.7   Ralph Oliffe's garden house in Maudlin Lane, Bristol (Source: Bodleian Library, Western MSS, Gough Somerset 2, fol.20)

Historical context confirms this interpretation. The first owners of these houses without exception regarded themselves as citizens and as parishioners of the city centre parishes. At his death in 1674 Cann was a parishioner of the city centre parish of St Werburgh. Joseph Beck was similarly a city merchant, a parishioner of St James with his main residence a house in the new St James's Square. For Cann's houses there is the additional evidence from the probate inventory made of his possessions in 1674. His main residence was in Small Street. The hall of his city centre house was a space used symbolically to denote the legitimacy and antiquity of his household, unheated but furnished with arms and armour indicative of his status in the city militia. The hall of the country

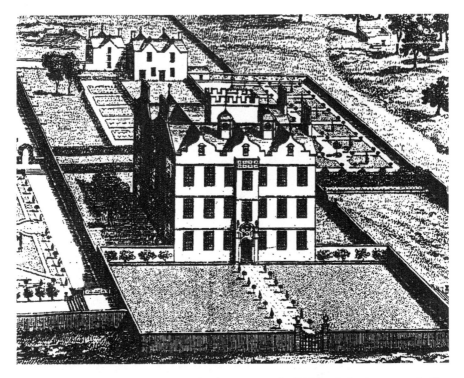

Figure 4.8 Sir Robert Cann's garden house at Stoke Bishop, Bristol, as extended by *c.*1708 detail from Kip's engraving published in Atkyns 1712, (Source: Bristol Central Library)

residence was in contrast a place of comfort. Here arms and armour were entirely absent (Leech 2000a: 8).

Medieval towns and especially cities have been seen as little islands of capitalism. We might see the investment of wealth in second residences as one facet of early capitalism, an investment that would bring both pleasure and fear for the safety of the investment.

Thus far I have drawn upon the city of Bristol to advance these ideas. London too might provide similar evidence. London merchants were heavily involved in investment in city property by the fourteenth century. With the acquisition of property came status for the family. In the 1470s the Stockers were one such London family, their properties at Ratcliff and Deptford conveniently placed on the riverside below London for easy access to city centre properties (Stocker 1999).

In 1612 three houses standing within large gardens in Coleman Street and Katherine Alley, noted as rare examples of lobby entrance houses in London (Schofield 1987: 59–62), might have been familiar to Londoners of the early seventeenth century as garden houses. The items to be found within these gardens might have been similar to those in the haberdasher John Goodyear's

Figure 4.9 Robert Hooke's garden house at Ashley, Bristol, detail from a print of 1795, (Source: Pritchard 1908: 305; see also Leech 2000a: 8)

garden in 1659. Goodyear's principal residence was in Walbrook in the very centre of the city. His second residence was a house and garden at Shadwell, complete with a statue, four flower pots and two rolling stones with iron handles (PRO PROB 2/643). The possession of a second residence complete with garden roller might be seen as another element of emerging modernity, one that in London and Bristol was certainly evident by the fifteenth century.

Attitudes to the possession of a second residence might too be seen as part of emerging modernity, and underline the juxtaposition of material culture and historical context. The diary of Samuel Pepys gives an insight into the thoughts of one London resident on the subject of second residences. On 14 July 1667, following a weekend visit to the Surrey countryside, Pepys recorded at length his reflections:

> My resolution is never to keep a country-house, but to keep a coach, and with my wife on the Saturday to go sometimes for a day to this place, and then quit to another place; and there is more variety and as little charge, and no trouble, as there is in a country-house.
>
> (Latham and Matthews 1974)

Pepys's thoughts, set within the context of the early modern city, have resonances for today. For those able to afford such luxuries, personal preferences will be weighed much as by Pepys in 1667. Pepys's thoughts on a second house were one viewpoint. Material culture and historical context together signal an opposite point of view. In Bristol and London, and probably elsewhere, the possession of a garden house as a second residence was very much an element of merchant culture and identity in the early modern city.

REFERENCES

Atkyns, R. (1712) *The Ancient and Present State of Gloucestershire*. London: W. Bowyer for Robert Gosling.
Carson, C. (1984) Wither vernacular architecture. *Vernacular Architecture* 15: 3–5.
Cooper, N. (1999) *Gentry Houses*. New Haven, CN and London: Yale University Press.
Defoe, D. [1724–6] (1971) *A Tour through the Whole Island of Great Britain*, ed. P. Rogers. Harmondsworth: Penguin.
Hall, M. (2000) *Archaeology and the Modern World, Colonial Transcripts in South Africa and the Chesapeake*. London and New York: Routledge.
Hayden, R. (ed.) (1974) The records of a church of Christ in Bristol, 1640–1687. *Bristol Record Society* 27: 1–315.
Johnson, M. (1997) Vernacular architecture: the loss of innocence. *Vernacular Architecture* 28: 13–19.
Kingsley, N. (1992) *The Country Houses of Gloucestershire Vol. 2 (1660–1830)*. Chichester: Phillimore.
Latham, Robert and Matthews, William (1974) *The diary of Samuel Pepys: a new and complete transcription, Vol. 8, 1667*. London: Bell and Hyman.
Leech, R.H. (1997) The topography of medieval and early modern Bristol. Part 1: property holdings in the early walled town and marsh suburb north of the Avon. *Bristol Record Society* 48: i–xxviii, 1–220.
—— (2000a) The symbolic hall: historical context and merchant culture in the early modern city. *Vernacular Architecture* 30: 1–10.
—— (2000b) The St Michael's Hill precinct of the University of Bristol. The topography of medieval and early modern Bristol, part 2. *Bristol Record Society* 52: 1–133.
Mowl, T. (1991) *To Build the Second City, Architects and Craftsmen of Georgian Bristol*, Bristol: Redcliffe Press.
Schofield, J. (ed.) (1987) *The London Surveys of Ralph Treswell*. London Topographical Society Publication No. 135.
Stocker, D. (1999) Notes on the Stocker family. Typescript privately circulated.
Yentsch, A. (1994) *A Chesapeake Family and Their Slaves*, Cambridge: Cambridge University Press.

5 Strangers below: an archaeology of distinctions in an eighteenth-century religious community

RON SOUTHERN

INTRODUCTION

In mid-eighteenth-century Yorkshire, a small settlement sprang up on a hill-side near the village of Pudsey, near Leeds. Named Lamb's Hill by patron Count Nichlaus Zinzendorf, it was populated by members of the Moravian Church, a group of Protestants who influenced the wave of conversion sweeping the country in the 1740s and 1750s. Lambshill, Gracehall, or Fulneck as it was later known, represented an outpost of a German-speaking foreign order that entered into contemporary debates about what constituted orthodoxy within the church and society generally. The Moravians had a vast international network of settlements and meeting houses which aided the free movement of their ministers, called Labourers, yet they worked closely with the people in the local area within which they settled, visiting in their houses, speaking their language, and trying to understand their ways without condoning what they saw as their ignorance. The Moravians were there to create a new world order: in the terms of one of their own metaphors, they were to rip up the weeds and seed new plants in ground freshly prepared. In this endeavour the Moravians thought themselves special, separate, as 'chosen'; and so they built a vast pile upon Lambshill, consisting of a central meeting hall flanked bilater-ally by two large houses, called 'Choir' houses: one for the young brethren to the west, and one for the young sisters to the east. Certainly the Moravians viewed their Choir Houses as their deepest enclosures from evil, and their members as sequestered under the strictest rule from the world. They were, in effect, like novices, protected behind the garden walls of a village monastery. As such the Choir Houses were a core part of what the Moravians considered to be their culture. They were proper places to facilitate proper feelings and thoughts. They were to be, their Principles of Practice stated, 'holy places where people become Anchorets and strangers to the world' (*Unitas Fratrum* (*UF*) November 11–15 1754, pt F: Principles in praxi, no. 161).

Gracehall, and its associated Choir Houses for their young women and young men, still stands on its artificial terrace a quarter of a mile long. To build their

Figure 5.1   Single Sisters' Choir

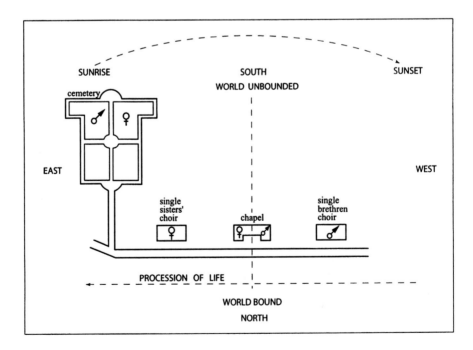

Figure 5.2   Phenomenology of Gracehall in the 1750s

settlement they drew upon finance from Saxony, gifts of wood from Norway (Hutton 1909: 309), and local bricks and stone. At the settlement there was always a confluence of normally distinct entities as the Moravians tried to meld what they believed and what they needed. The objects brought into the settlement, and how they were used and disposed of, indicate an entire range of relationships that distinguished them from, or associated them with, the landscape and people around them. This chapter will show, through their material culture, how the Single Sisters at Fulneck attempted to live a Christly life amongst the worldly of eighteenth-century Yorkshire.

PATHWAYS

A lifetime, for a Moravian, was a journey 'home' to be with Christ in eternity. Those who lived at Fulneck thus immediately set themselves apart by a semi-monasticism that distinguished a present time, tainted by a fallen, unfaithful, humanity, through which they passed, and a future timelessness, which would be experienced in the presence of Christ. Gracehall, completed in 1748, and the communal halls, their 'Choirhouses', completed in 1752, were an embodiment of their belief that they should live their lives as if Christ was bodily with them.

The Moravians occupied a paradoxical position; they were to consider themselves as a special, 'chosen' people, while at the same time a part of a community to be saved. This sense of being special was emphasised to the Single Sisters by the presence of Anna Nitschmann, the first Single Sister of Herrnhuth, the Moravians' headquarters in Saxony, at the laying of the foundation stone to their house in 1749 (Darley 1985: 46). She represented the plurality of connections which tied each Moravian to a greater diaspora; a connection that tied their alienated Englishness, as a chosen people in a religious Wilderness, to Sister Nitschmann's alienated Germanness. Laying the first stone, Sister Nitschmann began the foundation to a new order, a Christly order, that set itself against the world it occupied.

Rising above the politics of everyday life was the city on the hill, the material manifestation of Christ's grace operating in the world. For the Moravian, the act of cultivating a wild and distant land was an act of creation that turned a desert into a lush garden, the inhospitable into the hospitable and therefore social, the landless into the landed, the profane into the sacred. As the sacred land flowered and people found their God, the sea of godlessness, within which one could lose the chance of eternal life, retreated. The land thus prepared was fit to receive the city of God, the new Jerusalem, 'prepared as a bride adorned for her husband', and was the promise of Revelation fulfilled: 'Behold the tabernacle of God is with men, and he will dwell with them' (Revelations 21:3, 4). For the Moravian Sisters, the archetypal city on a hill, the land above the flood, was to become home.

In creating their House, they created a phenomenology of movement that juxtaposed those in the countryside around them as both the objects of their mission to present exemplary lives which could be copied, and as subjects and examples of the wayward, unChristly life in the 'world'. Within these buildings, with their tripartite arrangement along the constructed terrace and their bilateral facias making a clear guarding veneer between inside and outside, graded distinctions were made between polarities – the most fundamental being between the cardinal directions and the gender of the occupants.

Roberta Gilchrist (1994) reminds us that in Christian symbolism the south was readily associated with light and warmth, and the north with night and cold. These are natural – environmental – associations. According to Gilchrist, such distinctions became a part of a confluence of classical literature, medieval biblical exegesis and popular literary representation. In Gilchrist's work on the symbolism and physical spaces of seclusion in English nunneries, the Virgin Mary and female saints were consistently linked to the north of churches. Gilchrist formulates the distinctions made as 'north/moon/female/Old Testament and south/sun/male/New Testament' (1994: 133–4). Some confirmation of Gilchrist's interpretation is found in Austin Farrer's (1949: 219) work. Farrer, in his exploration of the symbolism of St John's Apocalypse, posits an association of the cardinal points in which South is associated with the summer solstice, North with the winter solstice, West with the autumn equinox and East with the spring equinox. A similar phenomenology operated at Fulneck. The settlement was divided into segments that may be considered stages in a pathway of spiritual development. Single brethren occupied the western part of Fulneck. Their domain ended in the western half of the meeting hall. From the eastern half of the Hall to the aisle of the burial ground on the eastern side of the Single Sisters' Choir House was the female domain of the settlement. Eastward from the aisle of the burial ground was again a male domain, being where the brethren buried their dead. The living dead, and the dead awaiting resurrection, thus enclosed Christ's special church, His 'Bride' on earth in time and eternity.

Symbolically the place of death lay with the single brethren at the western end of the settlement. Their place in the world, their confrontation with the world, made them by nature unsuitable for the spiritual life. Brethren, in their 'manhood', were perhaps generic 'Man', entities symbolically submerged in time and the death of the World. To live in the World was to be dead to God. Moving eastward was a movement toward God. Symbolic entry into the female domain, as pure, 'virginal', brides to Christ was, for the Moravian, associated with the entry of the Holy Ghost, the church mother, into the soul as guide and comforter. Spiritual awakening followed as preparation for the joining fully of the bride with the bridegroom. At Fulneck the symbolic journey that took brethren from the 'west', which has a Germanic stem meaning 'below' (*we*), was a journey to the 'east', the dawn and the rising sun/son, passing through the meeting hall where the scriptures were read and where Christ was praised. Here, within the Church below – the Bride – they could be reborn and grow into a fullness of spirit that would enable them to ascend to the Church above.

The orientations in the Burial Ground at Fulneck indicate some of the meanings that a Moravian might have attached to 'North' and 'South'. The burial ground was entered through a gateway in the centre of its northern wall. Funeral processions filed into what resembled the floor plan of a Roman basilica or early Anglo-Saxon church. The short transepts and apse-chancel or sanctuary are suggestive of a Roman church (Rodwell and Bentley 1984: 12–14). Where the axial orientation of a church would have been east–west, with sanctuary towards the east, the 'apse' of the Fulneck burial ground faces south. Therefore, at Fulneck the faithful were symbolically pointed in two directions: from west to east and from north to south. The orientation of the burial ground distinguished the bounded domain mediated by humanity to the north, and the unbounded domain to the south that was mediated by Christ and which could only be entered through faith. At burial, the lowering of the coffin was like entering the body of the Saviour: 'he to ye world did set like a little twinkling Star, whose Rising, shall be in that Heart all Hearts Comprising' (*Fulneck Congregation Diaries* (*FCD*) 5 November 1753). The unbounded heart swept aside all divisions and in that condition the true communion of the universal church prospered.

Emphasising the symbolic status of their settlement upon Lamb's Hill, compared with that of the surrounding world, the Moravians built a pathway that extended from the incoherence of the lower fields and woods up, in a straight line, to the terrace upon which stood their Meeting Hall, Gracehall, and their Choir Houses. On fine days the Sisters would walk together in the wood, and then walk up this central path 'in Procession . . . the Trumpets from the Battlement of the Hall' rendering 'this Walk still more solemn and respectable' (*FCD* 4 May 1759).

THROUGH A WINDOW

From the large attic window in the roof of their Choir House, the young Single Sisters of the settlement could see along the valley to the east and west, while immediately below them were their gardens and towards the bottom of a considerable slope lay their woods, the 'Sisters' woods'. When it snowed, the great arch of the valley shone in a luminescent greyness, the bare trees stark against bitter ground, while shrouded in drifting gloom Tong Hall disappeared and reappeared to view across the valley. Immediately to the east of them was the burial ground, with its small gravestones set in raised beds, face-up in rows, like flower-beds, or seedlings planted for a coming spring, all dug in the footprint of an Anglo-Saxon church, its apse drawn in an arch toward the south, while within its arms the congregation, men in the east, women to the west, slumbered untroubled by the weather or the ways of the world around them. A large western window looked out to the roofline of Gracehall. To the west, its presence swallowed by giant trunks of chimneys jutting from the high and wide-hipped roofline that girted the Hall, was the Single Brothers'

Choir House, both twin and different to that of the Sisters', of the earthly houses of God.

On 17 October 1750 pins were struck ceremonially by the chief ministers of the church as a first act to the raising of the Choir House roof. Raising the roof completed the constructed high 'ground' above the world that the settlement was supposed to be, and of which the Choir Houses were an important part. From this spiritual hilltop the faithful could look over a recovered domain. The roof set a limit on human perception and dominance, but was also a metaphor for the warm protection of Christ's body within whose fabric each individual was integrated. Without a roof over one's head each person was at the mercy of wind and rain, of an arbitrary nature encompassed by night. Once finished, the roof offered shelter, enclosure and protection. Beneath the roof companions could nestle out of harm's way.

Each of the Choir Labourers struck a pin with 'solemnity' as if participating in some part of Christ's crucifixion, and longed to see it 'quite completed' (*FCD* 16 October 1750). They perhaps saw themselves as carpenters building a new world. 'Raising the roof' connected these strangers who sang verses in German to the surrounding villagers. The pinning of the roof offered a ritual antidote to the alien aspects of Gracehall for villagers who probably still deposited mummified cats in attics to act as guardian spirits. An instance of such beliefs was reported in Leeds on Sunday, 31 July 1774:

> The sails of the windmill belonging to the Leeds Pottery fell down with a tremendous crash; which being looked upon as a judgement for the desecrating of the Sabbath, the proprietors resolved that the mill should never be allowed to be worked afterwards on the Lord's Day.
>
> (Donnel 1980: 35)

Here, under the rafters that had been so meticulously struck, the Single Sisters were to lay down their heads, dying to the world, beneath a great arch of a ceiling; but as if to remind them that they were not in the celestial realm of God, the ceiling cracked under its own weight, and it had to be modified to a more modest and truncated span (*FCD* 2 May 1751).

In pinning their roof so, the Moravians connected themselves to an entire lore of making and unmaking, in which being turned out and being unroofed were antitheses of the new world of the Moravians. Nowhere is this more clearly shown than in their relations with Mr Tempest, a local landlord, whose seat was across the valley at Tong Hall. Mr Tempest's campaign against the Moravians was a long and painful war of attrition. He denied them passage through his property, thus forcing them to carry dead brethren from nearby villages 'a great way'. He persecuted tenants who were brethren. He sent his people to force a way through the Single Sisters' garden to a field he had purchased. He perpetrated little discourtesies, hindrances, provocations. He made the Moravians feel ill at ease on their own land, threatening their perceived holy tenure.

Tempest's main concern seemed to be about property and the rights of property. The Moravians were also concerned with property, Christ's property, in this re-created landscape. Instructive is Mr Tempest's dispute with the Brethren over the usage rights of the beck, or stream, and the land immediately leading down to the beck, 'the Backs', upon which the Moravians had built a dye-house. The effluent from the dye-house no doubt polluted the waters of the beck, but the buildings, tanks for washing and the gardens of those who lived there impeded a common passage between isolated fields of Mr Tempest's 'Lordship'. Events came to a head when the Moravians sought judicial clarification of their right to use the 'Backs' and the water in the beck. The hearing, held in York, found in their favour.

Jubilation over their victory was overtaken by the finding of a 'murthered Child wrapped up in a Shift' in the beck. The dead child was taken to the nearby dye-house to await the arrival of the coroner. The portent of the murdered child was given greater emphasis by the conflict that it brought with Mr Tempest. Mr Tempest wanted the body buried quickly, and whether through mistrust of Mr Tempest's motives, or through a general disquiet over a distressing event, the people of Pudsey were 'alarmed', and wanted the Moravians to intervene on their behalf. Holding on to the dead child identified the Moravians with the villagers and their interests against those of Mr Tempest. They were adding insult to injury, and deepening their transgression into the domain of Mr Tempest. Not only was he seen to be challenged and defeated in court, transgressing against his presumed political and social authority, the Moravians challenged his authority before the town's people by becoming their advocates. What else could they do to insult him?

In April 1752 Mr Tempest began to persecute tenants who attended Moravian meetings. In his fury, Mr Tempest perpetrated acts of what E.P. Thompson (1993) considered to be almost of 'ritualistic significance' in the eighteenth century: a form of social excommunication, the unroofing of a house, which exposed all inside to the ravages of the world. Mr Tempest laid bare the 'poor Man's House' to the wind and rain that would dowse his fire and turn the once warm wall as cold as death. Tempest's wrath encompassed exclusion in the same way that, for the Moravians, Christ, in his kindness, included and protected. Despite this, even those supposedly in his pocket took a stand against him. At Tong: 'He turn'd the Clerk of the Church both out of his Clerkship and School' because he attended their meetings '& because he would not promise him to come no more'.

Through all the provocations, the test for the Moravians was not to be drawn into the violence perpetrated by Mr Tempest. They met his threats with their own rituals of exclusion. A sort of polite but firm stoicism disarmed his rationale for action, if not his simmering anger. When he went with about twenty men to cut the water supply to the dye-house, the Moravians obeyed the edict of scripture 'resist not evil' (Matthew 5:39), to remain 'still' and say nothing. We can see their method most clearly in their response to Mr Tempest's threat to evict the Sisters at Holme:

Mr. Tempest has been at the Sing[le] S[iste]rs Oeconomy at Holme with some others & threatened them that if they dont remove out of the House by Monday [ ], he will then come with some Constables and carry them all before a Justice of Peace, from whom he pretended he had already an order to send them away; the Sisters gave him a short and Modest Answer nor were they a tenth part so much flutter'd as he and his Companions.

(*FCD* 7 October 1752)

As they confronted Mr Tempest, the Sisters at Holme were no doubt well aware that they were trading their frail earthly tabernacles for a life under a greater roof in eternity.

PLANTS AMONG THE WEEDS

The Sisters at Gracehall were to live joyously spiritual lives, the sort of life they knew they would live if Christ was among them. The House itself was a metaphor for that life. Full of light and air (upon which observers of Moravian Settlements commented), and governed by rules which helped create a suitable environment, the House was cleaned daily, with an orderly disposal of refuse that was at odds with normal English practice in the eighteenth century. James Deetz (1995: 135), for instance, notes that it was still common for the English to scatter their rubbish about them, producing an archaeological signature that looks like a fairly uniform sheet of refuse around a settlement. Deetz's observations somewhat confirm elements of commentaries on the sanitary behaviour of the English, from Erasmus, in the reign of Henry VIII – who complained about poor ventilation, and floors covered by rushes and filled with 'spittle, beer, scraps, and other filth', from which, 'a vapour is exhaled very pernicious . . . to the human body' (Booth 1843: 237) – to mid-nineteenth-century advocates for better dwellings for the poor, who noted of Manchester in 1832 that:

The state of some of the streets and courts examined was found by the inspectors abominable beyond description, and exhibited a melancholy picture of the filthy condition and unwholesome atmosphere in which a large portion of the poor are doomed to live. In some districts the sewers were in a most wretched state, and quite inadequate to carry off the surface water, whilst the privies were in a most disgraceful state; inaccessible from filth, and too few for the accommodation of the number of people, the average number being 2 to 250 people.

(Booth 1843: 270–1)

In the Single Sisters' House, work-rooms were cleaned before breakfast in readiness for the day's industry. Sweeping and general cleaning was left until everyone had eaten. The 'Sleep-Hall' was probably swept first; and then each floor by Sisters who were appointed to the task: the flow of work moving from top to bottom, and finally, on the ground floor, from west to east. The dust was then taken through the eastern door to a special place to be shown by them 'by a Sister appointed to Look it out'.

Although there was what seems like a natural logic to the flow of work, one based upon the efficient use of objects, spaces, and time – nothing that was 'useless' was tolerated (*UF* 1819) – there was also an underlying schema to cleaning that coincided and overlapped with the profane rationale. At that fluid boundary between cleaning the physical body and cleaning the spiritual body, the top-to-bottom cleaning of the Choir House could also be seen in the terms of a hierarchy of spiritual cleansing. Cleaning the Choir House was a part of caring for the body of Christ's bride, and thus also caring for His body which was also their body: 'because he is our flesh and blood, and no one ever yet hated his own flesh, but nourisheth it and Cherisheth it' (Ephesians 5:29, *UF* 1754).

Having an 'airy' dormitory was a matter of some concern for the Sisters. Cleansing and caring for the House created the 'air' of fellowship for each Sister. The whole were satisfied by an airiness, a sweet flowing atmosphere, an airiness that was premised upon what 'may be aggreeable to Ev'ry one' (*UF* 1752, pt 3). This required a submission to the spirit of the 'Order' of the House as inculcated by their Mother, the Holy Ghost. Whereas each Sister washed her clothes as she chose, she did so on a day set aside for her room. Her daily work at the spinning-wheel, sewing or carding, was integrated into the chores of everyday living. She exercised free will about whether she washed that day, but had no control over the broader context which was set by the needs of the household. Time and facilities were allotted like the 'Victuals': 'so that Each may have an Equal Part of that which is Provided according As they shall find Proper, & Not that One take before the Others' (*UF* 1752, pt 3).

The House, at least on the ground floor, was probably cleaned from west to east. Sweeping purified. Dirt and the dark matter of the 'Back Passage' were the remnants of the unclean world that threatened to recontaminate the 'Body' of their abode. Sweeping was like the pedilavium, a purification of the floor of the house and the feet of the believer, contaminated by the insidious flow of a dissipating humanity. In the pedilavium, the feet were washed in the 'bloody Gore' from Christ's Body, and dried by his 'besweated Hair' (*FCD* 6 August 1755), in an act of purification before the taking of the Lord's Supper. They were adorned, like 'saphirs', with 'his own holy Blood and Water' (*FCD* 31 October 1755): absolved, cleansed of their 'Wants and Failings', of their sin, so they could partake of the food that so 'refresh'd and vivified' (*FCD* 1 September 1759). Similarly, they swept and washed the house of his 'Body', hoping that their 'Spiritual life' would be preserved (*FCD* 1 November 1755): 'May Jesu's Blood & Righteousness fill and adorn this Dwelling-Place' (*FCD* 26 July 1756). 'Order' meant to be 'clean in Soul and Body' (*FCD* 13 April 1756), which required a partaking of a Fountain '*open'd for Sin and for Uncleanness for the House of David and the Inhabitants of Jerusalem*' (*FCD* 13 April 1756). Cleaning the dust from the bodies fulfilled 'The Order to be Observ'd in the House', an 'Order' that prepared the way for Christ's presence.

CLEANING THE WORLD

Thrift and care were to be shown when cleaning. Nothing that could be used was to be thrown away. Their life was their faith, and their faith was always to be a practical endeavour, not full of theory. They were to feel the presence of God within, not just think about Him. Their gardening was tinged with the same ethos. Their tools were the common implements of gardeners: meant to be used, not just hung for effect. Inventories of garden implements mention only practical, workaday, utensils: three ladders (presumably for pruning and picking), a pair of garden sheers, three spades, two muckforks, two picks, two wheelbarrows, three 'hows', a scythe, watering pails, garden line for tying hay, hay rakes and forks (Fulneck Archives, *c.* 1760s). All these common tools were just the type to spread and mulch as well as weed and nurture: all were the physical extension of a practical faith.

In the domesticity of a practical faith, cinders, for instance, were kept for reburning. Spent ashes and dust from the cleaning, and refuse from the kitchen, were to 'go Out at One Door And that is in the End next the Burying ground' (*UF* 1752 b). Never wishing to waste anything useful, such refuse was probably used as mulch or compost for the vegetable gardens. In this the Sisters may have been just following the good garden practice known to them, but impregnated, as with all things in their Oeconomie, with their wish to create a domain fit for Christ. Here there is a mixing of earths. The gardener/philosopher/diarist John Evelyn was still read widely in the eighteenth century; his discourses upon the propagation of trees, and of the cultivation and creation of new 'earth' through selective mulches and fertilizers, highly regarded. It seems likely that the Moravians would have known of his theories and practices. Evelyn, had he lived in the 1750s, though, would probably have found the Moravian too much the Enthusiast for his taste (although he might have listened carefully for German gardening techniques, for which he had some regard), but would, nevertheless, have had the pit into which he threw the detritus to make compost, positioned to the north-east of the House. Into this pit all the 'rank *Weeds*' would be thrown, to be re-created as food for useful plants. In the terms of the phenomenology operating at Fulneck in the 1750s, John Evelyn's compost-pit would have been betwixt the eastern earth, by Christ's Grace awaiting its restoration to create new life, and the northern female domain, the enclosed earth; indeed, by one authority he follows, wonderful '*Menstruum*', highly effective in gardens, results (Evelyn 1706b: 44).

If the tools used by themselves and their gardening servants were common place, then what they sometimes grew in their gardens was not. Seeds for gardens often came from another part of the Moravian diaspora. From the structure of their design, it seems likely that the formal gardens below the Sisters' House were kitchen gardens. Flora Ann L. Bynum describes the gardens transplanted to the Moravian Settlement of Bethabra in North Carolina around 1753 onwards as resembling 'kitchen gardens of medieval and Renaissance Europe', which were characterised by 'large rectangular beds divided by cross paths'(Bynum 1996: 73). English garden design seem to integrate more diverse features. Gervase Markham, for instance, thought the 'garden, like the orchard, might be either be laid out as a single square, subdivided by cross paths into four quarters, or a series of squares, two, or three, or more, on different levels' (Blomfield and Thomas 1985: 42–3). Another gardener, William Lawson, thought that the kitchen garden should also have 'comely borders to the beds, with Roses, Lavender, and the like' (Blomfield and Thomas 1985: 46). Given the presence of Germans at Gracehall, both visiting and resident, there was probably a hybrid of design features, just as there was, no doubt, a mixture of local and imported seed planted in the garden. A 1768 plan of the settlement indicates as much, in its representation of divided squares and paths, as well as some concern for the aesthetics of garden symmetry and for the ornamental, as in the central feature of the Sisters' garden, an oval pond connected by pathways, its distinctiveness and beauty is nevertheless given the plain and practical name and purpose of 'reservoir'.

A 1759 list from Bethabra mentions areas 'planted only with seed which was brought personally from Germany' (Bynum 1996: 77), an earthily symbolic, aesthetic, as well as practical, connection with the centre of their religious world. The seed from Germany included that of 'Parsley, Turnip-rooted Parsley, Hamburg parsley, Onions, Red cabbage, Beets, Celery, Field salad or corn salad, Spinach, Garlic, Marigolds, Cress, Radish, Cabbage, Capper, Kohlrabi, and Marjoram' (Bynum 1996: 77). Compare this with the contents of the seventeenth-century English kitchen garden of Gervase Markham, a garden, like that on Lamb's Hill, set on the south side of the house, but which contained plants of more pungent and decorative scents. According to Markham, there should be a 'garden of herbs, set with a southern-wood, rosemary, hyssop, lavender, basil, rue, tansy, all-good, mariesome, pennyroyal, and mint' (Blomfield and Thomas 1985: 42–3). Moravian gardens, to the senses of a local Englishwoman, would probably have been full of unfamiliar shapes, colours and smells. The internationalism of their gardening was thus another way the Moravian Sisters distinguished themselves from their neighbours; it was also a way in which they created connections with the recreated world of Christ elsewhere in the world. Ashes and dust from an anointed house thus also nurtured the growth of a Christly diaspora.

COMMON DELIGHTS

In the England of Boswell and Johnson, however, social interaction was not confined to supping together, gardening or promenading; nor, in some areas of activity, was purposefulness in the disposal of refuse confined to the Moravians, and one is reminded by Roger Leech (1999: 21) of the purposeful procession of people to the common privy below London's Bristol Bridge – something that must have had analogues all over England. Given the human refuse allowed to wash into and collect in gutters and streams in the eighteenth century, one more pollutant would not have made much difference, and the beck was probably just one more sewer. We know from the fury and ease with which both Methodist and Moravian preachers were rolled in such common 'filth' – a reminder of what a potent presence it was – of the ubiquity of human faeces. Indeed its ubiquity no doubt added to its tolerance among certain parts of the populace , but equally its symbolic power in ritualised humiliation. Given the intensity of their efforts to create an airy and clean abode, it is unlikely that the Sisters would have deposited their night soil close to the House. Equally, they would have been aware of the consequences of using it in their garden. John Evelyn refused to 'enumerate' among his useful composts *Stercus humanum*, because of its propensity to 'perniciously contaminate the Odor of Flowers, and is so evident in the *Vine*, as nothing can reconcile it' (1706b: 33). As Evelyn reminded his readers, however, human manure was 'preferr'd by some before all other' (1706b: 33). Given its prevalent use in their persecution, a separation of earths is indicated: its non-use as fertilizer, one more way in which they distinguished themselves from the ungodly.

THE EARTHLY DORMITORY

The Sisters' walk within their woods, and their ascent to their House above, connected the wilderness that surrounded them to the domesticity of their home. Such notions would have resonated with John Evelyn's belief that a forest was a place of spirit, and a suitable place for a 'dormitory', a place of rest: of 'shady and solemn Places . . . *Emblems of Immortality*, and a reflourishing State to come, were not less proper to shade our natural Beds, (would our *Climate* suffer it) growing so like a *Shroud*, as does that *Sepulchral* Tree' (1706a: 337).

If the Single Sisters entered into a long, positive association with their forest, it is also probable that, in the eyes of some, they partook of some of its evils. We know that many of the neighbours were suspicious that the Moravians at Fulneck were Papists; that had Bonnie Prince Charlie reached Pudsey, they would have thrown in their lot with him. Indeed, their Lovefeasts in the Woods would seem like more '*Roman* Madness . . . Consecrated by *Faunus*', fanatics who 'resemble the giddy Motion of *Trees*, whose Heads are agitated with every *Wind of Doctrine*' (Evelyn, 1706a: 332). A contribution to this view would have been the way in which the domain partially occupied by their forest had become the source of disputation.

Down below, bordering the stream they called simply the 'beck', and bordering their forest, was a contested domain called the 'Backs'. Upon the 'Backs' the Moravians had built their dirtiest industry, a dye-house, with vats for soaking and washing cloth. Almost immediately it was built it created conflict with Mr Tempest, not so much for the pollution it caused, but because it interfered with a pathway between properties. Also, the Moravians had diverted the stream for their own use, and this interfered with the perceived 'common' rights of the Backs. Here the Moravians, as a unified individual entity, usurped the rights of the historical communities around them. For the Moravians the turning of the stream to the work of the Settlement was a transformation of it into a part of Christ's order, albeit of the lowest kind. Equally, down in their tree'd borderland, the Sisters' wood provided a common − ungodly − place to be visited and acclimatised ritually for Christ, a potent symbol of the world generally, while providing a private place where the most basic human functions may have been fulfilled.

For the Sisters, the 'Backs' was a metaphor for the struggle needed to create a Christly body out of their continuing humanity. Connecting each floor of the house was a central stairway within a 'Back Passage'. The 'Back Passage' was a conduit that both regulated and facilitated the flow of life within the house. Sisters descended to their 'Victuals' in the Dining Hall and rose to their beds in the Dormitory by this passageway. The raw materials from the wool chamber on the ground floor were carried out into the 'Back Passage' and then through the enclosing doors, or up the stairway, to the spinning rooms on the ground and second floors, while down the stairway came the debitage of earthly living − the remains of the daily cleansing, the tabernacles of the dead, and the finished products of human industry. The 'Back Passage' was a space of movement: a space tainted by the noise and bustle of the world, by the unfaithfulness of the outside within, in which the 'Backwardness' (FCD 8 January 1756) and 'irregularity' (FCD 27 August 1756) of the Choir confronted the desire for 'Stillness'; where, for instance, a Sister's 'backwardness in coming to meetings' could threaten the 'Family-Order' and where the 'back'-ness of such an action was 'Very prejudicial to their Spiritual Health & Growth' (FCD 7 November 1755). Lingering on the stairs could thus be seen as the action of an uncommitted Heart, of one who was not in a good state of health.

The Back Passage was equally a space of the liberty of movement, where the rights of the Commons, the 'Backs', the unenclosed waste, from their point of view, a right fought for in a dispute with Mr Tempest (FCD 27 July 1751), was held in tension by the need for enclosure, a need that would be unnecessary in the reconstituted world of Christ. The Back Passage, as with the 'Backs', was a place that opened up the house to the close interrelationship of a family, to the stream of connection that was their foundation and desire, as was access to and usage of the Beck which flowed through the Backs. The Back Passage was also a place that invited irregularity, a space between that contained all the possibilities of stray tongues and unobserved liaison; a place like the Backs from which could come the 'Mob' to threaten and to insult them in their quietude, where a 'Criticizing Spirit' (FCD 22 February 1757) might vent thoughts and where a 'Dryness' (FCD 22 July 1756) for fellow Sisters might arise. Their endeavour was to preserve their 'Soul and Body chaste' (FCD

1 November 1755), to remain 'Sweet Smelling', and thus to this end they daily 'Put the Place in Order', by cleaning 'where the Sisters wash themselves' and by cleaning that path between everything within the house . . . the Back Passage.

CONCLUSION

Within the cloistered order of their Choir House, the Single Sisters entered fully into their task of living a life stripped of the endless humiliations of a cruel world. What distinguished them from their neighbours were the eccentricities of their faith manifested in wilful displays, but also in more benign examples of the sort of hybrid lifestyles that were created when cultures were brought together in a living society of diverse resources; where, for instance, English flowers were mixed with German onions to create a very particular aesthetic. The selectivity of this closed cosmopolitanism required, however, some way of rendering the uncontrollable world that invaded their domain as refuse that could be left behind. This is what gave the Sisters their sense of being chosen, and their joyous apprehension of their special domain; for deep within their house, particularly in their dormitory, where they slept each night in the arms of Christ, they left the dirt and noise of normal life behind. This was played out in other aspects of their lives. Their walk from the woods, and the cleaning of their house, were integrated manifestations of their beliefs. Certainly, when the wood was in good order, they had Lovefeasts there, which concluded with an exultant assent to the chapel above them, symbolically leaving behind them the vulgarities of the world. But the Sisters' use of their allotted domain was more complex than a simple annexation of spaces to partic-ular purposes would allow. Balanced with this movement away from the world was their engagement, both negatively (as with their dispute with Mr Tempest) and positively (as with their advocacy of the rights of the local community in the case of the murdered child), with the potential of a recreated Christ-filled world. Through such acts the Moravians melded with their surroundings, becoming more English with each breath, while the English became Moravian, as their strange transcendence became the cosmopolitanism of a new world. Still, for some, their ways remained alien. In 1850, a proposal for a self-sustaining village for the poor, one meeting with the 'approbation' of authorities at Herrnhut and the Pope, was considered to be like a prison, or a lunatic asylum, and definitely contrary to the needs of the national character (*Illustrated London News* 24 August 1850). Perhaps Mr Tempest's England was still very much alive, alongside all the other Englands that have ever been. Between this world and the next, the Sisters at Fulneck were caught in the tensions of just making their way, which also indicates how we must approach them, within a tension-filled making our way; for when a garden is a dormi-tory becoming a grave, as well as the lit wounds of Christ, we must look to a sinuous context of changing meanings to approach the richness of fruitful historical lives.

ACKNOWLEDGEMENTS

I would like to acknowledge with thanks the assistance of librarians and archivists at Fulneck, John Rylands and the Ballarat Mechanics' Institute, without whom this work would not have been possible.

REFERENCES

Blomfield, R. and Thomas, F.I. (1985) *The Formal Garden in England*. London: Waterstone.

Booth, A. (1843) The dwellings of the poor. *The Builder*, 8 July, vol. 1: 270–1.

Bynum, F.A.L. (1996) Old World gardens in the New World: the gardens of the Moravian settlement of Bethabra in North Carolina, 1753–72. *Journal of Garden History* 16(2): 70–86.

Darley, G. (1985) The Moravians: building for a higher purpose. *The Architectural Review* 177(1058): 45–9.

Deetz, J. (1995) *Flowerdew Hundred: The Archaeology of a Virginia Plantation, 1619–1864*. Charlottesville, VI: University of Virginia Press.

Donnel, E. (1980) Who made creamware? In Paul Atterbury (ed.) *English Pottery and Porcelain: An Historical Survey*, 86–98. London: Peter Owen.

Evelyn, J. (1706a) *Silva: Or a Discourse of Forest-Trees*. London: Robert Scot, Richard Chiswell, George Sawbridge and Benjamin Tooke.

—— (1706b) *Terra: A Philosophical Discourse of Earth, Relating to the Culture and Improvements of Plants, &c. as it was Presented to the Royal Society, April 29. 1675*. London: Robert Scot, Richard Chiswell, George Sawbridge and Benjamin Tooke.

Farrer, A. (1949) *A Rebirth of Images: The Making of St John's Apocalypse*. London: Dacre Press.

Fulneck Archives (*c.* 1760s) An inventory of the furniture Fulneck Sisters' House. *Fulneck Congregation Diaries*, Fulneck Archives, Fulneck, Yorkshire.

Gilchrist, R. (1994) *Gender and Material Culture: The Archaeology of Religious Women*. London: Routledge.

Hutton, J.E. (1909) *A History of the Moravian Church*. London: Moravian Publication Office.

Leech, R. (1999) 'The processional city: some issues for historical archaeology'. In S. Tarlow and S. West (eds), *The Familiar Past?: Archaelogies of Later Historical Britain*. London: Routledge.

Rodwell, A. and Bentley, J. (1984) *Our Christian Heritage*. London: George Philip.

Thompson, E.P. (1993) *Customs in Common*. London: Penguin.

Unitas Fratrum (1752) The order to be observ'd in the House, Fulneck Archives, Fulneck, Yorkshire.

—— (1754) pt D: Minutes of the Provincial Synod at Lindsey House, May 13–20. Held by John Rylands special collection, University of Manchester, no. 69.

—— (1819) A brief view of the constitution doctrine & discipline of the Church of the united brethren, John Rylands special collection, University of Manchester.

6   The architecture of empire:
Elizabethan country houses in Ireland

ERIC KLINGELHOFER

A summertime scene of low Virginia countryside, with oven-hot fields, distant woods, and simmering swampland, seems to contain a mirage, a seventeenth-century English country house, somehow transplanted into the New World. It is Bacon's Castle, near Jamestown (Figure 6.1). The explanation for its presence, and for similar upper-class constructions in other English colonies, should be sought in England itself, which produced the model, and in Ireland too, which was England's first colony, the only foreign territory of English settlement after the loss of the Calais Pale in the mid-sixteenth century. Scholars have long studied the complexities of England's architectural history, and indeed the colonial homes of Virginia are well recognised as an important part of early American material culture. Sixteenth- and seventeenth-century Irish residences have received comparatively little attention, and were never surveyed as a group. This chapter augments the opinions found in those works covering the topic with my own observations of a select number of important houses. I suggest that patterns in their design and construction can be attributed to the socio-political factors of imperial and colonial expansion.

W.G. Hoskins proposed that in little more than a single generation, the turn of the sixteenth century to the seventeenth century, the majority of English manor houses were transformed from medieval open-hall types into essentially modern plans with chimneys, hall/parlour divisions and upper bedrooms (Hoskins 1953). While acknowledging the serious reservations made by Matthew Johnson, one could nevertheless suggest that the surge of new house construction on a large scale does indeed represent a 'Great' Rebuilding, but in a different context and with a different twist on the term 'great' (Johnson 1993). Whatever the case may be for and against Hoskins's generalisation, I would point instead to the pattern of large-scale constructions by which the 'Great' and 'Near-Great' remade their personal environments (Howard 1990, 1997). This rebuilding and new building is of course part of the *longe durée* evolution of residential architecture, which is given movement and direction from social and economic changes as new wealth, new families and new conditions appear (Girouard 1967; Airs 1975; Cooper 1997). Enough structures

Figure 6.1 Bacons Castle, Virginia: a planter's Jacobean cross-plan house

appeared in the period *c.* 1540 to *c.* 1640 – and have survived – to suggest a pattern to the architecture of the Tudor–Stuart élite. During the course of that century, architectural forms preferred by the upper class of England fell into three discernible styles: what has been called 'Tudor domestic Gothic' but may be better refered to as 'traditional Tudor', another that emphasised classicism and a third that promoted a chivalric image, which Timothy Mowl called neo-medieval (Castle 1927; Mowl 1993).

Several examples serve to illustrate this movement and the forms that it took. Representative of a 'traditional Tudor' style is The Vyne, in Hampshire, the seat of the Sandys family, courtiers who entertained Henry VIII three times there (Figure 6.2). The lively brick diapering survives from the original decorative scheme, which was maintained through later alterations, like conversion of a central tower into a gabled porch (Howard 1998).

Italian Renaissance classicism is associated with the Cecil family of William, Lord Burghley, and his son Robert, Earl of Salisbury, whose service to and rewards from the Crown put them atop the nobility of the robe. The Cecils used their residences of Burghley House (begun *c.* 1552) and Theobalds (begun 1563) to illustrate their position at Elizabeth's court. These courtier houses were massive in size and ornamental in decoration. Conspicuously consuming the wealth they drew from the Crown, the Cecils would swell Theobalds into the largest house in England. This proved too tempting a target for the jealous, acquisitive James I, who pressured Robert into exchanging Theobalds for an

Figure 6.2   The Vyne, Hampshire: with a central tower rebuilt as a gabled porch

early Tudor palace at Hatfield, where construction on a new, much grander Hatfield House began in 1608 (Cecil 1984). Here, Robert's allegiance to and mastery of the Renaissance state appears in the classical motifs used in the rich woodwork that dominates the interior. Outside, a façade of classical mass and regularity rises above Cardinal Wolsey's brick palace nearby, reduced to an ancillary function while retaining its medieval arrangement of hall, solar and porch tower.

These great residences of the Tudor and Stuart period have been called 'courtier' houses, in that power and wealth flowed from the monarch's court, but they may be more aptly called 'political' houses because it was their builders' service to – and power within – the state, rather than solely to the person of the monarch, that was celebrated in stone. Thus Montacute House, where the Phelips family marked their rise on the national scene, *c.* 1600, exudes even more classicism than that shown by the Cecils (Figure 6.3). As Speaker of the House of Commons, Sir Edward Phelips erected a wide-windowed east front where statues, niches, and round windows are complemented by a formal garden enclosed by exuberant balustrades and pavilions.

Castles reappear in the English countryside for the third architectural style, which is not found before the last decades of Elizabeth's reign and seems not to have continued beyond the life of her successor, James. The late sixteenth-century chivalric revival in general was part of the heightened social differentiation of late Renaissance courts, which revelled in such works as Ariosto's *Orlando Furioso*, but in England it may have been taken further than elsewhere.

Figure 6.3 Montacute House, Somerset: the south-west corner displaying large windows and the ornately decorated garden wall

Dedicated to Elizabeth, Spenser's *Faerie Queene* embodied the cult of Gloriana, but also spoke to the English victory over religious enemies like the Armada and the conquest of Ireland. Elizabethan culture required an explanation for virtue and vigour in a state headed by a female. Does it stretch the evidence to suggest that chivalric castellation flourished under an increasingly embattled Queen and died out with the last Elizabethan courtiers?

Much of the work, of course, was a refurbishment of existing medieval structures, such as Kenilworth Castle, where in 1575 the favourite, Robert Dudley, Earl of Leicester, entertained the Queen with the sort of chivalric pageantry typical of the Valois and Hapsburg courts (Renn 1991). Kenilworth may have inspired the Gothic Revival of Sir Walter Scott's romantic fancies, but the ruined works of both John of Gaunt and Robert Dudley can speak of earlier needs and ideals. In his treatment of the 'archaeologies of authorities,' Matthew

Johnson offered a spatial analysis of this castle, among others, but examined its medieval, not Elizabethan, elements and ideologies (1996: 122–31). Mowl distinguished between a naturally evolving late, late Gothic style that appears in the Smythson castlehouses in the north Midlands, and a foppish sort of 'play-castle' found in the south of England (1993: 108). Whether or not this distinction has value, I have chosen examples from the southern group, while conceding the importance of such buildings as Bolsover Castle in Derbyshire (Girouard 1967, Faulkner 1985).

Leicester's work is in ruins, but not so that of another favourite, Sir Walter Ralegh, who on the grounds of the antiquated Sherborne Castle in Dorset, erected a castellated lodge with polygonal corner towers. More impressive structures followed. Wardour Castle in Wiltshire, has a stern stone face, punctuated by some dangerously low windows and an interior court or light well that has classical decoration. The main castle entry has left the Gothic past but seems lost in the Renaissance, with banded (possibly Tuscan) columns that one hopes supported a missing architrave, and somewhere above, a figured niche (Figure 6.4). A last English example, Lulworth Castle in Dorset, completed early in James's reign, is a four-square structure with round corner towers (Figure 6.5). The arrangement of its rooms, however, owes little to the Middle Ages (Girouard 1967: 88–93). With the kitchen and its servants placed 'downstairs' with the cellar storage rooms, the 'upstairs' was unified by a central staircase rising over an entrance lobby. Older traditions did survive, in the 'hall

Figure 6.4 Wardour Castle, Wiltshire: symmetrical entrance façade, with Renaissance entablature

Figure 6.5 Lulworth Castle, Dorset: large round towers flanking the south façade and classical garden entrance (Photo courtesy Roger Leech)

and passage' format for formal dining, but the arched service doors have classical round openings above (Figure 6.6). This chivalric style is a pastiche of elements in a setting of formal gardens, like the jewellery worn by men and women of the Renaissance.

What architecture then passed from England to Ireland, and was erected by men of money and interest in new buildings? The builders would be those Irish families that managed to avoid the deep suspicion of the Tudor dynasty, and the English soldiers, clerks and even poets 'of fortune' who sought to make names for themselves in the island, often as colonisers. Elizabethan colonisation centred on the province of Munster, the south-west of Ireland, whereas renewed colonising under James took place later in Ulster, the north-east. Did colonial architecture duplicate that of the homeland, and if so, did it take one style over others? Unfortunately, these questions cannot be answered with any certainty. Only a small number of Irish sixteenth- and seventeenth-century buildings have been thoroughly surveyed; the necessary details have not yet been accumulated to propose a discrete typology. Nevertheless, observations of several important houses point to some potentially significant patterns of architecture design.

We must first recognise the presence in Ireland of the explorer, coloniser and courtier Sir Walter Ralegh. He was lord of a huge 'seignory' of lands that the Queen had confiscated from Irish rebels. On the south coast, his estates along the Blackwater River were served by its port town of Youghal, which

Figure 6.6 Lulworth Castle, Dorset: interior of great hall/dining room and double-entrance screens with round lights above (Photo courtesy Roger Leech)

followed the political winds and elected Ralegh its mayor. He built a home in the late 1580s beside the largest church in the area, St Mary's, and probably reused its collegiate buildings. The Myrtles stands today, only slightly altered from Ralegh's efforts to have a 'traditional Tudor' house, with steep roof, massive chimneys, and gabled dormers (Figure 6.7). Another example of this style in Munster is Dromaneen, an Elizabethan manor house with end chimneys, a pronounced upper-storey string course and the remnants of dormers (Figure 6.8). Even larger, with a long gallery on the upper floor and opulent fireplaces, is the well-known late Elizabethan residence that is part of the castle at Carrig-on-Suir (Waterman 1961: 252; Craig 1982: 113–14). As this was the seat of the Earl of Ormonde, who through the Boleyns was cousin to the Queen, the extraordinary wealth and power of the builder suggests that this was an exceptional structure, more an expression of personal taste and ambition than a model for Tudor architecture in Ireland.

Classical elements also appeared in early colonial Ireland. Far to the north on the Ulster coast, in James's reign, the Earl of Hamilton inserted a new residence in medieval Dunluce Castle (Figure 6.9). Though cramped by existing walls, this building had a regular front of large windows carried in multi-storey projecting bays, and on one side – facing inland – a crude little portico more suited to the Mediterranean than the North Atlantic. Renaissance influence also appears in a group of extraordinary structures, large, symmetrical houses with corner towers, similar to, but more house-like than such oversized

Figure 6.7 The Myrtles, Co. Cork: rear of house showing Tudor chimneys and dormer gables

tower-houses like Bunratty Castle. Looking back to the castle and forward to the country house, classical elements mix with the palatial, as in the Bishop of Dublin's Rathfarnam Castle (Craig 1982: 114–22). Kanturk Castle, Co. Cork, was built in the 1590s for the head of the McCarthy clan, whose ambition was displayed by the size of his residence as well as its defensive potential (Figure 6.10). The royal government worried about further rebellion and ordered construction halted before the roof was in place, and it has been left that way for four hundred years. There are machicolation at the top, gun loops at the bottom, even early elements like Gothic doorways inside. But its large windows and many fireplaces reveal a post-medieval concern for creature comfort, and the regularity of plan and elevation looks to contemporary English models, while the provincial effort to reproduce classical details in the main entranceway reflects the Renaissance in the dimmest light.

Figure 6.8 Dromaneen Castle, Co. Cork: residential block with gable-end chimneys, raised entrance, string course and dormers above

More commonplace than the transplanted architectural types are the many fortified houses of substance, usually of two or three stories. A good example is Durrus Court, out on the Sheepshead Peninsula, with a symmetrical U-shaped plan and end chimneys (Figure 6.11). Where the Tudors may have retained crenellation as a decoration for high status buildings, in defence-conscious Ireland both crenellation and machicolation appear regularly on residences. These were fortified manor houses, not quite castles, but not English manor houses either. And it was not a peculiarity of circumstances in Ireland that led to this difference, but actually that of England, which alone among the northern European countries built undefended country houses in the sixteenth century. To live successfully in Ireland, the English erected these and even more defendable residences, like the *c.* 1600 Mallow Castle of Sir John Norreys, President of Munster province (Figure 6.12). Polygonal towers, crenellation and gun loops through the walls all speak of a concern for defence alongside an expectation of comfort, as indicated by the wide rooms and numerous windows. Nevertheless, this hybrid form is in no way a 'play castle', as it was built by one of Elizabeth's best generals.

We have seen examples of 'traditional Tudor' and even some classical elements in Irish houses. But both types are few in number compared to the common fortified houses or castle-houses, which are built well into the seventeenth century. The grim reality of self-defence would seem reason enough to preclude examples of the chivalric style. Yet there may have been times when

Figure 6.9 Dunluce Castle, Co. Antrim: entrance to residential block displaying Elizabethan fenestration bays and string course

English dominance seemed certain, and led to over-confidence. Edward Spenser's rebuilding of Kilcolman Castle may be the exception that proves the rule. History tells us that it was quickly taken and burned by Tyrone's rebels in 1598, and recent excavation of the ruins determined that the Tudor construction was considerably weaker than that of the medieval builders (Klingelhofer 1999). Spenser's castle thus seems to have been more for show than real defence, certainly appropriate for the setting of Sir Walter Ralegh's visit and the first 'public' reading of *The Faerie Queene*.

How then does the architecture of colonial Ireland lead us on to America and the other English-speaking possessions? We have been examining the work of the first generation of colonisers, both English and the Irish who associated with them. These examples are admittedly a small selection. Yet I have been focusing not on lesser vernacular architecture, but on the architecture of the

Figure 6.10 Kanturk Castle, Co. Cork: main front, with five-storey flankers and raised Renaissance entrance

Figure 6.11 Durrus Castle, Co. Cork: three-storey house with gable-end chimneys and machicolation

Figure 6.12   Mallow Castle, Co. Cork: a reduced cross-plan house with polygonal tower and gun loops

Great, in that half-humorous reinterpretation of the Tudor/Stuart 'Great Rebuilding'. Such grand residences would always have been few in number, though naturally their numbers increased over the generations. On the one hand, the vast majority of the substantial houses erected in Ireland under Elizabeth and James belong to another architectural type, the defended manor house. On the other hand, the presence in Ireland of all three domestic Elizabethan architectural types suggests that, for some members of the élite, their houses represent something other than the fruits of colonisation, or colonialism in its basic sense.

Some definitions are in order. A colony is a dependent, secondary zone that is economically developed and politically controlled by an expansionist primary area. It is created for the benefit of the primary area, and is transformed into something else, something more productive. The transformation often entails social and political changes, which may then lead to a separation from the primary area, but this would be an unintended consequence. Transformation into a province is another possible, though not inevitable, consequence. A province of an empire, on the other hand, is equal to other provinces; that is the intent and functional goal of imperialism. Political and economic discrepancies notwithstanding, only a sense of equality (provided often by loyalty to an ideology or a monarchial figure) creates an imperial identity and those bonds of unity upon which successful empires rest. A colony transforms; an empire conforms.

The differences between 'colonial' and 'imperial' are thus significant, and especially so to the participants in colonial imperialism. Under the Tudors and Stuarts, the self-identified colonists saw themselves as planting settlements in a primitive, alien and dangerous land. The goal was first survival, and then economic success; adaptions to local conditions and adoptions from local cultures were common. The others who came to live in 'frontier' communities, whether idealistic or naive, built to English fashions and saw Englishness where there was only promise and potential. For them, it was less a colonial mind-set than an imperial mentality that determined their choice of building.

My observations here raise several vexing questions. What other aspects of these builders' lives did not fit into a 'colonial' mentality? What exactly is a colonial mentality or a colonial existence? How can we distinguish it from an imperial mentality? How is either demonstrated through material culture? Can such identities be archaeologically tested? Do these identities merge, or remain distinct, in a 'colonial empire'? These are the kinds of questions that will need to be addressed as comparative colonial archaeology – a sub-discipline in its infancy – develops models and methodologies. As for the Jacobean brick structure in the Virginia Tidewater, it is neither more nor less a mirage than is McCarthy's Renaissance mansion in the hills of north Cork.

REFERENCES

Airs, M. (1975) *The Making of the English Country House 1500–1640*. London: Architectural Press.

Castle, S.E. (1927) *Domestic Gothic of the Tudor Period*. Jamestown, NY: International Casement Company.

Cecil, Lord David (1984) *Hatfield House*. London: St George's Press.

Cooper, N. (1997) The gentry house in the Age of Transition. In D. Gaimster and P. Stamper (eds), *The Age of Transition: The Archaeology of English Culture 1400–1600*, 115–26. Oxford: Oxbow.

Craig, M. (1982) *The Architecture of Ireland*. Dublin: Eason.

Faulkner, P.A. (1972) *Bolsover Castle*. London: HMSO; republished (1985). London: English Heritage.

Girouard, M. (1967) *Robert Smythson and the Architecture of the Elizabethan Era*. South Brunswick, NJ: Barnes.

Hoskins, W.G. (1953) The rebuilding of rural England, 1560–1640. *Past and Present* 4: 44–59.

Howard, M. (1990) Self-fashioning and the classical moment in mid-sixteenth-century architecture. In L. Gent and N. Llewellyn (eds), *Renaissance Bodies: The Human Figure in English Culture c. 1540–1660*, 198–217. London: Reaktion.

—— (1997) Civic buildings and courtier houses: new techniques and materials for architectural ornament. In D. Gaimster and P. Stamper (eds), *The Age of Transition: The Archaeology of English Culture 1400–1600*, 105–13. Oxford: Oxbow.

—— (1998) *The Vyne*. London: National Trust.

Johnson, M.H. (1993) Rethinking the Great Rebuilding. *Oxford Journal of Archaeology* 12: 1, 117–24.

—— (1996) *The Archaeology of Capitalism*. Oxford: Blackwell.

Klingelhofer, E. (1999) The castle of the *Faerie Queene:* probing the ruins of Edmund Spenser's Irish home. *Archaeology* March/April: 48–52.

Mowl, T. (1993) *Elizabethan and Jacobean Style.* London: Phaedon.

Renn, D. (1991) *Kenilworth Castle.* London: English Heritage.

Waterman, D.M. (1961) Some Irish seventeenth-century houses and their architectural ancestry. In E.M. Jope (ed.), *Studies in Building History,* 251–74. London: Odhams.

Part II

The Second Empire: 1800–1945

7 Crossing Offa's Dyke: British ideologies and late eighteenth- and nineteenth-century ceramics in Wales

ALASDAIR BROOKS

> The Welsh have danced among these giant cogwheels before. Wales has always been now. The Welsh as a people have lived by making and remaking themselves in generation after generation, usually against the odds, usually in a British context. Wales is an artefact which the Welsh produce. If they want to. It requires an act of choice.
>
> (Williams 1991: 304)

Wales is the forgotten part of the British Empire's Celtic world. The Irish and the Scots are an unavoidable presence wherever the Union Flag once flew, and St Patrick's Day and Highland Games are celebrated and participated in from Vancouver to Wellington, but the Welsh often seem to vanish into the margins of the former Empire's collective consciousness. Yet the importance of Wales to the United Kingdom and the Empire should not be underestimated. To take but one example, the industrial coalfields of South Wales were a vital part of the economy of industrial Britain.

This chapter, however, focuses on rural Wales. The specific goal of this chapter is to demonstrate how the arrival of new forms and types of pottery into rural Wales in the late eighteenth and nineteenth centuries represents the spread of a new 'British' identity and its ideologies into Wales, and how those ideologies interacted with traditional Welsh behaviour. The implications of the status relationships between the created British identity and the traditional Welsh socio-cultural unit forms a vital part of this discussion. To demonstrate these points in more specific detail, this chapter engages in a study of pottery assemblages from four rural sites dating from the end of the eighteenth century through to the end of the nineteenth century, and located in the region of Cemaes in north Pembrokeshire, Wales. These sites are Llystyn Mill, Pwll Mill, Fron Haul and Parcau, a series of cottages and houses in the Clydach Valley, just outside Newport, Pembrokeshire (Figure 7.1).

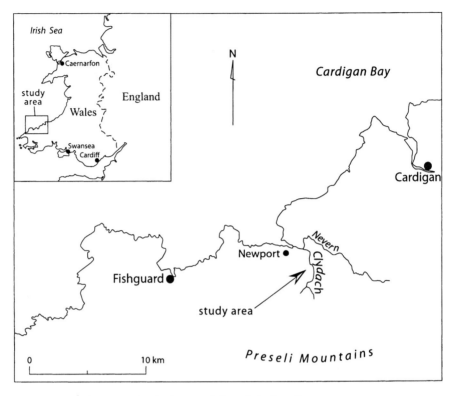

Figure 7.1 North Pembrokeshire and the Clydach Valley

WALES

Before discussing the pottery that forms the core of this chapter, it is necessary to provide some background to Wales and Welsh history, not just in the eighteenth and nineteenth centuries, but in the more distant past. This section should not be understood as arguing for the existence of an anachronistic Welsh nationalism before the late eighteenth century, nor does it seek to deny the importance of the centuries of cultural influence and exchange between Wales and England; it seeks only to emphasise and explore the roots of the long-standing perceptions of 'otherness' between these two parts of the island of Great Britain.

It would be disingenuous to draw a direct connection between the events of the fifth century and the later British Empire, but it can nonetheless be argued that the very formation of Wales is rooted in dispossession by an alien, conquering people. The specifics are rooted more in legend than fact, with Vortigern, Hengist and Horsa, Emrys Wledig (or Ambrosius Aurelianus) and – most potently – Arthur little more than names. Nonetheless, by the middle of the seventh century, the Brythonic peoples (the original 'British') had been largely confined to Wales, Cornwall and Stratchclyde by the Germanic invaders. The medieval Welsh histories record that by 682 '. . . the Britons lost the crown of the kingdom, and the Saxons won it' (Davies 1993: 56–62). At the end of the eighth century, Offa built his great earthwork, Offa's Dyke, to mark the border between the Brythonic princes and Mercia. To the Saxons, those to the west of the dyke were *weallas*, foreigners. These Welsh referred to themselves as *Cymry*, fellow countrymen, but after Stratchclyde was finally absorbed by the Scottish Kingdom (*c.* 1018), they had no fellow countrymen left but themselves (Williams 1991: 3; Davies 1993: 64–6).

This may seem an unusual digression for a chapter that is ostensibly about industrial-era pottery, but this background has been frequently manipulated within the ideology of Welsh identity ever since. The partisans of Owain Glyn Dŵr and Henry Tudor in the fifteenth century were particularly adept at manipulating the legends of the Welsh past. Most relevantly to this chapter, when in 1847 the commission on the state of education in Wales published its report drawing a connection between the Welsh language, Nonconformism and sexual immorality, the report came to be known as *Brad y Llyfrau Gleision*, the Treachery of the Blue Books. The name was a direct reference to the Treachery of the Long Knives, the legendary plot that had led to the slaughter of the Celto-British nobility by the Saxons (Davies 1993: 391).

CEMAES

This section offers a discussion of the wider social environment of the four sites included in this chapter. The focus is inevitably on Cemaes in north Pembrokeshire, but the situation in other parts of the county and Wales as a whole is also considered when relevant. The history of Cemaes can be traced back to the early medieval kingdom of Deheubarth. The region has always been recognisably Welsh in culture and language, and is indeed sometimes regarded as the 'heartland of the [Welsh] language' (Evans 1993: 13) in Pembrokeshire.

The late eighteenth and early nineteenth centuries were a traumatic period for all of Wales. While the problems that afflicted the rest of Great Britain and Ireland in this period are almost a commonplace in the historical record, Wales's demographic transformation is less well known. As John Davies wrote in his landmark history of Wales, 'All periods, of course, are "periods of change", but it is difficult to avoid the conclusion that the changes which the people of Wales underwent between 1770 and 1850 were of a fundamental nature' (1993: 320). In 1770, most of the Welsh population worked in a rural setting, but by 1851 this was true for only a third of the population. In 1770 it took days to travel from London to Pembrokeshire; in 1851 the same trip took hours. In 1770 Anglicans were the majority in most districts in Wales, but by 1851 eight out of ten of the Welsh population were Nonconformists. In 1770 Wales was quietly governed by the landed élite; by 1851 demands for mass representation were increasingly unavoidable. Finally, there were approximately 500,000 people in Wales in 1770. In the 1851 census, the figure stood at 1,163,000 people (Davies 1993: 319).

Most of these changes also took place in the rest of the United Kingdom (although the rise of Nonconformism was less dramatic elsewhere). In a wider imperial context, what really marks out Wales from the other components of the UK was the internal migration from the countryside to the coalfields. Wales never experienced the massive emigration to the New World that characterised Ireland, Scotland and England. Emigration did take place, but at its peak, only three Welsh per 10,000 left for North America annually. This compares to 12 English, 20 Scots and 77 Irish per 10,000. Indeed, by the 1890s, the hunger for labour in the coalfields led to Wales becoming a country of net immigration (Williams 1991: 178–80). Finally, the population of Wales only passed two million in 1901; even if Wales had experienced the emigration of the rest of Britain and Ireland, sheer lack of numbers would have prevented the Welsh from having the same wider imperial profile as the Scots, Irish and English.

Some of the seismic changes that both contributed to and resulted from the changing demographic patterns in Cemaes and Pembrokeshire were more specific to the region, though they were often rooted in and closely related to the wider events previously described. The population of the county grew rapidly, and then collapsed as the rural economy was unable to cope; many Cemaes parishes peaked in population between 1821 and 1841 before shrinking to nearly half of that peak by the end of the century (Lewis 1972: 301). Every bank in Pembrokeshire closed in the banking crisis of 1825–6, causing many farmers to lose their savings (Davies 1993: 355). Following the end of the Napoleonic Wars, market prices for the agricultural goods of north Pembrokeshire collapsed. Furthermore, the 1839–41 growing season was a disaster, further stretching farmers' limited resources (Howell 1993: 83–4) and leading to 'a state of semi-starvation and spiritual malaise' (Williams 1955: 185). The Rebecca riots of the late 1830s and 1840s were ostensibly rooted in turn-pike abuses, but they should be seen as a reaction against the disintegration of rural conditions in general (Davies 1993: 379). Significantly, local tradition has long popularly (though most probably inaccurately) identified the original 'Becca' as Thomas Rees of Mynachlog-Ddu – a parish of Cemaes (John 1984: 80; Williams 1955: 188–9). Finally, the expansion of the South Wales coalfields in the early nineteenth century only encouraged the internal migration from depressed rural areas to the new industrial regions (Davies 1993: 351).

The farm labourers of the Clydach Valley were near the very bottom of the Pembrokeshire social scale; only the landless rural poor encroaching onto the wasteland ranked lower. There were two categories of farm labourer in rural Pembrokeshire. The first category were the unmarried farm servants who would actually live on the farm premises. Of more direct interest to this study were the *gweithiwyr* ('workers'), the married labourers with their own cottages. These labourers were on a weekly wage and lived rent free or on a reduced-rate rented smallholding. Some were fed at the farmer's expense, others were paid more and fed themselves. Some worked directly for the landowner, others worked for the landowner's tenant. It is important to stress that most tenants were on yearly leases, not the life leases that had until recently characterised local rural life. As a result, the population of Cemaes was highly transient, a phenomenon exacerbated by the previously described rural disruption and the lure of the coalfields.

The farms of north Pembrokeshire were of a mixed nature, with an emphasis on livestock rearing and the corn harvest (Jenkins 1976: 20–1; Howell 1993: 78). Prior to the 1850s, farming in north Pembrokeshire was still largely 'unimproved' due to the inherent conservatism of the farmers, the lack of smallholder capital, the reluctance to invest what capital existed in case it led to an increase in rent, landlords who were themselves short on funds (or simply neglectful) and the rural unrest that often characterised the period (Howell 1993: 82–5). The *Pembrokeshire Herald* could with some justification state that 'It has truly been said that Pembrokeshire is half-a-century behind the English counties in the practice of agriculture' (cited in Howell 1993: 80). Pembrokeshire was frequently at the tail end of an east to west sweep of innovation and/or change in the British Isles, a pattern that can also be observed in the development of nineteenth-century cottage architecture in the county (Smith 1975: 313). Given the level of upheaval in rural Pembrokeshire in this period, one might well question whether any landlord could have significantly improved his small tenants' lot. In at least one case, well-meaning attempts by landowners to reorganise leased smallholdings to make sure that they were large enough to support their tenants only reduced the number of holdings available, thus inadvertently further encouraging migration from the countryside (Davies 1993: 355). It is within this context of uncertainty and poverty that the people of the Clydach Valley lived.

THE SITES AND THE POTTERY

Now that the social context is in place, this section will mention some of the specifics of the sites and the pottery. The four sites were excavated in the mid- to late 1980s under the direction of Dr Harold Mytum of the University of York. The pottery assemblages, in particular Llystyn Mill and Pwll Mill, have been the subject of ongoing analysis since 1991 (Brooks 1992, 2000), and this chapter is based on this past research. This section should not be considered as a full, formal publication of the assemblages, which is still forthcoming. Nonetheless this section of the chapter does provide background information on the assemblages, and this marks the first publication of any aspect of the materials. Table 7.1 contains brief lists of the vessels recovered from the sites.

It is also important to note one of the idiosyncrasies of the assemblages and site occupation which necessarily impacts all analysis. These assemblages were not generated by single households, but rather by a series of often intermittent

Table 7.1 Cottage pottery types

	Pwll Mill	Parcau	Llystyn Mill	Fron Haul
creamware	3	10	2	1
pearlware	9	12	12	7
whiteware	19	85	42	49
ironstone		7	4	3
white granite		3		
other white-bodied			1	
blue earthenware		3		
porcelain	6	46	23	32
Chinese porcelain	1			
black basalt		2		
refined redware	5	8	1	5
buff earthenware	1	9	3	4
buckleyware	11	13	7	13
tinglaze	1			1
manganese mottled	1			
North Devon	18	13	1	
Staffordshire-type slipware	2			
white saltglazed stoneware	1		1	
misc. other stoneware	3	11	8	10
redware	6	15	7	14
yellowware	3	12	6	7
TOTALS	90	249	118	146

Wares in bold are the tableware types used in the chapter's full analysis. Specific forms, however, such as figurines and chamberpots, were excluded from the tableware analysis.

A note on terminology: 'ironstone' was used for these assemblages as an ad hoc term to describe certain mid- to late nineteenth-century whitewares with a dense fabric. It is not to be confused with 'white granite' which is a specific ware (e.g. Ewins 1997) common to mid-to late-nineteenth-century American contexts, but very rare in contemporaneous British contexts.

households. This is only to be expected given the highly transient nature of occupation throughout rural Pembrokeshire, but it does mean that the assemblages are by necessity considered from the perspective of being representative of a localised social group rather than individual households. Fortunately, this chapter does indeed engage in a study of social groups rather than individuals, and thus this potential problem serves to strengthen the analysis.

The Fron Haul site is typical of the small cottages of south-west Wales. The cottage consisted of two sections: a main room featuring a fireplace at the far end, and a later addition containing the bedroom (Mytum 1988: 34). No traces of any partition survived by the time the site was excavated, but the main room was almost certainly subdivided into a kitchen and living-room section (the 'upper end') and a parlour (the 'lower end'), an arrangement known as *ty dau ben* or a 'two-ended house' (Jenkins 1976: 123).

The Fron Haul assemblage consists of 146 vessels across 12 basic ware types (Table 7.1). With very few exceptions, the wares recovered from Fron Haul post-date 1820. When a more specific date could be identified, usually through specific transfer prints or makers' and merchants' marks, these typically dated from the mid- to late nineteenth century. The existence of an early twentieth-century component also seems likely as there is at least one decal-printed porcelain saucer (TPQ 1892), and two of the marks on whiteware transfer-printed vessels are for makers or merchants who were in business from 1877 to 1921 and 1860 to 1915. In general, however, the overwhelming majority of the assemblage dates from the second half of the nineteenth century.

A few items, a single later creamware (*c.* 1780–*c.* 1830) jug, seven pearlware (*c.*1780–*c.* 1830) vessels and a fragment of tinglaze (*c.* 1600–*c.* 1800) pre-date the majority of the assemblage. Judging by its context, the tinglaze fragment is a stray sherd unrelated to the cottage. The creamware and pearlware were most probably display objects, and as such would not have been used on a daily basis. Significantly, the largely complete embossed shelledge pearlware plates feature almost no use-wear marks, while the creamware jug features an elaborate over-glaze transfer print with a farming theme.

The Pwll Mill site is, like Fron Haul, a *ty dau ben* cottage, and is another typical example of the genre. The 90 vessels of the Pwll Mill assemblage represent both the smallest and one of the more interesting Clydach Valley assemblages. The vessels occur across 16 basic ware types (Table 7.1). The Pwll Mill assemblage is the earliest of the Clydach Valley assemblages. The Chinese porcelain, creamware, tinglaze, manganese mottled ware, North Devon gravel-tempered ware, white saltglaze, Staffordshire slipware and pearlware, all ware types that pre-date 1830, comprise 36 vessels or 40 per cent of the total. The wares which definitively post-date 1820, namely the whiteware, yellowware and Chelsea sprig porcelain comprise 25 vessels or about 28 per cent of the total. The remaining third of the assemblage could belong to either period. Furthermore, the characteristic ware types and decorations of the middle of the nineteenth century, such as the highly fired whitewares often misleadingly described as 'ironstone' (see Table 7.1 captions for a quick definition of 'iron-stone' and 'white granite' in this context) and flow blue transfer prints, are entirely lacking, while decorations associated with the second half of the century, such as Guest and Dewsberry (1877–1921) 'Asiatic Pheasants' prints and cut-sponged wares are also almost entirely lacking (there is a single cut-sponged bowl). Unfortunately, no maker's or merchant's marks were identified, nor were any transfer prints (beyond willow) identified, so this additional information is lacking. The preponderance of evidence, however, suggests that the Pwll Mill assemblage was generated between *c.* 1790 and *c.* 1850. Given the small number of vessels recovered (even allowing for the presence of a nearby stream), it seems likely that occupation of the cottage was intermittent throughout this period.

The Parcau house is larger and more elaborate than the Pwll Mill and Fron Haul cottages, and is an excellent example of a *ty singl* or 'single house'. This type of cottage features two floors, with the rooms on both floors arranged in a row – much as for a *ty dau ben*; indeed, many single houses started life as a *ty dau ben.* The rear lean-to at Parcau, probably containing a dairy, is also typical of the *ty singl* (Jenkins 1971: 92; Mytum 1988: 35).

The Parcau assemblage consists of 249 vessels across 17 basic ware types (Table 7.1). This is by far the largest of the Clydach Valley cottage assemblages, with fully 103 vessels more than the next largest assemblage at Fron Haul. The Parcau assemblage contains vessels representing all periods of ceramics development from the late eighteenth century through to the end of the nineteenth century. Just under 10 per cent of the assemblage consists of tablewares dating from 1760 to 1830 (black basalt, creamware and pearlware), and a further 5 per cent consists of eighteenth-century North Devon gravel-tempered coarsewares. At the same time, there are mid-nineteenth century wares, represented by white granite and mid-century makers' marks, and late nineteenth-century/early twentieth-century wares, represented by at least one decal-print and vessels made during the Guest and Dewsberry period of the Llanelli pottery (1877–1921). The two white granite mugs are the only vessels of this ware type currently known from a domestic British site. The lack of any common mid-eighteenth century wares, such as white saltglazed stoneware and delftware, strongly suggests that occupation began after 1780, and – given the vagaries of time-lag in deposits – more probably after 1790. As a whole, the Parcau assemblage appears to represent occupation of the site across the late eighteenth and nineteenth centuries, but with most of the ceramics dating from the mid-through to the end of the nineteenth century. This may well be a function of increased availability and lower costs of pottery in the later period rather than a more intensive later occupation. As of this writing, it has not yet been identified whether the occupation of Parcau was constant or more intermittent, or how many households were involved.

The Llystyn Mill site is by far the most complex of the Clydach Valley sites. The site consists of a main cottage, an adjacent, smaller (almost certainly earlier) cottage and two further structures associated with a water-driven fulling mill (Mytum 1988: 36). The Llystyn Mill main cottage was almost certainly a *ty singl*, once again with an adjacent dairy. Efforts to distinguish between pottery associated with the main cottage and the earlier building by context were inconclusive, and the site assemblage is therefore considered as a whole.

The Llystyn Mill assemblage consists of 118 vessels across 14 basic ware types (Table 7.1). The vast majority of the Llystyn Mill assemblage dates from the middle and second half of the nineteenth century. This is particularly true of the identified maker's marks, the small quantities of highly fired whiteware/ironstone and stylistic features of the whitewares. However, there is a significant quantity of earlier materials, notably the 12 pearlware (*c.* 1780–*c.* 1830) vessels, that comprise more than 10 per cent of the assemblage. Given the near-absence of creamware and North Devonware (only one vessel each), it appears most likely that these earlier materials are the result of intermittent occupation of the site in the first three decades of the nineteenth century, but no earlier than 1800, and most likely in the 1820–30 period. The peak of occupation then dates to the middle (*c.* 1850–*c.* 1870) of the century. The lack of decal prints and potentially twentieth-century marks strongly suggests that Llystyn Mill was abandoned before the end of the nineteenth-century.

ANALYSIS

The comparative, interpretive analysis of material culture has been somewhat neglected in the literature of British post-medieval archaeology, but this type of study has had a strong tradition in wider historical archaeology for at least a quarter of a century. While his positivist agenda has never found any real following outside North America (Brooks 2000: 10–11), South's artefact pattern analysis marked perhaps the first attempt to build a coherent argument for comparative material culture studies between sites (South 1977: 83–164). Comparative studies of ceramics assemblages are also common in North America (e.g. Adams and Boling 1991) and indeed beyond (e.g. Brooks 2000; Klose and Malan 2000; Lawrence 2003). Furthermore, the use of ceramics and other material culture to study specific issues of socio-cultural ideology is also well attested, examples of which include the generation of a syncretic (or 'creolised') culture amongst African-Americans (e.g. Ferguson 1992), and the perception of ideological shift through changes in material culture use by single households (e.g. King and Miller 1991). Nineteenth-century Welsh identity has also been studied archaeologically, although past work in this regard has focused on gravestones, language and religion (Mytum 1994, 1999) rather than the material culture of domestic life. Despite the anthropological perspective of the North American elements of this past work, all of this research provides valuable context for the present study.

This analysis of the assemblages in this chapter focuses on the tablewares rather than the coarse utilitarian wares. Even more specifically, the analysis focuses on the plates, bowls and teas (cups and saucers combined). These three vessel forms are by far the most important diagnostic forms, and they also comprise the overwhelming majority of the tablewares at each site (Figure 7.2) – and at least 50 per cent of the total assemblages in three of the four cases.

The overlapping dates of the assemblages, the intermittent nature of the multiple-household occupations and the nature of the single-context middens from which most of the materials were excavated makes it impossible to place the Clydach Valley in a strict hierarchical temporal order. Pwll Mill dates before 1850 and Fron Haul dates after 1850, but the Parcau and Llystyn assemblages are far more problematic. While the majority of the materials at both sites post-date the middle of the nineteenth century, both sites – especially Parcau – contain important earlier elements. Despite these issues, the role of temporal shifts remains important, particularly as far as Pwll Mill is concerned. For example, the refined tablewares form a much smaller part of the Pwll Mill assemblage (under 50 per cent) than for the other three assemblages (about 70 per cent at all three – see Figure 7.3). As Pwll Mill largely dates from a

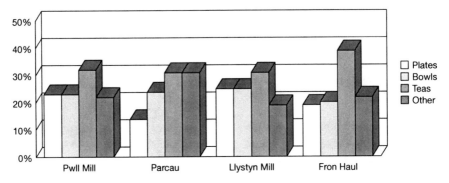

Figure 7.2   Plates, bowls and teawares as per cent of tablewares (MNV)

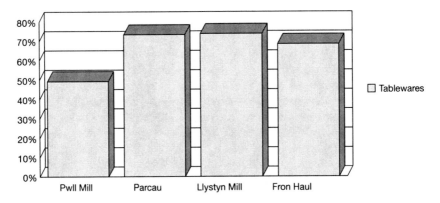

Figure 7.3   Tablewares as per cent of each assemblage (MNV)

period where refined tablewares were new and more expensive, the higher percentage of coarsewares in the assemblage – some in tableware forms – is only to be expected.

Returning to the plates, bowls and teas, a comparison of the most common types within each form reveals a rigid hierarchy of type, particularly for the three sites with important post-1850 components (Figures 7.4a–c). More than 50 per cent of the teas at each site are porcelain, a figure that rises to more than 70 per cent when Pwll Mill is excluded. More than 70 per cent of the plates – once again with the exception of Pwll Mill – are transfer-printed. Only 20 per cent of the Pwll Mill plates are printed; precisely half of the plates at this site are shelledged (hidden in the 'other' category). The bowls are less rigid in their decorative distribution, but as will be discussed, it is particularly significant that the overwhelming majority of these vessels at all four sites are types other than porcelain and transfer prints. With the exception of Llystyn Mill (where there are equal quantities of sponged and printed bowls), sponged bowls form the plurality of the bowls. Cut-sponged bowls are the most common of this sub-type.

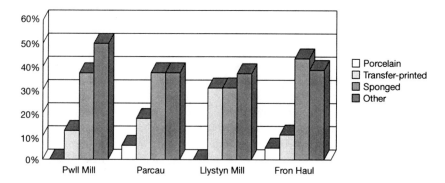

Figure 7.4a Bowl distributions (MNV)

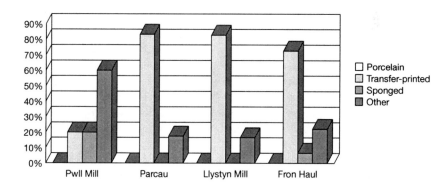

Figure 7.4b Plate distributions (MNV)

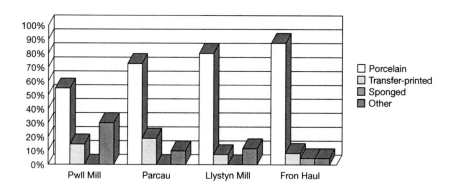

Figure 7.4c Teawares distributions (MNV)

Miller's work on the economic scaling of plates, bowls and teas (Miller 1980, 1991) is particularly important in interpreting the hierarchy of types revealed by Figures 7.4a–c. While Miller's CC indices are a valuable research tool in an American context, the specifics of the data do not translate in a transatlantic context (Brooks 2000: 210–11). Nonetheless, many of the general observations inherent his data are applicable for British contexts. In particular, porcelain is the most expensive type of tableware, transfer-printed wares are the next most expensive – though their relative value falls over the course of the late eighteenth and nineteenth centuries – and other types of decoration are less expensive than these first two types of tableware. Thus Figures 7.4a–c reveal that the teawares overwhelmingly occur in the most expensive tableware available, that after *c.* 1850 plates overwhelmingly occur in the next most expensive tableware and that (with the exception of Llystyn Mill) bowls rarely occur in the more expensive types.

At this point, where the relationship between certain forms and the relative value of their predominant types has been established, it is necessary to briefly step back and explain the context within which the interaction of British identity and ideology interacted with traditional rural Welsh behaviour. The purpose of this chapter is to look at how the arrival of these British identities into Wales, and the wider implications thereof, was partially formed and informed by a particular aspect of material culture, namely ceramics. As such, this is not a study of British identity itself, a topic which is more than adequately covered by existing literature, both for history (e.g. Colley 1996) and material culture (e.g. Brooks 1999). Nonetheless, a summary of the background in this regard is necessary.

'Britain', in its modern sense, is a comparatively recent creation. Wales was forcibly united to England by 1282 (though *de jure* only from 1536), and James I and VI adopted the title 'King of Great Britain . . . and Ireland' in 1604, but the Act of Union between Scotland and England dates from 1707, and the United Kingdom of Great Britain and Ireland was only created in 1801. Past research has shown how, following the Act of Union and creation of the United Kingdom, a new 'British' identity was forged. This new identity was based on several ideological concepts, prominent amongst which were the perceived need for national unity in the face of war with external powers (Colley 1996: 193–5, 339), and the need of the governing classes to portray a stable, prosperous, and calm Britain during a time of internal uncertainty (Brooks 1999: 54–6). This new 'British' identity, as formed and developed by the governing classes of the new nation, found expression in a range of material culture (Colley 1996: 193–5), including transfer-printed ceramics (Brooks 1999).

Amongst the important sub-themes that were drawn into and included in the wider ideology of the new metropolitan British identity, particularly amongst the ruling élite, were conceptions of order, gentility and refinement which originally rooted in the eighteenth century (Langford 1989). A small number of examples of the expression conceptions could take include transfer-printed plates showing 'stately homes dominating the rural landscape' (Brooks

1999: 54), the transformation of the Scottish Highland Laird from 'the leader of an extended kin group on the margins of the Scottish state to a commercial landowner connected to the wider networks of British capitalism' (Brooks 2000: 96–7; see also Hunter 1976: 10–11; MacInnes 1988: 72), and the association of tea-drinking with genteel, refined sociable behaviour (Weatherill 1996: 157–9; Richards 1999). North American archaeologists are probably most familiar with some of these concepts as part of Deetz's 'Georgian Worldview' (Deetz 1996: 62–4, 66–7), but despite the ideological overlap, this is a wholly inadequate term to use for the archaeology of rural Wales or the worldview of a Welsh cottager, and by the nineteenth century these themes had in any case been subsumed into the broader ideologies underpinning the new British identity.

Paradoxically, while the British identity was being formed, the late eighteenth and nineteenth centuries also saw the rise of a newly assertive sense of Welsh identity (Williams 1991: 162–7; Morgan 1992), a process that was, incidentally, even more visible for the Scottish Highlands (e.g. McCrone 1989; Clyde 1995). Much of the relevant imagery also found its way onto transfer-printed ceramics (Brooks 1997). However, the appropriation of much of the relevant imagery only served to demonstrate that 'the national minorities had been successfully appropriated to the point that they were considered symbolically "safe"' (Brooks 1999: 60). Certain aspects of Welsh and Scottish Highland culture were adopted and appropriated by the new British governing class, but Welsh and Highland culture as a whole remained conceptually marginalised. While it is certainly possible to speak of traditional Welsh behaviour for rural Wales, beyond its narrow intellectual base 'Welsh national identity' was a largely artificial concept until the mid-nineteenth century. To demonstrate this dichotomy with a Scottish example, Queen Victoria and Prince Albert's children could safely wear the Scottish kilt, but as recently as the 1930s *Antiquity* could publish a paper characterising the Hebrides as a 'cultural backwater' (Curwen 1938).

That the British and Welsh ideologies of this period found expression in material culture is a given. However, the many relevent transfer-printed ceramics mentioned throughout the previous discussion are rarely found on British archaeological sites for the simple reason that many of them were made for export (itself an interesting point, but one outside the purview of this chapter). Thus it becomes necessary to look at the wider assemblage, rather than individual examples. The previously observed correlation of certain forms with specific categories of tablewares becomes particularly revealing when the role of those forms within both traditional Welsh behaviour and the new British ideologies is taken into account. The most common element of the diet of the rural Welsh poor was *cawl*, a bacon and vegetable stew (Owen 1991: 10). For fairly obvious reasons, this stew would have required hollow vessels – namely bowls – for consumption. Significantly, at all of the Clydach Valley sites (even Llystyn Mill), the overwhelming majority of the bowls, the form most closely associated with traditional Welsh food, are the cheaper, less expensive materials.

The teawares, however, are a very different matter. In its origins, tea-drinking was very much an alien concept to the rural poor of north Pembrokeshire. Indeed, as briefly addressed earlier, tea-drinking's British roots lie in a sophisticated, almost ritualistic consumption associated with expense and status (e.g. Weatherill 1996: 158–9) originally advanced by the same governing élites who were developing the new British identity. Only in the late eighteenth and early nineteenth centuries did the industrialisation of ceramic production make teawares more widely accessible to the British public. Nonetheless, these forms maintained status connotations rooted in their broader ideological background (Brooks 2000: 178–9). Given the striking and sharp correlation between teawares and porcelain (Figure 7.4c), the most expensive tableware available, it is exceptionally clear that the specific connection between teawares and status remained valid for the rural poor of Cemaes, even if the broader nature of that connection within British society had shifted significantly over the previous century. There can be no clearer demonstration of the divide between the relative status of the new British identity and traditional Welsh behaviour than these sharp distinctions of type and decoration between the 'alien' teawares associated with the former, and the 'traditional' bowls associated with the latter.

The plates fall somewhere in between the bowls and the teawares. With the exception of Pwll Mill, the plates are overwhelmingly transfer-printed. Transfer prints were initially much more expensive than undecorated or sponged wares – in the United States, two to four times as expensive (Miller 1991) – although the relative price nonetheless fell gradually in Britain over the course of the nineteenth century (David Barker, personal communication, 10 May 2000). The process at work is nonetheless similar to the teawares: a type of ware that was initially more expensive and thus had certain status connotations is acquired once it became affordable and more accessible. Multiple factors were involved in that accessibility, including improved transport to western Wales, a dramatic increase in the number of 'china dealers' near Cemaes and possibly a sudden shift in American preferences from transfer prints to 'white granite' (Brooks 2000: 192–4). Yet it is important to note a significant difference between the status implications of the plates and teawares. For the teas, both the supposed primary function (tea-drinking) and the material (porcelain) held status implications. For the plates, it is solely the decorative technique (transfer prints). Plates were not the radical innovation in material culture that teawares were; however important *cawl* and bowls might have been to the Welsh diet, it can hardly be argued that plates were largely alien to rural poor Welsh material culture prior to the late eighteenth century in the same way that teawares were.

The role of the Welsh dresser within Welsh material culture is particularly relevant when considering the status implications of various vessel forms. The use of a wooden dresser as a vehicle for the display of pottery is well documented across the British Isles (e.g. Vincentelli 1992: 18–23; Webster 1999). Surviving examples complete with their original nineteenth-century pottery are frustratingly rare, but those examples that do exist typically feature a range of vessel forms, but with a emphasis very towards the upper end of the hierarchical types, namely porcelain teas and transfer-printed plates. Vincentelli further notes that:

> In the 18th century, it was fashionable for the gentry to collect porcelain and fine china and the spread of tea-drinking necessitated the production of all kinds of new ceramic forms . . . The new industrial methods of production of domestic ceramics and ornaments made them available to ordinary people. They too could enjoy the luxury of decorating their houses and their tables with brightly coloured pottery. They too, could take pride in their household choices and display their personal taste.
>
> (1992: 18)

By the nineteenth century, this fashion for display of 'brightly coloured' luxury pottery very much filtered down to the dressers of the poorer elements of Welsh society. While the presence of dressers in the Clydach Valley households can be neither confirmed nor denied, all of the available evidence suggests that the teawares, and in all probability many of the plates, were used for display. As noted earlier, some of the Fron Haul plates indeed provide direct evidence of this through their lack of use-wear marks. Furthermore, this use of plates and teawares for display only adds stress to the importance of the cheap and inexpensive bowls for traditional everyday food consumption.

On a final note, the rigidity of the hierarchy of form and type across the three later sites strongly suggests a level of conscious choice in acquisition by the Clydach Valley households. While to a certain extent there is a natural connection between some forms and some decorations and wares, this is by no means absolute – as indeed the larger percentage of transfer-printed bowls at Llystyn Mill demonstrates. Yet despite this conscious choice, it is not argued here that the presence of refined tablewares, in particular porcelain teawares, itself signals a conscious awareness of the new British identity and its associated ideologies by the Clydach Valley households. Nor is it held that the new identity replaced traditional behaviour in Wales or that their presence implies a conscious rejection of 'Welshness'. Instead, the spread of the new forms and types of pottery to rural Wales was a material expression of the wider spread of the new national ideologies of the late eighteenth- and nineteenth century to Wales and the ongoing development of a syncretic culture that combined both traditional Welsh behaviour and the new metropolitan 'British' identity and ideology. The comparisons of the different wares and decorations found on bowls, plates and teawares clearly demonstrates the tensions inherent in the creation of this syncretic culture and the different status assigned to its different contributing elements.

CONCLUSION

Before concluding, it is important to note that the processes described in the previous section are not unique to Wales – the importance of 'traditional' bowls and the arrival of 'alien' teawares has also been observed in the Outer Hebrides (Brooks 2000: 93–126). More comparative work needs to be done to see to what extent these observations are valid for England. Indeed, the lack of relevant assemblages in British archaeology may necessitate the re-evaluation of some of this analysis once more data becomes available.

What is unique, however, is the context, the shifting relationship between Wales and Britain. As has been noted throughout the last section, the assumption underlying much of this discussion has been that in the nineteenth century Welsh behaviour (as represented by the inexpensive *cawl* bowls) was perceived as 'low-status' while wider British culture, identity and ideology (as represented by porcelain teas and, to a lesser extent, transfer-printed plates) was 'high-status'. However outmoded this perspective may seem in the early twenty-first century, this was a widespread prejudice of its day, to the point of being a nineteenth-century truism. Nowhere is this better represented for Wales than in the *Brad y Llyfrau Gleision*, the Treason of the Blue Books. This government report on Welsh education (officially known by the more mundane title 'Report of the Commissioners into the State of Education in Wales') stigmatised Welsh culture, the Welsh language and Welsh religious Nonconformism as the causes of sexual immorality, stupidity, inadequate education and local obstructionism, while some London newspapers openly called for the extirpation of the Welsh from the British body politic (Williams 1991: 208; Jones 1992: 103–65; Davies 1993: 390–2). The wounds opened by the *Brad* can still cause tension; as recently as 1985, Gwyn Williams could write that 'The venom injected into Anglo-Welsh relations then, by this ego-trip of three arrogant and ignorant barristers probably buttonholed by some militant [Anglican] clergymen has never fully ceased to operate' (1991: 208).

The irony is surely that just at the moment that English and British attitudes to traditional 'Welshness' and the wider social turmoil of the period were radicalising political opinion in the principality, and a sense of Welsh national identity moved beyond being the preserve of the self-appointed Welsh intelligentsia, the advent of industralisation meant that Welsh material culture increasingly revolved around the standardised, mass-produced materials of the British imperial state. Few aspects of Welsh material culture can provide better evidence of this than the ceramics of the Clydach Valley sites. The relative amounts of each type naturally differ, but the forms, wares and materials are largely indistinguishable from those excavated from any other contemporaneous British site – and, indeed, most sites throughout the British Empire. While the specifics of decoration occasionally differ, even here standardisation becomes paramount: the most common definitively Welsh tableware decoration at the Clydach Valley sites are the 'Asiatic Pheasants' plates of the Guest and Dewsberry firm of Llanelli – a pattern that can hardly be described as a uniquely Welsh phenomenon. Furthermore, the tableware form most closely associated with traditional Welsh food (bowls) is overwhelmingly found in cheaper, low-status decorations, while that form most closely associated with an alien – in this case

British – culture (teawares) is overwhelmingly found in the most expensive, most high-status ceramic available.

Whatever the Williams quote at the beginning of this chapter might suggest to the contrary, the Clydach Valley sites date from the period when Wales had to become a conscious creation. Prior to the nineteenth century, Welshness could be subconscious for the majority of the population; distinctions between 'Welsh', 'English' and (post-1707) 'British' were largely abstractions for social and political élites. From the nineteenth century, however, industrialisation meant that 'British' material culture was accessible across all strata of society in a wholly new, dynamic and all-embracing fashion. A new syncretic material culture was formed, influenced by traditional Welsh behaviour and the new British identity, and the wider status perceptions of both of these elements. The ceramics assemblages of the Clydach Valley thus represent more clearly than most other aspects of everyday domestic material culture the fundamental shifts in the relationship between traditional Welsh society and the new British ideologies.

ACKNOWLEDGEMENTS

First and foremost, I would like to thank Harold Mytum for involving me with the analysis of the pottery from the North Pembrokeshire Historical Archaeology project, and for his help and assistance over the last few years with the materials. I would also like to thank the students and trainees of the 1992 and 1998–2000 Castell Henllys fieldschools and training excavations for their help with the processing of the assemblages. Though they may well have both forgotten having done so over the years, David Barker and Louise Henderson both helped with a couple of vessel IDs each. Susan Buckham's comments on the drafts of this chapter were invaluable (thanks, pal). Pwll Mill and Llystyn Mill were included in my doctoral thesis for which Harold Mytum (again), Lawrence Butler, Tania Dickinson and David Gaimster all provided useful suggestions on those assemblages in that context. Martin Hall made some suggestions on a late draft that I have attempted to address when appropriate. I am also indebted to Susan Lawrence for her editorial remarks. Finally, all errors of fact and perceived errors of interpretation remain – of course – solely my own responsibility.

REFERENCES

Adams, W.H. and Boling, S.J. (1991) 'Status and ceramics for planters and slaves on three Georgia coastal plantations'. In G.L. Miller, O. Jones, L. Ross and T. Majewski (compilers), *Approaches to Material Cutlure Research for Historical Archaeologists*, 59–86. Tucson: Society for Historical Archaeology.

Brooks, A.M. (1992) An analysis of eighteenth- to nineteenth-century pottery from southwest Wales. Unpublished MA thesis, University of York.

Brooks, A.M. (1997) Beyond the fringe: transfer-printed ceramics and the inter-nationalisation of Celtic myth. *International Journal of Historical Archaeology* 1(1): 39–55.

—— (1999) Building Jerusalem: transfer-printed finewares and the creation of British identity. In S. Tarlow and S. West (eds), *The Familiar Past? Archaeologies of Later Historical Britain*, 51–65. London: Routledge.

—— (2000) The comparative analysis of late eighteenth- and nineteenth-century ceramics – a trans-Atlantic perspective. Unpublished DPhil thesis, University of York.

Clyde, R. (1995) *From Rebel to Hero: The Image of the Highlander 1745–1830*. East Linton: Tuckwell Press.

Colley, L. (1996) *Britons: Forging the Nation 1707–1837*. London: Vintage.

Curwen, E.C. (1938) The Hebrides: a cultural backwater. *Antiquity* XII: 261–89.

Davies, J. (1993) *A History of Wales*. Harmondsworth: Allen Lane.

Deetz, J. (1996) *In Small Things Forgotten*, rev. edn. New York: Anchor Books.

Evans, M.B. (1993) The land and its people, 1815–1974. In D. Howell (ed.), *Pembrokeshire County History, Volume IV: Modern Pembrokeshire 1815–1974*, 3–38. Haverfordwest: Pembrokeshire Historical Society.

Ferguson, L. (1992) *Uncommon Ground; Archaeology and Early African America, 1650–1800*. Washington, DC: Smithsonian Institution Press.

Howell, D.W. (1993) Farming in Pembrokeshire, 1815–1974. In D. Howell (ed.), *Pembrokeshire County History, Volume IV: Modern Pembrokeshire 1815–1974*, 77–110. Haverfordwest: Pembrokeshire Historical Society.

Hunter, J. (1976) *The Making of the Crofting Community*. Edinburgh: John Donald.

Jenkins, D. (1971) *The Agricultural Community in South-West Wales at the Turn of the Twentieth Century*. Cardiff: University of Wales Press.

Jenkins, J.G. (1976) *Life and Tradition in Rural Wales*. London: J.M. Dent & Sons.

John, B. (1984) *Pembrokeshire*. Newport, Pembrokeshire: Greencroft Books.

Jones, I.E. (1992) *Mid-Victorian Wales: The Observers and the Observed*. Cardiff: University of Wales Press.

King, J. and Miller, H. (1991) The view from the Midden: an analysis of Midden distri-bution and composition at the Van Sweringen site, St. Mary's City, Maryland. In G.L. Miller, O. Jones, L. Ross and T. Majewski (compilers), *Approaches to Material Culture Research for Historical Archaeologists*, 331–53. Tucson, AZ: Society for Historical Archaeology.

Klose, J. and Malan, A. (2000) The ceramic signature of the Cape in the nineteenth century, with particular reference to the Tennant Street site, Cape Town. *South African Archaeological Bulletin* 55: 49–59.

Langford, P. (1989) *A Polite and Commercial People: England 1727–1783*. Oxford: Oxford University Press.

Lawrence, S. (2003) Archaeology and the nineteenth-century British Empire. *Historical Archaeology* 37(1): 20–33.

Lewis, E.T. (1972) *North of the Hills – A History of the Parishes of Eglwyswen, Eglwyswrw, Llanfair Nantgwyn, Meline, and Nevern*, privately published.

MacInnes, A. (1988) Scottish Gaeldom: the first phase of clearance. In T.M. Devine and R. Micheson (eds), *People and Society in Scotland, Volume 1: 1760–1830*, 43–51. Edinburgh: John Donald.

McCrone, D. (1989) Representing Scotland: culture and nationalism. In D. McCrone, S. Kendrick and P. Straw (eds), *The Making of Scotland: Nation, Culture, and Social Change*. Edinburgh: Edinburgh University Press.

Miller, G.L. (1980) Classification and economic scaling of nineteenth-century ceramics. *Historical Archaeology* 14: 1–40.

Miller, G.L. (1991) A revised set of CC index values for classification and economic scaling of English ceramics from 1787–1880. *Historical Archaeology* 25(1): 1–25.

Morgan, P. [1983] (1992) From a death to a view: the hunt for the Welsh past in the Romantic period. In E. Hobsbawm and T. Ranger (eds), *The Invention of Tradition.* Cambridge: Cambridge University Press.

Mytum, H.C. (1988) The Clydach Valley, a nineteenth-century landscape. *Archaeology Today* 9(3): 33–7.

—— H.C. (1994) Language as symbol in churchyard monuments: the use of Welsh in nineteenth- and twentieth-century Pembrokeshire. *World Archaeology* 26: 252–67.

—— H.C. (1999) Welsh cultural identity in nineteenth-century Pembrokeshire: the pedimented headstone as a graveyard monument. In S. Tarlow and S. West (eds), *The Familiar Past? Archaeologies of Later Historical Britain*, 215–30. London: Routledge.

Owen, T.M. (1991) *The Customs and Traditions of Wales.* Cardiff: University of Wales Press.

Richards, S. (1999) *Eighteenth-Century Ceramics: Products for a Civilised Society.* Manchester: Manchester University Press.

Smith, P. (1975) *Houses of the Welsh Countryside.* London: Royal Commission on Ancient and Historical Monuments in Wales, HMSO.

South, S. (1977) *Method and Theory in Historical Archaeology.* New York: Academic Press.

Vincentelli, M. (1992) *Llestri Llafar – Talking Pots.* Aberystwyth: University College of Wales.

Weatherill, L. (1996) *Consumer Behaviour and Material Culture in Britain 1660–1760*, 2nd edn. London: Routledge.

Webster, J. (1999) Resisting traditions: ceramics, identity, and consumer choice in the Outer Hebrides from 1800 to the present. *International Journal of Historical Archaeology* 3(1): 53–73.

Williams, D. (1955) *The Rebecca Riots: A Study in Agrarian Dissent.* Cardiff: University of Wales Press.

Williams, G. (1991) *When Was Wales?* Harmondsworth: Penguin.

8   An imperial people? Highland Scots, emigration and the British colonial world

JAMES SYMONDS

INTRODUCTION

Between the beginning of the sixteenth century and the last quarter of the twentieth century, over 50 million people made the westward transatlantic voyage to North America (Bailyn 1988: 5). Of the 17 million people who emigrated from the British Isles in the hundred years between the Battle of Waterloo and World War I, around 80 per cent moved to North America (Cohen 1997: 68). The remainder colonised the southern hemisphere, setting up home in Australia, New Zealand, the former Rhodesia and South Africa. Although numerically overshadowed by the outpouring of population from Ireland, which lost 25 per cent of its population in the famine years of 1845–51, Scottish emigration made a significant contribution to the settlement of the British colonial world.

In this chapter I will explore one aspect of the Scottish diaspora – emigration from the Outer Hebrides of Scotland. I have two main aims. The first is essentially programmatic. A number of North American scholars have suggested that historical archaeologies of European colonialism should adopt a global comparative perspective (Falk 1991; Deetz 1993; Orser 1996). This approach seeks to explain similarities in the patterning of material culture in different localities by invoking the influence of extended information flows and the spread of capitalist behaviour. Global networks of capitalism are powerful and durable structures. They both constrain and enable individual human agency, but in all cases arise out of a desire to exploit inverse power relationships. I argue that instead of reifying these abstract power structures we should instead focus upon how the processes of colonialism and capitalism were enacted in day-to-day practice within localised frameworks of meaning. Historical archaeology has the capacity to recover evidence from a range of historically specific worlds (Hodder 1999: 137). By 'plying backwards and forwards' between global structures and local responses it is possible to move beyond universal explanations and to understand the material conditions of individual lives in particular times and places (Hall 2000: 18) One of the key aims of historical archaeology should be to 'ironicise' the master narratives that commemorate colonial encounters by exposing the 'smaller, stranger, potentially subversive narratives of archaeological material' (Johnson 1999: 33–4). As I hope to demonstrate, a local scale of analysis provides an essential starting point that allows us to move beyond de-contextualised global inferences.

My second aim is to provide a series of case studies to show how historical archaeology can illuminate the experience of life in remote nineteenth-century North Atlantic communities, and the circumstances surrounding emigration and re-settlement. Case studies will be presented from the Isle of South Uist in the Outer Hebrides of Scotland, and Nova Scotia (Figures 8.1 and 8.2). It is my contention that far from being a homogeneous and homogenising process, Highland emigration between c. 1770 and 1870 had a variety of causes and an equally varied set of outcomes. It would be wrong to assume that those who made the transatlantic voyage in this period were a unified band of colonists, or even that they defined themselves as essentially 'British'.

BRITONS AND BRITISHNESS: MYTHIC HISTORIES AND IMAGINED COMMUNITIES

> Every culture dreams its present and re-imagines its past. (MacDonald 1994: 42)

The seemingly intractable problem at the core of this volume lies in the definition of the terms 'British' and 'Britishness'. As Matthew Johnson has stressed (this volume), identities are constantly re-created and re-negotiated. Historic formulations of British identity have resonance in present day political and cultural debates, making the task all the more difficult. The process by which national identities are produced and legitimised is complex and involves as much active forgetting as remembering (McCrone 1998: 63). When considering Britishness it is important to remember that whereas there was clearly an historic British state, there was never a British *nation*. It is therefore impossible to establish a fixed point in time when an authentic 'British people' first stood shoulder-to-shoulder and eyed up an unsuspecting world.

Some historians have placed the making of British consciousness as early as the Tudor and Stuart periods, in the years 1533–1707 (Bradshaw and Roberts 1998). The Act of Union of 1707, which linked Scotland to England and Wales to create the United Kingdom of Great Britain, provides a more widely accepted political starting point. Linda Colley (1994) has suggested that a British 'nation' and sense of Britishness was 'forged' between 1707 and 1837. Drawing upon Benedict Anderson's definition of a nation as an 'imagined political community' (Anderson 1991), Colley argues that political union enabled the constituent nations within Great Britain to find unity as a result of shared Protestantism and prolonged warfare with France. In essence, the peoples of the British archipelago had sufficient shared interests (or fears) to persuade them

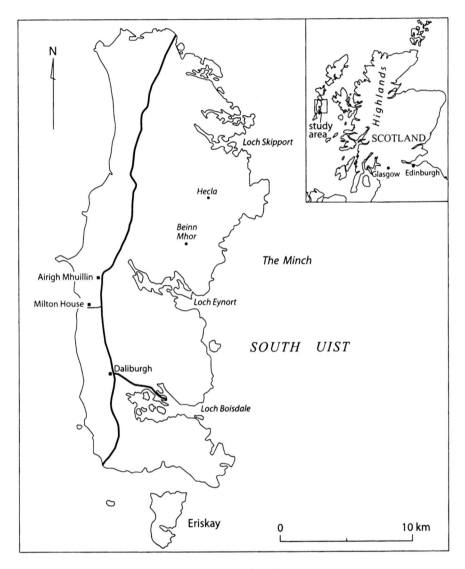

Figure 8.1 South Uist and places mentioned in the text

to act together as a 'multi-national conglomerate' to oppose the threat of a rival imperial power and the Roman Catholic Other beyond their shores (Bradshaw and Roberts 1998: xi).

Colley rejects the notion that this new sense of Britishness came into being through cultural uniformity, arguing that because Great Britain was 'invented' in 1707 it was 'inevitably superimposed on much older allegiences' (1994: 373). The open hostility and mutual suspicions that existed between Scotland and England, far beyond the suppression of the 1745 Jacobite rebellion, support this

Figure 8.2 Nova Scotia

point. Of course internal divisions based on language, geography, religion and class also existed *within* Scotland. The traditional rivalry between Highlander and Lowlander is one rather obvious example of this. If one accepts Colley's assertion that older beliefs and values were somehow submerged beneath a politically imposed imagined structure, then one is forced to ask 'whose imagination or invention and of what community?' (Bumsted 1999: 94).

A second, related, question is what happened to these 'older allegiances'? Were they inevitably subdued or transformed? Or did they continue to operate at a local and regional level much as before, only to be relegated to a position of lesser importance whenever the red coats were taken off the peg and the Union Jack unfurled? As Colley acknowledges 'Identities are not like hats. Human beings can and do put on several at a time' (1994: 6). It is perfectly possible to be partriotic to the British state, while at the same time being proud of a Scottish, English, Welsh or Northern Irish identity. This capacity for diversity within a unifying framework suggests that any analysis which takes an untheorised conception of Britishness as its starting point makes the mistake of approaching the problem back-to-front.

The patchwork of peoples that united in the service of the greater British state was diverse. Colley and other historians have tended to dwell on the question of how these British peoples came to imagine that they were *different* from other nationalities. Conversely, one might ask how did these people come to see themselves as the *same*? The mythic national histories that unite the British are a consequence of collective political action, rather than its cause. People come to see themselves as belonging together through acting together (Jenkins 1997). By the end of the nineteenth century the catalogue of joint endeavours had accumulated to the extent that it was possible to tell an 'island story' to illustrate the march of British progress. This narrative was based around the actions of heroic individuals: 'The Empire ... was biographical: India was Clive, Canada Wolfe, New Zealand Cook' (MacDonald 1994: 59; Kidd 1998: 321–42). Towering cultural icons such as Lord Nelson and the Duke of Wellington galvanised a sense of patriotism and engendered a feeling of inherent superiority among generations of British schoolboys. British history was the history of military victories.

Quite how this rising tide of euphoric sentiment was greeted by ordinary people in the more remote corners of the British Isles is difficult to gauge. Prior to the second quarter of the nineteenth century Britain was an essentially rural country. The majority of the population were illiterate, disenfranchised and living perilously close to the poverty line. The rhythms of agrarian life were not regulated by clock-time, or the news of distant military victories, but by the swish of the scythe and the sound of the church-bell. In such circumstances allegiance to family and local community were far more important than a sense of belonging to a fiscal-miltary state (Prest 1998: 91). When viewed in this way Britishness becomes something of an occasional side-show; a pall of smoke that surrounds the mouth of the cannon and temporarily obscures the local and regional identities which individuals ordinarily used to define themselves, and the communities to which they belonged. Perceptions of national belonging are rooted in local social and economic practices. These may follow, but are not determined by broader national trends. To quote the anthropologist Anthony Cohen: 'local experience mediates national identity' (1992: 13).

SCOT, HIGHLANDER, GAEL: CONVERGING OR CONCENTRIC IDENTITIES?

> Sometimes when seeing the end of our present our past looms larger because it is all we have or think we know.
>
> (MacLeod [1976] 1993: 203)

Elements of Scottish Highland culture may be found in every continent of the modern world. The skirl of the bagpipes and the parade of tartan-clad clansmen feature in Highland Gatherings from Sydney to San Diego. Scottish place names on maps document the spread of Highland settlers across the New Worlds. Free-market capitalism, rooted in the scholarship of Adam Smith and the Scottish Enlightenment, dominates Western economic activity. Scots traders and manufacturers led the way in establishing Britain's global commercial pre-eminence. It is no coincidence that the world's largest transnational fast-food corporation – McDonald's – trades under a Highland surname. The Scottish Calvinistic–Presbyterian religious faith, with its promotion of the Protestant work ethic, self-improvement and a sense of God-given 'steward-ship' over nature has been highlighted as shaping the spiritual beliefs and social practices of the colonies of settlement (Notestein 1947; Stanford Reid 1976).

The historian Hugh Trevor-Roper (1983) has argued that many of the symbols of Scottish Highlandism – including the short kilt – arose out of the 'invention of tradition' in the eighteenth century. Although his arguments are overstretched, this was certainly a formative period for the appropriation of Highland motifs and the development of 'tartanry' by lowland Scotland (Donnachie and Whatley 1992; Broun *et al.* 1998). Before this time Highlanders had been generally despised by lowland Scots. Highlanders were the wild and unwanted neighbours who inhabited the barren fringes of the kingdom, spoke an archaic language and persisted in pre-modern forms of clannish feuding.

The image of the Highlands and its inhabitants was transformed in the late eighteenth century. Improved access by road and sea allowed the more remote parts of the Highland region to be discovered by an increasing number of travellers. The primitive Highlander became something of an anthropological curiosity, a personification of the Enlightenment notion of the 'noble savage'. The Romantic interest in aesthetics enabled Highland landscapes, which had hitherto been dismissed by outsiders as barren wastes, to be viewed as sublime and picturesque (Withers 1992: 145).

The process by which 'Highlandism' was transformed and incorporated into the core of lowland Scottish culture was greatly assisted by contemporary Romantic fiction. Sir Walter Scott's highly sentimental representation of Highland culture served to rehabilitate the more rebellious aspects of the Scottish past by re-presenting them as a series of heroic failures (Ash 1980). As the cities of lowland Scotland became industrialised, the discovery of an appar-ently authentic Gaelic-speaking Highland race provided a culturally distinctive identity that was seized upon with enthusiasm. The myth of the Highlands provided a retrospective glimpse of how Scots life may once have been, a view that has arguably coloured all subsequent readings of the Scottish national past (McCrone 1998; Womack, 1989: 175; Withers 1992). The Scotland of tartan-clad warriors was able to take its place as a junior partner of empire alongside England, largely because its own history was 'deemed to be over'. Its identity lay firmly (and safely) in the past (McCrone 1998: 59). For progressive upper- and middle-class Scots this raised the possibility of dual or concentric identities. At a cultural and sentimental level they were Scots, but politically they were British and regarded themselves as 'enlightened, rational and forward-looking' (McCrone 1998: 60). Becoming British required the ability to switch between quite different sets of beliefs and values. The tensions that existed between Scots, as an imagined 'Celtic' race, and the English, who espoused supposedly 'Anglo-Saxon' values, may be expressed in the antinomies below (McCrone 1998: 58):

Celt	*Anglo-Saxon*
feminine	masculine
community	society
feeling	reason
nature	culture
left	right

SOUTH UIST: A CASE STUDY IN EMIGRATION

When questioned about their identity, modern-day inhabitants of South Uist respond by saying that they are 'crofters', 'Gaels', or 'Highlanders'. After this they acknowledge that they are Scots, but they rarely use the term British. Indeed, some vehemently object to being described as such. Identity is primarily constructed around a shared sense of territory (Smout 1994). Inhabitation establishes ties with real and imagined ancestors, and distinguishes them from outsiders or incomers. 'Britishness' is associated with negative aspects of state control and imperialism, two things which the strongly independent, deeply religious and anti-authoritarian *Uidhistich* are keen to distance themselves from. A brief examination of the circumstances of mass emigration from the island over the last two and a half centuries allows this suspicion and distrust to be placed in context.

In 1769 Colin MacDonald of Boisdale, proprietor of the southern part of South Uist and a convert to the Protestant Church of Scotland, expelled an Irish Roman Catholic priest from his estate. He then threatened to evict tenants from his estate if they refused to renounce their Catholic faith (Adams and Somerville 1993: 64). In an effort to enforce his will, Boisdale stood outside the Protestant church on Sundays and forced passers by into the church with the aid of a stick. The episode is recalled in South Uist folklore as *Cneideamh a' Bhata Bhuidhe* – the Faith of Yellow Stick (Hutchinson 1973: 10).

When Boisdale's actions came to the attention of the Roman Catholic Church in Edinburgh, Bishop George Hay set about devising a relief plan (Bumsted 1978: 513). Boisdale's impoverished tenants were offered the oppor-tunity to escape persecution by a scheme of assisted emigration. In 1772, 11 families left Boisdale's estate for the Island of St John (latterly renamed Prince Edward Island) in the Gulf of St Lawrence. The group was led by Captain John MacDonald of Glenaladale and was promised the opportunity to establish a Highland Roman Catholic colony in the New World. However, when the opportunity arose relatively few tenants opted to leave South Uist. Sentimental ties to kin and ancestral lands were clearly strong enough to make exile unthink-able, despite the apparent severity of the persecution and the offer of financial support from the Church.

A little over 70 years later, in 1846, South Uist was devastated by a cata-strophic failure of the potato crop. The potato was central to the subsistence practices of the tenantry and its failure caused widespread distress. The ensuing famine lasted for five years. South Uist had been purchased in 1838 by Colonel John Gordon of Cluny in Aberbeenshire. Faced with the burden of a starving population, Cluny instigated a programme of forced clearance and transportation. Between 1848 and 1851 more than 2700 people were shipped from his estates on South Uist and Barra to Québec (Hunter 1976: 81).

How did these episodes relate to the broader social and economic conditions created by the British state? In the Outer Hebrides, insulated by geographical remoteness and a strong regional Gaelic culture, notions of 'Britishness' were of little consequence to the labouring poor. However, exposure to the wider British economy meant that the lives of the tenantry were profoundly affected in indirect ways. The examples of emigration described above show how the specific actions of a small number of powerful individuals were able to transform the lives of the poor by displacing them, quite literally, to a New World. Plying between local and global scales of analysis it is possible to see how successive landlords attempted to make the most of external opportunities and to minimise any setbacks that threatened their income. Invariably this meant working against the best interests of their tenants.

The growth in trade with external markets was of paramount importance. The Union of 1707 created new opportunities for trade with England and the Highland region was seized upon as a ready source of manpower – first and foremost for infantry regiments – and raw materials. The supply of Highland-reared black cattle to English markets grew steadily throughout the eighteenth century, encouraged by the demand for raw materials from newly industrialised cities and the need to provision the Royal Navy with salt beef. By the first half of the nineteenth century the balance of exports had shifted in favour of wool, mutton and kelp, but the underdeveloped Highland region was firmly locked into a subordinate role. In essence, it had become an 'internal colony' of the British state, fuelling the expanding economy of lowland Britain (Devine 1988: 75; Macinnes 1988: 85).

The revolution in manners that accompanied the development of British industrial capitalism challenged the pre-existing Highland social order in other ways. Incorporation into English aristocratic circles encouraged members of the Highland élite to distance themselves from their customary obligations and allegiances. When John MacDonald, Chief of Clanranald, died in Edinburgh in 1794 he was succeeded by his six-year-old son, Ranald George. Ranald George married the daughter of the Earl of Mount Edgecombe, an English peer, and became Member of Parliament for the rotten borough of Pympton in Devon (Campbell 1994: 206). His island estates were held in trust and administered on his behalf by Edinburgh-based lawyers and accountants. Several years of high living in London society led Ranald George to accumulate massive debts and he was forced to sell his estates in South Uist and Benbecula to Gordon of Cluny in 1838.

The sale of the Clanranald lands reflected an overall decline in the traditional pattern of landholding in the West Highlands. By the early 1840s almost all of the islands in the Outer Hebrides were under new ownership (Devine 1988:

94). The new proprietorial class were incomers. They included lowland Scots capitalists and mainland Highlanders, enriched through careers in banking, trade and industry in the far corners of the British Empire. The purchase of a Highland estate paved the way for these self-made men to enter the Victorian upper classes. Owning a Highland estate 'gratified the same passion for possession as the collection of fine art or the acquisition of expensive and elaborate furniture' (Devine 1994: 81). The purchase of a Highland estate also posed a commercial challenge. It was an act of speculation designed to raise income from hitherto neglected and infertile lands. In this sense the pre-modern traditionalist world and modern capitalist world were brought into direct conflict.

DOCUMENTING THE DISRUPTION: HISTORICAL ARCHAEOLOGY AND EVERYDAY LIFE

The issue of access to land is central to any discussion of the social and economic transformation of South Uist. Agricultural improvement introduced radically different forms of land tenure to the island. It also struck at the very heart of subsistence practices and swept away customary farming practices. Two major economic re-orientations occurred as a result of the rise of commercial landlordism in South Uist. The first was a heavy investment in the production of kelp. The second was the drainage and enclosure of land for large-scale sheep farms.

Before the disruptions of the late eighteenth century, the population of South Uist lived in nucleated hamlets, or *bailtean*. The social hierarchy of the clan was based upon a patrilineal kinship network. Members of a clan offered allegiance to their chief in return for military protection and were united by a belief in a common ancestry and access to ancestral lands. Farming settlements were scattered along the fertile west coast of the island. Some of these farms were held as joint tenancies, but the majority were headed by close relatives of the chief, a gentry that was granted a lease on a *tack* of land in return for rent and military service (Dodgshon 1989: 169–98; Whyte 1995: 254). These 'tacksmen' or leaseholders derived their income from the sale of Highland black cattle to southern markets. Additional income was generated by sub-letting areas of their tack to sub-tenants. Farming was a communal effort. Sub-tenants grew their crops in open fields surrounding the settlement. Individual strips of land were allocated by lotting and changed hands each year. The hills beyond the settlement were held in common and provided summer grazing for cattle.

Archaeological research at Airigh Mhuillin, in the middle district of South Uist, has revealed the extent of the changes that took place between 1750 and 1850 (Symonds 1999a, 1999b, 1999c, 2000). The various attempts to reorganise the agricultural economy have left traces in the landscape. Roads, drains and stone field walls mark the expansion of enclosure onto the former common grazing grounds. Insights into the disruptions caused to everyday life by 'improvement' may also be gained by examining the form of houses and the evidence that they hold for the composition of household groups and the performance of routine activities. A third line of inquiry is provided by portable material culture. Artefacts recovered by excavation can be studied to assess the impact of imported factory-made products on indigenous patterns of production and consumption.

During the Napoleonic Wars (1793–1815) a French military blockade prevented the export of Spanish barilla to the British Isles. This led to a steady rise in the price of domestically produced alkalis. Kelp, an alkaline seaweed extract used in the manufacture of soap and glass, rose in price from £2 a ton in the 1760s to more than £20 a ton in the decade following 1800 (Hunter 1976: 16–18). The trustees of Clanranald's estate exploited this fact and mobilised the population of the island to gather seaweed from the coasts.

The growth of the kelp industry had a profound impact upon day-to-day life. Islanders were diverted from their agricultural tasks and forced to adopt a semi-industrial lifestyle. In the late spring and summer the workforce was concentrated on the east coast of the island. Here they cut, dried and burnt bubble-weed from the rocky inlets, living in makeshift turf huts. In the late autumn they returned to the west coast to gather the stick-like tangle that had been cast up by storms onto the sandy beaches. The processing of kelp for export to Liverpool and Glasgow took precedence over agricultural production and the population became heavily dependent upon potatoes for sustenance. Their rewards were few. Even at the height of the kelp boom the price paid to South Uist kelp-makers never exceeded £3.3s. per ton (Hunter 1976: 16).

The drive to increase profitability led to a sustained assault upon the established settlement pattern. The old communally farmed *bailtean* were dissolved and replaced by individual small-holdings or crofts. Crofts were set out over former arable and common grazing land, with little regard for customary rights. Individual crofts contained only a few acres of land and were not large enough to support a family. In a cynical act of rent racketeering the estate set rents at a deliberately high level. This compelled tenants to undertake seasonal kelp work in order to survive. Many of the structures that have been surveyed and excavated at Airigh Mhuillin were occupied by kelp-labourers at this time. The massive stone houses, which are up to 4m wide and 16m long, give an impression of stability and permanence. This was, however, far from the case. The majority of any family were only in residence in the winter months. At other times of the year all able-bodied individuals were employed in kelp making far away from the settlement.

Visitors to the islands frequently remarked upon the primitive appearance of the local dwellings. This perception has tended to obscure the ingenuity with which the houses were constructed using simple materials. The walls of the houses at Airigh Mhuillin are formed from undressed gneiss boulders with a tempered-earth core. There are few trees on South Uist and so the roofs would have been spanned using driftwood from the beach. This tent-like framework was covered with turf and thatch, secured with heather ropes and weighted down with stones.

Airigh Mhuillin is situated on the peat lands of central South Uist. The soils are heavy and poorly drained. Houses were therefore constructed on hummocks in the morainic drift, with their long axis running downslope. The houses did not possess chimneys, or windows, and were divided into three broad activity areas. The upper end of the house was set aside as a sleeping area. The middle of the house was a general living space where domestic activities focused around a peat fire. The lower third of the house, through which entry was gained, was used as a cow byre. Its position at the foot of the slope allowed animal urine to leave the byre through a drain in the end wall.

Martin Hall has suggested that historical archaeologists often find it difficult to recover material evidence for the lives of the poorest members of society (Hall 2000: 19). We are therefore fortunate in that the houses excavated at Airigh Mhuillin not only provide evidence of the hardships that were endured by the poor, but also of some of the strategies that they developed in response.

The first point that can be made is that the houses show evidence of adaptation. Prehistoric and medieval settlements in South Uist had concentrated on the sandy *machair* coastal plain. In this environment houses tended to have sunken floors cut into the sand and turf walls. The move to the former grazing grounds, which are strewn with Lewisian gneiss boulders, enabled stone walls to be substituted for turf. However, despite this innovation the house plan retained its traditional longhouse form. The capacity to shelter both humans and animals beneath one roof was central to the Hebridean conception of symbolically ordered domestic space. A similar oppositional logic seems to have structured the habitual space of peasant longhouses in other areas of upland Britain, such as Dartmoor (Austin and Thomas 1990: 43–78). The house may be viewed as a hierarchical representation of the human body. The upslope areas (the head and stomach) were reserved for human activity and the downslope (the bowels, complete with a drain for urine and excrement) was set aside for animals (St George 1998: 128–35).

The evidence from archaeological excavation and contemporary accounts suggests that houses were lightly furnished. The dresser seems to have been one favoured item of furniture. An upright dresser with plate-rack allowed ceramics to be displayed to effect in an upright position. It could also be moved around the interior space to provide a convenient temporary screen. Insecurity of tenure was such that even the roof timbers of houses were sometimes dismantled and removed by tenants when they were evicted.

The portable material culture recovered by excavations confirms the impression of poverty. Ceramics vessels are few in number and comprise the cheapest quality creamwares and pearlwares. Small bowls and shallow dishes predominate, indicating the importance of sloppy oat and potato based meals to the diet. The preference for bowls, as opposed to flatware, is striking. This suggests that imported vessels were selected on the basis of their ability to maintain customary ways of preparing and consuming food. Portions of food were dispensed from an iron pot on the central hearth and eaten with the hands from a bowl cradled in the lap. A high percentage of bowls show evidence of repair, stressing that care was taken to curate highly prized imported wares.

The economic recession at the end of the Napoleonic Wars in 1815 decreased the nationwide demand for cattle and kelp. A reduction of tax levied on salt by government further encouraged glass manufacturers to use salt in place of kelp. When the kelp industry finally collapsed in the late 1820s the estate sought new sources of revenue and turned to sheep ranching. The crofts occupied by the redundant kelp labourers in the middle district of South Uist were broken up and land was enclosed to form Milton Farm, an extensive holding that spanned the width of the island. The tenants evicted from Airigh Mhuillin were resettled on poor quality hill ground on the east coast of the island. This act of clearance, in the 1830s, broke the tradition of sharing houses with stock and forced the inhabitants to subsist primarily on potatoes and sea fishing.

HIGHLAND SCOTS: AN IMPERIAL PEOPLE?

British imperial colonies differed from those of Spain and France in two import-ant respects. First, little use was made of indigenous labour. In North America both British and later American planters employed slave labour from Africa. However, the process of colonisation was heavily dependent upon settler labour from England, Wales, Ireland and Scotland. Second, British settlement attempted to occupy *all* land, even that which initially appeared to be marginal (Lowenthal 1997: 227–36). Despite these differences the motivation for colon-isation remained the same. Colonies were primarily conceived as locations from which commodities could be extracted for export. Under these circumstances 'Local livelihood and ecology, indigenous or settler, were of no moment in themselves; all that mattered was producing as much as possible for the home market' (Lowenthal 1997: 230).

Scottish Highlanders were eager to take part in this colonial enterprise. In the popular imagination Highland emigration is often conflated into a single catastrophic episode: the forced evictions and transportations that followed the famine years of the 1840s. Events surrounding the traumatic dispersal of clansmen have been used by their descendants to construct an enduring lament for the loss of homeland and community (Craig 1990). The reality was rather more complex. Emigration from the Highlands in the mid-nineteenth century was part of a continuum and reflected a long-lived 'culture of mobility' in Highland society (Devine 1992). Recent scholarship has shown that emigra-tion affected all levels of society, but the majority of those who departed in the early nineteenth century were poor tenants. They left, sometimes against their will, but always in the hope that they would find new land and fresh oppor-tunities. Their choice of destination was often determined by correspondence with relatives engaged in military service or trade overseas. Highlanders in the British North American colonies, for example, have been described as 'the "shock troops" of empire, moving deep into the backwoods, doing the

rough work of pioneering, confronting and dispersing the indigenous peoples'
(Richards 1999: 123).

Bernard Bailyn's study of late eighteenth-century Atlantic migration identifies two distinctive patterns of emigration from Britain. The 'metropolitan'
pattern was characterised by young single males from London and other large
southern towns. In contrast to this the 'provincial' pattern was characterised
by family groups that contained both mature women and children. This group
typically emanated from a rural location in northern England or Scotland
(Bailyn 1998: 12–14). Group or 'chain-migration' – often involving whole
communities – was a common feature of Highland emigration to eastern
Canada and the Maritime provinces (see MacLean 1991). By the 1850s,
Highlanders were constructing 'remarkable inter-continental links' and even
the poorest individuals had become 'globetrotters, mobile spirits in the international labour market . . . these emigrants connected imperial outposts in ways
that orthodox histories of empire often discount. The Highlanders were an
imperial people' (Richards 1999: 122).

The following case study explores the experience of some of the poorest
Highlanders who emigrated to Nova Scotia. Permanent European settlements
had been established in Nova Scotia by the French in the early seventeenth
century. The influx of nineteenth-century Scots was therefore a relatively late,
albeit significant, phenomenon. Highland Settlers are unlikely to have questioned their moral authority to colonise a new land. Attitudes promoted by
nineteenth-century social Darwinism would have led them to believe that the
indigenous Mi'Kmaq, a people without agriculture or Christian faith, were an
'unfinished' society in need of advancement. This should not detract from the
fact that Highland settlers often unwittingly served as the instruments of British
colonial oppression. The physical dispossession of the indigenous population is
ironic given that many Highlanders were themselves fleeing destitution following eviction. Aside from the social hardships brought about by Scottish
colonisation, the introduction of new farming methods such as sheep farming
also had an impact upon the ecology of Nova Scotia. Alfred Crosby has commented that European settlers did not arrive alone in the New World, but were
accompanied by 'a grunting, lowing, neighing, crowing, chirping, snarling,
buzzing, self-replicating and world-altering avalanche' (Crosby 1986: 4).

NOVA SCOTIA: A CASE STUDY

A Highland Scot serving with the Fraser Fensibles is said to have answered a
French sentry's challenge in fluent French at the capture of Québec, avoiding
the alarm as General Wolfe's soldiers climbed the cliffs from the St Lawrence
River to the Plains of Abraham. Highland regiments played a major part in
British wars against the French and Americans. Some 23 regiments of the line
and 23 of fencibles (more than 48,300 men) were recruited from the Scottish
Highlands and islands between the outbreak of the Seven Years' War in 1756

and 1815 (Macinnes 1988: 83). Military service provided Highlanders with a stable, if hazardous, source of income and the promise of land in the New World when their regiment was disbanded.

After the American War of Indepedence many Loyalist soldiers retreated from New England to settle in the Minas Basin of Nova Scotia and Cape Breton Island. The size and shape of land grants offered to soldiers by the British government varied. Private soldiers were allowed 100-acre lots, married soldiers 200-acre lots and retired officers 500-acre lots (Hornsby 1988: 20). The colony of Nova Scotia had been founded in 1625 by Sir William Alexander of Stirling in an attempt to establish a Scottish plantation to rival those of the English in North America. Settlements were established at Baleine Cove in Cape Breton and Port Royal in the Annapolis Valley. However, in the face of hostility from rival French settlers neither settlement lasted more than three years.

The influx of disbanded Highland soldiers and New England Planters in the 1760s changed the character of Nova Scotia, which had previously been administered as the French backwater colony of Acadia. It also encouraged Highlanders facing economic hardships at home to opt for emigration. From the 1770s Roman Catholic Highlanders, led by their priests and tacksmen, populated Antigonish and Guysborough counties and the south and west coasts of Cape Breton. The first emigration of Highland Presbyterian families to Nova Scotia took place in 1773, when the *Hector* arrived at Pictou from Loch Broom. Settlement spread westwards into Colchester and Cumberland counties, to the east coast of Cape Breton and to the north and west of the Bras d'Or lake (Campbell and MacLean 1974: 35–75). Significantly, it is the arrival of the Presbyterian Highlanders aboard the *Hector* that has been chosen by the government of Nova Scotia to mark the founding of the province. A reconstructed sailing ship sits in Pictou Harbour and serves to reinforce the 'foundation myth', much as the *Mayflower* proclaims the pre-eminence of white Anglo-Saxon Protestant America in New England (Harper and Vance 1999: 20).

If authentic Scottish origins can be claimed to exist anywhere in the Maritime Provinces it is in Cape Breton Island, the 'Highland Heart' of Nova Scotia (MacNeil 1980). Census returns indicate that in 1871 50,000 of Cape Breton's 75,000 inhabitants were of Scottish descent (Hornsby 1988: 15). The majority of Highland emigrants arrived in Cape Breton between the years 1800 and 1840, preceding the mass emigrations of the famine years.

The development of the Maritime timber trade in the 1790s provided a vital catalyst. As new shipping routes were created linking Scottish ports to the eastern Maritimes, a growing number of the vessels that regularly ferried oak and pine to the home market offered passages to would-be emigrants on their return trip. The rise of this staple export had ambivalent effects. On the one hand, human cargoes were deposited in Cape Breton to lead the assault upon the virgin tree canopy. On the other hand, much of the wealth generated by timber flowed back to Britain and was invested in the substantial town and country houses of England and Scotland (McKinnon and Wynn 1988).

The influence of the Old World did not stop there. An analysis of the pattern of settlement allows us to return to the theme of how individual agency was constrained by broader economic processes. The economic divisions between 'frontland' and 'backland' farm plots in Cape Breton have their origins in the character and timing of emigration from Scotland. The few relatively prosperous *tacksmen* who arrived in Cape Breton between 1800 and 1820 acquired good quality 'frontland'. Typically these lots were rectangular, with a width ratio of 1–5, and bordered the coast, lakes or the fertile *intervales* along the river valleys. By the late 1820s the best of this land had been settled. Later arrivals, who were in any case generally less well off, were forced to accept 'backland', thin-soiled irregular plots carved out of the rocky uplands (Hornsby 1988). For many Hebrideans the dilemma was clear. Having escaped the injustices of their former existence they possessed land of their own, and were free from the influence of tacksmen and unsympathetic landowners. However, the ghosts that had reputedly followed them on their voyage to the west came back to haunt them, and they once again found themselves unable to subsist on marginal land. When the Colonial Office abolished free land grants in 1827 and imposed a price of £200 for a standard 200-acre plot, most were unable to pay. It has been estimated that in 1837 almost 20,000 of the 35,000 inhabitants of Cape Breton were illegally squatting on Crown Land (Bitterman 1987; Hornsby 1988: 20).

Highland settlers coped with this adversity with a combination of flexibility and conservatism. The residue of extended kinship networks transplanted from the Old World offered one means of mutual support. In the Margaree District of Cape Breton 71 per cent of the pioneer population were related to each other before they left the Highlands (Ommer 1977). Elsewhere communities turned in on themselves and practised close cousin and brother–sister exchange marriages, as a direct reaction to their radically changed circumstances, with 'no inclination to mix with strangers' (Molloy 1986).

As colonial settlers the inhabitants of the scattered backland farms were subjects of the British Crown, but regarded themselves to be first and foremost Hebrideans or Highlanders. Individual and group identities were maintained, for a while at least, by the Gaelic language, religious faith and musical traditions. Other aspects of traditional lifestyles did not survive the process of emigration. Stone-built Hebridean longhouses were abandoned in favour of New England style wooden-frame houses, and new agricultural methods were needed to clear and farm the densely wooded hillslopes of Cape Breton.

CONCLUSIONS

This chapter has stressed that British identity, in common with all other ethnic and political identities, should not be regarded as 'bounded' and unproblematic. Efforts to recover archaeological evidence for a 'British mindset' will always be met with failure. The British state was a multi-national and multi-ethnic conglomerate. The military and commercial success of this alliance can be attributed to its ability to allow diversity within a unifying framework. The presence of British manufactured goods in an archaeological context should not be taken to indicate the presence of uniquely British values or beliefs. As I have attempted to demonstrate in my case studies from South Uist and Nova Scotia, responses to the growth of British imperialism were varied and were derived from highly localised experiences.

ACKNOWLEDGEMENTS

I thank Susan Lawrence, Mary Beaudry and Victoria Parsons, who were all forced to wait far too long for this chapter to be finished. Research in South Uist was funded by the Earthwatch Institute, Boston University and the Catherine MacKichan Trust.

REFERENCES

Adams, I. and Somerville, M. (1993) *Cargoes of Despair and Hope: Scottish Emigration to North America 1603–1803*. Edinburgh: John Donald Publishers Limited.

Anderson, B. [1983] (1991) *Imagined Communities: Reflections on the Origin and Spread of Nationalism*. London: Verso.

Ash, M. (1980) *The Strange Death of Scottish History*. Edinburgh: Ramsey Head Press.

Austin, D. and Thomas, J. (1990) The 'proper study' of medieval archaeology: a case study. In D. Austin and L. Alcock (eds), *From the Baltic to the Black Sea: Studies in Medieval Archaeology*, 43–78. London and New York: Routledge.

Bailyn, B. (1998) *The Peopling of British North America: An Introduction*. New York: Vintage Books.

Bitterman, R. (1987) Farm households and wage labour in the north east Maritimes in the early nineteenth century. *Labour/Travail* 31: 13–45.

Bradshaw, B. and Roberts, P. (eds) (1998) *British Consciousnesss and Identity: The Making of Britain, 1533–1707*. Cambridge: Cambridge University Press.

Broun, D., Finlay, R.J. and Lynch, M. (eds) (1998) *Image and Identity: The Making and Re-making of Scotland Through the Ages*. Edinburgh: John Donald Publishers Limited.

Bumsted, J.M. (1978) Highland emigration to the Island of St. John and the Scottish Catholic Church 1769–1774. *Dalhousie Review* 58: 511–27.

—— (1999) Scottishness and Britishness in Canada. In M. Harper and M.E. Vance (eds), *Myth, Migration and the Making of Memory: Scotia and Nova Scotia c. 1700–1990*, 89–103. Halifax and Edinburgh: Fernwood Publishing and John Donald Publishers Limited.

Campbell, D. and MacLean, R.A. (1974) *Beyond the Atlantic Roar: A Study of the Nova Scotia Scots*. Toronto: McClelland and Stewart Limited.

Campbell, J.L. [1984] (1994) *Canna: The Story of a Hebridean Island*, 3rd edn. Edinburgh: Canongate Press.

Cohen, A.P. (ed.) (1992) *Belonging: Identity and Social Organisation in British Rural Cultures*. Manchester: Manchester University Press.

Cohen, R. (1997) *Global Diasporas: An Introduction*. London: UCL Press.

Colley, L. [1992] (1994) *Britons: Forging the Nation 1707–1837*. London: Pimlico.

Craig, D. (1990) *On the Crofters' Trail: In Search of the Clearance Highlanders*. London: Jonathan Cape.

Crosby, A. (1986) *Ecological Imperialism: The Biological Expansion of Europe, 900–1900.* Cambridge: Cambridge University Press

Deetz, J. (1993) *Flowerdew Hundred: The Archaeology of a Virginia Plantation 1619–1864.* Charlottesville, VI and London: University of Virginia Press.

Devine, T.M. (1988) *The Great Highland Famine.* Edinburgh: John Donald Publishers Limited.

—— (1992) The paradox of Scottish emigration. In T.M. Devine (ed.), *Scottish Emigration and Scottish Society*, 1–16. Edinburgh: John Donald Publishers Limited.

—— (1994) *Clanship to Crofters' War.* Manchester: Manchester University Press.

Dodgshon, R.A. (1989) Pretense of blude an plaice of thair dwelling. In R.A. Houston and I.D. Whyte (eds), *Scottish Society 1500–1800*, 168–98. Cambridge: Cambridge University Press.

Donnachie, I. and Whatley, C. (eds) (1992) *The Manufacture of Scottish History.* Edinburgh: Polygon Press.

Falk, L. (ed.) (1991) *Historical Archaeology in Global Perspective.* Washington, DC: Smithsonian Institution Press.

Hall, M. (2000) *Archaeology and the Modern World: Colonial Transcripts in South Africa and the Chesapeake.* London and New York: Routledge.

Harper, M. and Vance, M.E. (eds) (1999) *Myth, Migration and the Making of Memory: Scotia and Nova Scotia c. 1700–1990.* Halifax, NS and Edinburgh: Fernwood Publishing and John Donald Publishers Limited.

Hodder, I. (1999) *The Archaeological Process.* Oxford: Blackwell.

Hornsby, S. (1988) Migration and settlement: the Scots of Cape Breton. In D. Day (ed.), *Geographical Perspectives on the Maritime Provinces*, 15–26. Halifax, NS: St Mary's University.

Hunter, J. (1976) *The Making of the Crofting Community.* Edinburgh: John Donald Publishers Limited.

Hutchinson, R. (1973) Emigration from South Uist to Cape Breton. In B.D. Tennyson (ed.), *Essays in Cape Breton History*, 9–23. Windsor, NS: Lancelot Press.

Jenkins, R. (1997) *Rethinking Ethnicity.* London: Sage.

Johnson, M. (1999) Rethinking historical archaeology. In P.P.A. Funari, M. Hall and S. Jones (eds), *Historical Archaeology: Back from the Edge*, 23–36. London and New York: Routledge.

Kidd, C. (1998) Protestantism, constitutionalism and British identity under the later Stuarts. In B. Bradshaw and P. Roberts (eds), *British Consciousness and Identity: The Making of Britain, 1533–1707*, 321–42. Cambridge: Cambridge University Press.

Lowenthal, D. (1997) Empires and Ecologies: reflections on environmental history. In T. Griffiths and L. Robbin (eds), *Ecology and Empire: Environmental History of Settler Societies*, 227–36. Edinburgh: Keele University Press.

McCrone, D. (1998) *The Sociology of Nationalism.* London and New York: Routledge.

MacDonald, R.H. (1994) *The Language of Empire: Myths and Metaphors of Popular Imperialism 1880–1918.* Manchester: Manchester University Press.

Macinnes, A. (1988) Scottish Gaeldom: the first phase of clearance. In T.M. Devine and R. Micheson (eds) *People and Society in Scotland, vol. 1, 1760–1830*, 70–90. Edinburgh: John Donald Publishers Limited.

McKinnon, R. and Wynn, G. (1988) Nova Scotia agriculture in the Golden Age: a new look. In D. Day (ed.), *Geographical Perspectives on the Maritime Provinces*, 47–60. Halifax, NS: St Mary's University.

MacLean, M. (1991) *The People of Glengarry: Highlanders in Transition, 1745–1820.* Montreal and London: McGill Queens.

MacLeod, A. [1976] (1993) The road to Rankin's Point. In *The Lost Salt Gift of Blood*, 179–205. London: Flamingo/HarperCollins.

MacNeil, N. [1948] (1980) *The Highland Heart in Nova Scotia.* Antigonish, NS: Formac

Publishing Company Ltd.

Molloy, M. (1986) No inclination to mix with strangers: marriage patterns among Highland Scots migrants to Cape Breton and New Zealand, 1800–1916. *Journal of Family History* 1(3): 221–43.

Notestein, W. (1947) *The Scot in History: A Study of the Interplay of Character and History*. London: Jonathan Cape.

Ommer, R. (1977) Highland Scot migration to south western Newfoundland: a study of kinship. In John Mannion (ed.), *The Peopling of Newfoundland*. St John's: Memorial University.

Orser, C.E. (1996) *A Historical Archaeology of the Modern World*. New York: Plenum.

Prest, W. (1998) *Albion Ascendant: English History 1660–1815*. Oxford: Oxford University Press.

Richards, E. (1999) Leaving the Highlands: colonial destinations in Canada and Australia. In M. Harper and M.E. Vance (eds), *Myth, Migration and the Making of Memory: Scotia and Nova Scotia c. 1700–1990*, 105–26. Halifax, NS and Edinburgh: Fernwood Publishing and John Donald Publishers Limited.

Smout, T.C. (1994) Perspectives on Scottish identity. *Scottish Affairs* 6: 101–13.

Stanford Reid, W. (1976) *The Scottish Tradition in Canada*. Toronto: McClelland and Stewart Ltd.

St George, R.B. (1998) *Conversing by Signs: Poetics of Implication in Colonial New England Culture*. Chapel Hill, NC and London: University of North Carolina Press.

Symonds, J. (1999a) Toiling in the vale of tears: everyday life and resistance in South Uist, Outer Hebrides,1760–1860. *International Journal of Historical Archaeology* 3(2): 101–21.

—— (1999b) Songs remembered in exile? Integrating unsung archives of Highland life. In A. Gazinch-Schwartz and C. Holtorf (eds), *Folklore and Archaeology*, 106–128. London and New York: Routledge.

—— (1999c) Surveying the remains of a Highland myth: investigations at the birthplace of Flora MacDonald, Airigh Mhuilin, South Uist. In M. Harper and M.E. Vance (eds), *Myth, Migration and the Making of Memory: Scotia and Nova Scotia c. 1700–1990*, 73–88. Halifax, NS and Edinburgh: Fernwood Publishing and John Donald Publishers Limited.

—— (2000) The dark island revisited: an approach to the historical archaeology of Milton, South Uist. In J.A. Atkinson, I. Banks and G. MacGregor (eds), *Townships to Farmsteads: Rural Settlement Studies in Scotland, England and Wales*, 196–209 (Scottish Archaeological Forum). Oxford: BAR, British Series 293.

Trevor-Roper, H. (1983) The invention of tradition: the Highland tradition of Scotland. In E. Hobsbawm and T. Ranger (eds), *The Invention of Tradition*, 15–42. Cambridge: Cambridge University Press.

Withers, C. (1992) The historical creation of the Highlands. In I. Donnachie and C. Whateley (eds), *The Manufacture of Scottish History*, 143–56. Edinburgh: Polygon Press.

Womack, P. (1989) *Improvement and Romance: Constructing the Myth of the Highlands*. London: Macmillan.

Whyte, I.D. (1995) *Scotland Before the Industrial Revolution c. 1050–1750*. London: Longman.

9 Death and remembrance in the colonial context

HAROLD MYTUM

INTRODUCTION

British colonial expansion offered opportunities for personal development in many ways. For some, the freedom from religious persecution was a major attraction, for others the opportunity to establish a viable family business was the motivating force. Some colonists had little choice in their emigration, either as indentured servants or as convicts, but could still often build upon this unwelcome leaving of their native shores. Whether the result of a pulling or pushing force, most colonists assumed that their emigration was permanent. Expecting to live and die in their new environment affected the ways that they considered disposing of and remembering their dead. Burial grounds established by populations such as these have often become significant features in the landscape, and some continue to be used for burial today. Many individual memorials and burial grounds are given special significance by Western populations as evidence of the pioneering phases of British settlement. These are particularly noticeable in the eastern coast of North America and Australia.

Many British colonists, however, always intended to return to their homeland after a period abroad. The opportunistic tobacco grower, the mining prospector or merchant, the career soldier or civil servant, and even the missionary, hoped that after a period abroad comfortable retirement at home was in prospect. Alas, for a large proportion this was not to be their fate, and the colonies long remained a net importer of British population due to high mortality rates and, in areas under the first phases of Western settlement, low reproduction and high infant mortality rates. A few important individuals who died away from home could be shipped back to Britain, but most were buried close to their place of death. Some colonial burial grounds are largely formed of that part of the itinerant diaspora which was overtaken by illness and accident, and now lie largely uncared for by the local population. Only occasionally are such sites maintained by an historically aware minority within those countries and beyond. Such burial grounds are frequently found in the Indian subcontinent, south-east Asia and Africa, though isolated examples can be found in practically any country.

Interest in burial grounds and memorials in British colonies has varied greatly over time, but in recent years recording has become popular, and if linked to any more academic discipline, it has been to history. Archaeological approaches have, as yet, been rare in many parts of the world, though North America would be an exception to this. Many important questions could be asked about the particular places where the memorials are located, and the individuals and communities with which they are associated. Some examples combining simple recording with some general discussion of the historical context can be found. Examples can be given of such work in Australia (Weston 1989; Dunn 1991; Zelinka 1991), Malta (Welsh 1999), the Indian subcontinent (Yalland 1985), south-east Asia (Harfield 1984, 1985) and central America (Hammond 1999, 2000). Many studies of the material culture associated with death have not been archaeological in emphasis but rather from a background in history, art history, anthropology or cultural geography, but still offer much to the archaeologist (Mytum forthcoming a). A few more overtly archaeological studies have been carried out, notably early investigations by Deetz and Dethlefsen in North America (1965, 1967, 1971; but also Bell 1994 for later references), Gibraltar (Mytum 1993) and Italy (Rahtz 1987), as well as in Britain itself (Shoesmith 1980; Mytum 2000; Tarlow 2000). In this study, emphasis will be placed on comparing the British practices of burial and commemoration at home with those in a range of colonial contexts to offer a comparative overview from an archaeological perspective (Table 9.1).

FRONTIER DEATH AND BURIAL

The first areas to be colonised in North America replicated in many ways the British traditions of burial. Excavations around Jamestown church, Virginia, revealed a dense concentration of burials, many of them intercutting, inside and around the church. This was a pattern typical in British parish churches, and this tradition of repeated interment continues in many rural locations to this day. Burial of at least the more affluent was in wooden coffins; these came in a range of shapes, but the single break coffin became the norm. This is widely known from excavation evidence and from other sources such as funeral stationery and indeed designs on memorials.

Funerary rituals usually leave little direct archaeological trace, though the material culture trappings sometimes survive in folk-life collections and are described in historical sources. These show that there were great similarities between Britain and North America during the seventeenth and early eighteenth centuries (Rauschenburg 1990). Prior to interment, the coffin was covered by a rented pall cloth, varying in quality according to status. This was carried on a bier from the home of the deceased to the place of worship and then onto the burial location. Biers were normally carried by two men, but horse-drawn

Table 9.1 British colonial burial grounds (in part derived from Sloane 1991).

Name	Date	Location of graves	Layout	Design monuments	Most common	Ownership
Churchyard	9–20c	Around church	Organic plots	None, garden	Simple, iconographic, sculpture, plots, none	Religious
Frontier graves	17–20c	Site of death	None	None	None or simple	None
Homestead graveyard	17–20c	Farm field	Irregular rows	None, garden	Simple, iconographic, none	Family
Potter's Field	17–20c	City edge	Regular rows	None	None or simple	Public
Town/city cemetery	17–20c	City edge	Regular rows, plots	Formal garden	Simple, iconographic, sculpture, none	Public
Missionary burial ground	18–19c	Near to mission	Regular rows	None, garden	Simple, iconographic, native tradition, none	Religious
Rural cemetery	1831–70s	City edge, Suburb	Rows, plots	Garden, picturesque	Simple, iconographic, sculpture, mausolea, none	Private co, public
Chapel burial ground	19–20c	Near to church, at distance	Regular rows	Formal, garden	Simple, iconographic, plots	Religious
Churchyard, chapel ground extensions	19–20c	Near to church, at distance	Regular rows	Formal, garden	Simple, iconographic, plots	Religious
Lawn-park cemetery	1855–1920s	Suburb	Rows, plots	Pastoral, park like	Simple, sculpture, small monuments	Private, public
Memorial park	1917–present	Suburb	Rows, plots	Pastoral, suburban	Ledgers, plaques	Private

hearses were used by more affluent families. The wealthy also gave out gifts to mourners, varying from food or small amounts of money to mourning clothes, spoons or jewellery (Tashjian and Tashjian 1974: 27–30; Bury 1986); sumptuary laws were passed in 1721 to restrict these gifts in Massachusetts (Benes 1977: 225). Such laws in Britain were largely ignored in England, particularly as the new occupation of funeral directors encouraged expenditure. The increasing availability of mourning crepe produced by Huguenot weavers moreover allowed the expanding middle classes to indulge in mourning fashions (Llewellyn 1991: 91). Funeral sermons and graveside elegies became popular from the later seventeenth century onwards, and these could be printed and kept as memorials which have been studied for example in England (Houlbrooke 1998: 295–330) and New England (Tashjian and Tashjian 1974: 34–48). There was a great preoccupation with having a 'good death', with a respectable life well spent, a strong statement of Christian faith and a prayerful acceptance of death, often surrounded by the family (Llewellyn 1991; Houlbrooke 1999). Whilst the emphasis within the 'good death' changed over time, it remained an important factor in attitudes amongst many Protestant British at home and abroad from the seventeenth to the nineteenth century.

Churchyard burial grounds dominated Britain, but in the colonies the Anglican tradition was only powerful in some areas such as Virginia and in later colonies such as Australia. However, even in these places a diversity of denominational interests was soon manifested. In puritan New England, community burial grounds dominated from early on; they were originally established away from the meeting houses, but often were later relocated adjacent to the places of worship as the population became more dispersed (Brooke 1988). In large North American cities separate burial grounds were established for those who could not afford a seemly urban burial, and for slaves. These Potters' Field burial grounds, so called after the biblical reference to such cemeteries, were often later forgotten and built over (Sloane 1991: 24–5). Smaller towns could either have separate burial grounds or just different zones based on social status within the one community burial ground.

In sparsely populated regions without developed infrastructures, the methods of interment and memorial developed within the long-settled and highly structured British context could not be imitated, even if desired. Initially, isolated graves were dug at or near the place of death, and rarely were any markers used (Dunn 1991: 16–17; Sloane 1991: 14). Pioneer life and death, struggling with sometimes hostile indigenous peoples and the natural environment, led to many deaths and isolated burials. This was represented, for example, in some of the Australian art relating to death scenes, where links between death, burial and landscape were also emphasised (Fitzpatrick 1997). Here, the 'good death' was absent, making such deaths upsetting (Llewellyn 1991: 34–6), and requiring a romantic emphasis on colonial heroism in a world perceived as wild and uncivilised.

As settlement began to develop, farmstead burial was common, and this applied to all levels of society. Some examples have been excavated in the

Chesapeake region, Virginia. Earth-dug graves with or without coffins are found, usually arranged roughly east-west but with more variability than in more formal burial grounds; sometimes several clusters of graves can be identified, sometimes with some intercutting, suggesting that the location of earlier burials was not fully known (Gibb 1996: 196–202). African-American graves were sometimes spatially separated (Aufderheide *et al.* 1981).

Farmstead burial became the typical frontier burial style, and as settlement spread across the North American continent, so did this burial form. As the economic and social infrastructure developed in previously frontier contexts, so the burial patterns changed. Thus, the frontier pattern of burial was not a chronological one, but related to a certain initial stage of settlement development. Homestead burial therefore also occurred widely in British colonies in Africa and Australasia. It was an effective deathways response to harsh lifeways and limited opportunity for communal activities which could include funerals and burial in grounds designed for a wider population. Once population densities began to increase, there could be pressure from the local authorities for more regulation in burial. For example, fees for gravediggers and clergy were established in New South Wales by Governor Macquarie in 1810, and during the following year a series of burial grounds were established and farmstead burial in those townships officially prohibited (Dunn 1991: 17).

Memorials in frontier locations were often in perishable materials or were relatively crude, though it is worth noting that for much of Britain in the seventeenth century and most of the eighteenth century churchyard memorials were rare and, in some regions, also crudely carved (Burgess 1963; Willsher and Hunter 1978; Mytum 2000; Tarlow 2000). It is thus not surprising that so few early memorials survive from America, with the possible earliest extant example being that with a death date of 1653 from Dorchester, Massachusetts (Chase and Gabel 1997: 5). Another reason for few early survivals is the use of wooden grave markers. Wooden markers of a post and rail form survive in south-eastern England, particularly in Sussex and Essex (Burgess 1963: 117–18), and also in South Carolina (Rauschenburg 1990). Documentary evidence suggests that this form, and perhaps others which were more like headstones, were in use in these areas and in Georgia, Maryland and New England (Benes 1975; Crowell and Mackie 1990). Wooden boards similar in shape to simple headstones also survive in America, though their date is difficult to assess. Excavation has occasionally located post holes which could suggest grave markers, but until there are more excavations the prevalence of wooden markers is uncertain. Given the often limited time period of use for colonial burial grounds, this evidence is more likely to survive in these locations than in the heavily reused churchyards of Britain where later burial cuts will have destroyed all trace of earlier markers.

Once masons had begun to shape stones rather than just cutting initial letters on fieldstones, many early headstone designs were based on furniture designs or architectural features such as doorways, though others could be extremely esoteric and individual. Footstones were also often produced, but survive less frequently. Some memorials were flat ledgers which completely covered the grave. Dating the production of early stones cannot be based solely on the date of death of the person commemorated. Many with early dates were produced long after death once stone memorials had become popular, so phasing early memorial development can be more tentative than the later stages when the tradition was well established in a region (Mytum 2001). In a few areas such as Virginia, memorials were shipped from England, as indicated by documentary evidence (Crowell and Mackie 1990).

From the middle of the eighteenth century onwards, homestead burial grounds in the north-east of America could have carved headstones similar to those found at the larger communal cemeteries. The pattern of social segregation noted in the excavated Chesapeake burials can be mirrored in the stone locations, with the Chandler family graveyard in Pomfret, Connecticut, where a small stone to the slaves Cuff and Dinah is placed in the south-western corner of the walled plot (Slater 1996: 243).

In New England it is possible to chart the establishment of a funerary industry in a colonial setting from the late seventeenth century through to the first half of the eighteenth century. This involved the development of the undertaker's profession and the rise of a professional class of masons who, to varying degrees, relied on cutting memorials for their living. The masterful work by Slater (1996) on the carvers of eastern Connecticut can serve as a source of examples, though many carvers in New England have now been studied (see Chase and Gabel 1997 for examples and bibliography). The first carver with a distinctive, if crude, style to be identified in eastern Connecticut produced memorials which have survived in five towns, and who has been termed the Norwich Ovoid carver after the settlement with the overwhelming majority of his products. The stones have been shaped, and the inscribed face smoothed off, but have no decoration; dates range from the late seventeenth century through the first quarter of the eighteenth century (Figure 9.1). In the same area more sophisticated styles were brought from Essex County, Massachusetts, by the experienced carver Lieutenant John Hartshorne. His small stones show a range of types (Slater and Tucker 1978), but have decoration utilising a range of motifs and often incorporating a simply carved face. Thereafter more carvers became adept at decorative styles, and Obadiah Wheeler and Benjamin Collins are examples, the latter's son Zerubbabel continuing the family tradition beyond the War of Independence (Slater 1996: 7–10). During the first half of the eighteenth century, eastern Connecticut was provided with a range of able masons who could produce memorials, a situation reached over 50 years earlier in and around Boston, Massachusetts, but one not achieved till later still in many other regions. Memorials reflected the changing economic, social, cultural and ideological status of the evolving colony.

Deetz (1996) has offered a sequence of development in Anglo-America which has three phases. The first phase, before 1660, was marked by a culture closely modelled on England, though there is relatively little associated mortuary data. In the second phase, from 1660 to about 1760, Deetz identifies

Figure 9.1   Development of headstone design in part of eastern Connecticut (adapted from Slater 1996)

strong regional folk cultures developing in America, and these are manifested in mortuary monuments of New England which he claims are different from anything in England (Deetz 1996: 122). Whilst this is correct, he underestimates the extent of regionalism not only in America but also within England and, indeed, the rest of Britain and Ireland.

Mortuary styles in the eighteenth century were highly regional everywhere, and indeed continued to be so in some respects through much of the nineteenth century (Burgess 1963; Mytum 2000). The third Deetz phase begins from 1760, involving greater contact once again with England and the spread of the Georgian world-view. This led to an emphasis on the individual and on order and symmetry. In mortuary art this is represented by the urn and willow, introductory phrases (Deetz 1996: 99) and the move to limited family plots (Deetz 1996: 123). Again, this is part of a set of wider changes seen not only in England but across Britain and Ireland in a range of guises; the dominance of the urn and willow was a New England phenomenon. In Britain the urn alone, or in conjunction with one or more other neo-classical motifs, was far more common; regional preferences for various combinations and styles of treament for the motifs are striking in Britain and Ireland throughout the later eighteenth and early nineteenth centuries (Burgess 1963). Although some motifs in mortuary art might be seen to reflect American national identity (Clark 1989), these were still used within the genre of memorial type, shape and layout found throughout the English-speaking world formed by Britain and its existing or former colonies. Whilst memorials clearly reflected many forms of identity through form, symbol and text, those trends simplistically identified by Deetz can be studied at different levels. These can emphasise similarity or difference both within and between regions at any period. The simple idealist model of Deetz needs considerable development or should be abandoned.

DEVELOPED COLONIAL SITUATIONS

As colonists became more sophisticated in their tastes, and were able to indulge in fashions which could include those associated with mortuary behaviour, the nature of burial locations and the memorials within them became more formalised (Table 9.1). Repeated burial in the same plots was much less common than in Britain, and extensions or new burial grounds were frequently required in subsequent decades. This has had the archaeological benefit of preserving many relatively early stone memorials. In the major urban centres such as New York and Charleston, South Carolina, however, limitations of space led to the same overburying and churchyard overcrowding found in Britain (Sloane 1991: 19–20). The development of crypts for the deposition of large numbers of coffins occurred in post-independence America as it did in Britain (Sloane 1991), and would elsewhere later as the numbers of urban burials increased and the middle classes sought refuge from the burial conditions within the churchyard. Few such crypts have been investigated, though the Spitalfields, London example will form a useful basis for comparison (Reeve and Adams 1993). The concerns with a 'good death' could be undermined by an inappropriate style and context of interment, and for a time the crypts provided a solution, though these too then became full.

The response to overcrowding was fuelled by several powerful factors all pushing in the same direction. These can be listed as increasing concern over the health implications of intensive burial within an urban context, the individual's body and the fate of those remains, and the family's ability to mourn in an appropriate setting (Mytum 1989; Tarlow 2000). In Britain there were additional concerns over Anglican domination of the burial rite and location, with both theological and financial implications (Rugg 1998). This was less of an issue in colonial settings, though the establishment even there was often Anglican, and this coloured the choices which those in power might make with regard to burial provision. For example, conflicting interests delayed the establishment of a cemetery in Sydney, leading to a 20-year delay before Rookwood Cemetery was established in 1867 (Sigrist 1989).

Throughout the British colonies, cemeteries were established following the styles developed during the nineteenth century in Britain (Brooks 1989). The most dominant theme of the Victorian cemeteries was that of a rural association, fostered by careful planting of trees and other vegetation, and even by landscaping of the terrain (Curl 1972). Plans with an emphasis on the symmetrical or asymmetrical were chosen, and both can be found in colonial settings. Whatever the design, behind it lay a careful regimentation of carefully measured and numbered plots into which the ground was divided. Segregation

by religion and denomination was also normal. Similar trends took place at the
same time in the United States (Sloane 1991). Ownership of cemeteries varied,
with some in local or state government control, others under a board of trustees.
Private ownership was an option also taken in Britain and America. Cemeteries
also became widespread in Europe, but their style of management, and often
their appearance, was quite different from the models which became the norm
in Britain and its colonies.

The development of the funerary landscape of Sydney, Australia, illustrates
the shifts in nature of mortuary practice in a colonial setting (Zelinka 1991).
The Old Burial Ground adjacent to St Andrew's Church in the centre of
the town was established in 1793 (Dunn 1991: 15). This was a relatively small
area of land, bounded by George Street and Druitt Street, and expansion was
impossible. Burials were sometimes near the surface and the smell from the
decomposing corpses was apparent, suggesting that too rapid overburial was
leading to ever-more shallow graves being dug; over 27 years, about 2000
people were buried in the Old Burial Ground (Zelinka 1991: 24–6). In 1820,
Devonshire Street Cemetery was established by Governor Macquarie beyond
the then bounds of the town. At first, only four acres were allocated, with a
portion set aside for Jewish burials, following pressure from that small community. All Christians continued to be buried according to Anglican rights, with
the Anglican clergy continuing to obtain financial benefit from this arrangement. As ministers of other religions reached the colony, and as demand for
burial space increased, so the land set aside for the cemetery was increased by
a further seven acres, to make a substantial block adjacent to Carters Barracks
and the Benevolent Asylum. By 1825 areas were marked out for Anglican,
Catholic and Presbyterian burials, and Jewish burials had a new block away
from their original allocation by 1831 (Zelinka 1991: 26). Thereafter the
Wesleyan Methodists and Congregationalists obtained blocks, and in 1836 the
Quakers were also granted space (Figure 9.2). The Devonshire Street Cemetery
in turn became full, and temporary relief was provided by placing three feet of
soil over the Anglican portion, so that it could be overburied. St Stephen's
Church at Newtown opened for Anglican burial in 1849, and other churchyards were similarly available for Anglicans (Zelinka 1991: 29). The Catholics,
who were numerous amongst the early settlers, attempted to gain their own
separate burial ground from as early as 1822, as conflicts between the families
of the deceased, Catholic priests and the Anglican establishment were frequent
at this time. Within a few years they were successful in establishing St Patrick's
Cemetery, Parramatta (Dunn 1988: 9), and various Protestant sects were also
able to establish their own burial grounds. One private venture, Balmain Cemetery, was established without denominational and only price-based zoning, but
this was very unusual. All these developments were insufficient, however, in
providing sufficient burial space and demands for a new, large cemetery
continued to be made.

In 1867, the Rookwood Cemetery was opened, 11 miles from the centre
of Sydney, and reached by railway; special trains allowed passengers to travel

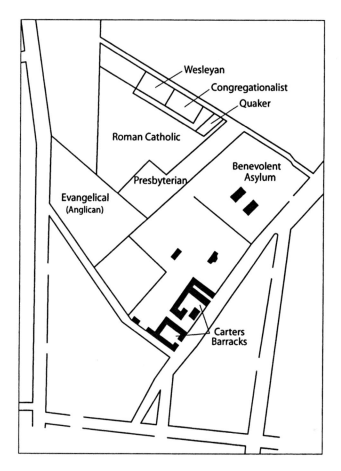

Figure 9.2   Plan of Devonshire Street Cemetery (adapted from Zelinka 1991)

to the cemetery along a branch line specially constructed for the purpose (Singleton and Kay 1989). Rookwood was an extensive garden cemetery, again with distinct religious and denominational sections, some now with distinctive chapels. The original area of 200 acres was gradually exended to its present 777 acres, making this the largest Victorian cemetery in the world (Weston 1989: 9). In 1901, a further Sydney cemetery was established, that of Botany Cemetery, and an adjacent area known as Bunnerong Cemetery, to which the human remains and surviving memorials previously found at the Devonshire Street Cemetery were moved in 1901 (Zelinka 1991: 29–32). Both these cemeteries once again were divided up into zones according to religion and denomination.

The Australian experience reveals the continuing Protestant concern with a 'good death'. This was manifested in the inscriptions found on memorials (Gilbert 1980), one which echoes those found in Britain. Whilst this was the case for settlers, surrounded by family and friends, the death of other British people far from home created unease. They were neither able to display piety appropriately, nor settle any disputes and put their affairs in order so that they may more easily rest in peace. It is perhaps for this reason that many memorials were raised by colleagues in the armed forces, administration or businesses in an attempt to create a familial structure to death and remembrance. Many inscriptions also give some identifier for the deceased, linking to an occupation or abode in Britain. This was often not necessary in British contexts as the person would have been known, and would be remembered, and at least their place of burial could be taken to indicate a location with which they had been associated. It is worth noting that many of those who died abroad were also commemorated on family memorials at home. One simple but typical example is that of Samuel Wimbush who was buried in the Church Missionary Society Cemetery at Brass, West Africa, but is remembered on his brother's stone in Terrington, Yorkshire (Mytum 2000: 49).

In some situations, British colonial deaths formed only part of the cemetery population, as with Gibraltar North Front Cemetery. Here the majority, even from its inception, were from the indigenous population (Mytum 1993). The contrast in monument choice was apparent from the beginning, with Gibraltarians erecting large family tombs (usually chest tombs of a form very familiar to those in Britain) which were then often used for generations, with the British chosing smaller monuments for individuals. Whilst this was partly due to the transitory nature of the colonial population, it also reflected the contemporary patterns of burial and commemoration in Britain in just a more extreme form. There, the chest tomb had been a popular choice for the later eighteenth and early nineteenth century, and could commemorate extended families and several generations, but by the time of the cemetery movement the memorial often recorded relatively few individuals, and many named only one. The separation by denomination within the cemetery also in effect segregated the native Catholic burial plots from those of the Protestant colonials, themselves having subdivisions according to denomination. Over time, and as lower-status native families began to desire memorials, a wider range of forms were produced, very much within a Mediterranean style, though with uniquely Gibraltarian emphasis. Many aspects of the funerary tradition were linked to Britain, where training is still taken for this trade, and certainly the above-ground loculi style of burial normal in adjacent Spain, and indeed much of Italy, is not part of the repertoire. The native burial styles at North Front Cemetery have thus been influenced by the colonial presence, but are not wholeheartedly part of it in the way that, say, Australian memorials were for the colonial period.

Segregation, which was widely carried out on religious and denominational lines within cemetereies, and thereby de facto separating the British and the Gibraltarians at the North Front Cemetery, was also explicitly enforced on racial grounds elsewhere. This matter has not been greatly studied from an archaeological perspective, but works by social geographers have shown the potential of this subject. Combinations of denomination and race were used to determine the appropriate sections of some cemeteries in nineteenth-century Port Elizabeth, South Africa, though many burial grounds were exclusive to one race (Christopher 1995). In Singapore, there was considerable conflict between the Chinese interests regarding burial and those of the colonial authorities (Yeoh 1991). Australian mission cemeteries offer exciting possibilities for the study of interaction of colonial religious beliefs and styles of memorial with indigenous traditions, but little work has been done and access may prove more difficult than is normally the case in the study of memorials (Wrightson 1998).

The pattern of increased memorial numbers over time would generally seem to be similar in Britain, Ireland and New England, though there were regional variations in the popularity (and indeed survival) of stone memorials. Depending on the region, memorials can be seen in increasing numbers particularly from the middle or later eighteenth century, though this also reflects growing living population densities. Where burial records have been compared with memorials, it would seem that a significant minority of the population were remembered on stones by the end of the eighteenth century, and half or slightly more were being commemorated by the later nineteenth century (Mytum forthcoming b).

In the late eighteenth and early nineteenth centuries, some memorial designs continued to be found widely throughout the world, within Britain, the colonies and the United States of America. Amongst the more elaborate memorials, table and pedestal tombs were common, and many neo-classical or Gothic-revival features can be found. These were often shipped out from Britain, though in centres with sufficient skilled craftsmen they could be locally produced. Many memorials were made with a mixture of materials, native stone sometimes being used for the body of the tomb and imported marble for particular decorative features and inscribed plaques. In the Indian subcontinent and south-east Asia, there were numerous relatively small cemeteries with such memorials (Harfield 1984, 1985). Whilst the simpler headstones were less common in such burial grounds compared with British contemporary churchyards, the individual monuments would rarely have been out of place in such locations back home. The only exceptions were some of the more elaborate memorials, ranging in date from the middle of the seventeenth to the nineteenth centuries, to be seen in South Park Street Cemetery, Calcutta and at Surat, India, where the highest officials of the East India Company had their tombs constructed (Curl 1980: 135–45; Williams 2000). Here indigenous architecture influenced some of the designs and also the decorative schemes, though some Christian symbolism was often included.

India was one of the few places where the British colonial memorial tradition was influenced by indigenous traditions. This did not happen in the Mediterranean (such as Gibraltar and Malta) where the classical influences came from the past rather than contemporary practice. But whilst the British fascination with Indian culture was reflected in architectural styles of memorials in India, these influences did not become popular back in Britain. The bias in memorialisation towards the more elaborate in these Asian cemeteries reflects the polarised wealth of the British in such places. The successful middle class merchants, administrators and military could afford monuments to match their station, but the rest of the British population in such centres were poor soldiers, sailors or lowly clerks hopeful of rewards which were not to be; they had simple memorials or none at all, and are even less well represented in memorials than their equivalents back home.

Some forms of headstone were also very widespread, and represent a style of memorial which was both simple and effective. It was almost always made from the local materials and by local masons. The type of phrasing and sentiment within the inscription was also remarkably universal, though idiosyncratic phrases are often found. The most common designs were those based around a semi-circular top to the headstone; often this was set on square or concavely cut shoulders. Subsequently, Gothic-revival headstones became popular. These shifts in style can be illustrated by comparing graphs from St John's Cemetery, Paramatta, Australia, with those from a group of Yorkshire graveyards (Table 9.2, Figure 9.3). The evidence from two opposite sides of the world show remarkable similarities in the periods of popularity of particular styles. The round-topped headstone, type 4100, has almost identical distributions over time, and a similar pattern can be seen with the Gothic style memorials 4200. The more complex shape 5107 has a long period of use in the Yorkshire sample, but has a clearer peak in the Paramatta cemetery. This deserves further analysis, as this is a style more popular at an earlier date in some parts of Britain and Ireland, and this may be an example of a somewhat outdated style which was used in Australia as stone memorials came into use for the first time there. Once the memorial production industry at Parramatta was established, it was adopting round-topped forms at the same time as in Yorkshire, and the Gothic-revival designs only slightly later.

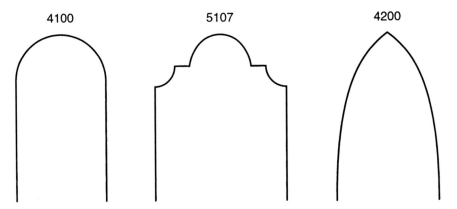

Figure 9.3 Headstone shapes in Yorkshire and Parramatta used in Table 9.2. Shape codes from Mytum 2000

Table 9.2 Numbers of memorials, by decade and shape,* in a sample of graveyards in Yorkshire (Escrick, Kellington, Riccal, Sherriff Hutton) and Parramatta, Australia (data abstracted from Dunn 1991).

Decade	4100		5107		4200	
	Yorkshire	Parramatta	Yorkshire	Parramatta	Yorkshire	Parramatta
1790–9	0	0	2	0	1	0
1800–9	0	1	8	1	4	0
1810–19	0	4	5	2	2	0
1820–9	2	2	7	13	2	1
1830–9	0	1	5	31	14	1
1840–9	0	1	3	15	19	2
1850–9	7	2	5	14	17	11
1860–9	25	12	5	0	9	11
1870–9	43	26	3	1	13	2
1880–9	31	15	4	0	15	3
1890–9	8	2	2	2	9	1
1900–9	7	2	1	1	7	0
1910–19	4	0	4	1	4	0
Total	127	68	54	81	116	32

*For headstone shapes see Figure 9.3, codes taken from Mytum 2000.

COLONIAL INFLUENCES IN BRITAIN

Whilst most cultural influences flowed out from the mother country to the colonies, there were ways in which the colonial experience affected aspects of mortuary behaviour in Britain. Three strands can be reviewed here, though with further research more aspects may become apparent where the interaction across the continents had an impact in Britain.

The most important early influence was undoubtedly that experienced by colonists in the Indian subcontinent who came into contact with another complex culture with its own mortuary traditions. The European trading stations established in the Indian subcontinent were great creators of personal wealth, but at very great risk. The environment of such trading posts was one extremely unfavourable for those who had not grown up in such conditions, and death rates were exceedingly high. In these contexts the British, along with their European rivals the Dutch, Portuguese and French, were much concerned with appropriate disposal of the deceased in a rapid, hygienic and yet befitting manner. The use of non-ecclesiastical cemeteries, laid out specially for the purpose and with architecturally visible structures erected over the graves of the most notable, was a solution borrowed from the native élites and which reached its apogee with the Taj Mahal (Curl 1980: 138–40). The architect Vanburgh spent some time in India during the 1680s and was fascinated by the mausoleum concept and design. This may have been a particularly important inspiration in Vanburgh's development of the aristocratic landscape burial, first played out in physical form at Castle Howard, Yorkshire (Williams 2000). This was an important challenge to the burial monopoly of the church, though it would be decades before this hold could be broken more widely.

The British colonial practice in India formed a model solution to the urban burial crisis in expanding British and European cities, and was no doubt conveyed by many of those who were fortunate enough to return from such climes. It also provided a model for the family churchyard mausoleum, which may have been a factor in their increasing popularity from the seventeenth century onwards, though these were also developing, apparently independently, within a European context from this time (Curl 1980; Colvin 1991). The experience of other colonial cemeteries such as the town burial grounds of New England also showed viable less extravagant alternatives with which many who had worked in the colonies would have been familiar.

The second result of imperial endeavours was the rise of the Egyptianising style in architecture. The imperial conflict in Egypt, where Napoleon had done much to arouse interest in the antiquities, led to the return to Britain of a number of highly influential artefacts such as Cleopatra's Needle and other smaller items which were housed in the British Museum. The link between Egyptians and death made this a particularly appropriate style for memorials and funerary architecture such as cemetery gates and chapels (Curl 1980). The style spread across the world (McDowell and Meyer 1994), but was initiated by colonial conflict and then appropriation of styles for use in the homeland.

The final example of British mortuary choices being affected by colonial development was in the importation of suitable materials for memorials. In the nineteenth century, whilst most architectural decoration was provided by British quarries, already Irish and more distant colonial sources began to be exploited. By the twentieth century, South African and then Indian granites were often used in a polished form, with the almost complete extinction of the Scottish granite memorial industry. The forms into which the materials were carved were within the British traditions, but the materials reflected the global economy. Whilst Italian Carrera marble memorials were exported all over the world and were not linked to colonial or post-colonial trading networks, the choices of granites reflected where British investment and knowledge of sources of raw materials could be matched with markets at home.

CONCLUSIONS

British burial traditions have had a profound effect on all the colonial and ex-colonial mortuary traditions around the world. This can be seen in the basic assumptions behind the disposal of the body, the styles of disposal, the attitudes to disturbance of the remains, and the manner and style of memorialisation. Some of these traditions relate to religious pursuasion and wider cultural forces, but even so, a range of typical solutions apparent within the regional variability of the British Isles can be seen to be the inspiration, and often the continuing reinforcement of colonial traditions. That regional variation also appears within the colonies should occasion no surprise; even here, however, rarely were radical alternatives taken, apart from those adaptations associated with frontier contexts alien to the homeland. In death more than in life, the colonial experience remained one grounded in British culture and tradition, a comforting familiarity which can still be experienced in visiting burial grounds around the globe.

REFERENCES

Aufderheide, A.C., Neiman, F.D., Wittmers, L.E., Jr and Rapp, G. (1981) Lead in bone II: skeletal-lead content as an indicator of lifetime lead ingestion and the social correlates in an archaeological population. *American Journal of Physical Anthropology* 55: 85–291.

Benes, P. (1975) Additional light on wooden grave markers. *Essex Institute Historical Collections* 111: 53–64.

—— (1977) *The Masks of Orthodoxy: Folk Gravestone Carving in Plymouth County, Massachusetts, 1689–1805.* Amherst, MA: University of Massachusetts Press.

Brooke, J.L. (1988) For honour and civil worship to any worthy person: burial, baptism and community on the Massachusetts near frontier, 1730–1790. In R. Blair St George (ed.), *Material Life in America, 1600–1860,* 463–85. Boston: Northeastern University Press.

Brooks, C. (1989) *Mortal Remains: The History and Present State of the Victorian and Edwardian Cemetery.* Exeter: Wheaton Publishers.

Burgess, F. (1963) *English Churchyard Memorials.* London: Lutterworth Press.

Bury, S. (1986) *Sentimental Jewellery.* London: Victoria and Albert Museum.

Chase, T. and Gabel, L.K. (1997) *Gravestone Chronicles,* 2 vols, 2nd edn. Boston: New England Historic Genealogical Society.

Christopher, A.J. (1995) Segregation and cemeteries in Port Elizabeth, South Africa. *Geographical Journal* 161(1): 38–46.

Clark, E.W. (1989) The Bigham carvers of the Carolina Piedmont: stone images of an emerging sense of American identity. In R.E. Meyer (ed.), *Cemeteries and Gravemarkers. Voices of American Culture,* 31–59. Logan, UT: Utah State University Press.

Colvin, H. (1991) *Architecture and the Afterlife.* New Haven, CN: Yale University Press.

Crowell, E.A. and Mackie, N.V., III. (1990) The funerary monuments and burial patterns of colonial tidewater Virginia, 1607–1776. *Markers* 7: 103–38.

Curl, J.S. (1972) *The Victorian Celebration of Death.* Newton Abbott: David and Charles.

—— (1980) *A Celebration of Death: An Introduction to Some of the Buildings, Monuments, and Settings of Funerary Architecture in The Western European Tradition.* London: Constable.

Deetz, J.F. (1996) *In Small Things Forgotten. An Archaeology of Early American Life,* exp. and rev. edn. New York: Doubleday.

Deetz, J.F. and Dethlefsen, E. (1965) The Doppler effect and archaeology: a consideration of the spatial aspects of seriation. *Southwest Journal of Anthropology* 21(3): 196–206.

—— (1967) Death's head, cherub, urn and willow. *Natural History* 76 (3): 29–37.

—— (1971) Some social aspects of New England colonial mortuary art. *American Antiquity* 36: 30–8.

Dunn, J. (1988) *The Parramatta Cemeteries. St Patrick's*. Parramatta: Parramatta and District Historical Society.
—— (1991) *The Parramatta Cemeteries. St John's*. Parramatta: Parramatta and District Historical Society.
Fitzpatrick, L. (1997) Secular, savage and solitary: death in Australian painting. In K. Charmaz, G. Howarth and A. Kellehear (eds), *The Unknown Country: Death in Australia, Britain and the USA*, 15–30. Basingstoke: Macmillan.
Gibb, J.G. (1996) *The Archaeology of Wealth: Consumer Behavior in English America*. New York: Plenum.
Gilbert, L.A. (1980) *A Grave Look at History: Glimpses at a Vanishing Form of Folk Art*. Sydney: John Ferguson.
Hammond, N. (1999) Outpost of empire: church monuments in Belize. *Church Monuments* 14: 129–39.
—— (2000) Beyond the Mexique Bay: church monuments in Belize, part II. *Church Monuments* 15: 89–102.
Harfield, A. (1984) *Christian Cemeteries and Memorials in Malacca*. London: British Association for Cemeteries in South Asia.
—— (1985) *Bencoolen. The Christian Cemetery and The Fort Marlborough Monuments*. London: British Association for Cemeteries in South Asia.
Houlbrooke, R.A. (1998) *Death, Religion and the Family in England 1480–1750*. Oxford: Clarendon Press.
—— (1999) The age of decency: 1660–1760. In P.C. Jupp and C. Gittings (eds), *Death in England. An Illustrated History*, 174–201. Manchester: Manchester University Press.
Llewellyn, N. (1991) *The Art of Death. Visual Culture in the English Death Ritual c. 1500–c. 1800*. London: Reaktion.
McDowell P. and Meyer, R.E. (1994) *The Revival Styles in American Memorial Art*. Bowling Green, OH: Bowling Green State University Popular Press.
Mytum, H. (1989) Public health and private sentiment: the development of cemetery architecture and funerary monuments from the eighteenth century onwards. *World Archaeology* 21: 283–97.
—— (1993) Death and identity: strategies in body disposal and memorial at North Front Cemetery, Gibraltar. In M.O.H. Carver (ed.), *In Search of Cult. Archaeological Investigations in Honour of Philip Rahtz*, 187–92. Woodbridge: Boydell Press.
—— (2000) *Recording and Analysing Graveyards*, Practical Handbook 15. York: Council for British Archaeology.
—— (2002). The dating of graveyard memorials: evidence from the stones. *Post-medieval Archaeology* 36: 1–38.
—— (forthcoming a) *Mortuary Monuments and Burial Grounds of the Historic Period*. New York: Plenum.
—— (forthcoming b) Rural burial and remembrance: changing landscapes of commemoration. In D. Cranstone and M. Palmer (eds), *The Archaeology of Industrialisation*. Oxford: Oxbow Books.
Rahtz, S.P.Q. (1987) The Protestant cemetery in Rome. Interim report. *Opuscula Romana* 16(10): 149–67.
Rauschenberg, B.L. (1990) Coffin making and undertaking in Charleston and its Environs, 1705–1820. *Journal of Early Southern Decorative Arts* 26(1): 19–63.
Reeve, J. and Adams, M. (1993) *The Spitalfields Project. Volume 1 – the Archaeology. Across the Styx*, Council for British Archaeology Research Report 85. York: Council for British Archaeology.
Rugg, J. (1998) A new burial form and its meanings: cemetery establishment in the first half of the nineteenth century. In M. Cox (ed.), *Grave Concerns: Death and Burial in England 1700 to 1850*, 44–53. York: Council for British Archaeology Research Report 113.
Shoesmith, R. (1980) Llangar Church. *Archaeologia Cambrensis* 119: 64–132.

Sigrist, J. (1989) A walk through history. In D.A.Weston (ed.), *The Sleeping City. The Story of Rockwood Necropolis*, 13–28. Sydney: Society of Australian Genealogists and Hale and Iremonger.

Singleton, C.C. and Kay, J. (1989) The Rockwood Cemetery Line. In D.A. Weston (ed.), *The Sleeping City. The Story of Rockwood Necropolis*, 44–53. Sydney: Society of Australian Genealogists and Hale and Iremonger.

Slater, J.A. (1996) *The Colonial Burying Grounds of Eastern Connecticut and the Men Who Made Them*, Memoirs of the Connecticut Academy of Arts and Sciences, Memoir 21, rev. edn. New Haven, CN: Connecticut Academy of Arts and Sciences.

Slater, J.A. and Tucker, R.L. (1978) The colonial gravestone carvings of John Hartshorne. In P. Benes (ed.), *Puritan Gravestone Art II*, 79–146, Dublin Seminar for New England Folklife, 3. Boston: Boston University Press.

Sloane, D.S. (1991) *The Last Great Necessity. Cemeteries in American History*. Baltimore, MD: Johns Hopkins University Press.

Tarlow, S. (2000) *Bereavement and Commemoration. An Archaeology of Mortality*. Oxford: Blackwell.

Tashjian, D. and Tashjian, A. (1974) *Memorials for Children of Change: The Art of Early New England Stonecarving*. Middletown, CT: Wesleyan University Press.

Welsh, A.N. (1999) *The Msida Bastion Garden of Rest. A Visitor's Guide*, 2nd edn. Valetta: Din L-Art Helwa.

Weston, D.A. (1989) Introduction. In D.A. Weston (ed.), *The Sleeping City. The Story of Rockwood Necropolis*, 9–11. Sydney: Society of Australian Genealogists and Hale and Iremonger.

Williams, R. (2000) Vanbrugh's India and his mausolea for England. In C. Ridgway and R. Williams (eds), *Sir John Vanbrugh and Landscape Architecture in Baroque England 1690–1730*, 114–30. Stroud: Sutton Publishing.

Willsher, B. and Hunter, D. (1978) *Stones: Eighteenth Century Scottish Gravestones*. Edinburgh: Cannongate Books.

Wrightson, K.K. (1998) Aboriginal Australian burials in Christian missions. *Markers* 15: 234–85.

Yalland, Z. (1985) *Kacheri Cemetery, Kanpur. A Complete List of Inscriptions with Notes on Those Buried There*. London: British Association for Cemeteries in South Asia.

Yeoh, B.S.A. (1991) The control of 'sacred' space: conflicts over the Chinese burial grounds in colonial Singapore, 1880–1930. *Journal of Southeast Asian Studies* 22(2): 282–311.

Zelinka, S. (1991) *Tender Sympathies: A Social History of Botany Cemetery and the Eastern Suburbs Crematorium*. Sydney: Hale and Iremonger.

10   Seeing each other: the colonial vision in nineteenth-century Victoria

JANE LYDON

Greater attention might not improperly be paid to the appearance of the area surrounding the settlement – no effort has as yet been made in this direction. The effect of tidiness, and *per contra* of untidiness, on the Aboriginal mind is most important; the inculcation of tidiness forms part of civilization as well as discipline.

(Royal Commission into the Aborigines, 1877: x–xi)

INTRODUCTION

Coranderrk Aboriginal Station, outside Melbourne, in the south-eastern Australian state of Victoria, was one of the most intensely negotiated sites of exchange between British colonisers and Aboriginal people during the nineteenth century. Following white invasion of Victoria in 1835, disruption of Aboriginal society was severe, and during the 1850s the colonial government pursued a policy of grouping surviving Aboriginal people on mission stations to be 'civilised' (Christie 1979; Cannon 1983; Lakic and Wrench 1993). In their attempts to 'civilise' the indigenous residents, white managers created a visual regime which intersected with Aboriginal ways of seeing, shaping forms of cultural exchange. From this sometimes obscured relationship, it emerges that British and indigenous identities were constituted through practices and attitudes grounded in the material realm.

British colonists sought to impose new ideas of order and time-discipline upon the residents through constructing the station as 'disciplinary machine', embodying technologies such as an orderly layout, a division between public and private space, and isolation from wider society. Aboriginal appropriation of European goods and practices was judged by white observers to be a straightforward index of their 'civilisation'. The visibility of people and landscape was a crucial element of this apparatus. While missionaries at other stations considered themselves successful in this enterprise, at Coranderrk, by contrast, white anxiety over control was a recurring theme, and the residents' protracted 'rebellion' was quelled only in the mid-1880s.

How do we explain this contestation? How was it played out against British visuality? Traditionally, Aboriginal visual conventions were important and elaborate, but differed fundamentally from European practices. Hence traditional values such as kinship persisted out of sight of official eyes, undermining the effectiveness of white surveillance. There were also convergences between white and black, old and new. The history of this complex visual, cross-cultural, negotiation defines the contingent, yet persistent nature of both British and Aboriginal identities. This study explores how European attempts to impose the disciplinary apparatus of the panopticon upon Coranderrk intersected with the traditions of the Aboriginal residents, the Kulin clans of central Victoria.

VISIBILITY AND CONCEALMENT: CORANDERRK AS DISCIPLINARY MACHINE

The Board for the Protection of the Aborigines sought to confine and isolate Aborigines on stations, and to impose corrective technologies of hierarchical observation and normalising judgement upon them which relied upon the visibility and demeanour of the residents. The impulse to control through surveillance and measurement is central to the European disciplinary apparatus first defined by Michel Foucault (1991). Its major tool was observation and its major effect 'to induce in the inmate a state of conscious and permanent visibility that assures the automatic functioning of power'. Specifically, this machine operated by 'dissociating the see/being seen dyad', so that 'power has its principle not so much in a person as in a certain concerted distribution of bodies, surfaces, lights, gazes; in an arrangement whose internal mechanisms produce the relation in which individuals are caught up' (Foucault 1991: 200–2).

Foucault elaborated this conception of the modern gaze in his account of the development of medicine at the beginning of the nineteenth century. While touch and hearing were an integral part of medical examination, they remained 'under the dominant sign of the visible', forming a kind of 'multi-sensorial perception [which] is merely a way of anticipating the triumph of the gaze that is represented by the autopsy' (1975: 165). This dominant, all-powerful gaze became the guarantee of truth, and in the endless task of defining the individual, the gaze became 'that which establishes the individual in his irreducible quality' (Foucault 1975: xiii–xiv).

Following this schema, one strand of colonial historiography has traced the imposition of white structures of sociality on indigenous people through the operation of Aboriginal stations as carceral institutions. Some scholars have examined the power relationships inherent in the spatial organisation of landscape: on slave plantations in the United States, for example, archaeologists have identified common patterns of clustering of service and slave buildings around the planter's central house, allowing overseers to maintain surveillance over their slaves (e.g. Leone 1984, Orser 1988; see also Kelso and Most 1990, Hood 1996). Others have compared these places with sociologist Erving

Goffman's (1961) 'total institution', characterised by closure, rationalisation and a hierarchical distinction between inmates and staff (Haebich 1988; Rowse 1993: 36–41).

For whites, the appearance of bourgeois civilisation was all-important, a straightforward index of progress. In a sense, the Board saw its Aboriginal settlements as machines, embodying an orderly spatial layout, a division between public and private space, and isolation from wider society. Through these technologies, it sought to impose new ideas of order and time-discipline upon the residents. The visibility of people and landscape was a crucial element of this apparatus: the importance of appearances, being *seen to be* clean, orderly and industrious, structured white policy and interaction between people. In one of the most evocative and concrete accounts of this scenario, historian Bain Attwood argues of the Aboriginal station Ramahyuck, in Victoria's east Gippsland, that

> fundamental to [the missionary Hagenauer's] reconstruction of Aborigines was a plan to produce a carefully defined and ordered social space . . . a didactic landscape, an instrument to transmit Christianity and 'civilisation', mould the conduct of Aborigines, and express a conception of what he wished the Aborigines to become.
>
> (1989: 7)

Hagenauer, a strict disciplinarian, saw the station operating like a game of chess, with the mission house, school house, 'native houses' and the tasks performed around them enabling 'each branch to work separately and yet to form part of the whole machinery'. The centre of this ideal landscape was the 'top of a gentle rise' surrounded by fertile landscape; the 'village' was designed to echo familiar European hamlets. At Ramahyuck the orderly, hierarchical arrangement of buildings, spaces and fences effectively governed movement and relationships between the residents, on the basis of race, age, rank and gender. Segregated space was an internal feature of buildings too, such as the chapel. Children were separated from their parents, boys from girls, in the boarding house. A chief goal of this apparatus, particularly the design of houses, was to redefine Aboriginal people as individuals, 'an integrated centre of consciousness', rather than 'being bound by the obligations of a kin-based society' (Attwood 1989: 7–19).

In Attwood's view, this physical apparatus transformed Aborigines, as the missionaries' 'ideas and values actually came to be imbricated in the very fabric of Aborigines' consciousness and way of being . . . becoming integral to their sense of themselves'. He argues that this order was consensual, and that 'the seeds of oppression came to lie within Aborigines as well as without' making liberation even more difficult. An alternative culture persisted but this came more and more to frame its resistance in the missionaries' language – 'their protest tended to reinforce the existing relationship rather than recast it on their terms. It was a reactive rather than creative power'. Attwood concludes that by the 1870s the goal of creating Ramahyuck as an isolated, self-contained island of reform had largely succeeded (1989: 29–31).

While Ramahyuck, as the Board's model establishment, may indeed have been effective in achieving missionary goals, by contrast at Coranderrk, white anxiety over control was a recurring theme, and the residents' protracted 'rebellion' was quelled only in the mid-1880s (Barwick 1998). This contestation can be better understood in the light of several analyses of Aboriginal settlements which query the effectiveness of institutional control, and show that aspects of traditional culture may in fact strengthen, and a separate, oppositional, social domain develop. Tim Rowse (1993: 34), for example, argues that even under very disciplinarian reserve regimes, comparison with Goffman's model of hermetic closure denies continuities between inmates' lives within and outside institutions. Traditions such as age and kinship relationships can find room to persist or even expand within institutional structures, either because of their importance to Aboriginal people, or because they are facilitated by new circumstances such as an increased marriage pool, an assured food supply or social distance from whites. Most importantly, 'there would seem to be something highly resistant, in the Aboriginal sense of kinship, to the degrading individuations of 'total institutions' (Rowse 1993: 39–47).

At Coranderrk a range of factors allowed the Kulin residents to organise themselves for the station's first decade, not least being its consensual establishment in partnership with missionary John Green in 1863. However, as at other Aboriginal stations, the ritual of inspection was conducted rigorously and often, providing the substance of the Board's annual reports, and defining its population in minute detail. These reports were at first approving, praising the station's location, layout and organisation. In 1865, the Board Secretary stated that he 'found the huts occupied by the blacks both clean and orderly. The adults were well-clad, the children were as neat and clean as Aboriginal children in a partially civilised state can be expected to be, and the infants seem to be well cared for' (Board for the Protection of the Aborigines 1865: 5).

The residents knew that they were to be prepared for inspection at any time, and complied with outsiders' expectations of cleanliness and order. Domestic space, under women's control, was a particular focus for scrutiny, and reports were uniformly approving. In 1869 it was said

> The garden in front of the [Greens'] house looks very well, and in every part of the station I saw improvement. I entered and examined a great many of the huts occupied by the married people, and it was gratifying to see so many marks of the change produced by domestication. The men were away at work in the fields or on the station, and the women were occupied in little offices in their homes. Objects indicating some taste and some pride in the appearance of their dwellings were not few. Their native baskets were hung up against the walls, the walls were here and there ornamented with pictures, their rugs and clothing were arranged in order, and their fires tidily kept.

All these little things serve to astonish those who are acquainted with the habits and feelings of the Aborigines.

(Brough Smyth 1869)

But there is also evidence that Aboriginal people asserted their own, traditional or innovative practices within the mission landscape. Coranderrk's equitable and culturally tolerant origins under the management of Presbyterian minister John Green shaped its spatial organisation and operation, thwarting later managers' intentions of keeping an eye on the 'village'. The first arrangement comprised a north-facing row of huts along the flat top of a ridge sloping to Badger Creek (Figure 10.1). To the west, a little downhill, a schoolhouse stood, with Green's better-quality house on its farther side. By 1866 the school teacher's house stood in front of the schoolhouse-dormitory.

One of the most persistent conventions of Kulin society was its placement of dwellings as a symbolic statement about land ownership: when tribal groups assembled for ceremonies, dwellings were oriented according to home territories, each facing the compass direction of its homeland (Howitt n.d.; Barwick 1998: 118–19). This organisation was maintained, in modified form, until at least the 1880s at Coranderrk, while the segregated dormitories were comparable to the Kulin camps for single young men and women. The men could still go away for days at a time to hunt. The Kulin retained some aspects

Figure 10.1 Charles Walter's view of the front of the Coranderrk settlement, *c.* 1865 (Page 1, Green Family Album, Museum Victoria XP 1937)

of traditional domesticity, co-existing with new, fixed, household routines. Green's more comfortable residence was sited away from the Kulin, which would have given both his family and the Kulin more privacy.

This settlement area was cleared of trees, as was a large, gently sloping space in front of it, which was used for playing games. Ethnographer and public servant Robert Brough Smyth (1878: 352) described a game he was shown in this space in 1873, where a bulbous-headed stem called a *wi-tch-wi-tch*, or *weet-weet*, was flicked across the ground to a great distance, as a stone may be skipped across the surface of water, resembling a hopping kangaroo. Brough Smyth (1878: 177) also described a form of football using a ball made from possum skin which was played here, and wrestling staged before elders. Photographs throughout the station's life show cricket in progress in this area. This highly visible public area of the settlement was where children played, visitors arrived and where visiting groups sometimes camped. This is also the site of public events, including the expression of anger and conflict (cf. Clarke 1996: 74–7). In some respects this space acted like the traditional British village green, but it was not a contained compound. The surrounding bush and the steeply sloping south side of the ridge, plunging behind the houses to Badger Creek, acted as a means of escape for people wishing to avoid restriction (e.g. Brough Smyth 1869; Green 1871).

This public space of interaction was linked to another key element of Coranderrk's initial organisation: the court formed by Green and the Kulin where those who broke rules – such as a ban on drunkenness – were publicly reprimanded, and where consensus was achieved. This was basically run by the residents themselves. As Green (1865) stated shortly after the station was founded: 'My method of managing the blacks is to allow them to rule themselves as much as possible. When there is any strife among them this is always settled at a kind of court, at which I preside.' When the residents were given a role in deciding on a rule or punishment, they would hold firmly to their decision, although they resisted the external imposition of rules (Royal Commission into the Aborigines 1877). In 1882 Green (Coranderrk Aboriginal Station 1882: 136) described how before this assembly he countered a rumour a little girl was spreading about his treatment of a patient who had died, and 'they were all perfectly ashamed of themselves for saying such a thing'. Green's important role as leader within this system of justice and collective management conformed to the paternalistic model of the Presbyterian Church, with Green as shepherd of a flock. Residents quickly adopted Christianity, attending prayers twice daily and keeping the Sabbath.

This system can also be understood as a continuation of the tradition of public shaming to maintain order, a traditional Aboriginal means of regulation and punishment which relies upon a person's sensitivity to the collective perceptions of a close-knit community well known to her or him. As one Aboriginal person explained recently to an anthropologist, 'You know when you are doing things in the open and you don't want it that way' (Heller 1982). Institutional life can paradoxically provide the conditions for the perpetuation of these practices, sometimes self-consciously in opposition to European practice. This awareness of being observed and assessed according to collective rules of behaviour seems to offer some points of similarity with panoptical control; it can make people conceal stigmatised customs such as dancing or language, always discouraged by missionaries. But instead of the individualising and distancing gaze of surveillance, designed to inculcate within each person the awareness of being continuously observed, there are signs that members of the Coranderrk community remained answerable to kin, not an internalised European code of conduct. Here, the public and visible spaces of communal action continued to be used according to Aboriginal tradition.

Some traditional practices, however, during the first decade at least, continued in private – in fact, probably relied upon their concealment. For example, Green described how

> They are a most remarkable people in their ideas of morality and chastity; and at a certain time, even after I built a house, or huts, the female had a little place at the back of the hut, where she had to sit apart from the men for a week every other month, and she would not touch with her hand anything belonging to the man, and the man would not touch a thing belonging to her while she was in that state . . . I got them to make two beds inside, and not to go outside, so that people might not ask me why they were sitting there, and so on.
> (Royal Commission into the Aborigines 1877: 86)

Obviously Green did not see these customs as interfering with his objectives at the station and assisted the residents to maintain them, although he too was aware of the importance of concealing non-European customs from visitors. In addition, some residents (especially the elderly) continued to defecate in the bush, believing that using the outhouses, by giving their enemies access to their excrement, made them vulnerable to sorcery (Coranderrk Aboriginal Station, 1882: 131; cf. Reynolds 1990: 87–9). For some years these practices did not enter the purview of Board surveillance.

Green also enforced certain European taboos, for example keeping children inside the fence, away from women who had lived as prostitutes before settlement at the station; he was proud of his control over the children's movements, stating that, 'I had forty or forty-five there, and just by a snap of the fingers I had them all in the school-house before you could count twenty' (Royal Commission into the Aborigines 1877: 87) These patterns of avoidance and movement across the station landscape indicate the tacit tolerance of cultural difference as well as transformation.

By the 1870s, however, the pleased tone of officials congratulating each other on the success of their 'experiment' was superseded by more critical reports, and further measurements of progress were imposed. For example, the visiting doctor, Gibson, suggested that 'the next supply of clothing for the children should be a little lighter in colour, so that it can at once be seen whether or not it is clean'. And he drew attention to the mia mias, which had formerly been suppressed, where possible, in visual and textual accounts of the station, stating, 'There are still five nomadic huts of the station, made of sheets of bark laid together; but these belong to elderly blacks, whose habits are difficult to deal with; but the interior of these is as clean and orderly as the circumstances will allow' (Board for the Protection of the Aborigines 1871: 11–14).

As conflict grew between residents and white allies such as John Green, on the one hand, and the Board, on the other, the village layout increasingly became a matter for contestation. Green was dismissed in 1874, and a successor sparked protest when he decided to build the hop-master Burgess's house in the middle of the vegetable garden, away from the two parallel rows of houses arranged by the Kulin. Observers began to find its overall appearance lacking, as an inquiry concluded in 1877: 'Greater attention might not improperly be paid to the appearance of the area surrounding the settlement – no effort has as yet been made in this direction' (Royal Commission into the Aborigines 1877: x–xi). It was at this time of conflict that the Board commissioned photographer Fred Kruger to produce a series of portraits which were intended to argue for its successful management of the station, and the 'tidiness' of its people, at least (Lydon 2000).

Between 1879 and 1881 conflict increased, as residents went on strike, held protest meetings, lobbied influential white supporters outside the station and finally sent a deputation of men to walk the 41 miles into Melbourne to bring their grievances to the Chief Secretary's attention (Barwick 1998: 165–210). Following this 'rebellion', which prompted a parliamentary inquiry into the Board's management of Coranderrk, major landscaping and re-building were carried out, intended to improve the station 'machinery' (Figure 10.2). This re-organisation made a new entrance road ending in a grand sweep at the manager's new two-storey brick house, completed in 1883. From this house, through the tall window lighting the staircase at its eastern end, a distant view could be had of the 'village', but this would not have allowed the manager to 'spy' on the residents from the house: managers described hearing distant 'disturbances' and 'going down into' the settlement to intervene.

This new relationship would have given residents relative privacy, and probably acted to maintain cultural differences. Social distance between white and black embodied in the spatial layout of living and working quarters has been observed to preserve Aboriginal tradition at modern settlements (e.g. Trigger 1986). Similarly, anthropologist Gillian Cowlishaw (1988: 232–44) argues for the development of an 'oppositional' culture, an 'arena of social meaning in an embattled situation' which provides a source of dignity, and a sense of honour, a 'defiant reaction to rejection'. Although whites often do not acknowledge the contrasting values of Aboriginal people as 'culture', Cowlishaw, like Rowse, sees 'the major contrast with white individualism, competition and material concerns' in Aboriginal family orientation (and see Morris 1988).

These studies suggest how spatial organisation and visual practices may have facilitated the preservation of traditional social practices at Coranderrk, and

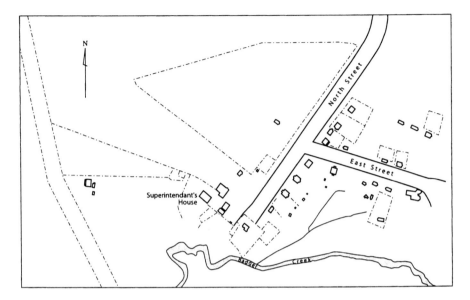

Figure 10.2 Plan of Coranderrk following landscaping programme, 1883. Notice the superintendant's substantial new residence some way to the south-west of the settlement

point to the ways the Kulin contested European disciplinary technologies. They also suggest that the formation of identity is best seen as a process comprising the play of representations *between* black and white, as well as *within* these categories. As Stuart Hall (1993: 392–403) argues, identity is a production which is never complete, and 'always constituted within, not outside, representation' (cf. Bhabha 1994). While Coranderrk's residents had not initially thought of themselves as belonging to the continent-wide category 'Aboriginal' (Attwood 1989), they rapidly understood white perceptions and capitalised on them when necessary. In 1884, for example, resident Sam Rowan left the station without permission. Visiting the Travellers Rest hotel in Blacktown, near Box Hill (then a township outside Melbourne), he pretended that he was a 'black tracker' in pursuit of a criminal, and persuaded the innkeeper's daughter to write a letter for him to this effect. A policeman reported: 'I believe this is not the first time they have been out imposing on the public by representing themselves as "blacktrackers"' (Hayes 1884). Rowan was clearly aware of the status accorded Aboriginal 'trackers' by white society, on account of their skilled bushcraft.

   Identification with traditional Kulin clans, such as Wurundjeri or Taungerong, continued to structure relations among the Aboriginal residents of Coranderrk. Anthropologist and historian Diane Barwick (1998: 163) traces the persistence of kin affiliation, arguing that conflict exploited by white manager Halliday in 1878 centred on antagonism between the 'Kulin pioneers' and newcomers, clan groups traditionally alien to the Kulin such as the

Burapper and Pangerang who also came to live at Coranderrk, although whites mistakenly attributed the nature of this hostility to 'blood', their own criterion. Yet white assessments of the nature of 'half-castes' by comparison with 'full-blooded' Aboriginal people were also taken up by the Aboriginal people; while such factionalism could be defined as Kulin versus the Burapper and Pangerang, the protagonists came also to employ the terms 'pure blacks' and 'half-castes' themselves. During one confrontation both systems of classification were invoked, as a Kulin speaker 'waved his hand over toward the newcomers in the most majestic manner and replied addressing them "Why you fellows, who are you, who are you anyhow, why you come here like a lot of scotch thistles!"', while another argued that 'Sir Henry Barkly [the Governor] gave this station to Mr Green for the *blacks*, not for the half castes' (Barwick 1998: 163)

Rather than assigning essentialised 'agent-positions' I seek instead to make visible the historical processes by which identities are ascribed, resisted or embraced (Scott 1991). Residents quickly came to see Coranderrk as home – both because of the ancestral connection between Wurundjeri and traditional lands, but also through a developing bond established through building their lives there; it was a refuge as well as an institution. The station's specific material and social organisation enabled residents to maintain important aspects of culture and identity.

Hence the effectiveness of the Board's 'machine' was undermined in ways it did not recognise. In March 1883 the acting manager William Goodall wrote about a difficulty which had arisen in building the new huts, as he reported:

> Johnny Terrick objected to any place being built there unless it was for himself as he looks upon that piece of ground as his own property and as I had already promised the cottage to another I could not grant it to him. I further found that if I persisted in the erection thereof it would cause a large amount of discontent and murmuring so I requested Mr Anderson to lay out the cottages near the original sites of the huts occupied by Bamfield[?], Morgan and Dunolly to whom I had promised the cottages when it was first decided they should be erected. This appears to give general satisfaction.

He concluded that 'having occupied any place for any length of time they become attached to it and do not like to be placed any where else' (1883). Unaware of persisting links to traditional country, he recognised the residents' new attachments to Coranderrk.

Another important goal of the Board's apparatus of control was to isolate and fix the Aboriginal residents: in 1877 the remote Framlingham station in western Victoria was thought to be ideal in this respect (Royal Commission into the Aborigines 1877: 105). But at easily accessible Coranderrk, just outside Melbourne, this was impossible to achieve. Coranderrk was unique amongst the Victorian stations in its level of contact with white society: the station's proximity to white settlement saw a constant flow of visitors towards it and travel of the residents away; the problem of maintaining the residents' seclusion was a constant theme. In 1874, for example, the Board referred to

> the great difficulty . . . in keeping them under control when they are induced by old associations or superstitions, or tempted by the lower class of whites, to wander from the spots where in health they are supplied with good food and clothing and in sickness tended with the same care as is bestowed on Europeans.
>
> (Board for the Protection of the Aborigines 1874: 3)

Visitors went to the station as to a laboratory or zoo, and the station's political importance as a site of Aboriginal–white struggle saw the production of visual representations in the form of photographs which, for whites, constituted certain 'truths' about Aboriginal people (Lydon 2000). Once it had satisfactorily enforced its assimilation policy in the mid-1880s, the Board allowed the station to become a showplace, open to visitors, and as tourism out of Melbourne developed, Coranderrk became a 'must-see' site on an itinerary which extended north-east into the Dandenongs mountain range. Residents benefited in various ways – by selling souvenirs to visitors to the station, or participating in sporting or cultural events in Melbourne. This contact also allowed residents to develop a sophisticated awareness of white discourse, which assisted them to contest the Board's attempts to increase its control during the 1870s. Aboriginal residents combined an acute grasp of the role of demeanour and visibility within white systems of control with a frequent disregard of its power, in struggling to retain their land and autonomy. In these ways Aboriginal people disrupted the ideal isolation imposed by the Board.

It is also possible to recognise the Aboriginal reformulation of Christian rituals, such as Christmas, celebrated with cake-baking, cricket and music. Many station managers sanctioned removal from the usual European routine at this time, and at Coranderrk in 1874 Green reported that 'The most of them like to get a few weeks to fish and hunt about the Yarra River Flats', the first record of what became a yearly ritual up until the end of the station's life (Board for the Protection of the Aborigines 1874: 7). Before European invasion the annual cycle of movement around their own country had concluded with the Kulin assembling at Merri Creek, a tributary of the Yarra, in December to conduct group business (Fels 1988: 30). Archaeologists note how Christmas camp sites often coincide with the pre-settler landscape, some appearing on 'prehistoric' coastal fishing and shellfish gathering sites which are marked by shell middens (e.g. Byrne 1996). These convergences were satisfying to black and white. They point to the creative intersection of two cultural orders, whence signifying practices could be read in more than one way.

Hence while power relationships may be inherent in the spatial organisation of a landscape, as Attwood argued of Ramahyuck, it is important not to overestimate its impact on the people who lived in it, despite its inertia and scale

(Hodder 1991). Aboriginal 'resistance' to control, or power to construct an 'oppositional domain', was limited, especially under those circumstances of oppression that characterise colonial relations, but evidence for strategies to maintain and conceal traditions, or to respond to new circumstances, serve to remind us that the process of cultural exchange is complex and situational. Aboriginal people have found inventive ways of maintaining or transforming identity within colonial society (Davison 1985; Read 1988; L'Oste-Brown and Godwin et al. 1995; Clarke 1996).

Coranderrk was founded in unusually consensual circumstances, which during its first decade permitted a degree of autonomy. There was space for Aboriginal objectives and traditions to co-exist with newer practices, and opportunities to reformulate them. Perhaps this is why in 1877 it was said that the residents' 'bearing and demeanour' was unique amongst the Victorian Aboriginal stations (Royal Commission on the Aborigines 1877: x–xi). The evidence suggests the co-existence of different cultural understandings of the station's physical landscape: white observers were pleased to note its orderliness and the civilising functions of schoolhouse and church, as well as the adoption of a new form of private domesticity measured through the appearance of nuclear households. The Aboriginal residents however maintained several forms of collective identity, reflected in their dwellings' spatial layout according to traditional land ownership, and forms of sociality such as group regulation. Some retained practices such as a camp lifestyle, betrayed by the presence of mia mias or more covert taboos.

In some cases such persistence was possible because Aboriginal practices were not recognised by whites, or, as in the case of Green's tolerance of beliefs surrounding menstruation and defecation, were not perceived by him to threaten Christianising objectives. Different conceptions of power or meaning may allow the co-existence of different cultural practices. As Rowse (1993: 26–7) notes, 'cultures differ in what they think "power" is. For many Aboriginal people it seems to include forces that are "spiritual" . . . we need a series of ethnographies and histories which illustrate the many contingencies of the relationship between old forms of power and new forms of power'. Here, given that Green himself was subject to monitoring by his Board employers and that their dissatisfaction with his management eventually led to his resignation, the *invisibility* of such practices, converging with their concealment by mid-nineteenth-century white society, probably also contributed to their survival, contrasting with the rapid abandonment of the higher-profile corroboree, for example.

Hence the complex process of cultural exchange enacted at Coranderrk was strongly shaped by visual practices. In its clashes, convergences and misrecognitions, the intersection of two visual regimes serves to reveal both British and Aboriginal subjectivity as contingent and relational. As historians of visuality have argued, different, sometimes incompatible, ways of seeing have prevailed historically, as different codes of viewing co-exist or compete (Jay 1988; Bryson 1994). Although the colonisers' perspective dominated, and has strongly shaped our own point of view, we must acknowledge that it was neither natural nor inevitable. How then, did nineteenth-century Aboriginal ways of seeing differ from what many modern Western readers accept as natural?

ABORIGINAL DISREGARD?

Aboriginal responses to white authority were shaped by tradition, and especially by a distinctively indigenous 'scopic regime'. Traditionally, Aboriginal visual expression and 'ways of seeing' were very important and elaborate, and as in Western society the sense of vision was accorded primacy (e.g. Sutton 1982; Langton 1993: 9). However, as the linguistic research of Evans and Wilkins (1998) demonstrates, there is a culturally variable relationship between the senses' metaphorical extension into the cognitive domain: in Aboriginal languages, it is hearing, not vision, which is extended to denote 'know', 'think' or 'remember', while 'see' is more likely to be used for specific forms of social interaction ('flirt with', 'love', 'supervise/oversee'). This reflects an Australia-wide Aboriginal tradition that the ear is the organ of intellection as well as hearing, explained by the emphasis in Aboriginal society on grasping language, stories or names as the key to socially transmitted information, and the summoning of verbal records in recollection. The resulting cognitive verbs extend to acts such as remembering or knowing faces, as well as names or sounds (Evans and Wilkins 1998: 37).

This linguistic pattern is linked to visual practices. In general, direct eye contact is far more communicatively loaded in Aboriginal communities than in European societies, and may be offensive or interpreted as a sexual advance (Hansen and Hansen 1992). Many communities have highly developed sign language systems. Where communal life entails a high level of continuous background noise, individuals tune in or out selectively. Conversational styles are not usually dyadic, or face to face, with the expectation of eye contact and control by the speaker; instead in remote Aboriginal communities, talk is 'broadcast', with no need for eye contact and with control held by listeners. This is related to complex kin relationships which often require that people are turned away from each other even when talking (Evans and Wilkins 1998). Elaborate rules existed for meetings with strangers which stressed formality, and the creation of a physical and temporal space of adjustment (a warning period) for host groups (Hallam 1983). Movement proceeded behind other people's 'lines of personal social presentation', such as paths of movement, vision or personal orientation (Trigger 1986: 99–117).

This visual subtlety and indirectness was perhaps related to the tendency for life to be lived in full public view, with participants engaging or disengaging when they chose (Walsh 1991). As I have noted, regulation of behaviour was traditionally effected through public 'shaming' of wrongdoers before their relatively close-knit kin, as laws are enforced by reference to an external referent rather than by individual self-mastery (Von Sturmer 1981; Heller 1982).

While it is difficult to discern such intangible and nuanced practices in the past, these observations have implications for thinking about the intersection of nineteenth-century visual and social systems at Coranderrk. The station's layout, as we have seen, provided spatial buffer zones in the form of public spaces, while the open, uphill approach toward the ridge-top station settlement would have helped maintain Aboriginal 'sight lines', allowing residents to prepare for visitors. The bush and creeks remained private Aboriginal spaces. The unmediated, face-to-face contact characteristic of the European visual regime, linked to a notion of the observation of external appearances as a realist measurement of things and people, would initially have been literally confronting to Aboriginal people. By contrast, looking relations within tradi- tional Aboriginal visual regimes were characterised by greater delicacy and tact. Meaning was found in a wider range of less overt signifying practices. This fundamental cultural difference in orientation initially determined represen- tational codes as well: European perspectival conventions relied upon the description of surface appearance, whereas Aboriginal art tended to emphasise the inside, in associating artists, place and ancestral power (Morphy 1991; Taylor, 1996; Morphy 2000).

CONCLUSION

Hence communication at Coranderrk was a complex process: European visual regimes emphasised outward visual form and observable practices as a measure of 'progress', effected by the imagined burden of a disciplinary gaze. But while British colonists' policy was to construct Aboriginal stations as 'discipli- nary machines', embodying technologies such as an orderly layout, a divi- sion between public and private space, and isolation from wider society, Coranderrk's spatial arrangement and internal organisation diverged from this ideal. Its residents' actions demonstrate that, within a society largely structured by non-visual conventions, Kulin behaviour can sometimes be understood as disregard, as they continued to pursue their own objectives. Traditional practices such as collective, kin-based forms of decision-making and authority were maintained, augmented by new customs. Through their intersection, Coranderrk's story of cultural negotiation reveals the contingent nature of both white and Aboriginal cultural identities.

ACKNOWLEDGEMENTS

I thank Susan Lawrence for her encouragement in developing this chapter. It draws from doctoral research at the Australian National University conducted in collaboration with the Aboriginal descendants of Coranderrk's residents, and I especially thank Jessie and Colin Hunter, Ian Hunter, Murrundindi, Bill Nicholson Sr, Joy Murphy, Vicky Nicholson and Brian Paterson for

their interest and support. For their advice on the arguments made in this
chapter, I thank especially Nicholas Thomas, Ann Curthoys, Howard Morphy
and Bain Attwood.

REFERENCES

Attwood, B. (1989) *The Making of the Aborigines.* Sydney: Allen and Unwin.
Barwick, D. (1998) *Rebellion at Coranderrk.* Canberra: Aboriginal History Monograph 5.
Bhabha, H. (1994) *The Location of Culture.* New York: Routledge.
Board for the Protection of the Aborigines (1865) *Fourth Report.* Melbourne: John
    Ferres, Government Printer.
—— (1871) *Seventh Report.* Melbourne: John Ferres, Government Printer.
—— (1874) *Tenth Report.* Melbourne: John Ferres, Government Printer.
Brough Smyth, R. (1869) Report of Brough Smyth. In Board for the Protection of
    the Aborigines, *Sixth Report,* Appendix II. Melbourne: John Ferres, Government
    Printer.
—— (1878) *The Aborigines of Victoria with Notes Relating to the Habits of the Natives of
    Other Parts of Australia and Tasmania.* Melbourne and London: John Ferres,
    Government Printer, and George Robertson.
Bryson, N. (1994) Art in context. In M. Bal and I. Boer (eds), *The Point of Theory:
    Practices of Cultural Analysis,* 66–78. Amsterdam: Amsterdam University Press.
Byrne, D. (1996) Deep nation: Australia's acquisition of an indigenous past. *Aboriginal
    History* 20: 82–107.
Cannon, M. (1983) *Historical Records of Victoria. Foundation Series. Volume 2B: Aborigines
    and Protectors 1838–1839.* Melbourne: Victorian Government Printing Office.
Christie, M. (1979) *Aborigines in Colonial Victoria, 1835–86.* Sydney: Sydney University
    Press.
Clarke, P. (1996) Aboriginal use of space in the Lower Murray, South Australia. *COMA*
    August: 74–7.
Coranderrk Aboriginal Station (1882) *Report of the Board Appointed to Inquire into and
    Report Upon the Condition and Management of the Aboriginal Station at Coranderrk.*
    Melbourne: John Ferres, Government Printer.
Cowlishaw, G. (1988) *Black, White or Brindle: Race in Rural Australia.* Cambridge:
    Cambridge University Press.
Davison, P. (1985) *The Manga-Manga Settlement, Phillip Creek: An Historical Reconstruction
    from Written, Oral and Material Evidence.* Townsville: Records of James Cook Univers-
    ity, Occasional Papers in Anthropology.
Evans, N. and Wilkins, D. (1998) *The Knowing Ear: An Australian Test of Universal Claims
    about the Semantic Structure of Sensory Verbs and Their Extension into the Domain of
    Cognition.* Institut fur Sprachwissenschaft Universitat zu Koln, Arbeitspapier Nr. 32
    (Neue Folge).
Fels, M. (1988) *Good Men and True: The Aboriginal Police of the Port Phillip District
    1837–1853.* Melbourne: Melbourne University Press.
Foucault, M. (1975) *Birth of the Clinic: An Archaeology of Medical Perception.* New York:
    Vintage Books.
—— [1975] (1991) *Discipline and Punish: The Birth of the Prison.* London: Penguin.
Goffman, E. (1961) *Asylums.* Chicago: Aldine Publishing Company.
Goodall, W. (1883) *National Archives of Australia*: 13/3/1883: B313, Item 204.
Green, J. (1865) *National Archives of Australia*: 28/7/1865: CRS B312, Item 9.
—— (1871) *National Archives of Australia*: B313, Item 182.
Haebich, A. (1988) *For Their Own Good.* Nedlands: University of Western Australia
    Press.

Hall, S. (1993) Cultural identity and diaspora. In P. Williams and L. Chrisman (eds), *Colonial Discourse and Post-Colonial Theory: A Reader*, 392–403. New York: Harvester Wheatsheaf.

Hallam, S. (1983) A view from the other side of the western frontier: or, 'I met a man who wasn't there . . .'. *Aboriginal History* 7(2): 123–56.

Hansen, K. and Hansen, L. (1992) *Pintupi/Luritja Dictionary*. Alice Springs: Institute for Aboriginal Development.

Hayes, Constable (1884) Report Victoria Police 6/9/1884, Melbourne. National Archives of Australia: B313, Item 216.

Heller, A. (1982) The power of shame. *Dialectical Anthropology* 6: 215–28.

Hodder, I. (1991) *Reading the Past: Current Approaches to Interpretation in Archaeology*. Cambridge: Cambridge University Press.

Hood, J. (1996) Social relations and the cultural landscape. In R. Yamin and K. Metheny (eds), *Landscape Archaeology: Reading and Interpreting the American Historical Landscape*, 121–46. Knoxville: University of Tennessee Press.

Howitt, A. (n.d.) *A.W. Howitt Papers*, MS 9356 (microfilm). State Library of Victoria, La Trobe Collection.

Jay, M. (1988) Scopic regimes of modernity. In H. Foster (ed.), *Vision and Visuality*, 3–23. Seattle, WA: Dia Art Foundation.

Kelso, W. and Most, R. (eds) (1990) *Earth Patterns: Essays in Landscape Archaeology*. Charlotteville, VI: University Press of Virginia.

Lakic, M. and Wrench, R. (eds) (1993) *Through Their Eyes: An Historical record of Aboriginal People in Victoria as Documented by the Officials of the Port Phillip Protectorate 1839–1841*. Melbourne: Aboriginal Studies Department, Museum of Victoria.

Langton, M. (1993) 'Well, I heard it on the radio and I saw it on the television . . .': an essay for the Australian Film Commission on the politics and aesthetics of film-making by and about Aboriginal people and things. Sydney: Australian Film Commission.

Leone, M. (1984) Interpreting ideology in historical archaeology: the William Paca Garden in Annapolis, Maryland. In D. Miller and C. Tilley (eds), *Ideology, Power and Prehistory*, 235–362. Cambridge: Cambridge University Press.

L'Oste-Brown, S. and Godwin, L., with Henry, G., Mitchell, T. and Tyson, V. (1995) *Living Under the Act: Taroom Aboriginal Reserve 1911–1927*. Brisbane: Department of Environment and Heritage.

Lydon, J. (2000) Regarding Coranderrk: photography at Coranderrk Aboriginal Station, Victoria. PhD thesis. Canberra: Australian National University.

Morphy, H. (1991) *Ancestral Connections: Art and an Aboriginal System of Knowledge*. Chicago: University of Chicago Press.

—— (2000) Inner landscapes: the fourth dimension. In M. Neale and S. Kleinert (eds), *The Oxford Companion to Aboriginal Art and Culture*, 243–8. Melbourne: Oxford University Press.

Morris, B. (1988) Dhan-gadi resistance to assimilation. In I. Keen (ed.), *Being Black: Aboriginal Cultures in 'Settled' Australia* 33–63. Canberra: Aboriginal Studies Press.

Orser, C. (1988) Toward a theory of power for historical archaeology: plantations and space. In M. Leone and P. Potter (eds), *The Recovery of Meaning: Historical Archaeology in the Eastern United States*, 313–43. Washington: Smithsonian Institution Press.

Read, P. (1988) *A Hundred Years War: the Wiradjuri people and the State*. Sydney: Australian National University Press.

Reynolds, H. (1990) *The Other Side of the Frontier: Aboriginal Resistance to the European Invasion of Australia*. Ringwood: Penguin.

Rowse, T. (1993) *After Mabo: Interpreting Indigenous Traditions*. Melbourne: Melbourne University Press.

Royal Commission into the Aborigines (1877) *Report of the Royal Commission into the Aborigines*. Melbourne: John Ferres, Government Printer.

Scott, J. (1991) Experience. *Critical Inquiry* 17: 773–97.

Sutton, P. (1982) Personal power, kin classification and speech etiquette in Aboriginal Australia. In J. Heath, F. Merlan and A. Rumsey (eds), *Languages of Kinship in Aboriginal Australia*, 182–200. Oceania Linguistic Monographs, No. 24, University of Sydney.

Taylor, L. (1996) *Seeing the Inside: Bark Painting in Western Arnhem Land*. Oxford: Clarendon Press.

Trigger, D. (1986) Blackfellas and whitefellas: the concepts of domain and social closure in the analysis of race-relations. *Mankind* 16(2): 99–117.

Von Sturmer, J. (1981) Talking with Aborigines. *Australian Institute of Aboriginal Studies Newsletter New Series* 15: 1–19.

Walsh, M. (1991) Conversational styles and intercultural communication: an example from northern Australia. *Australian Journal of Communication*, 18(1): 1–12.

11   Nineteenth-century ceramics in Cape Town, South Africa

ANTONIA MALAN AND JANE KLOSE

INTRODUCTION

In this chapter we outline the context within which the British occupation of the Cape impacted on the availability and use of tea and table wares in a 'Dutch' settlement, with reference to excavated ceramic collections and contemporary household inventories. The period considered can be broadly subdivided into three phases: (1) after the collapse of the Dutch East India Company (DEIC) during the 1780s, the First British Occupation and transitional years (1795–c. 1820); (2) early British Crown Colony (c. 1820–c. 1860); and (3) the British Cape (c. 1860–1910).

Studying the material culture of nineteenth-century colonies is related to a question of scale, ranging from the global dimension to richly textured local manifestations. An archaeology of the modern world must address the fact that objects, images and people circulated across oceans and through continents (Hall 2000). Like many other cities around the world, the archaeological record of mid-nineteenth-century Cape Town is marked by the presence of sherds of banded, printed and sponge-decorated ceramics manufactured in the potteries of Britain. These ceramics also lie in rock shelters in the mountains of the Cape Folded Belt, are found scattered outside the kitchen doors of farmsteads, nestle between the cobblestones of mission stations and protrude from the foundations of a 'Boer War' fort. It is an intriguing experience to pick up identical pieces in those vastly different contexts – to hold fragments of bowls, made in England but used and discarded by hunters, herders, slaves, farmers, shopkeepers, servants, housewives, governors and soldiers alike.

Until the end of the eighteenth century, Cape Town had been developing a Eurasian colonial identity under a century and a half of DEIC rule. It was created as an outpost for protecting and servicing Company ships and mariners, but the descendants of Europeans and African and Asian slaves slowly colonised the hinterland. Cape Town became part of the Second British Empire for similar strategic reasons, so that it was held safe in British hands to protect the passage to India.

The wave of emigration of British people throughout the colonies during the nineteenth century was represented in South Africa by working-class Irish, Scottish and English immigrants as well as the more 'respectable' merchant and professional class. These mid-nineteenth-century migrants came from a very different society than their Dutch period colonial forebears, and they carried with them the material culture of a triumphant 'bourgeois revolution' (Said 1994). Susan Lawrence (1999) has suggested that mid-nineteenth-century South Africa should reflect a British imperial pattern that is shared with Australia, Canada and later with New Zealand – the 'new' colonies of the Second British Empire. At the same time, there should be regional differences. The colonies were the homelands of a diversity of indigenous and settler people 'who were far from passive victims of the colonial process' (Beaudry 2000).

CAPE TOWN AND ITS HINTERLAND DURING THE NINETEENTH CENTURY

Cape Town lies half-way along the sea route between Europe and Asia and marks the extreme south-western outpost on the Indian Ocean maritime circuit. It was an economically minor but strategically important port of call, governed through the DEIC headquarters in Batavia (Jakarta) from 1652 until the First British Occupation in 1795. The First British Occupation was largely a military presence, however, and the colony was passed back to The Netherlands (Batavian Republic) in 1802. In 1806 Britain decided to regain this strategic post on the route to the East, and eventually declared the Cape a Crown Colony in 1814.

At that time the population of Cape Town consisted of about 16,000 people, just over half of whom were either slaves or 'free blacks' (freed slaves or descendants of slave mothers) who had their origins in India, Asia and south-eastern Africa. They worked as labourers, commercial and domestic workers, and artisans. The Europeans had antecedents throughout the Company's recruitment network, but were predominantly German or Dutch.

In the last quarter of the eighteenth century the DEIC as a major Indian Ocean trading power declined rapidly, especially in relation to the British and North Americans plying the 'country trade' (Copeland 1990; Staniforth and Nash 1998: 6–7). Cape burghers were officially allowed to purchase their own ships and import goods from 1792. An opportunity thus arose for merchants in Cape Town to prosper and acquire leading positions in local government (Pama 1977: 9–14). Previously, the richest burghers had gained their wealth through servicing the DEIC as farmers and franchise-holders, but now major import houses emerged that were linked to British partners. Certainly a visitor in 1793 found the Capetonians' buying habits interesting enough to comment on, reporting that 'de kabinetten, stoelen, kasten en tafels zijn uit Holland, het glaswerk en tafelservies uit Engeland, en ider moet het duurste hebben' (the cabinets, chairs, cupboards and tables are from Holland, the glasswork and table services from England, and each must have the most expensive) (De Jong 1793: 140). Commercial restrictions favouring British goods were brought in after about 1815.

During the First British Occupation of the Cape strategic marriages were arranged between the daughters of the eighteenth-century official and social élite and eligible British military and merchant bachelors (Bird 1823: 170; Worden et al. 1998: 86–102, esp. 98). There was a resulting flurry of new goods, new money and renewed intimacy with Europe through merchants, immigrants and sojourners. The transitional years, from about 1790 until about 1820, saw a combination of modification of the cultural landscape, using monumental and official town planning and architecture, fashion and language, alongside variable manifestations in less overt areas, such as domestic life, house-hold furnishings and tablewares (Malan 1993a).

The Cape in the 1820s was still a heterogeneous, small-scale society, depen-dent for much of its cultural and material well being on passing ships, and it was also prey to fluctuating fortunes (Pama 1977: 2). While a vernacular language (that became formalised as Afrikaans in the twentieth century) and architecture may have developed during the eighteenth century, it displayed a regional colonial rather than a national quality (Malan 1993a). Robert Semple (visiting from Boston, USA in 1803) remarked that 'as yet the people of the Cape are only about to assume a character. They are neither English, nor French, nor Dutch. Nor do they form an original class as Africans, but a singular mix of all together which has not yet acquired a conscience, and is therefore almost impos-sible to be exactly represented' (quoted in Worden et al. 1998: 89).

In 1820, most of the free 'white' population of Cape Town itself was still of Dutch or German origin, but by the middle of the century 'Cape Town had become an identifiably British colonial city' (Worden et al. 1998: 153). British authorities now controlled official language, education and high culture and 'it became the rage to copy everything English' (Worden et al. 1998: 132). A group of immigrants, known as 'Indians' or 'Hindoos' – white officers and offi-cials retired from military service in the East – influenced middle-class taste, and the town was full of British soldiers and sailors. British entrepreneurs and working men were also being encouraged to emigrate to the colonies, and a variety of settler parties arrived, the best known being those who landed in the eastern Cape, 'the 1820 Settlers' (Winer and Deetz 1990; Worden et al. 1998: 88–97). At the same time, an indigenous, syncretic underclass cultural matrix was developing, centred in Cape Town (Bank 1991: 101). After the full eman-cipation of slaves in 1838, many newly freed people migrated from rural areas to join their brethren in the town. Irish, English and Scots craftsmen and working-class men and women added to their numbers.

In Cape Town's wine, cattle and wheat farming hinterland, and in more distant or less favourable areas, there were varying levels of response to the British regime by the local gentry, farmers and villagers. Some collaborated closely, most adopted what benefited them and others took action against inter-ference in their lives and their labour relations by 'trekking' to new pastures, and establishing 'Boer' republics such as the Orange Free State and Transvaal. Some rural gentry flaunted the new regime in more subtle ways. In 1820, for example, Hendrik Hendriks (who lived about 50km from Cape Town) defiantly built his new farmstead in old-fashioned late eighteenth-century Cape style and layout. However, by the time he died in 1848 the household incorporated a few 'British' elements such as mahogany bedroom furniture and cream-coloured tablewares. Further away from the port, the supply of ceramics depended initially on itinerant peddlers or periodic visits to Cape Town, and only in the 1840s did retail outfits establish stores along the much-improved wagon routes to the interior.

Though Cape Town's inhabitants had pointedly ignored the coronation of Queen Victoria in 1837 (Pama 1977: 1), they were apparently won over by the time she sent her son Prince Alfred to open the city's new harbour in 1860, and enthusiastically celebrated the Queen's Diamond Jubilee in 1897, reflecting 'a sense of imperial solidarity and order' (Worden *et al.* 1998: 263). Shortly afterwards, the South African (Boer) War (1899–1902) devastated such comfortable attitudes, but the outcome of the conflict also postponed 'Boer' nationalist ambitions and finally led to the Union of South Africa in 1910. By that time there was virtually nowhere in Southern Africa that lay beyond the reaches of the Second British Empire's trade, commerce, military patrols and missionary work, and – like Coca-Cola bottles in the twentieth century – Willow-patterned ceramics tangibly marked the global expanse of a nineteenth-century empire.

NINETEENTH-CENTURY CERAMICS AT THE CAPE

Until the twentieth century Cape Town did not have a fine ceramic or glass manufacturing industry of its own. Only coarse-bodied, low-fired earthenwares (mostly cooking pots) were made locally (Jordan 2000). Though the Cape Colony had been well supplied with a range of coarse and finer quality ceramics from Asia, the advent of British rule in 1795 coincided with the arrival of mass-produced ceramics from Britain. It is notable that the first British ceramics to arrive in the Cape were very ordinary export wares. We seldom find examples of the better quality British ceramics manufactured around the turn of the nineteenth century. This is also the case for eighteenth-century Asian porcelains excavated at the Cape, which are predominantly everyday quality and types (Klose 1997). It is also notable that even the poorest household in the Cape was using Chinese porcelain vessels during the DEIC period.

Until about 1800 or 1810 the majority of the porcelains used in the Cape were from China, with a few from Japan. Asian porcelains continued to be imported well into the nineteenth century, however, and specific nineteenth-century types include Chinese 'ginger jars' and tea and tablewares decorated with 'Canton' or 'Nanking' borders. These are examples of the type and quality of porcelain made for export to the United States (Mudge 1981; Wall 1994:

133; Staniforth and Nash 1998). Before 1800, most stonewares (except for glazed Asian stoneware storage jars) were salt-glazed wares from Europe (Germany). The small amount of white- and coloured-bodied refined earthenwares and refined stonewares were from England. After this date, and until the mid-1900s, the majority of fine ceramics in the Cape were of British manufacture, and household inventories indicate that they circulated quickly, at least among urban dwellers (Malan 1993a).

At the Cape, therefore, the relationship between imported Asian and European ceramics in particular correlates with changes in trade networks from the late eighteenth-century DEIC era through the early British occupation to the second half of the nineteenth century. The ceramics from the site of Sea Street (Table 11.1) clearly illustrate this process (Klose 1997: 142). The proportion of Asian porcelain to refined earthenwares in a collection is also significant for relative dating purposes.

Table 11.1 Ceramics excavated from Sea Street

James' House	Phase 1		Phase 2		Phase 3		Phase 4	
	MNV	% MNV	MNV	% MNV	MNV	% MNV	MNV	% MNV
Chinese export porcelain for European markets	8	61.5	333	39.0	72	18.0	29	20.0
Japanese export porcelain	–	–	13	1.5	4	1.5	1	0.7
Chinese porcelain for Asian market	4	30.8	100	11.7	17	4.3	5	3.4
European porcelain	–	–	–	–	–	–	1	0.7
Bone china	–	–	–	–	–	–	1	0.7
Asian stoneware	–	–	10	1.2	3	0.8	–	–
German stoneware	–	–	35	4.1	16	4.0	4	2.8
British stoneware	–	–	1	0.1	–	–	1	0.7
European tin-glazed earthenware	–	–	10	1.3	–	–	–	–
Euro/Cape manufactured coarse earthenware	1	7.7	90	10.6	29	7.3	5	3.4
Asian/African earthenware	–	–	1	0.1	–	–	–	–
Refined industrial wares (RIW) – cream coloured	–	–	163	19.1	139	35.0	50	34.5
RIW – pearlware	–	–	45	5.3	46	11.6	16	11.0
RIW – white wares	–	–	30	3.5	66	16.6	28	19.3
RIW – other	–	–	6	0.7	1	0.3	4	2.8
RIW – refined stonewares	–	–	3	0.4	1	0.3	–	–
Totals	13	100%	853	100%	397	100%	145	100%

For Cape sites, the post-1800 British ceramics can be divided into two main branches: mass-produced bone china ('English porcelain') and industrial white-bodied wares (cream-coloured ware, pearlware and industrial white wares). As Robin Hildyard (1999: 99) puts it, by the 1820s bone china 'had become, in fact, the porcelain equivalent of creamware'. Stronger, denser and white-bodied industrial wares (such as 'stone china' and 'ironstone') were developed in Britain from the beginning of the nineteenth century and had a long temporal span. 'White granite', a type of ironstone developed in the mid-nineteenth century, was manufactured specifically for export to North America but has not yet been identified in the Cape (Klose and Malan 2000).

Identification and chronology of nineteenth-century ceramics in Cape Town

Much of our work on nineteenth-century ceramics in Cape Town is based on a range of collections from urban sites that include samples of material that accumulated in neighbourhood middens. People disposed of their household debris close to their homes, often dumping in waterways, ditches or depressions in the vicinity. Features deliberately excavated for trash containment are rare occurrences before the end of the nineteenth century in Cape Town. Many of the town's streams and canals, and the shores of the bay, gradually clogged up with debris, sometimes dumped informally and sometimes as deliberate landfill.

Together, these ceramic collections span a hundred years, though none are tightly dated. The upper layers from Sea Street, at the edge of Table Bay, date from the later eighteenth into the early nineteenth century (Archaeology Contracts Office 1991a; Klose 1997). The Jackson's Yard collection was deposited at the bottom of a water course during the first four decades of the nineteenth century; and the Tennant Street collection accumulated around the middle of the nineteenth century (Archaeology Contracts Office 1996; Klose and Malan 2000). We also refer to collections from Harrington Street, Cape Town (deposited on the banks of a stream running down Canterbury Street in about 1860 (Archaeology Contracts Office 1991b; Malan 1993b)), and ceramics derived from urban developments in Pretoria, Transvaal (dating around 1900 to 1920), and surface collections from nineteenth-century sites in the Grahamstown area of the eastern Cape. Despite the imprecise temporal, social and economic contexts of the collections, we maintain that the ceramics from such sites can be meaningfully compared within Cape Town and around Southern Africa and also to contemporary sites throughout the Second British Empire.

We use a methodology and standard terminology applicable to analysing eighteenth- and nineteenth-century ceramic collections in the Cape in which our findings are expressed as 'ceramic profiles'. The analysis is based on frequencies and percentages of ceramic taxa, based on ware, decoration, form and function (Klose and Malan 2000). Though appreciating that there is 'no ready-made, one-size-fits-all analytical scheme' (Potter 1992: 20–1), this has enabled us to compare ceramic collections within the Cape, and has the potential for comparisons at a wider scale. 'Ceramic profiles' also play a role in contract work by providing a standard against which practitioners can quickly and simply recognise chronological periods in the field. The Sea Street 'ceramic profile' (Table 11.1) illustrates the arrival of British manufactured tea and table wares in Cape Town (Klose 1997: 49). The ceramics salvaged from Jackson's Yard (Table 11.2) represent the tail end of the Euro-Asian ceramic trade, together with British imports dating to the first decades of the nineteenth century. As a comparison, the Tennant Street site (Table 11.2) represents the ceramics in use during the middle of the nineteenth century (Klose and Malan 2000).

Ceramic collections derived from 'open' sites like Jackson's Yard and Tennant Street include intrusive sherds and detailed 'ceramic profiles' cannot be fully compared to 'sealed' and stratigraphically excavated sites like Sea Street. We have therefore tabulated table and tea wares and ceramic types that are definitely associated with the temporal span represented by these assemblages.

Lady Anne Barnard, wife of the Secretary to the first British Governor at the Cape, noticed 'brightly shining Staffordshire plates in their glass cupboard' at Pieter du Toit's farmstead near Wellington as early as 1797 (Lewin Robinson 1973: 17–18). We believe that at that date and place, however, the light was as likely to have been reflected off high-fired late eighteenth-century Chinese blue-and-white porcelain (the inspiration for Willow pattern). Continuing involvement in the Asian 'country trade' is evident in both Sea Street and Jackson's Yard. The Chinese porcelain wash basins and American-market enamelled wares are similar to those traded to Australia at the end of the eighteenth century (Staniforth and Nash 1998). At Jackson's Yard we still find Asian market ware 'coarse' porcelain bowls and shallow dishes. These were made in China for local eastern markets, and rice-based cuisine, but were traded by the DEIC and became a typical component of the eighteenth-century Cape ceramic signature (Klose and Malan 1999). At Jackson's Yard the Asian market wares comprise common forms and decorations manufactured in the eighteenth century, as well as later designs.

Tablewares were listed in detail in the household of Amelia Martha van de Kaap in 1821. They included silver, silver-plate, clear and blue glass, Asian porcelain, German stoneware ('keulsche potten') and numerous vessel types made of 'porcelyne als aarde' (porcelain as well as earthenware). There were also 'swart' and 'wit' earthenwares. 'Swart aarde' (black earthen) vessels (all teawares, such as jugs, bowls, sugar pots and teapots) had been listed in inventories since the 1790s, and were kept on display. For example, Catharine Verbeek placed hers in the 'galdery' (dining-room) wall-cupboard, a typical Cape feature designed to show off special possessions. In the Sea Street collection there were black basalt and Jackfield-type teapots, jugs and slop bowls – both black in appearance – and at Jackson's Yard there is a black basalt bowl. 'Swart aarde' was most probably black basalt (see Detweiler 1982).

Table 11.2 Ceramics (tea and tablewares) from Jackson's Yard and Tennant Street

	JY MNV	TS MNV
ASIAN PORCELAIN		
Chinese export	54	18
Japanese export	–	–
Chinese for Asian market (coarse/provincial)	22	5
Unprovenanced Asian porcelain	1	1
Sub total	77	24
EUROPEAN PORCELAIN		
Bone china		
white with gold	1	1
lustre and/or enamel	–	3
moulded	–	3
printed	–	1
lilac sprig	–	1
other/undecorated	1	3
Sub total	2	12
REFINED INDUSTRIAL WARES		
Refined white-bodied wares: combined		
cc ware, pearlware & industrial white wares		
painted (underglaze – u/g):		
blue only	17	1
'soft' colours	30	1
'harsh' colours	2	33
white & gold (painted/enam/print)	2	–
enamels (overglaze -o/g) –	4	–
cream-col.		
enamels + lustre	2	–
lustre only	2	1
printed overglaze – single	–	1
colour		
transfer printed (u/g):		
blue: Willow	40	97
blue: other	138	106
single colour	6	50
flow	–	28
multi-coloured	2	4
'print & paint' (o/g & u/g)	–	15
slide-on printed (decal) (o/g)	–	–
printed unidentified	–	2
industrial slipwares	40	78
sponged ware	–	9
lined – cream-coloured	5	–
lined – white ware	–	–
undecorated – transitional*	162	95
undecorated – white ware	–	–
modified edge (shell edged)	20	6

Table 11.2 continued

	JY MNV	TS MNV
relief decorated – rim only	1	3
Other	2	–
Undiagnostic	–	6
coloured glaze(s)	–	5
moulded + green glaze	–	–
relief moulded + painted coloured glazes	–	–
Refined coloured-bodied wares		
black glaze + red body		
'teapot' ware	1	2
lustre (red body)	–	3
stained body	–	–
Industrial refined stoneware		
English white salt-glazed	–	–
red stoneware	–	–
basalt/cane	1	–
jasper/jasper type	–	–
19th century:	1	1
plain/moulded/tinted		
Sub total	478	547
TOTALS	557	583

*'Transitional' denotes the mixture of late pale and almost white cream-coloured wares, pearlwares and early white wares found in the Cape in the first half of the nineteenth century

Blue-and-white Chinese export porcelain is still abundant in the Jackson's Yard collection, but it is now associated with almost identical forms of Staffordshire-made blue printed wares decorated with Willow pattern. This not only indicates the contemporary use of Asian and British ceramics of similar forms for tablewares – i.e. dining 'sets' – but also suggests that people at the Cape were combining blue and white 'Nanking' and 'Canton' decoration and early Willow-patterned wares together on the dining table. At Tennant Street there is considerably less blue and white Chinese export porcelain, which was probably still being used but not necessarily purchased. There are only residual Asian market ware bowls and dishes. The presence of Chinese porcelain 'ginger jars' is typical of a nineteenth-century Cape site. European bone china at Tennant Street is represented by white and gold and lilac sprig decorated sherds. There is white and gold at Jackson's Yard, but no lilac sprig.

There is a chronological progression in the appearance of the rims of pale cream-coloured earthenware plates. At Sea Street the plates in early levels have 'modified' edges, i.e. royal pattern and feather-edged rims, together with some with plain rims. By the upper level of Sea Street, the 'modified' rims have all but disappeared. The sequence tends towards completely plain rims, which we subdivide into raised (or 'Bath'), concave and flat, but the relative proportions of these types do not appear to change through time (Don Pottery 1983: 4). For shell-edged plates there is no obvious sequence. There are shell-edged plates and dishes at all three sites, though in diminishing amounts through time. They are mostly blue, but we find some green. The plates at Sea Street have rococo and scalloped edges but no straight-edged plates, Jackson's Yard and Tennant Street have all three types, and Tennant Street also has one plate with a straight edge but without any moulding at all. Embossed plate rims occur at Tennant Street on semi-vitreous white industrial ware and are a sign of the later period.

A few of the cream-coloured plates at Jackson's Yard are marked with impressed Spode marks with impressed numbers, which date to before 1833 (Copeland 1997: 51), and one has an impressed James & Ralph Clews mark, used between 1818 and 1834 (Godden 1972a: 53). To date, the earliest unambiguous documented evidence for the presence of cream-coloured earthenware in Cape Town is the household inventory of Hendrik Justinus de Wet. De Wet was the third-generation Cape-born son of a well-established family and had been president of the Burgher Council and member of the Council of Justice. At his death in 1802 the family and about twenty slaves lived on the corner of fashionable Heerengraght and Castle Streets in a three-storey house. De Wet was also a trader, storing large amounts of goods on the third floor. Cape retailers operated out of their homes and, as a British visitor described them, 'the wholesale Shops are called Stores, they are usually up one Story and make no shew on the outside' (Eaton 1818). 'Witte aarde' as well as porcelain was listed in De Wet's 'porcelain kamer', and 'witte aarde' was stored for family use in the household pantry.

What is interesting at the Cape is the status of cream-coloured ware, even from its first introduction. The inventories show that it was invariably kept in the pantry or storerooms rather than on display. The cream-coloured wares in De Wet's pantry are all dining vessels – soup tureens, serving dishes, table plates, pots and a cruet – probably like those illustrated in the Don Pottery pattern book (Don Pottery 1983). Lieutenant-Colonel Hendrik Cordes, a widower who died in 1804 at the Colonel's quarters at the Castle (the military headquarters), had 'wit aarde' listed in his pantry. In this case, however, the vessels included a tea and coffee set. At Jackson's Yard, as in the majority of the documents, the pale cream-coloured wares are mostly plates, with some bowls and serving dishes, jugs and chamber pots. By the time of Tennant Street there are only a few pieces of pale – almost white – cream-coloured earthenware. The other non-porcelain white-bodied wares from Tennant Street are generally more highly fired refined industrial ware and lighter in colour.

The majority of decorated refined earthenwares at Jackson's Yard are still obviously pearlwares, but by this period, for analytical purposes, we give precedence to identifying the type of decoration rather than the body. We recognise early pearlware at the Cape through a combination of decoration, the dry lightness of the body and blue-tinted glaze. By Tennant Street the pearlware bodies are developing into white wares, so the vitrification and 'blue gather' are no longer reliable identification tools.

Almost all the 'markers' we use in recognising and analysing blue printed wares only produce relative dates. There is no reliable way of dating blue patterns through manufacturing techniques, nor can blue colour be used except that pale blue and flow blue are relatively later developments (Copeland 1990: 13). The presence of certain items can provide a more precise *terminus post quem*. For example, there are documented dates for first use of certain patterns (see, for instance, Samford's study (1997)), and Copeland (1990: 12) points out that small tea plates were not introduced into tea services until after 1840.

Decoration also becomes more significant because of the 'Willow pattern factor'. On Cape sites we recognise a sequence based on the presence and/or proportions of Willow versus floral/scenic patterns and the occasional eastern scene, in combination with certain vessel forms, and the presence/absence of certain hand-painted blue decoration and printed chinoiserie motifs. Painted blue chinoiserie precedes painted blue flowers and leaves, and printed chinoiserie patterns appear before printed floral patterns with birds and rural scenes. Willow pattern gradually dominates the blue printed wares and is then joined by flow blue.

It is interesting to contrast the ceramic profiles of Sea Street and Jackson's Yard with Diana Wall's study of ceramics excavated from New York sites dating from the 1790s to the 1840s (Wall 1994: 92–208). The dominant choice of wares and designs within chronological periods in New York are: early – royal pattern earthenware vessels; middle – blue or green shell-edge earthenware dishes; and later – 'Canton' pattern Asian porcelain tablewares. Wall came to firm conclusions about the relationship between decoration of ceramic tablewares and the changing mode of eating in New York households. During the earlier period (from 1780s) food was highly visible, presented in plain open dishes on a table where quantity was more important than specialisation. During the first decade of the nineteenth century, women elaborated and specialised family meals, using plain white, completely undecorated plates only for the most mundane meals, but shell-edge for more important occasions. Then, while there was still some focus on food contents, vessel rims became highly ornate. By the 1820s, courses were more numerous (minimum of three) and specialised, and dishes served as symbols in a ritual and food was kept covered until served to diners. Intensification of decoration expressed changes in the meaning of a meal, that is decorative lids covering the dishes and busy blue chinoiserie decoration replaced food in importance. Chinese 'Canton' porcelain, however, was reserved for special occasions (Wall 1994: 147–9).

Robert Percival's, admittedly jingoistic, comments suggest that there were also changes in Cape Town, which may be reflected in the ceramics in Cape sites:

On the first introduction of the English officers at the Cape into the Dutch houses . . . they were for a considerable time obliged to conform to their hours, customs, and manner of living, which certainly was very unpleasant to Englishmen . . . By degrees, however, . . . alterations took place, and our countrymen persuaded the Dutch to adopt more of the English customs . . . so that there was a mixture of manners half English, half Dutch, in the hours of dining, and in the mode of dressing the victuals. . . .

The victuals at the Dutch houses are latterly [in 1801] much better dressed, a great deal of that stinking butter and grease left out, and at least two or three dishes roasted and boiled *a la mode Angloise*. The breakfast hour was altered to 9, dinner to 4, and supper to 10.

(Percival 1804: 257–8, 267)

Willow-pattern ceramics at the Cape are tablewares. Unlike the cream-coloured tablewares, which look different to Asian porcelain even if they include similar forms and sizes, the first Willow-pattern tableware vessels are visually similar to, and are combined with, blue and white Asian porcelain. British potters purposely copied Chinese porcelain decorations and shapes to fill the void left by the decline in imported Chinese porcelain at the end of the eighteenth century. At the same time, Spode and others cleverly exploited an opportunity to produce matching but cheaper replacements for broken Asian porcelain (Copeland 1990: 12–13). We also have evidence from Sea Street for a Staffordshire saucer decorated in a matching design to an enamelled Chinese porcelain saucer.

British tea sets, however, are completely different to the Chinese export porcelain cups and saucers used at the Cape, introducing new decorations and new forms and sizes. For example, tewares of the earlier period include black basalt vessels and painted and printed pearlware sets, with distinctive cup shapes and sizes. We also see a contrast between delicate and pretty hand-painted refined earthenware tewares produced in the early nineteenth century and those produced for mass export after about 1815. At Jackson's Yard there is some chinoiserie decoration in pale blue on cups and saucers, but the dominant decoration is a range of English rural scenes and flowers and birds with floral rims (mostly unmarked), and some floral hand-painted wares. The vessels are small and medium bowls, saucers, large handled cups and a teapot.

The earliest white on gold tewares at the Cape were bone china. Later, similar gilded tea services were made of white-bodied refined industrial wares. Less expensive versions were produced by British manufacturers by the mid-nineteenth century, when suitable industrial white wares and cheaper gilding techniques were developed. Gilding on white vessels was recorded in the Cape as early as 1831, in Francis Hawkins's deceased estate at The Vineyard, Newlands. He had a white and gilt tea set and a 'large and handsome gilt edge and handled dinner and desert set'. This fulsome description suggests that the appraisers were evaluating a type still uncommon in the Cape.

At Tennant Street there is predictably less chinoiserie teaware and there are still a few English rural scenes, but there the tableware is predominantly Willow pattern, and frequently marked 'stone china' or 'ironstone'. We have noticed that the body of many so-called 'stone' wares are as porous as common quality earthenwares. There is also the readily identifiable flow blue found on matching cups, saucers and plates, and apparently purchased in sets with a range of cup sizes. After about 1840, lilac sprig, lustre and gilding was used to decorate bone china used on the tea table at the Cape (Klose and Malan 2000).

Colours other than blue only become common by the Tennant Street period in the Cape, when there is a range of colour printed tableware. Another major group of ceramics that provides us with broad 'markers' based on colour are the hand-painted and industrial slipware bowls. There is a shift from natural earthy to the new brighter harsh colours. At Jackson's Yard, therefore, we find the 'soft early' colours, used on pearlware cups and small bowls, saucers and a large 'gebloemde' (flowered) bowl, but there are only two sherds with 'later' reds. At Tennant Street the proportions are reversed (Klose and Malan 2000). Muted colours such as browns and tans predominate at Jackson's Yard for lined, mocca, finger-trailed and blobby slip decorations on bowls and two handled mugs or jugs. At Tennant Street a bright blue is noticeable in industrial slipware decorations, and sponged polychrome decoration is now present.

Reconciling the documented and excavated records

The household inventories are often frustratingly imprecise records of decoration and vessel form. A 'gebloemde aarde' ('flowered earthen') tea set, listed in the 'galdery' of a Stellenbosch home in 1817, could be hand-painted or printed. Frans Bresler of Grave Street had 'delph' serving vessels, plates and a jug. It is not clear what these were made of, or if the description denotes a particular design. They were no doubt made from a type of blue-and-white refined earthenware and were probably hand-painted pearlwares. In 1838, Thomas Hunter, who established the first iron foundry in Cape Town, had 'chinaware' teaware – probably bone china – and 'delph' tableware, further defined as earthen and blue earthen. The Breslers also had a 'black earthen' breakfast set. Baron Willem Ferdinand van Reede van Oudtshoorn, residing at a peri-urban estate named Saasveld, chose a combination of Chinese porcelain and 'Staffordshire green-and-white' table services in 1822. What is significant, perhaps, is that the household appraisers all chose to distinguish between black, green and blue ceramics.

We have noticed that the brightly coloured and gilded bone china tea and coffee sets of the early nineteenth century (see Berthoud 1990) are seldom evident in the archaeological record at the Cape. There are some in a collection from an '1820 British Settler' household at Salem, in the eastern Cape (Winer 1994: 278–83). Perhaps this family brought such wares with them directly from England. Though there is a tendency towards relegating ceramic appraisal to vague categories of 'sets', 'services', 'china' or 'crockery' during the nineteenth century, some specific ceramic types are occasionally listed in the documents. Samuel Hudson, who decided to list his possessions in his journal (Hudson 1826), first came to the Cape in 1796 as general factotum to the Secretary to the first British Governor and later decided to return to work in the customs office. He described his tableware partly by origin and partly by decoration: 1 blue table service, 1 dozen French coffee cups, 1 (unspecified) tea and coffee set, 1 Worcester china dessert service, china plates, 'basons' and butter pots, 1 dozen Batavia saucers and 10 Queensware pots. 'Batavia' is an English term for Chinese export porcelain decorated with a brown glaze exterior, which is commonly found on eighteenth-century Cape sites. Thomas Lawson, magistrate of Albany and living in Grahamstown in the eastern Cape in 1828, had a dinner set of 'stone china' that was carefully itemised by vessel, an unspecified dessert set and tea set, glass, plate and silver dishes, and a 'blue earthen' table and tea service. He also had two 'stone' jugs. Relief-moulded refined stoneware vessels are found at both Jackson's Yard and Tennant Street. They were mass-produced for British consumers and exported from the 1820s (Henrywood 1992: 19–24).

A fashionable household inventory of the 1840s, such as that of Maria Berendina Becker (wife of a Swedish immigrant, Jacob Letterstedt) at Mariandahl, Newlands, had table, tea and breakfast services of white and gold, a tea and coffee service of purple and gold, as well as blue table and dessert services. There were finger glasses, custard glasses and silver tea and coffee sets. Silver-plated covered serving dishes and hot water dishes kept the food warm, and there was a 'compositie' teapot and milk jug. This inventory reminds us that the British also brought with them a popular fashion for silver-plate tableware, which seldom reaches the archaeological record. Silver and plate largely replaced the, often colourful, Asian porcelains (Japanese and Chinese enameled wares) that had been displayed in glass-fronted cabinets in the Cape. Cut and pressed glassware became widely available too. In 1839, William Robertson, residing at Haasendaal in the smart suburb of Rondebosch, kept his 'plate' tableware locked in his dressing room, but displayed a blue Tournai (European porcelain) dinner service of 111 pieces in the dining room. His neighbour, Carel Becker of Wolmunster, sported all his silver in the dining room, but the bone-china gilt-edged table and tea services and various dinner services were relegated to the pantry.

It is important, too, to place these artefacts in the context of all the other things people could buy, sell and own. Ceramics may be far more important to historical archaeologists today than they were to the people who used them in the past (Potter 1992). Inventory studies can be regarded as over-emphasising the possessions of the propertied, even though rich and poor households alike were recorded in the Cape. It must be pointed out that the poorer household often had very little ceramic tableware at all, and it was seldom in the form of sets or services. For example, the Beckers had five children, but their Long Street house inventory listed only five plates and three dishes in their front room, and Christina Kreil, the widow Visser (a 'freeblack' fisherman), had three dishes and six plates in the 'passage', and four plates, five small 'basons' and a single small plate in the front room. The *chineesch* Asamko's possessions, when auctioned after his death, included four earthen pots, three small pots, a dozen saucers, nine cups, a bowl, twenty plates and four dishes, while the Burgers, a dirt-poor couple with five children living on a farm near Clanwilliam, made do with five dishes, three small bowls, a saucer, milk jug and pewter teapot.

Mass-production and consumption in the later nineteenth century

The first Great Exhibition of the Industry of All Nations, held at the specially constructed Crystal Palace in London in 1851, epitomised the scale, variety and popular appeal of mass-produced items (Snyder 1994: 33–4). These were strongly marketed to the *nouveaux riches* and middle classes, skilled craftsmen and wage-labourers alike. English ceramics from the Staffordshire district dominated the market in the United States and Canada from the late eighteenth century until late in the nineteenth century (Schiffer 1987: 103). In the latter half of the nineteenth century more than a third of Staffordshire exports were shipped to the United States, with the remainder going to Canada, Australia and other areas of the British Empire (Godden 1972b: 7). The 1860s in Britain saw another major transformation of mass-produced ceramics and glass objects as industry became more mechanised. By this time a wide range of factories were in hot competition for the home and overseas markets and so manufacturing techniques, marketing and transport systems were more sophisticated.

The period 1860 to 1880 marks the height of 'Victorian' taste for an enormous range of styles and shapes for every type of object. Mail-order purchasing through catalogues became possible from Cape Town, especially for items of mass-production from Britain's industrial centres, such as architectural components, household and table wares and Birmingham trinkets. By 1880, department stores like Garlicks, Thorne, Stuttaford & Co. and J.W. Jagger & Co., and other emporia, were well established in Cape Town (Picard 1969). They printed their own versions of British catalogues to publicise available imports. Unfortunately, however, we do not have the equivalent household inventory sources for the period after 1850, so our contextual understanding of ceramics in daily use is limited.

The significant 'markers' of the later nineteenth century are based on developments in mass-produced decoration, such as slide-on (decal) prints and the presence of printed Japanese porcelains. Other typical decorations are lines around the outer rims of plain white well-vitrified tablewares, brightly coloured cut-sponge 'printed' and hand-painted *kommetjes* (small bowls) and serving vessels, open floral and geometric designs and asymmetrical ('Japanese') motifs (particularly popular in the 1880s). Brown, pink, grey and green transfer prints are present. Bone china with central clover leaf design is found on late nineteenth-century to early twentieth-century sites, as are vessels decorated only with thin gold lines or washed with a broad pink band or decorated in gold, silver or copper lustre. Again, these are everyday ceramics that were widely available (Bosomworth 1991; Klose and Malan 2000). There are also increasing numbers of back-marked sherds with datable makers' names and registration marks.

These later nineteenth-century ceramics are typified in collections excavated from Harrington Street in Cape Town (Malan 1993b) and Melrose House in Pretoria (Van Schalkwyk *et al.* 1995). Most of the more substantial ceramic collections from this period remain unpublished. For instance, contract excavations in Minaar Street, Pretoria, Transvaal (Anton von Vollenhoven, personal communication) and at Alphen, in Constantia, Cape Town, produced well preserved collections of late nineteenth- to early twentieth-century ceramics. A town dump excavated in Grahamstown includes many examples of commemorative and institutional wares typical of the turn of the twentieth century (Lita Webley, personal communication).

Explorations of regional identity

The extent of our research into nineteenth-century ceramics at the Cape has reached the stage of producing more questions than answers. We have described the arrival of 'Staffordshire wares' in a 'Dutch' Cape, and by the middle of the nineteenth century they had become ubiquitous. In 1814 the Cape was declared a British Colony and could be expected to absorb an increasing volume of its products, but why did British ceramics first arrive so long after their appearance on the North American market? Was it choice or restraints of trade? We have pointed out that the Cape ceramic profile of the eighteenth century is generally 'Eurasian', but we desperately need comparative collections from the East to test whether this is a broader 'Indian Ocean rim' pattern, and to track the introduction of British ceramics to India and the East Indies. There also appears to be a clear distinction between the density of ceramics on the ground and in sites of the early period and the years after about 1860. We are not sure if this is a local pattern or linked to British ceramic production and marketing, and global distribution.

On the other hand, the documentary record may have some clues for future investigation. On a sheep farm near Uitenhage called Honeyville, the immigrant William Tyssen built a house with parlour and two special-purpose bedrooms. In 1848 he was using a formal service of earthenware (three vegetable dishes, a dozen dinner plates, a dozen cheese plates, six soup plates, four egg-cups and a butter pot), which was stored in the kitchen. Tyssen's 'Boer' contemporaries, the van Wyks of Cafferkuilsrivier, Riversdale, also sheep farmers, had four pots and two dozen plates in the main (living- and bed-) room of their two-roomed house. Perhaps further research could reveal if there is in fact any difference between 'Boer' and 'Brit' households.

Similarly, the three cooks in the de Wet household (1802) were slave men imported from Ceylon, Madagascar and Mozambique, and the cook and baker in the van Reenen household (1827) came from Mozambique. What implications does the long tradition of domestic slavery have on the choice of Cape kitchen and tableware in the early nineteenth century, compared to, for instance, Australia? Since Cape cooking still today retains its Indian Ocean flavour, why were the porcelain saucer-dishes commonly used at the Cape not replaced or supplemented by the British and European-made ones which were made especially for the eastern market and rice-based cuisine? Scottish and Dutch potteries specially produced brightly sponge-printed and painted saucer-dishes for the eastern market in the same forms and combinations ('nests') that the Asian market porcelain kilns previously supplied. For example, those labelled 'sponge rice dishes' and 'painted rice dishes' in the Silber and Fleming catalogue of about 1883 (Bosomworth 1991: 180) are identical to a set purchased by one of the authors from a Sri Lankan junk shop in 1997. To date, we have not identified a single such saucer-dish at the Cape.

The majority of refined industrial ware vessels at the Cape are plates and bowls. We have found it difficult to ascertain the function of these bowls, especially where there are many incomplete vessels. Cape sites of all types and in all areas produce numerous *kommetjes* decorated in 'industrial slipware' and 'painted harsh colours' (*boerenbont*), especially after mid-century, but their function is ambiguous. Lynne Sussman (1997: 75) found scarce evidence for their use in North America, but concluded that they were 'appropriate for taverns and cottages'. We find them on all sites. Do these bowls indicate an equal preference for bowls or plates for eating at the Cape? Bowls can be associated with communal meals, where a central dish such as stew was served, or they could be for food preparation rather than consumption. They are similar to porringers, but lack the horizontal handles that typify that form. Were these handle-less bowls also used for drinking tea, coffee and chocolate, as in continental Europe today, or were they merely ubiquitous and multipurpose utensils? Why did they become an icon for Afrikaner folk culture during the twentieth century? For example, among the ceramics made in England and Europe to commemorate the Great Trek, in 1938 and 1988, many were in the form of *kommetjes*.

What, if any, relationship do the nineteenth-century refined industrial ware bowls of *kommetje* size have with the eighteenth-century Asian-market coarse porcelain bowls of similar or slightly larger size that are common on eighteenth-century Cape sites? Christiaan Jörg (1982: 194) has noted the lack of studies of the 'social function' of porcelains, and so this question will require thorough research into both eighteenth- and nineteenth-century sources.

CONCLUSION

The ceramic collections, echoed by the inventories, demonstrate a clear transition from Asian porcelain-dominated tea and table wares deposited before 1800 to those containing the British transfer-printed ware signature of the nineteenth century. This transition is linked to the change from DEIC trade to that of the Second British Empire, but is not simply a matter of a change of regime. There are more subtle things going on in the households of the Cape affecting the way ceramics filter into cupboards and stores. The documentary evidence from inventories provides contextual evidence for the use of ceramics at the Cape and the relationship between different types of wares. Not distinguishable in the documents, however, are the hand-painted chinoiserie and sponged or industrial slipware vessels. In the Cape the history of cream-coloured wares, pearlwares and industrial slipwares relies heavily on excavated evidence.

We also raise some broader questions with reference to anomalies in our excavated and documented collections. Is the distinction we make between pre-1840 and post-1860 a local or general observation? Why do we not find early Staffordshire wares and rarely see 'élite' British/European ceramics at the Cape? Does the 'Willow-pattern factor' apply outside the Cape? What are the proportions of porcelains to British wares in nineteenth-century Asian sites? How were bowls and dishes used in Asia? These questions can only be answered through discussion with our colleagues from the other colonies of the Second British Empire, and through comparison of similarly analysed collections from Europe, the East and other colonies.

While demonstrating the fruitful potential of integrating the different resources of information about ceramics at the Cape, we need considerably more systematically researched comparative information from here and elsewhere. Work is progressing on the early nineteenth-century collections, but we lack the evidence necessary to take interpretation any further. In particular we require archaeologically excavated, well-provenienced, single-household collections. One restriction is that physical separation based on race, class or address was not clear-cut in nineteenth-century Cape Town (Ross 1989) and there is a strong tradition of 'handing down' unwanted ceramics. Another is that there were no newspaper advertisements or specialised shops until after about 1820, which limits our source of documentary business records. The later period, however, remains a rich untapped resource for ceramics research.

REFERENCES

Archaeology Contracts Office (1991a) Archaeological work at Sea Street, Cape Town. Unpublished report, Archaeology Contracts Office, University of Cape Town.
—— (1991b) Archaeological excavations at 109 Harrington Street, The Granite Lodge. Unpublished report, Archaeology Contracts Office, University of Cape Town.
—— (1996) Phase 1 archaeological assessment of open State land in District Six. Unpublished report prepared for the Transitional Metropolitan Substructure of Cape Town.
Bank, A. (1991) The Decline of Urban Slavery at the Cape, 1806 to 1843, Communications No. 22. Centre for African Studies, University of Cape Town.
Beaudry, M. (2000) Discussant's comments: archaeology of the Second British Empire, Society of Historical and Underwater Archaeology Conference, Québec, Canada.
Berthoud, M. (1990) A Compendium of British Cups. Great Britain: Micawber Publications.
Bird, W.W. (1823) The State of the Cape of Good Hope in 1822. London: John Murray.
Bosomworth, D. [1883] (1991) The Victorian Catalogue of Household Goods. London: Studio Editions.
Copeland, R. (1990) Spode's Willow Pattern and Other Designs After the Chinese. London: Studio Vista.
—— (1997) Spode and Copeland Marks and Other Relevant Intelligence. London: Studio Vista.
De Jong, C. (1793) Reizen Naar de Kaap de Goede Hoop, Ierland en Noorwegen in de Jaaren 1791 tot 1797. MS in African Studies Library, University of Cape Town.
Detweiler, S.G. (1982) George Washington's Chinaware. New York: Harry N. Abrams Inc.

Don Pottery [1807] (1983) *Don Pottery Pattern Book.* Doncaster: Doncaster Library Service.
Eaton, S.N. (1818) Journal. MSB 177, National Library of South Africa, Cape Town.
Godden, G. (1972a) *The Handbook of British Pottery and Porcelain Marks.* London: Barrie and Jenkins.
—— (1972b) *Jewitt's Ceramic Art of Great Britain, 1800–1900.* London: Barrie and Jenkins.
Hall, M. (2000) *Archaeology and the Modern World: Colonial Transcripts in South Africa and the Chesapeake.* London: Routledge.
Henrywood, R.K. (1992) *Jugs: Shire Album 287.* Princes Risborough: Shire Publications Limited.
Hildyard, R. (1999) *European Ceramics.* London: V & A Publications.
Hudson, S.E. (1826) Inventory: furniture, books, pictures, linnen, plate of S.E. Hudson, 1826. A602 vol. A11, National Archives, Cape Town.
Jordan, S. (2000) The 'utility' of coarse earthenware: potters, pottery production and identity at the Dutch colonial Cape of Good Hope, South Africa (1652–1795). Unpublished PhD dissertation, Rutgers, State University of New Jersey.
Jörg, C.A. (1982) *Porcelain and the Dutch China trade.* The Hague: Marthinus Nijhoff.
Klose, J. (1997) Analysis of ceramic assemblages from four Cape historical sites dating from the late seventeenth century to the mid-nineteenth century. Unpublished MA dissertation, University of Cape Town.
Klose, J. and Malan, A. (1999) Ceramics of the southwestern Cape 1652 to 1900: A guide to the analysis and interpretation of ceramic assemblages excavated from archaeological sites. Historical Archaeology Research Group Handbook No. 1 (2nd edn), University of Cape Town.
—— (2000) The ceramic signature of the Cape in the nineteenth century, with particular reference to the Tennant Street site, Cape Town. *South African Archaeological Bulletin* 55: 49–59.
Lawrence, S. (1999) The nineteenth century British diaspora. Unpublished paper presented in symposium 'The archaeology of the British' at the Fourth World Archaeology Conference, Cape Town, January.
Lewin Robinson, A.M. (ed.) (1973) *The Letters of Lady Anne Barnard to Henry Dundas from the Cape and Elsewhere, 1793–1803, Together with Her Journal of a Tour into the Interior and Certain Other Letters.* Cape Town: A.A. Balkema.
Malan, A. (1993a) Households of the Cape, 1750 to 1850: inventories and the archaeological record. Unpublished PhD thesis, University of Cape Town.
—— (1993b) Catalogue of artefacts of the 1860s displayed at the National Monuments Council, Harrington Street, Cape Town.
Mudge, J.M. (1981) *Chinese Export Porcelain for the American Trade, 1785–1835.* E. Brunswick: Associated University Presses.
Pama, C. (1977) *Bowler's Cape Town: Life at the Cape in Early Victorian Times, 1834–1868.* Cape Town: Tafelberg.
Percival, R. (1804) *An Account of the Cape of Good Hope by Captain Robert Percival.* London: C. & R. Baldwin.
Picard, H.J. (1969) *Grand Parade: The Birth of Greater Cape Town, 1850–1913.* Cape Town: C. Struik.
Potter, P.B. (1992) Middle range theory, ceramics and capitalism in nineteenth century Rockbridge County, Virginia. In B.J. Little (ed.), *Text-aided archaeology*, 9–23. Boca Raton: CRC Press.
Ross, R. (1989) Structure and culture in pre-industrial Cape Town: a survey of knowledge and ignorance. In W. James and M. Simons (eds), *The Angry Divide: Social And Economic History of the Western Cape*, 40–6. Cape Town: David Philip.
Said, E.W. (1994) *Culture and Imperialism.* New York: Vintage Books.

Samford, P. (1997) Response to a market: dating English underglaze transfer-printed wares. *Historical Archaeology* 31(2): 1–30.

Schiffer, M.B. (ed.) (1987) *Advances in Archaeological Method and Theory*. San Diego, CA: Academic Press.

Snyder, J.B. (1994) *Historic Flow Blue*. Atglen, PA: Schiffer Publishing Ltd.

Staniforth, M and Nash, M. (1998) *Chinese Export Porcelain from the Wreck of the Sydney Cove (1797)*. Australian Institute for Maritime Archaeology, Special Publication No. 12.

Sussman, L. (1997) Mocha, Banded, Cat's Eye, and other factory-made slipware. *Studies in Northeast Historical Archaeology* 1.

Van Schalkwyk, J.A., Meyer, C.J., Pelser, A. and Plug, I. (1995) Images of the social life and household activities at Melrose House. *Research by the National Cultural History Museum* 4: 81–100.

Wall, D. DiZ. (1994) *The Archaeology of Gender: Separating the Spheres in Urban America*. New York: Plenum Press.

Winer, M. (1994) Landscapes of power: British material culture of the Eastern Cape frontier, South Africa, 1820–1860. Unpublished PhD dissertation, University of California at Berkeley.

Winer, M. and Deetz, J. (1990) The transformation of British culture in the eastern Cape, 1820–1860. *Social Dynamics* 16(1): 55–75.

Worden, N., van Heyningen, E. and Bickford-Smith, V. (1998) *Cape Town: the Making of a City*. Cape Town: David Philip Publishers.

Inventories are filed at the National Archives in Cape Town (CA) under the Master of the Orphan Chamber, MOOC8 (deceased estates) and MOOC7/1 (wills and appraisals), and also under STB/1 (Stellenbosch region) and MOIC (insolvencies). Estate auctions are located in MOOC10.

Date	Reference	Name	Place
1800	MOOC8/23.12	Catharina Verbeek	6 Plein Street, CT
1802	MOOC8/23.40_	Hendrik Justinus de Wet	14 Heerengragth, CT
1804	MOOC8/24.11	Lt Col. Hendrik Cordes	Colonel's Quarters, Castle, CT
1817	MOOC8/33.35	Maria Groenewald	Stellenbosch
1820	MOOC10/35.82	The *chineesch* Azamko	Cape Town
1821	MOOC8/36.8	Amelia Martha van de Kaap	37 Strand Street, CT
1822	MOOC8/37.51	Baron Willem Ferdinand van Reede van Oudsthoorn	Saasveld, Gardens, CT
1825	MOOC8/40.23	Christina Kreil	15 Riebeeck Street, CT
1825	MOOC8/44.7	Frans Bresler	14 Grave Street, CT
1828	MOOC 8/44.10	Thomas Lawson	Grahamstown
1831	MOOC8/46.44	Francis Hawkins	The Vineyard, Newlands, CT
1838	MOOC7/1/144.29	Thomas Hunter	56 Longmarket Street, CT
1838	MOOC7/1/144.97	Carel Becker	61 Long Street, CT
1838	MOOC7/1/144.129	Cornelis Burger	Langefontein, Clanwilliam
1839	MOOC7/1/150.19	William Robertson	Haasendaal, Rondebosch, CT
1844	MOOC7/1/178.31	Carel Becker	Wolmunster, Rosebank, CT
1847	MOOC7/1/190.134	William Tyssen	Honeyville, Uitenhage
1848	MOOC7/1/192.61	Johannes van Wyk	Cafferkuilsrivier, Riversdale
1848	MOOC7/1/193.59	Maria Berendina Becker	Mariendahl, Newlands, CT
1848	MOOC7/1/194.113	Hendrik Hendriks	Land-en-Zee Zigt, Somerset West

12 At home in the bush: material culture and Australian nationalism

Susan Lawrence

INTRODUCTION

At home and abroad, popular representations of Australian identity have come to emphasise the bush as a central aspect underpinning Australian character. Most recently, this was expressed during the opening ceremonies of the 2000 Olympics in Sydney, which featured a choreographed assembly of horse-riding bush men and women clad in Akubra hats and long dri-za-bone oilskin coats. Such stereotypes draw on a pervasive mythology of tough individuals in harsh conditions, mateship and, above all, a particular version of masculinity. The bush legend emerged at the end of the nineteenth century during a period of intense nationalism and political debate that culminated in Australian federation in 1901. Although widely criticised, the stereotype has been and continues to be widely influential in shaping cultural discourse.

Critiques of the bush legend have largely focused on the perspectives and backgrounds of those responsible for its popularisation. The urban base, sexist and racist attitudes, and misogynism of its leading proponents have all been singled out as problematic (Davison 1978; White 1981; Lake 1986; Goodman 1994). Few, however, have sought to get beyond the representation in order to explore the dimensions, material or otherwise, of bush life itself. The material traces of nineteenth-century bush life stand in marked contrast to the legend which purports to describe it. Archaeological evidence from nineteenth-century rural sites in Australia indicates the commonplace usage of refined ceramic tablewares and other accoutrements of simple but respectable domestic dining etiquette. The inspiration for such practices can be found in contemporary British and colonial notions of decency, hard work and self-improvement that characterised the Victorian age.

This chapter seeks to document aspects of the material worlds of bush settlers, and to examine factors that led to the erasure of elements of domestic respectability and femininity within nationalist discourses of identity. These factors are related to the positioning of white, male bush workers as quintessential Australians. 'Australian', as defined in the terms of the stereotype, provided an obvious contrast to the more mundane, and more British, character of Australian colonial settlement, and indicates the deliberate creation of a demonstrably non-British iconography at a time when Australian nationalism was burgeoning. In order to establish a distinctive Australian identity, some of the realities of bush life had to be written over and forgotten.

THE BUSHMAN AND HIS CRITICS

'The bush' is a catch-all phrase with wide currency in Australia. Initially it referred specifically to patches of thick vegetation and generally to uncleared country beyond the first British coastal settlements. The meaning of 'bush' gradually became enlarged to encompass all the rural territory between the cities and the 'outback', the latter being the stereotypically harsh and unsettled centre of the Australian continent. Neither metropolitan nor wilderness, the bush is the region of farms, forests, mines, and provincial towns and villages that supports Australia's primary and export industries. More than that though, the bush has mythic stature as the 'true' Australia, and the source of what it means to be Australian. This is despite the fact that Australia is one of the most urbanised countries in the world, and that since the first British settlement in 1788 most of its settler population has lived in cities on the coastal fringe.

Much of the iconic power of the bush is epitomised by the rugged bushman (Ward 1958), long a figure of Australian fiction and popularised overseas in such films as *The Man from Snowy River* and *Crocodile Dundee*. Ward traced the origins of this image to the traditions of itinerant bush workers, beginning with convict shepherds and already largely defined by the time of the gold rushes in the 1850s (1958: 167). From the convict period the trajectory of the bushman ideal could be traced through gold miners, shearers and finally the heroic Anzac soldiers of the First World War. Forged in a physical environment that demanded toughness and strength of body and spirit, the bushman was unfailingly loyal to mates, independent and egalitarian, eschewing and deriding notions of superiority by birth or fortune, and avowedly anti-authoritarian. The bushman 'swears hard and consistently, gambles heavily and often, and drinks deeply on occasion' (Ward 1958: 2). Rough and unpolished, the bushman was genuine, his character undisguised by the veneer of refinement and manners. The bushman was also by definition male, which Schaffer (Schaffer 1988) argues has symbolised the masculine, European domination of an Australian landscape conceptualised as feminine.

This mythic figure was popularised in the nationalist debates of the 1890s, a period when the separate Australian colonies were preparing to join together as a federated state (White 1981). Prominent among those leading the debates, and establishing the legendary bushman, were a group of writers associated with the *Bulletin* magazine and a group of artists known as the Heidelberg school. The writers included people such as Banjo Patterson, who wrote 'Waltzing Matilda' and 'The Man from Snowy River', and Henry Lawson, who wrote numerous short stories about rural life. Heidelberg artists such as Tom Roberts and Frederick McCubbin produced highly romanticised images such as 'Shearing the rams' and 'Down on his luck', which have since achieved iconic status, decorating everything from place mats to playing cards. Where Ward (1958) understood the source of the legend to lie in the affinity for the bush amongst the literary and artistic intelligentsia, subsequent analyses by historians such as Graeme Davison (1978) and Marilyn Lake (1986) have critiqued this origin myth both for its urban roots and its masculinist bias. The contested nature of masculinity itself has been the subject of analysis by historians such as David Goodman (1994).

Davison (1978) has examined the personal histories of those Ward identified as key contributors to the bush legend. He has convincingly documented the lack of bush experience among them, and their position within the bohemian and determinedly urban culture of inner-city Melbourne and Sydney. Davison argues that their depiction of the bush arose from their own alienation from the city, rather than from their understandings of, or participation in, the folk traditions of the bush itself.

The historical specificity of the masculinist ideal underlying the bush legend, and the anti-domestic/anti-feminine culture of the *Bulletin* writers and the Heidelberg artists, has been documented by Marilyn Lake (1986), who at the same time pointed to the masculinism inherent in the legend as a distinct historical position (Allen 1987: 617). When making this identification, Lake argued that the 1890s were characterised by a struggle for the national culture between feminist social reformers and a particular, and relatively recent, version of masculinity characterised by the *Bulletin* writers. While Lake does not fully describe the masculine ideal she calls 'Domestic Man', which preceded the *Bulletin*'s Bushman, she does suggestively argue that it was grounded in evangelical constructions of respectability and domesticity with their source in the colonists' British origins.

The domestically oriented masculinity that prevailed during much of the nineteenth century is more fully articulated by David Goodman (1994), writing about the gold rushes of the 1850s. He provides a more detailed analysis of the ideology of Lake's Domestic Man, and describes a manhood derived from and centred on the family hearth. This interpretation articulated masculine achievement in terms of responsibility, dependence and interdependence within a network of kinship (1994: 167). A manly figure was one who took responsibility for his family and dependants and was able to provide for them. He was industrious on their behalf and of good moral character. At mid-century, a well-rounded man enjoyed and sought the company of women and the quiet pleasures of the sitting room.

Goodman (1994: 8) also examines the gold rushes as one of the sources for the bush masculinity later popularised by the *Bulletin*. Together with the pastoral industry, and its reliance on armies of itinerant shearers and stockmen, the 'roaring days' of the gold rushes were the most potent settings of the stories and poems in which the Bushman was developed. Goodman credits the

construction of the 'roaring days' to Lawson and his contemporaries, and identifies it as a source of their more general bush mythologising. While the writers
came from largely urban backgrounds, several of them, including Lawson, had
been raised in goldfields towns and this at least was something with which they
did have real familiarity. However, the height of the rushes was already a
memory by the time Lawson's generation was growing up, and his stories of
the goldfields are fictionalised accounts tinged with the nostalgia for childhood.
As the *Bulletin* writers were using pastoral workers as iconographically heroic
figures, they were also using their memories of the gold rush to create a
legendary era of masculine mateship and independence from domestic bonds.

    These later representations of bush life are predicated on assumptions about
the conditions that prevailed there. Lake argues that for the men's press, 'home
influence was emasculating', and the bush was the idealised place of freedom
and revolt (1986: 118). To function in this way as a successful antithesis of
domestic ideals, the bush had to be constructed as rough and uncivilised.
Davison has demonstrated that the construction was not based on any real familiarity with the bush, nor was this necessary. In White's word's, 'The bush simply
provided a frame on which to hang a set of preconceptions' (1981: 99). In this
context of preconceptions and representations, material culture returns our gaze
to the experiences of the participants, the bush workers themselves and the
conditions of their lives.

ARCHAEOLOGY IN THE BUSH

People in the bush were active in their consumption of material goods and
they were motivated by the same culture of domestic respectability and comfort
that pervaded Victorian life. Archaeological remains of rough bush camps
includes hand-painted teacups, delicate sherry glasses and even a fragment of
floral wallpaper. It is evidence that is certainly at odds with the heroic images
evoked by the *Bulletin* writers, and it challenges some of the most fundamental
understandings of Australian identity. The physical traces suggest similarity with
contemporary middle- and working-class urban dwellers and their concerns for
evangelical piety, neat, well-ordered dining, a love of colourful decoration and
the pleasures of gambling and a shared drink that have been documented in
archaeological sites in Sydney and Melbourne (Karskens 1999; Murray and
Mayne 2003).

    Case studies from three bush industries provide evidence for arguments
about the material culture of bush life (Figure 12.1). Material is drawn from
excavations at two shore whaling stations in Tasmania (Lawrence 1998a, 1999),
a pastoral outstation (Murray 1993, 2000) and a gold-mining settlement
(Lawrence 1998b, 2000). These represent the three most important industries
in nineteenth-century Australia, economically and iconically, all of which
contributed in some way to contemporary experiences and understandings of
the bush and bush workers. The sites typify the kind of life that was being

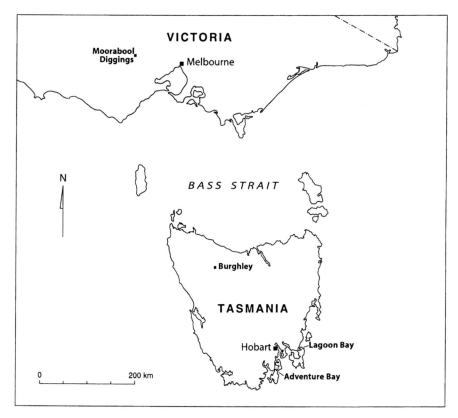

Figure 12.1   Locations discussed in the text

romanticised by the 1890s. They are in isolated, rural locations, with rudi-
mentary accommodation. They were populated by groups of transient white
men who, according to the later Australian legend, revelled in a life of
bohemian freedom from the constraints of domesticating ideologies.

The whaling stations, one at Adventure Bay on Bruny Island and one at
Lagoon Bay on the Forestier Peninsula, were both owned by Captain James
Kelly, in partnership with Thomas Lucas at the former station and with Thomas
Hewitt at the latter. They operated intermittently between the 1820s and
the 1840s, when crews of 20–30 men occupied them over the months of the
southern winter while hunting southern right whales. Excavations were carried
out at Adventure Bay in 1997 and at Lagoon Bay in 1999. At Adventure Bay,
an area of 287.75 square metres was excavated, sampling the manager's quarters, crew barracks, a storage hut and the tryworks where oil was rendered. At
Lagoon Bay, a total of 285 square metres was excavated from the crew barracks
and manager's quarters. At both sites artefacts were recovered from shallow
sheet deposits associated with the buildings and were from interior and exterior contexts. No sealed pit deposits were located.

The pastoral site of Burghley was an outstation of the Van Diemen's Land (VDL) Company and was located in the uplands of central Tasmania. It was occupied between the late 1820s and approximately 1839 by a small group of indentured servants and assigned convicts, all of whom worked as shepherds and labourers on the VDL Company's sheep runs. Excavations by Tim Murray (1993) in 1988 and 1990 uncovered 141 square metres of the main residential structure and associated yard areas. Again, all artefacts were recovered from sub-floor deposits and sheet deposits outside the building. The gold-mining settlement is that of the Moorabool diggings south of Ballarat, Victoria, which was occupied between the late 1850s and the 1880s by semi-itinerant miners working the low-grade alluvial gold deposits in the area. Four house sites were sampled during excavations in 1991 and 1992, and a total of 86 square metres were excavated. No intact pit features were found and the artefacts were recovered from shallow sheet deposits in and around the buildings.

Most of the archaeological evidence recovered from the sites can be described as household rubbish – broken jars and bottles, empty tin cans, broken dishes, discarded bones from meals eaten. Some of the rubbish suggests that life in the bush did correspond with heroic myths. There was plenty of glass from broken beer and gin bottles, with some wine and schnapps thrown in for good measure. Alcohol was also purchased in bulk – iron hoops from a small cask at the whaling station are about the right size for a keg of brandy, and at both the whaling station and the Moorabool diggings spigots were found that were used to tap barrels. There were also plenty of broken clay pipes, reminders that smoking was a favourite vice of the working man and woman.

However, a consideration of the minimum number of bottles recovered from the sites for which data is available suggests that the drinking was not necessarily to excess (Table 12.1). At Adventure Bay, broken alcohol bottles were disposed of at the rate of approximately 1.8 per year, from a population of 20–30 men. At Lagoon Bay, with a similar-sized crew, the rate was higher and approximately 5.2 broken bottles per year were dumped on site. Figures for the Moorabool diggings are harder to assess, as the number of residents at each house is not known, and as houses were unlikely to have been occupied for the entire period that the diggings were settled. However, with four houses occupied at most for a thirty-year period, only 0.9 bottles per year were discarded at each house. For all the sites the figures are largely meaningless, as they do not take into account site sampling, bottle re-use and re-cycling, the purchasing of alcohol in bulk containers like wooden casks that have not survived archaeologically and the consumption of alcohol off-site. However, the figures do provide a useful reminder that despite what appear to be large quantities of broken glass in the archaeological assemblages (e.g. 25 per cent of artefacts by weight at Adventure Bay), when translated to vessel numbers the rates of consumption are negligible.

Other rubbish is more perplexing, and more distant from the legend. Fragments of tableware have much to tell about customary ways of preparing and serving food, and about bush workers as users of consumer goods. One of

Table 12.1   Bottles and jars recovered (shown as minimum number of vessels)

	Adventure Bay	Lagoon Bay	Burghley	Moorabool
condiments	12	5	na	12
medicine		2	na	9
beer/wine	20	28	na	58
champagne				10
whiskey				5
gin	3	3	na	29
other spirits				3
soft drink				5
stoneware bottle	1		na	
stoneware jar	1	2	na	
Total	37	40	na	131

the things evident from the quantities of broken plates, cups and bowls is that bush workers preferred the fashionable transfer-printed earthenwares to more durable tin, or cheaper but old-fashioned creamwares, despite their migratory lifestyles and low wages (Table 12.2). It also indicates that the consumer revolution had succeeded in making these delicate goods so ubiquitous that they reached even the most marginal of places, and penetrated all levels of society. From the wide range of decorative patterns found on the dishes, it can be concluded that modern tastes for using matching sets of dishes were not yet well established. It might be supposed that bush workers picked up bits and pieces in their travels, rather than all at once as settled city dwellers could, but urban sites of the period also contain a range of unmatched dishes (Lydon 1998).

The functions of the different types of dish reflect diet, but also the social rituals of eating and drinking. All of the sites had more plates than bowls represented in the fragmentary pieces excavated. Chops and roasted meats were probably more frequently served than soups, although the deep rims of the plates would have held stews. Alcoholic beverages were also consumed, as we know from the amount of bottle glass. If the tablewares are any guide, for the most part they were associated with the informal customs of working people sharing a circling glass, rather than the highly structured middle–class rituals that required a range of separate types of differentiated glasses. Glass tumblers and cheap industrial slip mugs were the most common drinking vessels found. At the two whaling stations additional drinking equipment was found which suggests more elaborate social rituals.

One of the buildings excavated at Adventure Bay was a large, two-roomed stone structure. One end of the building had been converted into an apartment for the station manager. In the rubbish associated with the building portions of two delicate sherry glasses were recovered. An earthenware jug was found at Lagoon Bay which was probably used for serving beer or ale. It was fancifully decorated with moulded scenes that depicted camels, elephants, griffins and people in exotic dress. Neither of these sites had anything

Table 12.2 Glass and china tablewares (shown as minimum number of vessels)

		Adventure Bay	Lagoon Bay	Burghley	Moorabool
glass					
	stemmed glass	2		na	
	tumbler	4	1	na	
Total		6	1	na	
ceramics					
Transfer print	plates	4	10		14
	cups	9	1	1	23
	bowls		1		
	cup/bowl		3		2
	plate/saucer				15
	serving dish		1		
	sugar bowl			1	
	vase		1		
	unidentified	2			
Shell edge	plates	5	2	2	
Ironstone	plates				1
	cups				3
	plate/saucer				3
	jug		1		
Chinese Export	plates	1			
Porcelain					
Hand painted	cup		1	1	
Cream coloured	plates	1			
	cup		1		
	chamber pot	1		1	
	unidentified				4
Banded	cup	1			
	bowls				4
	plate/saucer				1
Sponged	bowl		1		
Rockingham	teapot				1
Basaltware	teapot		1		
Industrial slip	mug			2	
	bowls		1		
Total		24	25	8	71

approaching a full middle-class set of glassware, but these goods suggest that on some occasions at least something approaching that level of formalised drinking etiquette was observed. It is more than likely that these occasions included visits from the station owners, James Kelly and Thomas Lucas. Each owned a number of stations as well as numerous other business enterprises, so the day-to-day running of the station was left to a manager or headsman. However, the Adventure Bay station was within a few hours sail from Hobart, and Kelly, a captain and ship-owner, probably visited periodically.

Tea drinking was part of other customs of visiting and entertaining among the middle classes and working people alike. As part of day-to-day life it was deeply embedded in a complex set of customary beliefs and practises, and it required the manipulation of another elaborate set of social conventions and consumer goods. By the early nineteenth century tea drinking was a well-established part of British culture (Shammas 1990: 84). Its permeation of all social levels was facilitated by the repeal of the high import duties on tea in 1784 (Emmerson 1992: 10–12), and inexpensive, though decorative, earthenware cups, saucers, teapots, and other accoutrements produced by the potteries in the Midlands. The necessary equipage for the tea ceremony was ubiquitous at all the sites. A wide range of transfer-printed and hand-painted cups and saucers were found at each site, in a variety of patterns and colours. At Burghley a sugar bowl and teacup were part of a matching set, and one other teacup was found as well. Fragments of at least nine teacups, all in different patterns, were recovered from the Adventure Bay whaling station, and three from the Lagoon Bay station. Pieces of an ornate black basalt-ware teapot were also found at Lagoon Bay. On the Moorabool diggings, in addition to fragments of 21 teacups, other tea equipment included fragments of a brown Rockingham teapot and an electroplated silver sugar spoon. Fragments of pressed-glass dishes were also found there, including a stemmed serving dish possibly used for serving cakes.

Along with this variety of tablewares are other household furnishings. One of the huts at Lagoon Bay was ornamented with a delicate whiteware vase decorated with a sepia transfer print. At the Moorabool diggings furnishings include an ornate brass clock case, once gilded bronze, and a piece of floral wallpaper. These items indicate an attention to levels of comfort and decoration at odds with the tiny 3m × 5m bark huts in which they were found, and at odds with our expectations of bush life.

Dining, home furnishings and social drinking of tea and alcohol are all semi-public arenas shared with other people. In the more private matter of personal hygiene there is also some evidence that bush workers were concerned with decency and propriety. Creamware chamber pots were found at Adventure Bay and Burghley, although in very small numbers. It may be that they were used by the managers, another example of behaviour that demarcated them from the men under their supervision. Their absence from the Moorabool is curious, but it may be that tin was acceptable for that purpose.

MASCULINE DOMESTICITY

There are two aspects about this evidence of respectability which require further discussion. The first is the need to understand them in their own terms, and to consider what they might suggest about bush life. The second aspect is to consider the ways in which bush life as it was lived became transformed into the bush life represented in the Australian legend, and the reasons why such a transformation was necessary.

Goods used in the bush are indicative of prevailing notions of masculinity and femininity. One temptation when finding goods such as refined teawares and sherry glasses is to assume that the goods were associated with women who lived on the sites and attempted to create the kind of domestic environment appropriate within ideologies of domesticity. White women were almost certainly present in the goldfields homes of the Moorabool diggings, where census records indicate that the majority of the population was living in nuclear family homes, and where fragments of women's shoes and jewellery were found during the excavations (Lawrence 2000: 36–8, 151–5). White women may have been present at Burghley and at the whaling stations. Documentary evidence does not specify who lived at those sites, and there was no archaeological evidence of women's clothing or accessories. However, the VDL Company brought women as well as men from England as indentured labourers and had female assigned convicts (Murray 2000: 151). Other whaling stations in Western Australia and South Australia were home to the wives and children of the men who managed them (Gibbs 1998: 46; Staniforth 1998: 62–3), and it is possible that this also occurred in Tasmania. Aboriginal women were present at Burghley and at Adventure Bay, and were involved more generally in the pastoral and whaling industries, but their involvement was quite different to that of white women and would not be associated with signs of domesticity in the same way.

However, simplistically identifying the goods as signs of women's presence denies the possibility of seeing different versions of masculinity. Whether or not white women were there, goods to facilitate domestic respectability were certainly present and were used by men. When understood within the framework of mid-century constructions of masculinity, the presence of such goods in masculine environments is less problematic. While it may have been perceived and expressed differently by men and women, domestic ideals ultimately transcended gender. They were internalised as much by men as by women, and hence had power as a cultural system. It may be that in the bush respectability was located most firmly amongst the aristocracy of labour, the managers and skilled workers. Nevertheless, what we see in the consumer goods at these bush sites is the enactment of a locally understood respectability.

Whalers, miners and pastoral workers were physically remote from the mainstream of society, but they were nevertheless integrated with it. Domestic ideology and domesticated masculine identity informed the lives of men and, when present, women in the bush. Men acquired and used a range of consumer goods that were incorporated into their expressions of participation in broad cultural systems. Bush spaces were masculine places, but the masculine identities that were created there were not uniform. They were complex amalgams that at times emphasised dissolution and mateship, and that also enabled the acknowledgement of domestic respectability.

By the end of the nineteenth century representations of bush life were simplifying this complexity. Domestic masculinity in the bush did not fit the new images of Australian identity being created. The artists and writers who popularised bush imagery at that time had little bush experience and were uncomfortable with women and what they perceived as domestic constraints. Accordingly, when re-creating the bush, they located their own rebellion and dissatisfaction there as well. In order to contest the 'emasculating restraint' of domesticity, bush life had to be stripped of any genteel, domestic overtones, and rendered in an alien, essentialist roughness. While this transformation may have had a personal logic for individuals, it also served a useful national purpose.

FEDERATION AND AUSTRALIAN ICONOGRAPHY

Australian federation took place in 1901. The preceding decade had been one in which Australians actively considered what it meant to be Australian, and how being Australian might be different to being British. Australians were attempting to articulate a new national identity that co-existed with loyalty to the Empire. Responding to, even rebelling against, a colonial, British past, people were seeking distinctive and unique attributes from which to form a new identity. Accordingly, they selected those items which were most radical, and which emphasised originality and difference. Richard White (1981: 98–9) has already drawn attention to the bush as a ready-made source of local colour, and the self-conscious ways in which writers and artists alike encountered the bush.

Australian motifs, drawn from the landscape and the native plant and animal life, also began to appear in architecture and fashion. Moulded plasterwork designs used in ceiling roses and cornices began sporadically incorporating Australian flora in the 1850s and 1860s. They became very popular in the 1880s and 1890s, with designs including waratahs, flannel flowers, gum nuts, wattle, ferns, kookaburras and lyrebirds (Capon 1993). Between the late 1880s and the end of the First World War the most popular style of housing in Australia was the 'Federation house', a local adaptation of English 'Queen Anne', Arts and Crafts, and Art Noveau influences (Fraser and Joyce 1986: 10–11, 20). Motifs from the Australian bush were used extensively in the decorative treatment of exterior timberwork, red clay roof finials and ridgecapping, and stained glass, and on interior tiles and wallpapers. Even personal names took on a new Australian flavour, with Tasman and the feminine Tasma, Huon (a variety of native pine tree) and Sturt (an early explorer) all chosen for children.

In this process of defining a national image, bush workers were peculiarly amenable to re-shaping (White 1981: 103). Australia's contribution to Empire, and the source of its export earnings, was the raw materials of wool, minerals and, earlier, whale oil. All of these goods at different times were used as symbols of the nation, as wool was used extensively in the celebratory parades and displays that marked Federation itself in 1901 (Cremin 2000: 198). The workers who produced these goods were themselves even more appropriate symbols of

Australia and models for the development of a national persona. They had
the added advantage of being sufficiently distinctive from urban workers and
English farm workers that they could be considered uniquely Australian. However, they could only be uniquely Australian if stripped of any British characteristics. Linda Young (1998) has argued that gentility and domesticity were
originally practised because they were universalising cultures that maintained
Britishness in the colonies. Thus, one of the necessary features of constructing
the Australian bush was that it be made less comfortable and less domestic.
Women and children were removed from the narrative or relegated to its
margins. The lone men in 'Waltzing Matilda' and the painting 'Down on his
luck' drink tea from tin billy-cans, not basalt-ware teapots and fine transfer-
printed teacups. When they drank alcohol, it was straight from the bottle, not
from delicate stemmed glasses.

CONCLUSION

It might be assumed that the selection of bush imagery as a representational
device in the service of national identity honoured the Australian landscape
and those who lived there. Ironically, that was not the case. The manner in
which the iconography was created by urban observers obscured many of
the realities of bush life, while at the same time silencing the voices of those
who experienced it. 'The bush' was made rough, uncouth and 'other', although
those who lived there laboured mightily to maintain the signs of their
respectable status. Although they lived on the frontiers of the Empire, they felt
themselves firmly integrated within it. The goods they discarded and left behind
speak of the ceremonial serving of tea, the refined consumption of alcohol,
the careful acquisition of fashionable tablewares. These hard-won symbols of
respectability were all the more prized because of the physical and emotional
cost of achieving them. A new Australia that based its claims for identity on
the bare and elemental character of the bush denied the struggle of bush workers
to claim civility in their lives.

REFERENCES

Allen, J. (1987) Mundane men: historians, masculinity and masculinism. *Historical Studies*
    22(89): 617–28.
Capon, J. (1993) Decorative plasterwork in New South Wales, 1800–1939. *Australasian
    Historical Archaeology* 11: 43–51.
Cremin, A. (ed.) (2000) *1901: Australians at Federation, An Illustrated Chronicle.* Sydney:
    University of New South Wales Press.
Davison, G. (1978) Sydney and the bush: an urban context for the Australian legend.
    Historical Studies 71: 191–209.
Emmerson, R. (1992) *British Teapots and Tea Drinking.* Norfolk: Norfolk Museums
    Service and Twinings.
Fraser, H. and Joyce, R. (1986) *The Federation House: Australia's Own Style.* Sydney:
    Lansdowne Press.

Gibbs, M. (1998) Colonial boats and foreign ships: the history and archaeology of nineteenth century whaling in Western Australia. In S. Lawrence and M. Staniforth (eds), *The Archaeology of Whaling in Southern Australia and New Zealand*, 36–47. Canberra: Brolga Press for the Australasian Society for Historical Archaeology and the Australian Institute of Maritime Archaeology, Special Publication No. 10.

Goodman, D. (1994) *Gold Seeking: Victoria and California in the 1850s*. Sydney: Allen and Unwin.

Karskens, G. (1999) *Inside the Rocks: The Archaeology of a Neighbourhood*. Sydney: Hale & Iremonger.

Lake, M. (1986) The politics of respectability: identifying the masculinist context. *Historical Studies* 22(86): 116–31.

Lawrence, S. (1998a) Preliminary report on archaeological excavations at Kelly and Lucas' whaling station, Adventure Bay, Tasmania. Unpublished report for Department of Parks and Wildlife Tasmania, Hobart.

—— (1998b) Towards a feminist archaeology of households: gender and household structure on the Australian goldfields. In P. Allison (ed.), *The Archaeology of Household Activities*, 121–41. London: Routledge.

—— (1999) Preliminary report on archaeological excavations at Hewitt and Kelly's whaling station, Lagoon Bay, Tasmania. Unpublished report for Department of Parks and Wildlife Tasmania, Hobart.

—— (2000) *Dolly's Creek: An Archaeology of a Victorian Gold Rush Community*. Melbourne: Melbourne University Press.

Lydon, J. (1998) Boarding houses in the rocks: Mrs Ann Lewis' privy, 1865. In M. Casey, D. Donlon, J. Hope and S. Wellfare (eds), *Redefining Archaeology: Feminist Perspectives*, 138–46. Canberra: Research School of Pacific and Asian Studies, Australian National University.

Murray, T. (1993) The childhood of William Lanne: contact archaeology and Aboriginality in Tasmania. *Antiquity* 67(256): 504–19.

—— (2000) Digging with documents: understanding intention and outcome in northwest Tasmania 1825–1835. In A. Anderson and T. Murray (eds), *Australian Archaeologist: Collected Papers in Honour of Jim Allen*, 145–55. Canberra: Centre for Archaeological Research and the Department of Archaeology and Natural History, Australian National University, with the Department of Archaeology, La Trobe University.

Murray, T. and Mayne, A. (2003) (Re) constructing a lost community: 'Little Lon', Melbourne, Australia. *Historical Archaeology* 37(1).

Schaffer, K. (1988) *Women and the Bush, Forces of Desire in the Australian Cultural Tradition*. Cambridge: Cambridge University Press.

Shammas, C. (1990) *The Pre-Industrial Consumer in England and America*. Oxford: Clarendon Press.

Staniforth, M. (1998) Three whaling station sites on the west coast of South Australia: Fowler's Bay, Sleaford Bay and Streaky Bay. In S. Lawrence and M. Staniforth (eds), *The Archaeology of Whaling in Southern Australia and New Zealand*, 57–63. Canberra: Brolga Press for the Australasian Society for Historical Archaeology and the Australian Institute for Maritime Archaeology, Special Publication No. 10.

Ward, R. (1958) *The Australian Legend*. Melbourne: Oxford University Press.

White, R. (1981) *Inventing Australia*. Sydney: Allen & Unwin.

Young, L. (1998) The material construction of gentility: a context for understanding the role of women in nineteenth century sites. In M. Casey, D. Donlon, J. Hope and S. Wellfare (eds), *Redefining Archaeology: Feminist Perspectives*, 134–7. Canberra: Research School of Pacific and Asian Studies, Australian National University.

13   The British material presence in Cyprus (1878–1960): display for whom? Visibility, accessibility and adoption

KYLIE SERETIS

INTRODUCTION

This chapter addresses the important role played by the British Empire in the construction and development of Cypriot cultural identities by looking at how the Empire used material culture such as architecture and the ordering of space to reinforce its position on the island. It also considers the physical impact that the culture and ideology of the British Empire had upon the visual and conceptual landscape in the global/public sphere, and why this was not always adopted into Cypriot culture at the local level.

The purpose of this chapter is to show both the variety and ambiguity involved in the study of cultural difference and identity, in particular that of cultural identity, when investigated through material culture. The aim is not the generation of a universal definition, model or explanation for cultural difference under colonialism, but to begin to draw out and document the complexity involved in the study of how culture is transferred and understood between groups of people.

IMPERIAL LANDSCAPES

For Said (1993) imperialism can be defined as the theory and attitude of the dominant ruling class, and colonialism the articulation of imperialism, in invaded or settled territories. Thus when addressing the role of empires we have at least three things to think about – the mental templates of the coloniser, the actual physical articulation of this attitude within the colony and the experience of those peoples who were colonised. Through the examination of different cultural identities and the ways they interrelate within colonial contexts, we are provided with a means to explore the ways in which people within colonised communities, differently engaged and empowered, appropriate (or re-appropriate), contest and lay claim to their landscape.

Distinct attitudes were imbued in the British imperial order, resulting in very distinctive forms of colonialism. Jacobs (1996: 38) suggests two forms of colonial expansion. The first occurs where colonisation is based on a permanent territorial expansion, destroying the existing society and constructing a new society modelled on that of the imperial homeland. The second form of colonial expansion is one designed to maintain the indigenous society but re-orientate it in the service of the coloniser. The first form is applicable to countries such as Australia, the United States and Canada. Cyprus, due to the perceived 'Europeanness' of the island, falls into the second category alongside colonies such as India.

Cyprus, located in an important strategic geographic position in the eastern Mediterranean, has a history characterised by consistent foreign rule and intervention (Figure 13.1). As a result Cyprus has been home to people from a multitude of cultural and religious groups, including Christian Orthodox Greeks, Muslim Turks and Arabs, Christian Maronites, Latins, Armenians and the British. With exception of the British, these same groups have been in Cyprus since at least the sixteenth century. The numerous political and religious groups that have controlled the island of Cyprus over the last 500 years have had a considerable impact upon the identity of the inhabitants.

In 1571 Cyprus was annexed as a province of the Ottoman Empire, the island having previously been under Venetian control. The Ottoman period saw the introduction to Cyprus of a Turkish-speaking population from all over the Ottoman Empire. Under Ottoman control the status of the Roman

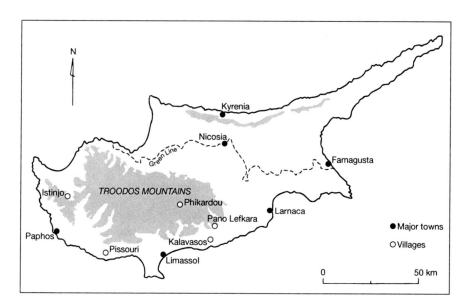

Figure 13.1   The location of Cyprus in the Mediterranean and places mentioned in the text

Catholic Church was diminished and the Venetians persecuted. Cathedrals in Nicosia and Famagusta were converted to mosques, and the others together with monasteries were either abandoned or sold to the Greek Orthodox Church (Jenness 1962: 57). The millet system (recognising the autonomy of different religious communities) was introduced, and gave the Greek Orthodox Church a position of dominance after a period of approximately 500 years. The Church was given the power to collect taxes on behalf of the Ottomans, and its power base within the Greek community was established (Anthias 1992: 34).

It is important to note that in the period prior to the British occupation of Cyprus insubordination, in the form of protests, could be organised and carried out under other, non-ethnic-related identities. During this period ethnicity was not necessarily the important identity under which 'communities' or groups could or would come together. Looking briefly at the history of the Ottoman period gives a reasonable indication that class struggles between the rural peasants and the urban élite could in some cases be more significant identity than any form of religious or ethnic identity. An example of this is when in 1764 Muslims and Christians came together to kill the new governor of Cyprus in response to a decision to double taxes. Therefore identity in Cyprus is not always ethnic, and thus the use of the 'past' as a basis to organise identity is not necessarily useful or relevant.

Prior to the British annexation of the island in 1878 cultural difference could be asserted through the practice of religion, the two main religious groups being Christians and Muslims. The two main ethnic groups were Greek Cypriots and Turkish Cypriots. In their religious practice they can be seen to be very different, although on a general level there are similarities between the two religions. Within both religious communities, religion was not seen as separate from secular life, and education was male dominated and conducted through the religious institutions. This could usually be seen in architecture with the religious building (either a church or mosque) having a school located within or nearby.

LANDSCAPES OF EMPIRE: MAP, SURVEY, CENSUS

In 1878 the island of Cyprus was leased by the Ottoman administration to Britain and from then was considered part of the British Empire. At this time Britain considered the occupation of Cyprus as a strategic move, positioning itself in a location close to two regions of potential conflict, the Russo-Turkish confrontation, and Suez and the Tigris-Euphrates Valley (Patrick 1976: 5). The British interest in Cyprus was further cemented in the 1920s when Cyprus became a Crown colony. British rule saw administrative roles, such as the collection of taxes, transferred to the foreign power. This was unlike the Ottomans' administration where indigenous peoples (religious leaders in the case of Cyprus) were in charge. Under the British, control was moved from the religious domain to that of the secular.

There are several factors that are shared as a part of the 'colonial experience': the importance of mapping the 'unknown' territory, classifying the indigenous inhabitants (usually through the census), the transfer of European town planning and architectural styles, and the development of a colonial administrative system. This can almost be seen as a template of the British Empire. In Cyprus the British constructed buildings, roads and bridges across the island. In the villages they built water systems to provide water, police stations, jails, schools and post offices. They also introduced an independent system of currency, established new judicial systems and enacted a representative Legislative Council.

The British created one of the first maps of Cyprus to show religious division (between Christians and Muslims). Between 1878 and 1882 under the instruction of the Foreign Office, Captain H. H. Kitchener conducted a survey of the island to compile a 'scientific map' for the administration and development of the island (Kitchener 1882). The people of Cyprus were demarcated and classified alongside the land. This map annotated mixed villages with mosques and churches and indicated Muslim and Christian cemeteries, thus effectively dividing the communities by the physically visible 'religious' difference (i.e. the presence of a mosque and/or church), and therefore contributing to the manufacturing of difference. It also helped by providing the administration with a classificatory system, enabling the collection of taxes alongside the recording of the census. In the taking of the first census in 1881, colony and people are divided into districts, religions, sexes, professions, languages, and so on. This was then open to manipulation within the villages. For example, it was the mukhtar (headman) of the village who filled in the initial census forms for the village as the majority of villagers were illiterate. There exists the possibility that forms could then be filled in for the mukhtar's own purpose or benefit, especially since this was used for taxation purposes as well as the supply of amenities and services.

The British administration oversaw the establishment of separate schools for the two communities, with Greek Cypriot schools teaching Greek history and Turkish Cypriot schools teaching Turkish history (Talbot and Cape 1914). The school buildings are important areas where difference, national, ethnic and religious, can be seen. From the 1920s the architecture of Greek Cypriot school buildings reflect in particular the Greek Cypriot nationalist movements of this period (Given 1997). Greek Cypriot schools, designed by Greek Cypriots, often hearkened back to a classical Greek past complete with pediments and columns (see Figure 13.2). Turkish Cypriot schools in contrast were plain, the design more in line with modernist movements in Turkey (see Figure 13.3). Bryant (1998: 58–9) points out a very marked difference in the ideology behind Greek Cypriot and Turkish Cypriot nationalism. Greek Cypriot nationalism looked to the past 'to restore an imagined former order of the greater Greek world', hence the Greek revival style in Greek Cypriot schools. Turkish Cypriot nationalism (along with Turkish nationalism and Atatürk's reforms) looked toward the future, through modernisation and progress (Bryant 1998: 58). This can also be seen for architecture more generally, for example with regard to

Figure 13.2   Greek Cypriot School, Pano Lefkara

Figure 13.3   Turkish Cypriot School, Istinjo

some Turkish Cypriot villages, and it is visible in both public and private architecture (although since the external façade of a house is in fact visible outside, it too can count as public).

THE PHYSICAL LANDSCAPE

Through the investigation of the physical remains of the British period it is possible to say that many of the items themselves are often homogenous. A water cistern in one village does not vary from that of another. The roads, whether the early stone-constructed variety, or the later tarred roads, do not differ in techniques of construction between villages. The construction of government administrative buildings such as courthouses, police stations and official residences all follow a very generalised colonial style, with only occasional local influences. Today these buildings may get lost amongst the more recent streetscapes of the 1960s-90s period, but at the beginning of the twentieth century and earlier, these would have been very imposing and prominent new structures on the Cypriot landscape. In the villages at least, they were also of very different scale and design from the older, more familiar buildings. For example, police stations were often built in prominent and highly visible locations. The villages of Kalavasos and Pissouri, built within naturally mountainous landscapes, have police stations that not only have wide-ranging views but are also prominently in view.

The provision of amenities such as both improved and more numerous roads as well as a postal service means that villages once isolated could take part in the wider communication networks across the island and beyond. This effect is not just limited to the period in which the construction took place as it has continued into the present. The British provided the infrastructure for modernisation. This distinctly British infrastructure made the process of industrialisation and modernisation that took place from the early twentieth century onwards possible, and has allowed Cyprus to take that step into the modern era more easily than some of its eastern Mediterranean neighbours. However, inevitably (but not necessarily intentionally) the same infrastructure played a role in the construction of Cypriot identities – Greek and Turkish – and the development of nationalist sentiments.

After the Greek War of Independence in 1821, Greek Cypriot religious leaders began to express the desire to merge with the 'Motherland', Greece. Under British rule, the desire for freedom and Enosis (union with Greece) was mainly articulated by the Church leaders and a few of the newly emerging merchant élite, and did not penetrate into other sections of the population. Enosis was seen as an opposition to British rule. The British were viewed as political oppressors and economic exploiters, preventing the development of the local economy. Enosis was also an affirmation of Greekness, as opposed to Turkishness. However, while Greek Cypriots sought freedom from British colonial rule, the aim was not independence but union with another nation-state – Greece.

British rule is often seen as instrumental in the development of nationalism
and the creation of inter-ethnic conflict in Cyprus. The political system that
the British introduced in the 1882 constitution was founded on the assumption of persistent ethnic conflict and formalised ethnic divisions (Anthias 1992:
41). In 1915 Britain offered to cede the island to Greece, with the proviso that
Greece aid the allies in Serbia. At this time, possibly as a result of the pro-
German King Constantine, the offer was declined (Patrick 1976: 5; Crawshaw
1978: 23). In 1931 the first episode of violence broke out – the burning down
of Government House by a group of Greek Cypriot demonstrators.

Many of the early British governors and officials in Cyprus had a classical
British education, learning of the rise of the West through the development of
the Greek world. These men, the governors and rulers of the island, were
taught to read Latin and Greek. Cyprus, with its large Greek-speaking population, was in the minds of the British administration ultimately tied to Greece
and by extension to ancient Greece. Thus while one-fifth of the population
was Muslim, for the British the island had a past that was inherently 'Greek'.

This belief can be seen throughout discussions within the colonial records
regarding Cyprus. In 1880 an exchange took place between the High Commissioner of Cyprus, Colonel Biddulph, and the Secretary of State for
the Colonies, the Earl of Kimberley, regarding the teaching of English. Lord
Kimberley refused Biddulph's argument that it 'was only through learning
English that the Cypriots would attain a higher civilisation and acquire access
to every branch of human knowledge'. Kimberley's reply was that the Greek
language afforded 'ample means not only for an ordinary education but for the
attainment of a high degree of mental culture' (Georghallides 1979: 47–8).

For the British administration segregation was the favoured method of
dealing with the two major religious groups on the island. Although in other
colonial situations one of the key aims of the British administration was to
'civilise' and educate indigenous populations in a British manner, usually
through the introduction and teaching of Christianity, this was not the case in
Cyprus. This is clearly reflected in the education policy in which the Colonial
administration established separate schools for the two communities (Talbot and
Cape 1914). There were also separate Muslim and Christian electoral lists
(Georghallides 1979: 45). In mixed communities there was a headman for each
community, with two separate meetings relating to village issues (Anonymous
1929: 2). Unlike in earlier periods of British colonisation, the aims were not to
'civilise' the local community, just to bring it under imperial order and control.

The 1940s and 1950s saw the emergence and development of Enosis as a
mass movement amongst the Greek Cypriots, along with a parallel development of nationalism, Takism, by the Turkish Cypriots. The 1950s and 1960s
were marked by a period of aggression and violence. Between 1955 and 1959
the EOKA struggle (National Organisation of Greek Cypriot Fighters), under
the leadership of Grivas Dighenis, only added to the fuel of nationalist
movements. In 1958 the T.M.T (Turkish Defence Organisation) was formed,
a Turkish Cypriot nationalist movement under the direction of the colonial

government. These organisations were not just concerned with nationalism: political parties within each were vying for support.

The Republic of Cyprus was founded on 21 August 1960, with Archbishop Makarios III elected as President and Dr Kutchuk as the Vice-President, and the introduction of a new constitution. The constitution divided the power of the Greek Cypriots and the Turkish Cypriots and, importantly, according to the Greek Cypriots, gave the Turkish Cypriots power considered disproportionate to their numbers in the population. In November 1963 Makarios proposed 13 points to amend the constitution (Crawshaw 1978). The proposal was an attempt to amend what the Greek Cypriots saw as the 'negative' elements in the constitution. The end result of this, and the nationalist movements, were intercommunal riots.

MATERIAL CULTURE IDENTITIES

An important aspect that needs consideration is that material culture can have multiple meanings and is not a simple reflection of the culture in which it is produced. Importantly, meanings of objects, places and spaces change through time. The architecture of a town or village, indeed the settlement pattern itself, often outlasts not only the generation that built it but also the ideology behind their creation. Through the successive use of buildings through time we can clearly show that the ideology that created the material culture is not followed and does not necessarily have to be experienced or believed by the successive users.

A good example of this is the House of Hadjigeorgakis Kornessios, currently a museum in Nicosia. The material culture relating to the eighteenth-century Greek Cypriot Hadjigeorgakis Kornessios, a dragoman under the Ottoman Empire, can be interpreted in a number of ways. The role of Office of the Dragoman was one of communication between the Ottoman government and its subject populations. The duties of the dragoman were mainly financial and included the collection of taxes from the Christian population of the island (Rizopoulou-Egoumenidou 1993: 11). Hadjigeorgakis's *konak* (house) contains the *kiosk* (enclosed wooden balcony), the *oda* (reception room) and a *hamam* (bath-house). Within the *konak* there are portraits of Hadjigeorgakis that show him with a *firman* (edict) and wearing the official headgear. But at the same time, Hadjigeorgakis was a practising Christian Orthodox Greek, he paid for the construction of an Orthodox church and his name can be seen on donor inscriptions. His house, the *konak,* reflects the 'Ottomanising' that took place throughout the Ottoman Empire and it clearly shows that on a spatial material level Greek Orthodox Cypriot houses, in this case of high status, can be no different to those of Ottoman Muslims of a similar status. Today these houses are being purchased, restored and refurbished by Greek Cypriots for a multitude of uses, such as offices, classrooms, homes or as museums. The meanings and the use of the buildings are no longer the same, despite the same external façade and similar internal features.

There can be no denying the impact that the British had on the health, education and lives of townspeople and villagers over the period 1878–1960. Fresh piped water, the clearing of wasteland, the eradication of malaria, the construction of roads, bridges and public buildings all had major impacts on their lives. Not only did the health of the population improve, the programme of public works such as building and road construction provided jobs (especially in the post-war periods of economic decline), and once constructed, provided faster access and communication between people and places. Although while roads were considered of the utmost importance, it was roads between the major towns that were the British administration's first interest, not the roads between villages. The increase in the number of schools saw literacy rates across the island improve, in particular in the more isolated rural areas.

However, the imposed colonial rationality and order within the colonies was not always followed. In practice it could be denied, and colonial law and order could be transformed or transgressed. What was intended and what came about through practice were not necessarily the same. The meanings intended by the coloniser and how it was understood by the colonised at the local level did not always neatly correspond.

In comparison to other colonial situations the extent of adoption of 'British' portable material goods in Cyprus during the late nineteenth and early twentieth centuries does not appear widespread through all classes on the island. It appears to have been mostly restricted to the urban élite, or those who aspired to belong to this group. However, in this context it is useful to remember that it is often those aspiring to belong to a particular group that are more concerned with identity and associated material culture than those who demarcate the boundary and who can in reality transgress it. Within the upper class of Cypriot society it could be suggested that the British influence is visible in both the adoption of European styles of clothing and other forms of material culture such as the furnishings of the period (for examples, see Marangou 1995: 117, and the Leventis Museum, Nicosia). But it should also be remembered that Cyprus, alongside other countries, was already aware of, if not a part of, European society before the British arrived in Cyprus. Unlike the pre-colonial situations of Australia or North America, Cyprus was already linked to European culture, trade and, therefore, importantly in this context, material goods. At this time in places such as Australia and North America the widespread adoption of items such as transfer-printed ceramics (whether foreign imports or locally produced) is seen as an imitation of British society, a way of displaying identity, and is adopted by many different socio-economic groups.

Generally my data comes from the following areas: the physical surrounds; ethnographic museums/collections; textual evidence – both primary and secondary sources; photographic and pictorial evidence, including lithographic drawings, paintings, and so on; and verbal communication. Due to the current political boundary, access to villages located in the north was not possible. On a specific level a quantitative approach has been adopted. *Material culture* is treated as the physical evidence of a changing relationship between communities on the island, and this analysis is not limited to coloniser/ colonised or ethnic/religious divisions, but also investigates regional, rural/ urban and agriculture/industrial factors. Through an investigation of public and private space within villages, architecture has been selected as one main focus.

In total, 47 villages in the southern half of the island were studied as a part of my research. Prior to the events of 1974, 18 villages were Turkish Cypriot, 14 Greek Cypriot and 15 were mixed communities of Greek and Turkish Cypriots. Of these villages, two villages remain mixed communities today (see Table 13.1). Villages were selected using the available British maps that divide cities and villages by their government districts to ensure spatial diversity (and this corresponded on the whole to how the British census was collected). Once selected the villages and/or towns were subject to more detailed research. A brief survey was made in regard to previous historical research: photographs, maps, travellers' accounts, and so on. Various spatial and chronological infor- mation was mapped when available – including who lived where, size of houses, families, location of religious or administrative buildings, and the presence of schools, shops and cafés.

The analysis of portable material culture proved to be particularly difficult, as there is very little left in the deserted villages, and modern villages that are still occupied give a distorted picture of the pre-1970s landscape. Not only have doors and windows disapeared, but so too have door lintels and stone. Many villages are used as animal pens, further confusing the archaeological record. Internal furnishings and fixtures are incredibly rare. As a means to understand what would have furnished houses, how space may have been divided and the possible repertoire of material in homes, the main ethnographic museums on the island were visited. The houses that belonged to individuals (such as the

Table 13.1 Villages surveyed as part of thesis

Village Type	No. 1 pre 1963–74 (status)	No. 1 after 1974 (status)
Greek Cypriot	12 occupied by Greek Cypriots, 3 abandoned (natural causes)	12 occupied by Greek Cypriots, 3 abandoned (natural causes)
Turkish Cypriot	17 occupied by Turkish Cypriots	6 abandoned, 1 still occupied by a single Turkish Cypriot family, 7 are used as farms or occupied by a single Greek Cypriot family, 3 have been reoccupied by refugees
Mixed	14 occupied by Greek and Turkish Cypriots	10 occupied by Greek Cypriots, 2 are abandoned, 2 still mixed
Refugee Settlement	–	1

House of Hadjigeorgakis in Nicosia and the Patsalos House in Lefkara) are only a general representation of a particular class of Cypriots (wealthy upper class). The village of Phikardou counteracted this a little. A general field sheet was devised to record the main elements/features of artefacts. An artefact was considered to encompass any material culture from buildings, roads and water cisterns, to shelves, fireplaces and other built features.

To date, of villages investigated across the island as a part of this study, none have surface evidence of large quantities of mass-produced ceramics, in contrast to the overwhelming amounts of village/local produced pottery. Most of the villages that do have mass-produced wares are those where occupation has continued after 1964. The majority of these wares appear to date from the mid-twentieth century and not the nineteenth century.

The British colonial administration, unsuccessfully in the long term, attempted to introduce a formalised grid plan design into the future organisation of towns and villages in Cyprus. Even in Australia, where from the beginning towns were planned European constructions, the grid plan did not last long. In 1809 Governor Lachlan Macquarie's grid plan for Sydney was outlined. By the 1830s Sydney's growth was more influenced by topography than the Governor's plans. In the villages of Cyprus today village planning and house construction continues to be heavily influenced by the surrounding topography. Within the government, the employment and training of Cypriots exerted a local influence on some of the government-constructed buildings (Schaar et al. 1995: 101–4), suggesting that the interaction between coloniser and colonised was not a simple one-way transfer of ideology and culture. Thus colonialism, the local articulation of the global concept of imperialism, is always contextual and tied to a particular place and time.

It is relatively difficult to tie material culture to a particular cultural or ethnic group (for a comprehensive account, see Jones 1997). And even when a particular item of material culture is linked to a specific group, the use of it by a different 'cultural' or 'ethnic' group does not have to mean the adoption of the belief system of that culture. In pre-1960s Cyprus it was not uncommon for Turkish Cypriots living in villages where there was no mosque nearby to worship in an Orthodox Church. This phenomenon is not uncommon in the Mediterranean world, and similar practices have been witnessed in northern Greece (Jane Cowan, personal communication). The important factor was that the building symbolised a place for worship, not whether it was Orthodox or Muslim.

CHANGING SPACES

The physical landscape of Cypriot villages today, can be divided up in to public and private space. In the past the notion of 'public' was not as we understand it today, so in an attempt to deal with this I will use the term 'communal' for the early period and 'public' for the later. Communal is used in the wider sense of access: it is public in the sense that it is not a private home or yard. It can include places of worship, and should further include the narrow paths, lanes and roads that surrounded houses and led to nearby villages, wells, water mills and the like, which the communities traversed throughout their lives.

In some but not all villages the 'identification' of Orthodox Christian or Muslim was visible through the display of symbols. In the case of Orthodox Christians it is a cross, sometimes with the date of house construction carved on the lintel above the entranceway to a house or courtyard. This same form of identification, using a different set of symbols, occurs in Muslim houses and courtyards, although here there is a wider range of symbols, such as a crescent, star or pine tree, as well as letters and numbers. These symbols occur in Orthodox Christian villages and Muslim villages, as well as villages that are mixed. As yet it is not clear whether there were earlier equivalents in wood, or whether this was something that denoted an important person in a village but was later adopted across a wider group and took on a wider meaning. But it is certainly the case that by the 1890s these images could be seen in the wrought-iron grates (above the doors) that continued into the next century and became popular with the wider community.

Up until the early twentieth century a village would have consisted of farmers, shepherds, their families, and sometimes a priest and a schoolteacher (often the same person). A typical village may have consisted of several one- and two-room mudbrick houses grouped together along narrow tracks and surrounded by fields. Courtyards – which today can often be places of social gathering – were where animals were kept and work was done. Often these lacked verandahs, or private spaces, doors to houses were left open, chairs were placed in the street and villagers sat outside, visible to all who walked by. For illustrative examples from the time, see village photographs in Thompson (1985), Malecos (1992) and Ohnefalsch Richter (1994). Not every village had a school, and by no means could all children attend. Prior to, and including the early years of the British control, mainly boys attended school.

At a certain point in time – differing across the island – within Cypriot society we get a changing notion of space, and the development of the idea of public space (and, by its very nature, the opposite, private space) to replace what I have termed communal space. Within the village it is seen in the slow development across the island, village by village, through the opening of coffee houses, the creation of village squares, the appearance of schools, religious and political monuments, local stores, cinemas and community halls. It can also be seen in small changes, even something as simple as the closing-off of court-yards. These become private enclosed spaces within the homes that no longer serve a functional purpose and the courtyard also becomes a place for social-ising. This is true of both the Orthodox and Muslim communities: it goes beyond the religious, and later ethnic and nationalist changes. At the same time borders were being drawn between neighbours, and there was a shift from thinking of 'difference' as that between Orthodox Christians and Muslims, to becoming Greek and Turk.

This changing notion, or the development of public space, is an important issue possibly tied to the development of nationalism and a nationalist sentiment. Prior to this, society appeared to operate at a more personal and individual level. It is only after the arrival of the British that this seems to change. It is possible that the very physicality of British colonisation – Government House, the police stations, post offices, and so on, combined with greater access to amenities, roads, print media and a world beyond the village – led the Cypriot villagers to act similarly.

My research has shown that through the material record of the general growth and changes experienced in Cypriot villages over the last century we can see the development of forms of ethno-nationalism amongst the two communities. But these communities themselves have also changed and developed over this time. The traditional architecture and spatial layout of Cypriot villages experienced major changes during this time. Some villages, such as the Turkish Cypriot villages of the northern Paphos region, embraced modernity, and the houses, schools and material culture associated with them demonstrates this. Others, such as the villages around Atheinou to the east, instead chose to keep a more traditional style but adopted some of the urban and neo-classical styles also seen in Nicosia.

CONCLUSION

Questions of empire and colonialism need to address not just the impact of empire on the subject colony, but also to take into consideration how empires encounter and are transformed by those cultures they seek to dominate, thus considering the multiple perspectives and points of view of all involved in the colonial process. It is dependent upon what the empire in question hopes to gain from the territory it is taking over. The local articulation of the global concept of imperialism – colonialism – is always contextual and tied to a particular time and place.

It is important to understand that the British Empire was not a timeless unchanging monolithic entity. The role and aims of the British Empire towards the end of the nineteenth century in Cyprus are very different from the role and aims of the British Empire that established colonies in North America in the early seventeenth century and in Australia in the late eighteenth century. In October 1907, after a visit to Cyprus, Winston Churchill, then Under Secretary of State for the Colonies, described British occupation as 'quite unworthy of Great Britain, and altogether out of accordance with the whole principles of our colonial policy in every part of the world' (Georghallides 1979: 17). In many aspects Churchill was right, however, it is clear that Britain considered the occupation of Cyprus as a strategic move, positioning itself in a location close to two regions of potential conflict – the Russo-Turkish confrontation, and Suez and the Tigris-Euphrates Valley (Patrick 1976: 5; Georghallides 1979).

However, for whatever reason, the British chose not to attempt to alter two aspects of Cypriot culture – language and religion. Although English was the language used at an administrative level, it was not a compulsory language taught in schools. This played a fundamental role in the development of Greek Cypriot and Turkish Cypriot identities throughout the twentieth century. Thus, regardless of the administrative changes, cultural difference between the coloniser and the colonised was not eroded. If anything we can see that the British administration played a role in the development of the nationalist causes on the island. This is perhaps most easily seen in the development of ENOSIS amongst the Greek Cypriots.

It would appear that in the establishment of the British Empire in Cyprus during the later nineteenth century, the government policy relating to religious difference created and fostered cultural diversity along ethnic lines, as opposed to homogeneity amongst the peoples on the island. This diversity existed until the 1960s and the creation of the Republic of Cyprus. The period from 1968 to 1972 saw a series of unsuccessful inter-communal negotiations. What was to follow was the invasion of Cyprus by Turkey on 20 July 1974. This resulted in the division and occupation of the northern part of the island by Turkish Cypriots and mainland Turks. In 1975 the 'Federal Turkish-Cypriot State' was proclaimed, and the so-called 'Turkish Republic of Northern Cyprus' was declared in 1983. (The Turkish Republic of Northern Cyprus is recognised only by Turkey.) Official and unofficial communications have occurred between both sides but to no avail; sadly Cyprus remains a divided island, with no tangible solution in sight. The year 2000 marked 40 years since Cyprus became an independent republic; perhaps there has not yet been enough time for the full effect of the British Empire to have emerged.

ACKNOWLEDGEMENTS

My PhD research has been funded in part by a University of Glasgow PhD Scholarship. Sections and ideas within this chapter have benefited from discussions on identity with Louise Hitchcock, Gloria London and Tessa Poller. I would like to thank Aileen Friel for reading and commenting on a draft of this chapter. Any errors remain my own.

REFERENCES

Anonymous (1929) *The Mukhtar's Handbook*. Nicosia: Government Printing Office.
Anthias, F. (1992) *Ethnicity, Class, Gender and Migration. Greek Cypriots in Britain.* Aldershot: Avebury.
Bender, B. (ed.) (1993) *Landscape, Politics and Perspectives*. Oxford: Berg.
Bernal, M. (1994) The image of ancient Greece as a tool for colonialism and European hegemony. In G.C. Bond and A. Gilliam (eds), *Social Construction of the Past: Representation as Power*, 119–29. London: Routledge.

Bond, G.C. and Gilliam, A. (eds) (1994) *Social Construction of the Past: Representation as Power*. London: Routledge.

Bryant, R. (1998) An education in honor: patriotism and rebellion in Greek Cypriot schools. In V. Calotychos (ed.), *Cyprus and Its People: Nation, Identity, and Experience in an Unimaginable Community (1955–1997)*, 53–68. Boulder, CO: Westview Press.

Calotychos, V. (ed.) (1998) *Cyprus and Its People: Nation, Identity, and Experience in an Unimaginable Community (1955–1997)*. Boulder, CO: Westview Press.

Crawshaw, N. (1978) *The Cyprus Revolt: An Account of the Struggle for Union with Greece*. London: Allen and Unwin.

Georghallides, G.S. (1979) *A Political and Administrative History of Cyprus, 1918–1926. With a Survey of the Foundations of British Rule*. Text and Studies of the History of Cyprus IV, Cyprus Research Centre: Nicosia.

Given, M. (1997) Star of the Parthenon, Cypriot *mélange*: education and representation in colonial Cyprus. *Journal of Mediterranean Studies* 7(1): 59–82.

Jacobs, J.M. (1996) *Edge of Empire: Postcolonialism and the City*. London: Routledge.

Jones, S. (1997) *The Archaeology of Ethnicity. Constructing Identities in the Past and Present*. London: Routledge.

Kitchener, H.H. (1882) 'A trigonometrical survey of the island of Cyprus, executed and published by command of H.E. Major General Sir R. Bidulph . . . High Commissioner, under the direction of Captain H.H. Kitchener, R.E. Director of Survey, hillshading by Lieutenant S.C.N. Grant, R.E., 1882'. Scale of one inch to one statute mile 1:163,360. London: Edward Standford.

Malecos, A. (ed.) (1992) *Cyprus of J.P. Foscolo*. Nicosia: Cultural Centre Cyprus Popular Bank.

Marangou, A.G. (1995) *Nicosia A Special Capital*. Nicosia.

Ohnefalsch Richter, M. [1913] (1994) *Greek Customs and Traditions in Cyprus*. Nicosia: Cultural Centre Popular Bank.

Patrick, R.A. (1976) *Political Geography and the Cyprus Conflict 1963–1971*. London, Canada: Department of Geography, University of Waterloo.

Pihler, M. (ed.) (1993) *A Dragoman's House: The House of Hadjigeorgakis Kornesios in Nicosia*. Cyprus Museum, Department of Antiquities of the Republic of Cyprus and the Royal Danish Academy of Fine Arts, School of Architecture, Department of Restoration, Copenhagen.

Rizopoulou-Egoumenidou, E. (1993) The Dragoman of Cyprus Hadjigeorgakis Kornesios. In M. Pihler (ed.), *A Dragoman's House: The House of Hadjigeorgakis Kornesios in Nicosia*, 10–16. Cyprus Museum, Department of Antiquities of the Republic of Cyprus and the Royal Danish Academy of Fine Arts, School of Architecture, Department of Restoration, Copenhagen.

Said, E.W. (1993) *Culture and Imperialism*. London: Chatto and Windus.

Schaar, K.W., Given, M. and Theocharous, G. (1995) *Under the Clock. Colonial Architecture and History in Cyprus, 1878–1960*. Nicosia: Bank of Cyprus.

Seretis, K. (forthcoming) 'Identities and empire: Cyprus under British rule.' Unpublished PhD thesis, University of Glasgow.

Shennan, S.J. (ed.) (1989) *Archaeological Approaches to Cultural Identity*. London: Routledge.

Silberman, N.A. (1989) *Between Past and Present. Archaeology, Ideology, and Nationalism in the Modern Middle East*. New York: Henry Holt.

Smith, A.D. (1988) *The Ethnic Origins of Nations*. Oxford: Blackwell.

Talbot, J.E. and Cape, F.W. (1914) *Report on Education in Cyprus 1913*. London: Miscellaneous Official Publications.

Thompson, J. [1878] (1985) *Through Cyprus With the Camera in the Autumn of 1878*. London: Trigraph.

Wilson, T.M. and Donnan, H. (eds) (1998) *Border Identities, Nation and State at International Frontiers*. Cambridge: Cambridge University Press.

14 Staging history, inventing heritage: the 'new pageantry' and British imperial identity, 1905–35

PETER MERRINGTON

Brother Copas is a novel (1911) by 'Q' (Sir Arthur Quiller-Couch), set in King Alfred's ancient capital city of Winchester, where hangs, in the cathedral, what is reputed to be the Round Table of King Arthur and his knights. This novel deals with the planning and presentation of a pageant, an instance of the genre of 'new pageantry', by the brothers and staff of Saint Cross Hospice, that ancient institution which lies in the water-meadows below Winchester College. A girl child, Corona Bonaday, arrives at Southampton by steamer (the *Carnatic*) from America, to stay with her uncle, a brother in the Hospice. It is a return to her roots in England, where she had been born, as well as a challenging but valuable rediscovery of her real father. At the same time, she is cast in the pageant as Queen of the May, and so her experience is a paradigm for the rediscovery of 'Englishness'.

'Q's' fictional pageant at Winchester follows the production of an actual pageant in this city in 1908. Many hundreds of similar pageants were performed throughout England, and in other parts of the British Isles and the 'dominions' of the Commonwealth, in the first three decades of the twentieth century. Quiller-Couch was a co-author of the *Pageant of Bradstone*, which was produced in 1929, and he appears to have been involved in numerous other such projects over the years. Various other authors adopted the idea of a historical pageant as a model on which to structure their histories and their novels. Perhaps most notable here is Virginia Woolf, whose final novel, *Between the Acts* (1941), set on the eve of World War II, is composed around the performance of a local historical pageant at a small country town, while her fictional tribute to Vita Sackville-West, *Orlando* (1928), is constructed as if it were a historical pageant of English letters. Woolf's friend and peer as a modernist author, E.M. Forster, wrote the scripts for two pageant performances, *Abinger Pageant* (1934) and *England's Green and Pleasant Land: A Pageant Play* (1938). During the historical moment which we call 'modernism' there is a paradoxically contrary preoccupation with 'Englishness', with heritage, roots and the archaic, albeit, as in Woolf's case, ironic.

In material stemming from the first two decades of the twentieth century we thus encounter a deliberate archaising of British identity, partly in reaction to the pressures of cosmopolitan modernisation, partly in line with contemporary trends in the archaeology of the antique world and partly parallel to a similar archaising of national identity in, for instance, Germany. We find, during this period, considerable interest in topics such as British pre-history approached from the perspective of myth and legend. National myths and legends such as those associated with King Arthur, the extraordinary claims of the cult known as the 'British Israelites' (promoted by some of the more fanciful of early Egyptologists such as Charles Piazzi Smyth, Astronomer Royal for Scotland (1865)), and the legends surrounding Glastonbury Abbey find prominent support. At the same time and partly from a range of more respectable individuals and institutions we note a widespread resurgence of interest in Shakespeare, in the 'spacious days of Good Queen Bess', and in all things Tudor.

These archaising trends are encountered during the period in literature, in popular histories, in biography, in the visual arts and architecture, and in performances of various kinds, notably in the performance genre of 'new pageantry'. This popular performance genre was used to invent and to reinforce a sense of national 'heritage', not only for the English but also (within the context of British imperial feeling) for the new nations of the Commonwealth such as South Africa and Australia. It is argued that the concept of heritage enjoyed its apogee in the early decades of the twentieth century and was a persuasive if conservative means of articulating national identity. The two concepts of 'pageantry' and 'heritage' (along with that of 'romance') were in fact often regarded as synonymous with the idea of 'history', evinced in the titles of popular historical works such as *The Pageant of Parliament*, *Romance of World History* and *Our Royal Heritage*, and of course numerous works of fiction such as the novel by Vita Sackville-West entitled *Heritage* (1919).

HERITAGE

> The life for us all, especially for the artist and the actor, is a kind of lampadephoria, in which the runners, swift or slow, short-lived or enduring, pass on the torch, radiant or flickering, from hand to hand.
> (Frank Benson, quoted in Trewin, 1960: 11)

It is evident from a variety of fields and kinds of social discourse that the concept of heritage, at present a leading concept in schools of cultural studies and historical archaeological studies was, in fact, a dominant trope with a richly layered and active set of meanings in the late nineteenth and early twentieth centuries. A considerable number of books appear in this period with titles such as *A Goodly Heritage* (a popular title taken from Psalm 16:6), *The Heritage of the Spirit* (1896), *The Common Heritage* (1907) and *Our Heritage: Individual, Social and Religious* (1903). Two quotations from this last work (which specifically refers to all then-current interpretations of the theme, from orthodox Christian theology to Darwin, Herbert Spencer, Lamarck and Galton) offer a sense of the cogency, and the ethical flavour, with which this trope was used:

> Thus we are born into a nation, into a great heritage of national history, national temperament, national privilege, as well as into a family and a home. . . .
>   Every generation leaves to its successors a valuable legacy. That inheritance is stored up in some institution, in some Art, in some accumulated wealth of Utility, in some Inheritance of History, or Poetry, or Science, or Literature, which make the world richer than they found it.
>
>   (Bruce 1903: 14, 93)

The chapters in Bruce's book are titled 'Our individual heritage', 'Heredity and responsibility', 'Our social heritage', 'Our educational heritage', 'Our civil and political privileges: the patrimony of civil and political privilege' and 'Our trusteeship of the great heritage'. It is impossible here to explore the range of expressions of this trope during the period in question, but it needs to be emphasised that the considerable force of the heritage tropology derives from its varied provenance: questions of legal right, laws of inheritance, succession and property ownership, speculations within social Darwinism and eugenics, concepts of national duty as 'trusteeship', national destiny, spiritual inheritance and the ubiquitous usage of metaphors of the family to describe social and international relations (the family of nations, sister states, brother races, and so forth) all sustain the idea of heritage as a model for social relations and for possession and empowerment. Its spiritual-evolutionary dimension, furthermore, was expressed in such eccentric, though popular, period fads as the movement called the British Israelite Truth, which published works with titles such as *The Covenant or Jacob's Heritage* (1877), *Our Great Heritage, With its Responsibilities: How and Where to Find the Title Deeds* (1927, 1937) and *The Heritage of the Anglo-Saxon Race* (1941), in which Britain was made out to be the lost tribe of Judah, and her imperial mission to be a spiritual destiny. Here we encounter a distinct attempt not only to claim a 'heritage', but also to fashion a 'genealogy' that would 'legitimise' this claim. As a controlling motif the idea of 'heritage' needs to be analysed for its discursive historical dimensions which, predominantly, indicate a sense of patriarchal imperial genealogy. As a partial synonym for 'public history' the idea of 'heritage' needs to be understood to entail a legacy of meanings that is not only far from neutral but is, in fact, remarkably dated and, by and large, conservative.

The idea of 'heritage' implies a narrative – a life-story with a teleological emphasis on the value of patrimony. This narrative structure is fundamental to the classic English novel from the eighteenth century on, but seems to emerge as a particularly self-conscious theme in the late nineteenth century even as the old Tory tradition of landed gentry becomes patently a thing of the past. It is taken to task by Thomas Hardy in *Tess of the D'Urbervilles* (1891) and by Samuel

Butler in his Lamarckian satire *The Way of All Flesh* (1903). It appears as social fantasy in Mark Twain's *The Prince and the Pauper* (1882) and his tale of 'racial' heritage *Pudd'nhead Wilson* (1894). As Anne McClintock has demonstrated, it is a motivating factor for Alan Quatermain in H. Rider Haggard's *King Solomon's Mines* (1885). It emerges in 1901 in Kipling's *Kim*, and in *The Inheritors*, a fantasy by Joseph Conrad and Ford Madox Ford which satirises King Leopold of Belgium and Cecil Rhodes. It is the theme of Vita Sackville-West's first novel *Heritage* (1919), and it appears as a belated coda to this epoch in the elegiac pessimism of Evelyn Waugh's *Brideshead Revisited* (1945). Besides these well-known authors and classic texts, a host of lesser pot-boilers and thrillers enters the new mass-readership market for consumable romance in Britain during this period, with titles such as *The Heir Without a Heritage* (1887), *Gilbert Freethorne's Heritage: A Romance of Clerical Life* (1888), *Frank Horton's Heritage, or, A Yoked Bondage* (1889), *The Heritage of Langdale* (1894), *An Unsought Heritage* (1896), *The Dual Heritage* (1908), *An Empty Heritage* (1908), *The Persistent Heritage* (1925) and *The Inheritance* (1928), this last by Florence Young, an expatriate South African writer of romances. Apart from these overt references, a great deal of English literature of the turn of the century celebrates a sense of 'Englishness' through the motif of the country house, the vernacular tradition, the Elizabethan or Stuart house set in mellow lawns, gardens and woods. Kipling's *Puck of Pook's Hill* (1906) and *Rewards and Fairies* (1910) represent English history and 'heritage' in terms of the English countryside.

'ARCHE' AND THE ARCHAIC

In 1911 a book appeared on the topic of *The Shakespeare Revival and the Stratford-upon-Avon Movement*. The book was written by Reginald R. Buckley, proponent of the concept of 'music drama' in England, or an English version of Wagnerian national opera. It had sections on the topic of folk art, as well as a foreword by the doyen of Shakespeare repertory, F.R. (Frank) Benson. Buckley, in collaboration with the composer Rutland Boughton, produced an Arthurian cycle of 'music drama', and planned to found a national theatre for England, on the lines of Bayreuth, to be situated at Glastonbury Abbey. In his book on the 'Shakespeare revival', Buckley waxes visionary, entering the heritage discourse with an emphasis on archaic Englishness and a preoccupation with eugenics, blood and soil:

> The time has come to speak out: to say to the singers and players of England, 'The Round Table is spread'; to the dramatists, 'The Sword of Power that was Shakespeare's is set in the stone four-square. Let him that is king among you draw it forth!'; to the educationists, 'Behold in Stratford all that England can do in the way of Art. . . .
>
> To those who have eyes to see and ears to hear it is abundantly evident that there is to-day an awakening throughout the length and

breadth of England. It is an awakening of national consciousness and of national responsibility. It involves a race-consciousness that will overcome class prejudice, and that will unite the dwellers in all parts of the Empire in that it means a new Imperial ideal. . . .

The evidences of this awakening are all around us in England to-day. In cities and in towns young men and women are spending the hours of recreation in singing the folk-songs and dancing the folk-dances evolved from the tillers of the soil, as an expression of race-consciousness in religious ceremonial . . .

(1911: 175, 204, 205)

In *Music-Drama of the Future* (1911) Buckley and Boughton supply a pictorial image of the 'future' which is at the same time an archive of the past (Figure 14.1). This image depicts an arch or vault, enclosing an altar with a sacred fire. The arch is called 'the gate of the future'. In curious combination the names of 'Watts, Angelo, Morris, Sophocles, Shakespeare, Wagner and Beethoven'

Figure 14.1 'The Gate of the Future', from Boughton and Buckley's *Music-Drama of the Future* (1911)

are inscribed on the arch. This image of the arch with altar is derived from a
high 'degree' of Freemasonry, known as 'Royal Arch' masonry, which was
presided over at the time by the Prince of Wales. It occurs again, with reference to the public sphere and public ceremonial, as the frontispiece to the
autobiography of the British imperial architect, Herbert Baker (Figure 14.2).
Baker too had a strong commitment to the folklorish aspects of vernacular
culture, to vernacular architecture, to 'arts and crafts', to Englishness and the
idea of Empire, and to initiatives such as Ebenezer Howard's 'garden city'
movement and the English National Trust.

The significance of Baker's and Buckley's images is made clear from the
Freemasonic meaning of the idea of the 'Royal Arch'. This is based on a
pun, in which the root meaning of 'arch', from the Greek *arche*, both origin
and authority, is linked to the Latin *arca*, coffer or bow, from whence the

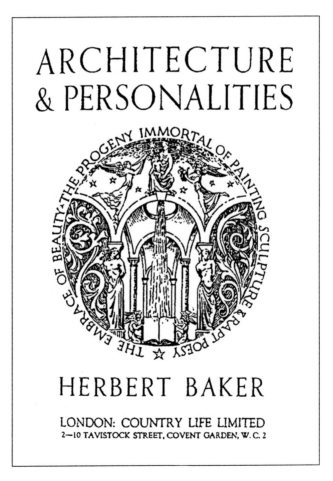

Figure 14.2 Frontispiece to the autobiography of Herbert Baker

engineering concept of the arch as structure is derived. A Freemasonic hand-book offers the following translation of the opening words of the Gospel of John: 'In the *arch* was the Word.' Thus the visual image fuses the idea of begin-nings and authority together with the idea of an architectonic form, a physical shelter or repository, a site for the safe-keeping of sacred meaning. Archivism or the safe-keeping of the nation's heritage and memory becomes a sacred and ceremonial performance which recursively reasserts the *arche*, the archaic, or origins as authority. For Buckley this is done through 'Music drama', choral works on Arthurian legend, on Uther, Igraine and Merlin, and antique Cornwall. For Baker, this is achieved through massive national and imperial architectural achievements which are studded with various sets of historical symbols, notably the Union Buildings in Pretoria, South Africa (*c.* 1908–11), the huge project of New Delhi in India, undertaken in collaboration with Sir Edwin Lutyens between 1912 and the mid-1920s, some of the World War I cemeteries or 'cities of the dead' in northern France, South Africa House in Trafalgar Square and Rhodes House in Oxford, which is an archive in all of the above senses.

PAGEANTRY AND BRITISH IMPERIAL IDENTITIES

> Pageantry for Art's sake, and for History's sake, and for the sake of Patriotism, national and international, . . . pageantry for the sake of human understanding and universal brotherhood.
>
> (Darnley 1932: 48)

Just as 'heritage' is used in the titles of books, so we find from the same epoch the recurring usage of 'pageant' or 'pageantry' to indicate a work of partisan history. Examples abound such as *The Pageant of British History* (1908) or *Pageant of Parliament* (1934). A later example (*c.* 1945) is Wilfrid Castle's social history of Syria and Palestine entitled *Syrian Pageant*. The term also has its literal and distinctly historical dimensions. In 1905 Louis-Napoleon Parker, a French-born son of expatriate American parents, 'invented' a new performance genre in England with, as he calls it, the 'Mother of all Pageants', the 'Historical Pageant of Sherbourne', in England. Parker's 'New Pageantry' swept North America for several decades, an early instance being the Québec Tercentenary Pageant produced in 1908. An American Pageantry Association was rapidly formed, to preside over the burgeoning industry, to regulate the new theatre scholarship generated by the pageants and to produce handbooks for 'pageant masters' (Glassberg 1990; Prevots 1990). The 'New Pageantry' was used for the cele-bration of founding anniversaries and jubilees, and inaugural occasions, in Britain, the United States and the imperial dominions. An Oxford-educated thespian, Frank Lascelles, 'Lord of the Manor of Sibford Gower' in Oxfordshire, became – like Parker – a celebrated 'pageant master', friend of royalty and imperial proconsuls, producer of imperial pageants and durbars. Lascelles, who produced the Oxford Historical Pageant in 1907 (with Kipling and Mark Twain in attendance), was invited to produce the Québec Tercentenary Pageant, held on the Plains of Abraham above the St Lawrence River (the scene of Wolfe's victory over Montcalm in 1759). The Chief Justice of the Cape Colony and Chairman of the National Convention (for the drawing up of a constitution for the new state of the Union of South Africa), Sir J.H. de Villiers, attended in lieu of the Union prime-minister elect, Louis Botha. De Villiers recommended this performance as the best way to inaugurate the South African Union in 1910, and Frank Lascelles was commissioned to produce the Union Pageant in Cape Town that year (Merrington 1997, 1999; Kruger 1999). Among the many other pageants produced by Lascelles was the 1911 Pageant of London staged at the great coronation year Empire Exhibition, and the Calcutta pageant which accompanied the coronation durbar at Delhi in early 1912 (Ryan 1999). His Harrow Historical Pageant (1923) enjoyed a list of aristocratic and distinguished patrons, which included Winston Churchill, Sir Oswald Mosley and Rudyard Kipling.

The term 'pageantry' displays an etymology (independent of the historical dimensions of the genre) that is virtually a paradigm for the 'colonial project'. It is derived from the Latin *pagus* meaning both a 'field' and a 'page'. This in turn stems from the verb *pangere*, to sow, plant, establish, record, pledge and covenant (which also happens to be the root of *pax* – a reminder of the Victorian ideal of '*Pax Britannica*'). Thus we find a paradigm of chronicling, occupying and settling the land, and covenanting: activities that are fundamental to what might be generalised as the 'colonial enterprise'. The scripts of the Cape Town and the Québec pageants (published as the 'Book of Words', or the 'Book of the Pageant') are compiled by local and national historians and antiquarians, and prefaced with dedicatory remarks from viceroys and premiers. The most significant historical episodes in the pageants are those dealing with landfall and settlement, as well as moments of dedication, covenant between settlers and God, or the signing of treaties between them and the 'natives'.

As the epigraph at the beginning of this section indicates, immense claims were made, at the time, for the social value of the 'new pageantry'. Again, here is a statement describing the 1910 Union of South Africa Pageant: 'Hottentots, Basutos, Zulus, Portuguese, Dutch and British all joined in. Now, no religion could have forged this unity, no patriotic appeal – nothing but a great drama in which races could act their own share in the epic story of a modern world's making.' 'History' and 'Art', patriotism, universal understanding and brotherhood, unity, the making of the modern world: these generous ideas are embodied in an epic and dramatic narrative; and this neo-Hegelian concept of progression towards a social ideal of universal wisdom is further inflected with social-Darwinist concepts of racial gradation.

In his first performance (produced in 1905 for the 800th anniversary of the founding of the town of Sherbourne in England), Louis Napoleon Parker included a procession of Freemasons singing Masonic hymns, and again there was a considerable Freemasonic aspect to the South African Pageant of Union:

late Victorian and Edwardian social tropologies of 'human understanding' and 'universal brotherhood', of national and racial origins and 'heritage', of helio-centric enlightenment and renewal such as were enacted in contemporary creed-systems like Freemasonry, are a ready stock of universalist concepts and images from which to construct the iconography of imperialism, whether it be in South Africa, Québec or Newfoundland, Egypt or Australia.

While the imperial pageants enjoyed this iconic and allegorical dimension, they were, however, not as programmatically allegorical by nature as were the instances of the 'new pageantry' that were produced in the United States – such as 'The Pageant of Darkness and Light' (Boston, 1911), 'A Pageant of Patriotism' (Taunton, MA, 1911), 'Pageant of American Childhood' (Worcester, MA, 1913) and 'The Romance of Work' (Philadelphia, 1915). The British and imperial pageants (including those of Québec and Cape Town) tended to focus more on historical re-enactment, on the presentation of canon-ical histories which emphasised founding episodes, while 'the American type made free use of allegorical interludes' (Beegle and Randall 1916: 19). An-other early commentator claimed that American pageants 'lean more towards advancing community ideals than in England and especially in featuring symbolism and prophecy' (Davol 1914: 28). Despite this distinction in style and content, the pageants in both the United States and the dominions of the Empire nonetheless were equally reflections of colonial or settler identity, and of spiritual-evolutionary discourses such as were popularly propagated at the turn of the century in the contemporary international climate of neo-Hegelian idealism. Both the Cape Town pageant and the Québec pageant laid emphasis on motifs of Christian enlightenment, civilization, the 'taming' of 'barbarous' lands and peoples.

Pageantry drew heavily on nineteenth-century ethnic typology. In both the Cape Town and Québec pageants the indigenous peoples are represented as of timeless tribal types: 'Bushmen', 'Hottentots', Zulus, Iroquois and Huron. These are distinguished by stereotypical characteristics – the 'Bushmen' are childlike, the 'Hottentots' cunning, the Zulus warlike, the Iroquois bloodthirsty and the Huron loyal. All are frozen in an ethnographic time-capsule, whereby (apart from exemplary individual cases of Christian conversion and change in lifestyle) they serve as a constant symbol of avowed racial, cultural and cogni-tive difference. They are a showcase to illustrate picturesque regionalism or to offset by pointed contrasts the 'civilization' of the colonisers. A comment on the back of a postcard from the Québec festival entitled 'At Home with the Caughnewanga Iroquois, who played their ancestors' parts in the pageants' reveals distinctly the racism of the period:

It is remarkable that, in spite of the centuries which in passing have done their best to civilize the Indian tribes of Canada, these people retain so fully the characteristics and habits of their ancestors. Ordinarily dressed as our white men, and living on farms, in ordinary houses, they fall with the utmost readiness into the spirit as into the garb of the aboriginal Indians. Their acting of savage progenitors is intensely real, and reveals depths of originality seldom seen among our white Thespians. It is the influence of their traditions, and shows that the later influence of our civilization is superficial. Their home is the wigwam, their dress the deerskin.

One particular emphasis in the 'new pageantry' is on the European Renaissance, and in particular on 'Elizabethanism', which served at the turn of the century as a motif for English identity, for the 'organic' values of a pre-industrial age ('The Spacious Days of Good Queen Bess') and for the idea of the fully rounded English gentleman (Girouard 1981). The following comment from a contributor to *Our Modern Orpheus*, the *festschrift* for Frank Lascelles, puts the contemporary viewpoint clearly:

> True pageantry is the modern counterpart of the spirit which inspired the Elizabethan renaissance, the period when Britain's greatness was founded, when her Imperial impetus was established.
>
> In that age, pageantry, from becoming a function of the trade guilds, virtually assumed control of the British nation. The Elizabethan was an era in which the whole nation expressed its life in a pageant of expansion. Nothing was too great for the dreamers of that age and nothing too difficult for them to accomplish. Thus it came to be evident that the highest and truest function of pageantry is to inspire the race to greater achievement. This constitutes its importance as a modern imperial influence.
>
> (Darnley 1932: 124)

It is a motif that recurs frequently in the writing of such figures as Rudyard Kipling and John Buchan (who, with his daughter Alice, wrote the *Book of the Words* for the Oxfordshire Historical Pageant at Kidlington in 1931), and it is consonant with the contemporaneous idea of the vernacular revival in domestic architecture. 'Elizabethanism' strongly inflects all ideas of English national 'heritage' at the time. It would seem no accident that the first serious modern exponent of Shakespeare (Shakespeare as a national bard, his plays as evidence of national character) should be A.C. Bradley, the brother of the Oxford neo-Hegelian F.H. Bradley, whose work on the idea of the 'organic' state is arguably a philosophical underpinning to the period obsession with a lost English Arcadia. According to Buchan, the gentleman-adventurers of his class and generation who rode with the imperial forces in the South African War, and who attended Milner in his Anglophone 'reconstruction', were such 'Elizabethans'. An example from Buchan's memoirs, *Memory-Hold-the-Door*, turns an individual life into an allegorical interlude from a grand historical pageant:

> The phrase 'Elizabethan' too casually applied, can be used with truth of Basil [Blackwood]. He was of the same breed as the slender gallants

who singed the beard of the King of Spain and, like Essex, tossed their
plumed hats into the sea in joy of the enterprise, or who sold their
swords to whatever cause had daylight and honour in it. His like had
left their bones in farther spaces than any race on earth, and from their
unchartered wanderings our empire was born.

He had the streak of Ariel in him, and his fancy had always wings.
'For to admire and for to see' was his motto. In a pedestrian world
he held to the old cavalier grace, and wherever romance called he
followed with careless gallantry.

(Buchan 1941: 107)

It is curious that the idea of historical pageantry with its emphasis on peri-
odicity and on origins should have exerted such influence on the popular
imagination in the decades that are known, generally, as the age of 'modernism'.
Two exemplary modernist authors, T.S. Eliot and Virginia Woolf, borrow from
the genre for the form of their poetry and fiction, and their peer E.M. Forster
scripted two actual instances of this performance genre. Early twentieth-century
'modernity', it seems, depended as much on a sense of the imaginary recuper-
ation of past ages as on a necessary sense of rupture with the past. Dressing up,
costume balls and the performances of the *Ballets Russes*, introduce a risque
carnival of imperial 'otherness' into the proprieties of 'home'. Pre-eminently,
however, the 'new pageantry' was intended to act as a means of reinforcing
social responsibility, civic and national pride, and the idea of modern 'democracy'. In his memoirs the pageant master Louis Napoleon Parker stresses the
ideal that the pageants should be socially inclusive; and the organising of
the Union Pageant in South Africa was an unprecedented coup in public relations, logistics and the control of mass casts and mass audiences.

The Times of London (14 July 1910), in an extended notice of the South
Africa Union pageant, says the following: 'The idea underlying the pageant is
to create from the outset of the Union a tradition founded on the actual history
of the races of which the "last-born nation of the British empire" is made up.'
The understanding was that a public tradition may be invented out of the raw
material of 'actual history' in order to forge a sense of national, racial or civic
identity. The following editorial from *Cook's Travellers' Gazette, Excursionist and
Tourism Advertiser* (September 1910) exemplifies the sense of civic and imperial
ceremonial, and the idea of 'history' as ideologically approved public spectacle.
It also reminds us of the very substantial touristic dimension to 'public history'
which emerged in the second half of the nineteenth century with the rise of
mass tourism and the phenomenon of the Great Exhibitions, *Expositions
Universelles* and World's Fairs:

Visitors to the Cape during the early part of November will be able
to add an extra item of exceptional interest to the usual programme
of sightseeing, viz, the Pageant at Cape Town, arranged in order to
celebrate the opening of the Union Parliament, at which the Duke of

Connaught will be present. The various scenes in this great spectacle will be presented at the foot of Table Mountain, on a scale closely resembling that held on the Plains of Abraham in Canada last year. The mastership of the Pageant has been entrusted to Mr Frank Lascelles, who is organising the Festival of Empire and Pageant of London to be held at the Crystal Palace next year.

The episodes, dating from 1486 right down to the Union of the South African Colonies, will include, amongst others, scenes illustrative of Primordial Savagery; Discovery of the Cape; Embarkation of Vasco da Gama; the Coming of Van Riebeeck; the Building of the Fort of 'Goede Hoop'; First English Occupation; incidents of the Great Trek, etc, terminating with an Allegorical Finale representing the consummation of the Union.

There were hundreds of instances of historical pageants performed in Britain between 1905 and, roughly, 1935, some of them on a huge scale such as the 1911 Pageant of London, and others performed on the stage of a village hall. They all tended to follow the model set by Louis Napoleon Parker, with the remarkable consequence that this genre seems to have shaped a popular public understanding of what is meant by 'history'. History, according to the formula of the 'new pageantry', is a partisan sequence of episodes (including myth and legend) which focus on famous men and women; history is in every sense affirmative of a clearly given set of values and perspectives; and history moves towards a grand 'consummation' or finale. There are moments of origin, and moments of 'first encounter', all of which emphasise the archaic, the original and the authoritative within national identity. History is made into a courtly performance, a set of symbolic acts and a national ritual. The final section of this chapter sketches the substance of four British pageants, three from England and one from Scotland, which illustrate this idea of ceremonial archaism.

ARCHAISING THE BRITISH

Louis Napoleon Parker's second pageant, the Warwick Pageant (2–7 July 1906), was produced 'in celebration of the 1000th anniversary of the conquest of Mercia by Queen Ethelfleda'. Sir Herbert Beerbohm Tree 'lent the heavy armour'. The pageant was staged in parkland under the walls of Warwick Castle with a glimpse of the River Avon. It was composed of 11 historical episodes, with a prologue in the form of a druidical chorus, and an epilogue and final tableau. Here is the opening druidical chorus, which was sung around a druidical altar:

Sages of the sea-girt isle,
That Clas Merddyn hight erewhile –
Nook of water-guarded green,

Where the age-hewn oak is seen
And the moon-eyed mistletoe –
All that earth or heaven can show
By our cryptic art we ken,
Wisest of the sons of men:
Seers and prophet-bards are we,
Priests of death and destiny.

Round the rock-built altar go,
Chant it darkly, foot it slow!
Bring weird water from the well!
O'er men's spirits cast a spell –
Mystic herb and scathing fire,
To be memory's funeral-pyre
Fashion of the fumes a veil,
Till both sight and hearing fail:
Dim their senses, lest they be
Masters of our mystery!

Fling we here, as doth behove,
Blossoms of the midnight grove,
Blent with fearful drops that fall
From the wrath-rimmed thunder-pall,
When the moon is hearsed in cloud!
Foot it faster, chant it loud!
Now the potent charm is sped,
Now the spell is perfected!
Eyes that slumber, wake! and see
Visions of the things to be!

The first episode is entitled 'dawn' and it features 'Kymbeline, Caradoc, and the Romans'. The second is evidently a play on the Warwickshire coat of arms, 'The Bear and Ragged Staff', dealing, *c.* AD 500, with 'Britons, Picts and Scots'. Then comes Ethelfleda, daughter of King Alfred, who routs the invading Danes. After this we encounter Guy of Warwick (AD 920), the 'Return of Roger de Newburgh, Earl of Warwick, from the Crusades in 1123 with Templar Knights', scenes from Marlowe's *Edward II* featuring Piers Gaveston, Warwick the 'King Maker' in 1464 and Prince Edward, King Edward IV, the Duke of Clarence, the Earl of Somerset, the Earl of Oxford and Queen Margaret. The eighth episode deals with the 'Charters' in 1546, that is the incorporation of the town of Warwick, and royal charters for local churches, and for the King's School of Warwick. Then comes the 'Nine Days' Queen' (1553), with Lady Jane Grey, Queen Mary and Thomas Fisher. Episode 11 represents the fire in 1694, but the tenth, the penultimate episode, is convulsive in its celebration of the Elizabethan era:

A new world opens on our sight,
A world of ampler life and light –
Hope beckoning from beyond the seas,
And dauntless spirits spurning ease
For vast adventure; mighty names
Made mightier by heroic aims;
Freedom that dawns above the deep,
And knowledge wakening from her sleep

. . .

And in the orient, dewy-dim,
Scarce lifted o'er the horizon-rim,
The kindling of new stars to flame
High in the firmament of fame;
While Europe hangs upon the breath
Of England's great Elizabeth

Elizabeth visits Warwick with a huge cast – Dudley, Seymour, Burghley, Howard of Effingham, Sidney and Spenser, local burgesses, the bailiff of Stratford and his son (John Shakespeare and little William), the guilds of Warwick, a chorus, youths, lords and ladies, dancers, and so forth. Madrigals are sung and there are both stately and grotesque dances, and the state barge proceeds down the Avon.

At the close of the pageant a narrative chorus and the chorus of druids combine, then 'enter Britannia with her escort of colonies, then the girls of the high school with flowers and garlands and sing the song of the high school, then enter other schools, and combined choruses now sing the "Triumph Song" by James Rhoades, "Sons of Warwick, of your fathers' fame arise and sing the pean!"'

Lords of war, or lights of learning, meet to match with man or devil,
Gallant knights and stately ladies, mighty teachers, bards sublime,
Parr and Owen, Field and Greville, classic Landor, princely Neville,
Loved your Burg in all its beauty – made more beautiful by time —
Touched to rapture by the holy hand of time.

Elizabeth's barge then returns up the Avon, with the Queen and Leicester, and from various entrances all the characters who have figured in the pageant march on with their attendants in groups.

They form a huge semicircle . . . now enter the fourteen colonial and American Warwicks represented by young girls in appropriate costume. Lastly enter a stately figure representing Warwick, attended by pages . . . She mounts the pedestal, wearing a masoned crown, typi-fying the castle. In her right hand is a model of St Mary's church, and in her left hand a shield with arms of the town. There follows a great shout of welcome. The junior Warwicks offer her their gifts. The entire crowd bursts into 'The Old Hundredth':

All people that on earth do dwell,
Sing to the lord with cheerful voice
Him serve with fear, his praise forth tell,
come ye before him, and rejoice

This is followed by the National Anthem; then to the strains of solemn music, the march past begins, and the last figure left on the arena is that of the little boy William Shakespeare. As he goes out he kisses his hand to the audience in token that the pageant is ended.

The Scottish National Pageant of Allegory, Myth and History was held in Edinburgh in June 1908 'in aid of the Scottish Children's League of Pity'. It began with an 'allegory of the city of Edinburgh', in which appeared the following set of figures:

The Arms of the City, halberdiers and trumpeters, the River Forth (her long train upheld by fishwives), the City of Edinburgh, Divinity, supported by two Angels, Faith, Hope, and Charity, followed by a monk, a nun, two choirboys, a Doctor of Divinity, and two students carrying a model of St Giles; Law & Learning; Medicine, Valour; agriculture; manufactures; commerce, a stately figure carrying the model of a ship, the four cables from which are held by an Esquimaux, African, Chinese and Canadian, to represent the North, South, East and West of the Globe; Architecture, Sculpture and Painting; Science comes last to guide her in things worldly; a strange and mystic figure bearing the Terrestrial Globe, crowned with the Aureole of the sun, her dark robes covered with Astronomical, Chemical and Algebraical signs. She is followed by her young son, Electricity, shimmering in silver, a brilliant light on his forehead and forked lightnings in his hand, and her youngest child Radium still in his nurse's arms. The Burghs of Scotland further support the Royal City: their representatives, a man and a maid, walk two by two, bearing the Burgh Banner.

This civic allegory is followed by a group of 'The Gods' – 'Bride (the hearth), Angus Og (youth, beauty and courtesy), Lir (Oceanus), and his children (Fionnuala, Conn, Aodh, Fiachra, changed into swans), Aoife (stepmother of the children of Lir); Lugh of the Long Hand (a sun-god) – The Sidhe (spirits of light, life, joy) – The Riders of the Sidhe carrying the Stone of Destiny, the Glaive of light, the Goblet of Abundance; Queen Maeve, and assorted fairies, male and female; the Formorians, Demons, Goblins and Sorceresses, the witches of Skye', and other lesser beings.
These are succeeded by groups of legendary mortals:

Scota, daughter of Pharaoh, married to Nel (from this Queen the Scots
derive their name), Nel (one of the 70 chiefs who built the Tower of
Babel), Eriu (a daughter of the Greeks, who gave her name to Erin);
the Cuchulainn Cycle; the Ossianic Cycle; The Arthurian Legend –
group of the Holy Grail; those who followed the quest of the Holy
Grail; King Arthur's group; knights of the Round Table; the two kings
Ban and Bors who fought for King Arthur; the group of kings who
fought against Arthur; the Questing Beast and the Knights of that quest;
Queen Guinevere and her group; Isolde's group; group of the Queen
of Orkney; group of the Four Queens under the Canopy (Queen
Morgan le Fay, Queen of the Eastlands, Queen of the Outer isles,
Queen of North Galis); escort of 12 knights; group of the Dead Elaine.

After these there appears a sequence of historical groups: Romans; Vikings;
the early Church – Palladius, Ninian, Patrick, Columba, Mungo and his disciples; King Malcolm III; Donald Bain; Duncan II; Edgar; Sir William Wallace;
King Robert the Bruce and Queen Isabella; all the way to the Stuarts, the
Marquis of Montrose, and to Charles II and Queen Catherine, William and
Mary, George I; covenanting gentlemen; and finally Jacobites of the 1715 and
the 1745. The pageant concluded with an allegorical 'Masque of the Seasons'.
    By the 1930s, some 25 years later, the genre had become a national institu-
tion. In this decade of growing international tension much of the Celtic twilight
was excised from the pageants, and the emphasis lay on Britain's, and England's,
public historical virtue, on military triumphs, on pacts and treaties, and on
the supremacy of the Protestant succession. The introduction to the *Book of
the Words* of the Pageant of England (1935) makes it plain that pageantry is
intended as a form of national propaganda:

> Our pageantry is set between these two periods: that coronation a 1000
> years ago when the grandson of Alfred, who was to defeat the northern
> princes on the bloody field of Bremesbrugh, took the oath to preserve
> peace at Kingston-on-Thames, and so kept his word that his alliance
> was courted by all the princes of Western Europe to the end of the
> 18th century, just before England emerged from the world chaos
> caused by the Napoleonic wars with her ancient institutions and her
> monarchy uninjured.
>   We have chosen, in our limited time, to show you of these 800
> years, not the broils and confusions, the debates and strifes, but the
> splendour and the beauty, the drama and the romance best suited to
> our English summer scene.

The Pageant of Runnymede (9–16 June 1934) was advertised as a celebration of English democracy, calling attention to the constitutional moment when
King John was obliged by his lords to sign the Magna Carta. Royal patrons
were the Prince of Wales, the Duke and Duchess of York, and the Earl of

Athlone (Governor-General of South Africa, 1923–31) and Princess Alice. A prologue was written by John Drinkwater and spoken by Dame Sybil Thorndike, and an epilogue spoken by Irene and Violet Vanbrugh. The eight scenes ran as follows: the 'Roman Conquest', the 'Sacking of Chertsey Abbey', King John's 'Granting of the Great Charter', a 'Tournament on St George's Day', 'Henry VIII entertaining the Holy Roman Emperor', 'Charles II hunting in the royal forests', 'Queen Anne opening Ascot Races' and 'Rural England after Waterloo'.

The 'Pageant of England' was staged by Marjorie Bowen and Gwen Lally (who was also the pageant master of the Runnymede Pageant) at Langley Park, Slough, from 28 May to 11 June 1935, the silver jubilee year of George V and Queen Mary. There were performances 'daily at 2.30 and 8.30 pm, floodlit at night'. The pageant consisted of 'seven episodes and a grand finale of Empire, in which British visitors from overseas will take part'. Marjorie Bowen describes the setting as follows:

> The scene chosen for this pageant has been its inspiration, and forms not only the background but the central theme; this space of wood-land where we set our scenes has been little subjected to change, and so preserves some manner of immortality. It has the authentic magic of the English landscape, and thus serves as the perfect setting for any glimpse of English history. England then is, perforce, our theme, the England that, sending her sons and daughters to the utmost reaches of the world, was and is the cradle of the empire over which His Majesty King George V now rules. No spot in this little island – where every spot is hallowed, or haunted – is more hallowed and haunted than this; within sight of the most magnificent and famous residence of the sovereign of England, Windsor Castle, our stage is within a few miles of those reaches of the Thames where stood noble abbeys and gorgeous royal dwellings.

The first episode is set in AD 925 with the crowning of Athelstan at Kingston-on-Thames. Then comes 'the Return after Poitiers', with Edward III, in 1357. The third episode represents Richard II and the Wat Tyler rebellion of 1382; after which is an elaborate portrayal of the Field of the Cloth of Gold (1520), which is followed by the requisite Elizabethan scene, 'the Triumph of Gloriana':

> Queen Elizabeth's courtiers and suitors include 'Shakespeare', as well as 'navigators and adventurers' – Sir Philip Sidney, Sir Francis Drake, Sir Walter Raleigh, Sir Humphrey Gilbert, Lord Cobham (warden of the Cinque Ports), Sir Martin Frobisher, Sir John Hawkins, and others of their peers. This episode is a symbolic representation epitomising the golden age of Queen Elizabeth, in which Gloriana is shown surrounded by her court and suitors. Citizens assemble to see the

'progress' of Queen Elizabeth and acclaim various members of the city companies, with their banners. Sir Francis Drake and noted sea captains surround the model of his famous ship, the Golden Hind. The queen knights the 'brave Lady Cholmondeley'. A group of citizens sing a madrigal; dancers form a rainbow and follow the queen as her procession leaves the arena.

The sixth episode depicts the marriage of the daughter of Charles I to William of Orange, while the seventh and final episode deals with Lord Howe's naval victory of the 'Glorious First of June' (1794) in the reign of George III, which includes an 'Indian group' (female Indian dancers):

This episode presents to us a scene after 'Morland', the 'Festival of the Haysel'. Decorated farm waggons with milkmaids, and country folk make merry. Celebrities and townsfolk arrive on the scene on foot and in various vehicles, to enjoy a day in the country. A post-boy rides on bringing news of Lord Howe's naval victory on the Glorious First of June. Entrance of King George III, Queen Charlotte, the Prince of Wales and princesses in open carriages, followed by other members of the royal family, who join in the general merrymaking, and are entertained at the village inn by tumblers, and dancing, etc. After greeting various friends, they drive off to the strains of 'Rule Britannia'.

The 'grand finale of empire' has a 'symbolic figure of the colonies' and a 'symbolic figure of peace' in which a 'Rose Garden of England' is acted out. Lady George Cholmondeley took the role of the rosebud, and Mr Paul Jones the leaf, while there were numerous 'petals'. The programme notes provide a deliciously bathetic description of this symbolism:

For centuries the rose has been linked with England's history. Not only is the rose our national emblem, but it grows far better here than in any other country in the world. To-day rose growing is a flourishing home industry employing many thousands of persons. In London's rose garden in Regent's Park 20,000 British-grown roses flower each summer. One of our largest rose growers markets 1,000,000 doz cut roses in a year.

Other pageants from the 1920s and 1930s also reflect this amusing leap from the symbolic and archaic to the modern: 'In the interests of public health, this Pageant is being disinfected throughout with Jeyes' Fluid'; 'refreshment marquees and bars by Mecca Cafés Ltd'; 'advance bookings by large network of agents'; cushions by the London Cushion Co'; 'seating capacity 7,500: 2,250 uncovered and unreserved at 1/6, 5,250 covered and reserved at 2/6, 5/–, 10/6'; 'The control and amenities of car accommodation at this Pageant have been entrusted to the Morris Garages Ltd'. Virginia Woolf, in her pageant novel

Between the Acts, mingles an 'Anglo-Saxon chorus' that winds among a row of trees in the backdrop with the sullen roar of a flight of aeroplanes heading toward France and the ticking of a wind-up gramophone that plays jazz hits in between the episodes.

What is required, above all, at the pageant performances, is a willing suspension of disbelief on the part of the large audience. Spectators themselves become part of the performance as they accommodate home-made costumes and props, 'black-leaded knotted twine' for chain mail, 'steel helmets fashioned out of discarded bowlers, flint-locks out of deal' (Parker, 1928: 286), and indeed where they accommodate distinctly selective and partisan versions of local or national history. Theatre is illusion, and this is all the more apparent where the conventions of theatrical realism or naturalism are unavailable. For this kind of historical pageantry to succeed there would have had to be a collective will. The repeated pageant themes concerning co-operation and patriotism and communal spirit extend to the required behaviour and deportment of the audience. Those who attended the performance would, surveying and approving their own past rehearsed before them, and paying active homage through the singing of national anthems, themselves be cast as players in the national drama.

CONCLUSION

Raymond Williams's concept of 'subjunctive' performance applies effectively to the idea of national identity as performed identity. In 'subjunctive' performance events are not presented in the standard 'indicative' mode but are potential rather than actual. The subjunctive mode deals with volitional states of activity such as hoping, wishing, praying, believing, blessing, and so forth. It is a possibility that this grammatical category of the 'subjunctive' mode, which is a mode that seems appropriate to describe the implications of pageant performance, is also most apt for describing the way in which citizens become implicated into discourses of national identity. The 'nation', as numerous commentators have made abundantly clear, is an invention. It takes considerable powers of persuasion, or a considerable degree of polite acquiescence (such as seems unavailable in our postmodern world), for the large-scale casts and audiences of the 'new pageantry' to don the ruffs and embrace the archaisms, to chant the Te Deum and sing the anthems, laying upon their pre-war modernity the eager guise of Anglo-Saxons and Elizabethans. This could only be possible where there existed a rich social 'discourse' of archaising identity, which was in fact the case, partly by virtue of the pageants themselves, but also deeply held from a great variety of sources. These included the lingering influence of William Morris's Arts and Crafts movement, the existence of a strong tradition of philosophical, ethical and spiritual idealism, the emergence of English literature as a university subject and the concomitant interest in sixteenth- and seventeenth-century theatre and literature, the expansion of the Shakespeare memorial movement at Stratford-upon-Avon, and the numerous ways in which a heritage discourse, as sketched earlier in this chapter, was held before the public. In the late twentieth and early twenty-first centuries, the past does indeed seem like 'another country', but for the Edwardians and Georgians of pre-war England, the past seems to have persisted into the present in vivid and immediate form.

REFERENCES

Beegle, M.P. and Randall, J. (1916) *Community Drama and Pageantry*. New Haven, CN: Yale University Press.

Boughton, R. and Buckley, R.R. (1911) *Music-Drama of the Future*. London: William Reeves.

Bruce, W.S. (1903) *Our Heritage: Individual, Social and Religious*. London: Blackwood.

Buckley, R.R. (1911) *The Shakespeare Revival and the Stratford-upon-Avon Movement*. London: George Allen and Sons.

Darnley, Earl of (ed.) (1932) *Frank Lascelles, Our Modern Orpheus*. Oxford: Oxford University Press.

Davol, R. (1914) *A Handbook of American Pageantry*. Taunton, MA: Davol Publishing.

Forster, E.M. [1934] (1936) The Abinger Pageant, in *Abinger Harvest*. London: Edward Arnold.

—— [1938] (1940) *England's Green and Pleasant Land: A Pageant Play*. London: Hogarth Press.

Girouard, M. (1981) *The Return to Camelot: Chivalry and the English Gentleman*. New Haven, CN: Yale University Press.

Glassberg, D. (1990) *American Historical Pageantry: The Uses of Tradition in the Early Twentieth Century*. Chapel Hill, NC: University of North Carolina Press.

Kruger, L. (1999) *The Drama of South Africa: Plays, Pageants and Publics since 1910*. New York: Routledge.

Lee, H. (1996) *Virginia Woolf*. London: Chatto and Windus.

McClintock, A. (1995) *Imperial Leather: Race, Gender and Sexuality in the Colonial Contest*. New York: Routledge.

Merrington, P. (1997) Masques, monuments and masons: the 1910 Pageant of the Union of South Africa. *Theatre Journal* 49: 1–14.

—— (1999) 'State of the Union': The 'New Pageantry' and the performance of identity in North America and South Africa, 1908–1910. *Journal of Literary Studies* 15: 238–63.

Parker, L.N. (1928) *Several of My Lives*. London: Chapman and Hall.

Piazzi Smyth, C. (1864) *Our Inheritance in the Great Pyramid of Egypt*. London.

Prevots, N. (1990) *American Pageantry: A Movement for Art and Democracy*. Ann Arbor, MI: UMI Research Press.

'Q' (Sir Arthur Quiller-Couch) (1911) *Brother Copas*. Bristol: J.W. Arrowsmith.

Ryan, D.S. (1999) Staging the imperial city: the Pageant of London, 1911. In F. Driver and D. Gilbert (eds), *Imperial Cities: Landscape, Display and Identity*, 117–35. Manchester: Manchester University Press.

Trewin, J.C. (1960) *Benson and the Bensonians*. London: Barrie and Rockliff.

Williams, R. (1979) *Politics and Letters: Interviews with New Left Review*. London: New Left Books.

Woolf, V. (1928) *Orlando*. London: Hogarth Press.

—— (1941) *Between the Acts*. London: Hogarth Press.

15 The institutional ware found in the basement of the firm A. E. Vallerand, Québec

CLAUDE LAFLEUR

INTRODUCTION

The fortunate discovery of a large deposit of material, lying in nothing but a little bit of straw, is at the base of this research. This deposit was excavated in 1991 by archaeologists working for the City of Québec. It was recovered from the basement of an old warehouse located at the corner of Dalhousie Street and St-Antoine Street in downtown Québec, which held the A.E. Vallerand business for more than a hundred years (1883–7) (Figure 15.1). The archaeologists were able to recover 80 per cent of the deposit, which comprised about 450 boxes of material such as lamp parts (stems and chimneys, shades, etc.), glassware and ceramics of all sorts. The deposit has been dated to between 1883 and the 1940s, which roughly corresponds to the use of the crawl space located under the first floor of the firm for the disposal of material unfit for sale. With the help of the many inscriptions on the ware (such as makers' marks, manufacturers' agents, logos and mottos), along with surviving documents, interviews with ceramic specialists and previous owners of the firm, and some contacts on the Internet, it has been possible to place the hotel ware in its cultural context.

ABOUT THE FIRM A.E. VALLERAND

After working for a few years as a manufacturers' agent for his brother, André E. Vallerand opened up his own store in 1883 on the corner of Dalhousie and St-Antoine Streets. In 1915 he gave up his business because of sickness, and a person named G. Gingras took control of the store for a few years. Then, in 1919, the firm was bought by Ferdinand Douville. With his three sons, and eventually his grandson, Denis Douville (an informant in this study), Ferdinand Douville was to own and manage the company until 1987. In that year the firm A.E. Vallerand declared bankruptcy, leaving everything in the store, including an old chest containing many papers and souvenirs from the beginning of the business 104 years earlier, but which were subsequently either lost or destroyed.

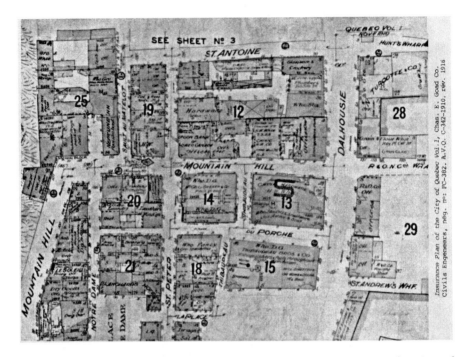

Insurance Plan of the City of Quebec Vol.1, Chas. E. Good Co., Civils Engeneers, nég. n°: FC-382. A.V.Q. C-342-1910, rév. 1916

Figure 15.1 Insurance plan of the city of Québec in 1916, showing location of A.E. Vallerand (neg. no. FC-382. A.V.Z.–1910, rev. 1916)

THE ARCHAEOLOGICAL CONTEXT

The building in which the deposit was uncovered was erected in 1820 by John Chillas on the site of the Hunt's wharf. The north section was a stone-built warehouse and the south section was a brick shed housing cooperage, sail-making and artisanal activities, which continued until 1850. The property was then used by wholesale businesses until 1876 when the city undertook the construction of Dalhousie Street, partly demolishing the building in so doing. New brick façades were then erected and, in 1883, André E. Vallerand started his import business in this building.

The crawl space (Figure 15.2), located under the first floor of the old ware-house, was 4m wide by about 15m in length, and approximatly 1m high (Simoneau 1991: 65). There, the employees were able to discard the broken material from a trap located in the floor and they would regularly level the deposit to ensure good use of the space below. The objects were found in a good state of conservation due, probably, to the low height of the basement ceiling which reduced trampling to a minimum.

Because of the colossal amount of material found, the digging was done in arbitrary units. Following the Tikal system, the deposit (CeEt 110–4X) was first

Figure 15.2 View of sub-operation 4X (West) and of the highest point of the Vallerand collection deposit (courtesy of Québec City Communications Services)

divided in half and then in 15 sections of 1.20m, each named alphabetically, allowing the recovery of a good sample of the material without too much breakage (Simoneau 1991: 69) (Figure 15.3).

The institutional ceramics discussed here correspond to approximately 15 per cent of the sampled deposit, and show very distinctive characteristics such as thickness, multi-coloured annular bands, the presence of logos and mottos, and manufacturers' agents' names printed on it. A total of 190 individual vessels are represented, of which 126 are decorated with an advertising logo.

THE EVOLUTION OF THE HOTEL WARE

One of the most important nineteenth-century developments in earthenware bodies was the ware generally known as 'ironstone', which is intermediate between earthenware and porcelain. It was strong and hard wearing and, in its later stages, very cheap (Collard 1984: 125).

Josiah Spode II and his nephew, Charles James Mason, are the ones who made a success of a fine earthenware fired at high temperatures approximating the body of porcelain. Spode created 'stone china' in 1805, but Mason

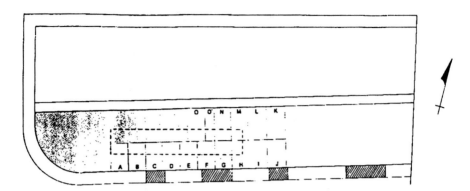

Figure 15.3   Plan-view of areas where surface finds were collected in sub-operation 4X (courtesy of Québec City Communications Services)

is actually the one who introduced the 'ironstone china' around 1813. His product was much like Spode's, except that the preparation of the body was supposed to contain iron slag. More recent analysis of the fabric (Atterbury 1978: 263) indicates that it did not contain any iron, but the name 'ironstone' remained nonetheless in general use throughout the years, perhaps more because of its association with hardness and durability, than because of the assumed iron content of the body itself.

At first ironstone was very much inspired by oriental wares in its decoration and also by the choice of colours imitating porcelain. Then it became heavier, more sturdy, thicker and also cheaper, but still very durable. Many different names were given to this ware, such as 'patent stone china', 'white stone', 'imperial ironstone', 'opaque porcelain' and then, 'semi-porcelain', even though the body itself showed little changes, if any at all (Collard 1998, personnal communication). This highly vitrified earthenware is the one which gave birth, between 1860 or 1880, to the institutional ware known as 'hotel ware' (Boger 1971: 310), probably because it was found in most hotels and steamships of the nineteenth century (Collard 1984: 131).

The first hotel wares produced contained more sand, making them more fragile. But then the potters included more feldspar in the preparation, giving the ware its vitreous quality and its hardness and also its ability to resist chipping, a quality particularly emphasised by both manufacturers and purchasers. 'All [hotel ware] plates have been specially rounded and reinforced to minimize edge chipping' (Royal Doulton 1995: 11). Manufacturers Dunn Bennett & Co. also drew attention to this, adding the phrase 'unchippable surface dinner plates' to some of their marks. The quality of the hotel ware is such that it will resist stains and acid, will not alter the taste of foods or taste like the last meal, will not crack or chip and will stay intact after years of service (Luckin 1987: 31).

It had to be sturdy, to stand up to the rigors of train service, and yet attractive, for the pleasure of the diners . . . [This ceramic] is basic, heavyweight, institutional grade ware. It is the same china used by hospitals, cafeterias and restaurants. 'Fat china', [is] a good description [for it]. With its heavy rolled edges, stout bottom rims and 'bullet-proof' thickness, the basic ware is far from attractive, but very well-suited for its surroundings. Yet, through the use of beautiful patterns and the application of colorful company heralds, the railroads turned this utilitarian ware into china that was deserving of the elegant surroundings in which it was used and of the epicurean delights that were served upon it.

(McIntyre 1990: 4)

When André E. Vallerand started his business in 1883, a great variety of decorative bands were available. For the first decades of the twentieth century, the clients' favourite decorations were the red annular band, which did very well with the customers, the green annular band like the 'green band' pattern used by the Canadian Pacific Railroad Company, the blue annular band, as well as a mix of all these (Denis Douville, personnal communication). But there were also floral bands like the 'California poppie' used by the Boos Bros Co., geometric bands such as the 'check' or the 'derby ware', which seem to have been quite popular in Australia, and the base white ceramic, which was often found.

THE MANUFACTURERS' MARKS

The repertoire of manufacturers' marks has helped to verify the dating of the deposit. It shows that the most intense production of hotel ware is located in the first two decades of the twentieth century. It is clear that such ironstone was manufactured before and even after this period, but most of the objects in the Vallerand deposit date from the beginning of the century.

The English products had a very good reputation with Quebecers, judging by the significant quantities of British ceramics found on archaelogical sites in Québec. Most of the objects in the Vallerand deposit were made by manufacturers located in the Potteries District in England, such as the Cauldon Potteries Ltd, Dunn Bennett & Co., Furnivals, the Globe Pottery, Grindley Hotel Ware, and John Maddock & Sons. These companies were all founded at the turn of the twentieth century, either a few years before or after 1900.

Denis Douville, grandson of Vallerand's successor Ferdinand Douville, has said that the products made by the Grindley Hotel Ware Co. and by John Maddock & Sons Co. were very popular with his clients. The John Maddock & Sons Company manufactured 'white granite ware' in great quantity for the American market (Llewellyn 1883: 458). It was initially appreciated for the thickness of the body of its ware, but then also lost its popularity because of it in the 1970s (Denis Douville, personnal communication). Around 1940, the Canadian importers started to do business more locally, mostly because of the price of the ceramics that kept getting higher, the duty and transport costs they had to pay, the time it took to cross the sea (up to three months) and because more than 25 per cent of the ceramic was broken on arrival. By then, the quality of the ceramics made in the United States was very similar to the English product, and at a much lower price.

ANDRÉ E. VALLERAND, AN IMPORTANT MANUFACTURERS' AGENT?

When the study of this hotel ware collection began, we were quite amazed to see what an important distributor A.E Vallerand was. Many logos were printed on this ware, advertising institutions located around the world such as Australia, Africa, United States, England, etc. But it was clear on second thoughts that Vallerand did not have clients overseas. Why, then, would English manufacturers send him this stock, which was often of low quality, and meant for institutions unknown to Quebecers in Canada?

Denis Douville explained that, in his grandfather's time, the British manufacturers would send several boxes of ceramics samples to their agents to show to their customers. The firm A.E. Vallerand did not have to ask for them but they were regularly sent to help promote sales. The presence in our collection of 'test plates' are proofs that manufacturers were sending such samples. One object (Figure 15.4) is a plate with different colours painted on it with identification numbers written under them as well as the name 'Blythe colours'. Another one carries the name 'Wengers, dark blue', and the last one (Figure 15.5) has the name 'Trent' written on it with a green pencil, as well as the date (24/7/22) and 'no. 10'. The samples decorated with a logo and a motto most certainly came from stock excess or of a lesser quality stock that the manufactures had not been able to sell.

From the begining of the Vallerand business the ceramics which did not meet the quality standards were discarded in the crawl space located under the first floor of the firm. The dating of some of the marks and the logos shows us that André E. Vallerand, as well as G. Gingras and Ferdinand Douville, used this place from the beginning of the business in 1883 through the first three decades of the twentieth century. The introduction of new laws in 1924 concerning the collection of garbage probably explains why fewer items were discarded in the basement afterwards (A.V.Q., Séries conseils et comité-. 1849–1929: Vidanges, règlement 51, 1 octobre 1924). To get rid of the hotel ware samples Vallerand could not store any more, a woman would regularly come with a trailer to buy a large amount of this ware for $200 and would then sell it at flea markets, allowing it to be spread all over the country. Religious institutions in Québec as well as charitable societies were also very happy to buy this solid ware at low prices even if the logos did not match.

The influence and importance of the Vallerand firm was therefore far from being as vast as first thought. It really did not have clients in Sudan, Africa, Australia or Brazil. Instead, to promote its sales, until the 1970s the Vallerand

Figure 15.4   Test-Plate 'Blythe colours', CeEt110–4X-300

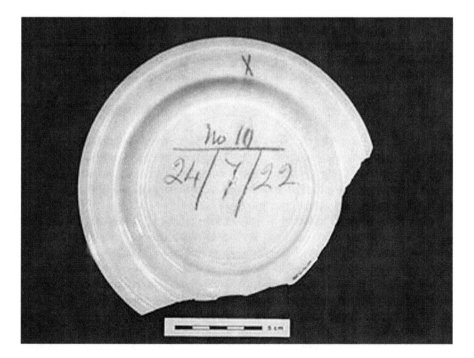

Figure 15.5   Test-Plate 'Trent, no. 10, 24/7/22', CeEt110–4X-200

company used travelling salesmen throughout the province, in Beauce, Abitibi, and in the Bas-du-Fleuve, with samples of ceramics received from the British manufacturers. Vallerand was nontheless very much appreciated by its clients in the Québec vicinity.

THE LOGOS OF THE VALLERAND DEPOSIT

Thanks to the logos and mottos printed on the institutional ceramics found in the Vallerand deposit, we are able to witness a new society emerging at the turn of the twentieth century as well as a new world of advertising. Part of the consequences of the Industrial Revolution is mass production. With the massive production of manufactured goods exceeding demand, advertising became a necessity. 'In the 1890s, a cluster of new techniques in communications and the complementary developement of modern advertising and consumer capitalism signaled a further phase in the history of leisure' (Bailey 1978: 2).

Hotel ware is, of course, an object meant for the consumption of food. But this very object, when it is decorated with a logo, may become a talked-about and effective marketing tool.

> . . . to the railroads, dining car china was much more than a food sevice item; it was a valuable promotional tool. Often times the china spoke of the region through which the train passed; . . . speaking enticingly of the road as any advertisement could. China also touted name trains and commemorated historic events . . . Frequently, the ware simply had the name of the railroad placed on the top as a friendly reminder of the traveler of who was providing them with the smooth ride, fine scenery and good food.
>
> (McIntyre 1990: 4)

The manufacturers created a cheap ware, easy to produce in large quantity, but with different designs. The consumers bought them no longer according to need but also for the simple desire to be up to date with the fashion industry. Hotel ware became a commercial object, satisfying at the same time the consumer's desire to express individuality.

Every item of hotel ware in this collection relates to urban life. Indeed, in the nineteenth century the rural population decreased continually. The land was no longer a saviour, so the people turned to the city where the industries offered good jobs and many working opporunities. With these advertising logos we are witness to the social change of the society, the industrialisation of the transportation system and mass consumption, as well as seeing the influence of the large British Empire that ruled a good part of the world at the turn of the twentieth century. In the Vallerand collection there are five distinct categories of logos: the catering industry, transportation, hostelries, institutions and other miscellaneous wares.

THE CATERING INDUSTRY

The Vallerand collection has 16 logos from the catering industry. Included are logos from restaurants, cafés, cafeterias, caterers and specialised food stores. With people now working in the cities and having no piece of land to grow food, many restaurants of all sorts take root near the workplaces. It is thus not surprising to see the United States itself represented by three logos from cafeterias. In Washington, cafeterias appeared about 1915 and increased rapidly in numbers during the crowded days of the war (Root and De Rochemont 1981: 317).

Australia and England are also represented by logos advertising cafés, such as 'National Café' in Adelaide, 'Fox's Café' in Darlington, 'Beach Café' in Bournemouth and the 'Café & Cocoa Room'. These special little cafés, where one could sit and relax, are also new to this period. The new middle-class society, having more money and time to rest, increasingly took advantage of such places. The catering business seems to have been active at the turn of the twentieth century with two caterers in Africa: 'The African caterer [. . .]' and 'Johnston the Caterer', as well as one in Holland represented by the 'Monnickendam Ltd. Caterers'. The 'Restaurants Garbers Delicatessen' logo, and the 'Rôtisserie Sportsman' in São Paulo are examples of specialisation, but also prove that the population was opening up to a new culture and that it was not uncommon to find ethnic restaurants or stores at the turn of the twentieth century.

THE TRANSPORTATION INDUSTRY

We see the importance of this category by the many logos included in it, such as the 17 steamship logos, seven train companies and a motorcycle company. With the new working opportunities in town, people had to transport themselves to work and back home. So the transportation industry grew rapidly to serve them but also to enable freight to be sent to destinations in a short period of time. Most of the steamship companies found here were operating between the United Kingdom and its colonies, as well as with the countries where commercial trade was significant. Some companies were also equipped for the transportation of passengers, either for leisure or work, such as the 'New England Steamship Company' doing business in the Great Lakes area in Canada, the 'P & O' and the 'Bibby Line'.

The Victorian era is the period where British emigration was most active, with migration to the United States, but also Australia, New Zealand, Africa and Canada. This phenomenon is seen through the logos of transportation companies meant for Australia and New Zealand, such as the 'N.S.W.G.R. RRR', the 'N.Z.R.', the 'McIlwraith & McEacharn Line', the 'South Australia Railways' and the 'New South Wales RRR'. Most of the others belong to English companies, except for the Canadian Pacific Railway ('C.P.R.') (Figure 15.6) and the Canadian National Railway ('C.N.R.'). The presence of so many

Figure 15.6   Logo of the Canadian Pacific Railway, CeEt110–4X-89

train and steamship companies from around the world indicates that the Industrial Revolution touched England and its colonies at the same time and rapidly shaped our countries as we know them now.

At the turn of the twentieth century, the car and motorcycle industry was starting to spread out and to influence social life. The Excelsior Company was an American company building motorcycles. At first seen as curiosities, these means of transport then became a social symbol of the élite. People no longer had to walk, ride a horse or take public transport for long distances, and they really appreciated it. An Excelsior motorcycle was the first to reach 100 miles per hour, in 1912. From the mark on the back of the vessel, this one could come from a New Zealand retailer.

THE INSTITUTIONS

Included in this category is everything relevant to the state or the government, such as banks, schools, hospitals, military institutions, and clubs and societies. The desire to join a club or society was not new at the turn of the twentieth century, but what was new was the increase in club membership and its popularity with the middle class (Thompson 1990: 395). Institutions such as the 'Naval and Military Club' and the 'Navy, Army & Air Force Institute (N.A.A.F.I)' were clubs or co-operatives where soldiers could find food, cigarettes, tea, and so on, and everything necessary for them to feel good enough to win a war, and at low prices. With new jobs, and thus new income, people also felt the need to invest their money and take insurance. Such companies are represented in the collection by the 'Metropolitan Life Insurance Company', and the '[. . . ugs] Bank'. The hotel ware logos such as 'Towers District Hospital', the 'Royal Prince Alfred Hospital', the 'South Western District Post Office' and 'The Holiday Camp' in Douglas are also symptomatic of this middle-class age and its preoccupation with wealth, elegance, utility and practicalities. Everything that is favourable to the well-being of the citizen is encouraged. These clubs or societies were 'an organisational form of enormous significance in the supply of leisure: it brought together a group of people, normally men, for the pursuit of a single activity or for leisure more generally' (Thompson 1990: 325).

In addition to the three schools found in our deposit, the 'YWCA' (Young Women's Christian Association) demonstrates that women were slowly looking for vocations other than marriage and family. Many were now aspiring to a professionnal title or to join groups or social clubs providing them with a place where they could meet, eat and play without having to drink alcohol.

HOSTELRY INDUSTRY

This is another important category of logos found in the Vallerand deposit. There are 32 advertising logos meant for hotels, inns, rooms, and so on. The railroad innovation is probably the most important factor in this growing industry, since all the railroad tracks led to a city centre. The train also had a tremendous impact on seaside resorts and paved the way for the vacation concept, mostly for middle-class society. For a little while, middle-class people traded their working clothes for the chic clothes of the upper class, tried their food, restaurants and extravagant ways of spending money, and their time of leisure in stylish hotels. The 'Palace Hotel' at Southend-on-Sea, the 'Waverley Hotel', and the 'Queen's Hotel' at Westcliff-on-Sea were all located in seaside resorts. It is interesting to see that the motto (a partly indecipherable Latin inscription mentioning health) of an artefact with the logo 'Beach Café', located in Bournemouth, is directly related to the health-giving reputation of this coastal resort.

Only one hotel represents Australia, the 'Belfast House' in Katoomba, and its appearance is known to us thanks to the logo printed on the plate. Another logo, meant for 'The Grand Hotel' in Khartoum (Sudan), takes us back in time to 1898 when Britain conquered this territory. There are two logos printed for Canadian institutions, the 'Cascade Inn', located in Shawinigan near Québec, which was a prestigous hotel attracting the upper class at the beginning of the twentieth century, and the 'Hotel St. Charles', probably located in Winnipeg, which seems to have been famous at that time. The United States is represented by two lines of hotels still existing in that country, 'Hilton's' and the 'Americus Hotel'. At the turn of the twentieth century these hotels, which were meant for the upper class in the first place, were so popular with the middle class that the upper class, looking for elegance and exclusivity, did not visit these places much any more (Howell 1974: 145).

IMPERIALISM

In the nineteenth century, the UK had an empire of 32 million square kilometres and 450 million inhabitants, which represents one quarter of the entire human race at that time. This emerging culture of British imperialism inspired feelings such as the quest for power, the lure of money, pride, religious feelings and humanitarian spirit (Bédarida 1990: 204). This imperialism is detectable through the logos and mottoes of the collection. The 'Royal Hotel' logo includes the motto from the Royal coat of arms, '*Honni soi qui mal y pense, Dieu et mon droit*', which clearly states the importance of God, and thus authority, to the Victorians. Mottoes such as *Vivit post funera virtus* ('Virtue lives on after death', *semper paratus* ('Always ready'), *Semper sursum* ('Always upward'), as well as *Servitor servientum* ('Servant of the servants'), are all examples of a society influenced by patriotic and virtuous feelings. We can also see this imperialism from the presence of two military clubs: the 'Naval and Military Club', and the 'Navy, Army & Air Force Institute'. The 'Holiday Camp' in Douglas, on the Isle of Man, was meant for boys, but in times of war, it would transform itself into a military camp where Canadian troops would receive a training before going to action. It apparently also served for the internment of the enemy aliens during World War Two (Nigel Malpass 1997, personnal communication).

The British navy helped make Great Britain a great empire (Bédarida 1990: 232). In the mind of the British, their power was based on apparently indestructible forces, being the sea, their fleet and the Empire. This huge feeling of pride in maritime endeavours, as well as this pratical and efficient way to transport goods and people probably explains the presence in the collection of such a large number (17) of steamship lines. The majority of companies represented were commercial lines, such as the 'Elders & Fyffes Ltd.', the 'Bibby Line', the 'Clan Line Steamers Limited', and so on, or were linked to the mail delivery between the British colonies such as the 'Union-Castle Line' and the 'P & O'.

Even after obtaining nominal independence, British colonies seem to have kept the commercial bond between them which gave the UK only more power. The presence of the logo from the 'Grand Hotel' in Khartoum indicates the strong influence of the Empire in this country. The 'Hong Kong Hotel' and 'Johnston The Caterer' in Africa are clear evidence of the influence of the British Empire in the colonies. The presence of the British flag in distant countries was very appealing for British people and filled them with pride to be privileged citizens of a vast empire (Charlot and Marx 1978: 43).

The result of this imperialism and colonisation is clear to see through the logos of the hotel ware. The UK had therefore many colonies that were still connected by solid cultural, economical and military bonds. The presence of

English hotel ware in Québec indicates participation in the same processes of industrialisation, mass consumption and the new ways of transportation, along with the other British colonies around the world.

BRITISHNESS AS A FORM OF IDENTITY

After the British conquest of Québec in 1759, Canada became British in many ways. And even though there were probably closer ties with the United States, in a practical way at least, Canadians felt a certain pride in being a member of the Commonwealth and having a British cousin across the ocean, and they most likely felt as well a sense of loyalty to Britain. This, and the dominance of the British manufacturers, is perhaps the reason why Vallerand continued his business with British ceramic industries up until the 1940s. After that period, the importer from Dalhousie Street decided to deal more locally, but only for economic reasons. By then, the products made in America were very similar to the English products, and at a much lower price, which apparently finally persuaded Vallerand and his sons to negotiate with the United States instead.

The British colonies, even after obtaining their independence, seemed to have wanted to keep their commercial bond alive. And we can also presume that Britain still wanted to control an informal empire with her colonies around the world. Consequently, Britain, by way of encouraging the importers to do business with her, sent Vallerand large quantities of ceramic samples. Part of the excess stock was then sold in flea markets, given to institutions, to charity, or simply thrown in the basement. Eventually, pieces of hotel ware were found all over the country, promoting, in some way, the wonderful way of life of the British and the new changes in twentieth-century society.

This assemblage of ceramics is a sign that the Quebecers were embracing the way of life of the British. Travel, railways, steamships, leisure, migration, commerce, and so on, all encouraged the building of a sense of common identity. There was a British heritage here in Canada, and apparently Canadians were trying to replicate some of the social structures of Britain. Being British was an infinitely precious thing, since all that emerged from Britain at that time was to be admired. Most of the technical revolution had crossed the ocean and those new ways of transport were now available in Canada. The middle class, this professional non-manual working class of citizens that grew in numbers at the turn of the century, promoted this industrialisation in some ways. They had to work hard just to appreciate the new luxury of leisure time and vacation. They were the ones who filled the restaurants, hotels and railways. Commerce was therefore stimulated at that period, and with mass production, the way of life improved.

With some of the logos meant for Québec's institutions, there is proof that the vast middle-class group of citizens were engaged in recreational activities in this continent as well. They had the desire to access the élite of the upper class, and their sumptuous worldliness, just like they did in Britain. In the meantime, some people in Québec were still eating five-course meals in restaurants, on fashionable plates, but maybe hoping one day to have a feast in porcelain serving dishes.

CONCLUSION

The archaeological dig that took place in 1991 in downtown Québec revealed a rich deposit of various objects, notably the hotel ware. The heavy china dinnerware, made specificaly for use in hotels, institutions and restaurants, offers a ceramic ware of great hygienic quality resistant to heat, breaking and chipping, that would not absorb the taste of food, and that would not stain, even after years of service.

The change from rural to urban life stimulated many changes at the heart of the society at the turn of the twentieth century. We can see many of these changes through our institutional ware collection, such as the use of the new modes of public transportation, the rise of the middle class, the blossoming of the restaurant and the hotel business, the increase of social clubs and seaside resorts, new concepts such as vacation and leisure, and the expansion of the British Empire.

The development of new ways of transportation opened doors to a panoply of choice concerning leisure, tourism and vacation. These means of transport abolished frontiers and allowed travellers to see new horizons featuring fabulous hotels, restaurants, seaside resorts, cafés, and so on. The modernisation of a society is identifiable by characteristics such as industrialisation, mass consumption, urbanisation and technological innovation. This ceramic deposit demonstrates therefore very well the advent of modernity and the desire for Quebecers to be contemporary at the same time as Britain, Australia or Africa at the turn of the twentieth century.

REFERENCES

Archives de la Ville de Québec, Séries Conseils et Comités-. 1849–1929: Vidanges, règlement 51, 1 octobre 1924.
Atterbury, P. (1978) *English Pottery and Porcelain, an Historical Survey.* New York: Antiques Magazine Library, Universe Books.
Bailey, P. (1978) *Leisure and Class in Victorian England:Rational Recreation and the Contest for Control, 1830–1885.* Toronto: Toronto University Press.
Bédarida, F. (1990) *La Société Anglaise du Milieu du XIXe Siècle à Nos Jours.* France: Édition du Seuil.
Boger, L.A. (1971) *The Dictionary of World Pottery and Porcelain.* New York: Charles Scribner's Sons.
Collard, E. (1984) *19th Century Pottery & Porcelain in Canada,* 2nd edn. Kingston and Montreal: McGill-Queen's University Press.
Lafleur, C. (1993) *La Vaisselle de Table et de Service en Verre de Couleur du Marché Vallerand.* Québec: Mémoire de Baccalauréat en Arts et Traditions Populaires, Université Laval, document inédit.

—— (1999) *La Céramique Institutionnelle du Dépôt de la Firme A.E.Vallerand*. Québec: Mémoire de Maîtrise, Université Laval.

Llewellyn, J. (1883) *The Ceramic Art of Great Britain*. London: J.S. Virtue & Co.

Luckin, R. (1987) *Teapot Treasury (and Related Items)*. Colorado: RK Publishing.

McIntyre, D. (1990) *The Official Guide to Railroad Dining Car China*. Cleveland, OH: Walsworth Press Company.

Root, W. and R. De Rochemont (1981) *Eating in America, a History*. New York: Ecco Press.

Royal Doulton (1995) *Hotel and Airline Division, Stock Patterns, Price List*. Ontario: Royal Doulton Canada Limited.

Simoneau, D. (1991) *Ilot Hunt: Fouilles Archéologiques*. Québec: Service de l'Urbanisme, Division du Vieux-Québec et du Patrimoine.

Thompson, F.M.L. (1990) *The Cambridge Social History of Britain, 1750–1950, vol. 3: Social Agencies and Institutions*. Cambridge: Cambridge University Press.

Watson, N. (1990) *The Bibby Line 1807–1990: A Story of Wars, Booms and Slumps*. London: James & James.

Webster, D. (1971) *Early Canadian Pottery*. Toronto: McClelland and Steward.

16 Are we re-inventing the wheel? Archaeological heritage management in Sri Lanka under British colonial rule

GAMINI WIJESURIYA

INTRODUCTION

This chapter attempts to deal with a different subject from those discussed elsewhere in this volume. Irrespective of its merits or demerits, transformation of Sri Lanka – the little island nation in the Indian Ocean, formerly known as Ceylon – from its own traditional social system, which had its origins in the pre-Christian era, to its present status is attributed to British colonial rule. It is manifested in all aspects of life: political and administrative systems, architecture, settlements, and so on, but its effects on archaeology have yet to be understood. In the massive effort of organising the public sector in colonised countries, the British introduced a range of subjects relevant to the governance of the society. 'Archaeology' itself was among them. In the public administrative sector, we can still hear the phrases such as 'like the time of the *sudda*' ('*sudda*' is the local synonym for 'white') or 'work like *sudda*'. These are reminders of imperial power, reflecting certain attributes of the public sector that existed.

The British introduced their own systems to the newly colonised countries, thus abandoning or disregarding the traditional systems that already existed there. In the process, however, they had to struggle to come to terms with local needs as well. For instance, at the peak of the move against the restoration of monuments in England in the late nineteenth century, the colonial power in Sir Lanka sought the assistance of the Royal Asiatic Society of Great Britain for the restoration of Buddhist monuments. This inquiry into archaeology within the context of the public administrative system introduced by the British will contribute to the comprehension of Britishness and the British Empire.

Archaeology as a subject was introduced to the public service in newly colonised Asian countries at very early stages of their occupation. Since its introduction to India and Sri Lanka, archaeology has been entirely a management discipline. Archaeology remained in the hands of the public sector and was controlled by the civil service of the respective countries rather than by the academic community. (In Sri Lanka, for example, the first university programme on archaeology started only in 1960.) The system existed for a century under colonial rule and another half a century with very little modifications under the national governments. One hundred and fifty years of archaeological practices have added invaluable experiences and made a significant impact to the management of the archaeological heritage in this part of the world. This however, has not been sufficiently acknowledged by the wider academic and professional community except in occasional remarks on certain aspects (Cleere 1984, 1989).

Over the last two decades, archaeology as a management discipline has gained rapid momentum throughout the world. It brought a new area of inquiry into the domain of archaeology and reflects a profound shift in archaeologists' attitude towards their role. This particular transition from an academic discipline of archaeology to a real world profession is seen in the Western world as relatively new, though, this chapter argues, such is not the case in South Asia.

The question of whether we are 'reinventing the wheel' arose when my recent visit to the Institute of Archaeology, University College London provided the opportunity to re-examine the heritage management model of the colonial world. In fact, the founder of the institute, Sir Mortimer Wheeler, was one of the strongest links between archaeology under the British in the colonial world and archaeology in Britain. The present director of the institute, Peter Ucko (1989: xi), had already pointed out that 'archaeology as a discipline would be foolish to allow the current divisions which exist in many countries between the academic, the field worker and legislator, to continue'. Undoubtedly, such divisions existed in many parts of the world, particularly where archaeology was an academic discipline and management of the archaeological heritage was the responsibility of a different group. On the other hand it is the combination of these three – academic, field worker and legislator – that provides the fundamental framework for archaeological heritage management to evolve from archaeology.

Long before this evolution came into effect in modern terms, the combination referred to existed under colonial rule. We found the evidence from the records of the institute itself. Wheeler's own career demonstrated this. All agree that he was an academic, field worker and legislator when he was the head of probably the largest single organisation managing the archaeological heritage under the colonial rule: the Archaeological Survey of India. Interestingly, that was more than half a century ago. This and many other examples suggest that the fundamentals of archaeological heritage management existed under British colonial rule in India, and had its parallels in Sri Lanka. Cleere (1989: 7–8) endorsed this when he stated 'ex-colonial powers often left their newly independent ex-colonies a legacy of excellent heritage management legislation. During their two centuries of rule the British endowed India with excellent protective legislation and a well-organised antiquities service, both of which continued after independence in 1947.

All of this prompted me to elaborate on the archaeological heritage management model which exists in certain South Asian countries, with special reference to the case in Sri Lanka where British colonial rule established the Archaeological Department of the Government in 1890. This chapter would not be sufficient for me to present a comprehensive account of the model, which was drawn predominantly from a colonial endeavour, but an attempt will be made to highlight the essential features in comparison with modern notions of archaeological heritage management.

There is in fact an identity issue in archaeological heritage management. The modern British prefer to call the management aspects of archaeology 'archaeological heritage management' (AHM) as against its pioneer 'cultural resources management' (CRM) started in the USA (Cleere 1989; McManamon and Hatton 2000). This, however, is not a subject for debate in this chapter while recognising the rationale as the prerequisite for archaeologists to enter the area of inquiry dealing with the management of archaeological heritage (Wijesuriya 1993: 123). It should be mentioned here that twenty years of experience in heritage management in Sri Lanka while working in the public sector established by the British and overseas, including participation in several academic programmes, numerous international congresses and service within WAC and ICOMOS, has provided the in-depth knowledge required for this chapter.

FROM INDIGENOUS TO A COLONIAL
PRACTICE OF CONSERVATION

Conservation and management of the monuments and sites constituted an essential component of the entire social process in the ancient past (Wijesuriya 1993: 10–15). However, four hundred years of colonial rule and the unstable political atmosphere in the period immediately preceding it have resulted in the wiping out of all such traditional practices. A new system of managing the archaeological heritage emerged with the arrival of the British colonial power, which was responsible for the establishment of the Department of Archaeology.

Inspired by Buddhism, the past played a major role in the life of the community. Events of the past are often quoted in Buddhist stories as a medium of explaining complex issues and also as a strong vehicle of inspiration for the present and future. For this purpose, going back to the past lives of the Buddha, his disciples, rulers and even ordinary people often recurs in Buddhism (e.g. Buddha's previous birth stories known as *jataka* amount to 550 in number – these bring many values, explanations and good examples to follow and bad ones to avoid in present day lives). Building memorials in the form of *stupas* by depositing relics began soon after the death of the Buddha. Subsequently, there were other types of memorials such as image houses which added to the massive monastic building complexes. The depositing of relics of the Buddha and his disciples made all these edifices sacred, always to be 'monuments' and to last forever (Wijesuriya 1993: 15), thus becoming places of worship and of constant attention. Returning to those places became a normal feature in people's lives. The older the place, the more it is valuable to the worshippers and pilgrims. In fact, pilgrimages by people in Sri Lanka and other parts of the world to the birthplace and other associated places of the Buddha were a millennium-old tradition (Rahula 1960: 191). This required the rulers and the public to protect, maintain and restore those monuments and places and to adopt formal procedures for the purpose.

A chronicle shows how a ruler ordered his own death sentence in the second century BC because he caused damage to a monument (Geiger/*Mahavamsa* 1960: 21, 22–5), thus highlighting the type of punishments which were available to those who harm monuments. Lithic inscriptions have laid down rules for the regular maintenance of the temple properties and monuments (Wijesuriya 1993: 13). There were properties assigned to gain income to support maintenance and restoration. Experts on restoration were settled in exclusive villages. There were officers and ministers in charge of conservation and rehabilitation of ruined monastic complexes. Principles of conservation and restoration were found in the ancient treatises in architecture (Dagens/ *Mayamatha* 1985). These are now a part of the lost heritage.

Sri Lanka became a British colony in 1815. By this time, principal human settlements were in the wet zone or south-western part of the country. A large number of major settlements established from the pre-Christian era to the sixteenth century AD had fallen into ruins and gone under forest. These consisted of ancient Buddhist monastic complexes and administrative centres. Buddhism as a religion, on the other hand, was still practised in the areas occupied by the people.

Although British colonial rule did not openly destroy religious centres like its predecessor, the Portuguese, certain actions such as erecting large-scale, disproportionate buildings and the introduction of incompatible uses around temple complexes led to their systematic deterioration (Bandaranayake 1996: 181–2). However, certain British colonial administrators were astonished by the richness of the heritage both hidden in the jungles and surviving in settled areas, and started to record them in diverse forms. In 1868, the government sent its chief architect to Anuradhapura (capital of the country from the sixth century BC to the eleventh century AD), in order to document the monuments neglected and hidden in the jungles. The government established the Archaeological Survey of Ceylon in 1890 in line with its counterpart in India (Wijesekera 1990). This was a central government organisation directly funded and staffed by the state. Such organisations hardly existed in England or any other European countries at that time. Although the UK passed its first Ancient Monuments Protection Act in 1882, it is considered a 'relatively toothless measure compared with the earlier (1863) law that had been enacted in Imperial India' (Cleere 1989: 1). The original mission of the Archaeological Survey was the documentation of the monuments and sites but this soon expanded to cover the areas of preservation and maintenance with supporting legislation and the necessary institutional framework.

Since independence in 1948, minor changes within the Department of Archaeology have taken place but the fundamentals of the colonial model continue to dominate. Presently, the Department is responsible for the management of the entire archaeological heritage of the country (Deraniyagala 1996: 1–6). It is a central government organisation supported by adequate legal provisions (*Antiquities Ordinance*) to deal with the entire spectrum of issues related to the archaeological heritage management of the country and its territorial waters. It is headed by a qualified archaeologist (since 1940, all the Heads of the Department have qualified with PhDs). Under the umbrella of the Head (Director-General), there are highly trained and experienced specialists to handle research and policy as well as the operational aspects of inventorisation, investigation including excavation, conservation (objects, monuments, sites) and presentation, maintenance, public awareness, and so on. There are also permanent staffs to carry out all the field operations. They gain their training and experience on site, locally and abroad.

Heritage under its purview covers anything from the prehistoric, proto-historic and historic periods (Deraniyagala 1996: 1). The historic period ranges from the sixth century BC to the sixteenth century AD, followed by the colonial periods of the Portuguese, Dutch and British. These include extensive archaeological sites, ancient cities, living cities and living religious monuments. Among them are six World Heritage Sites.

Functions of the Department of Archaeology as provided in the *Antiquities Ordinance* are as follows:

(a) to formulate a national archaeological policy and co-ordinate and implement such policy after it is approved by the Government;

(b) to inventorise the archaeological heritage of Sri Lanka;

(c) to protect and maintain such archaeological heritage;

(d) to conduct research into every aspect of the archaeological heritage of Sri Lanka and specially, into the prehistoric, proto-historic, early historic, middle historic and late historic periods and into general or specific theory, method and practice;

(e) to enhance public awareness of the archaeological heritage of Sri Lanka through appropriate displays of antiquities, publications and by other means;

(f) to levy an entrance fee where it is necessary at selected sites or visitor centres;

(g) to conduct archaeological impact assessment of areas that may be affected by development, industrial or other projects proposed by the government or lay person and implement any mitigatory measures that may be required.

AN ARCHAEOLOGICAL HERITAGE MANAGEMENT MODEL

The list of functions and the type of specialists mentioned above reflects the wide scope of the Department, its power and capability to handle all aspects of heritage management of the country. Although the list was formulated recently, the overall nature of the model remains as an advancement of the original model developed during the colonial period. The discussion of the model from here onwards, will follow the articles of the Archaeological Heritage Management Charter of ICOMOS. The Charter has a series of recommendations, sometimes together with justifications, under different topics related to archaeological heritage management. There may be disagreements and needs for improvements on the model anticipated from the charter but at present, it can be counted as a reasonably developed reference point. Articles of the charter are summarised and presented in their original sequence, followed by a discussion.

Article 1: Definition and Introduction

In addition to the introduction to the charter, this article contains a definition of the archaeological heritage:

> 'archaeological heritage' is that part of the material heritage in respect of which archaeological methods provide primary information. It comprises all vestiges of human existence and consists of places relating to all manifestations of human activity, abandoned structures, and remains of all kinds (including subterranean and underwater sites), together with all the portable cultural material associated with them.

The above is a modern definition but its colonial predecessor had followed the style of the time, covering all known, unknown, movable and immovable cultural properties within their domain. Accordingly, all movable objects discovered underground irrespective of their location belonged to the state. Underwater sites were also covered.

Article 2: Integrated Protection Policies

This article of the charter highlights the need for archaeological heritage protection policies to integrate with land use and development planning, environmental and educational policies of a given country. The need to create archaeological reserves is recommended. Policies are to be made to provide access to information by the public (including indigenous people) and to seek their active participation in decision-making.

Integration of archaeological heritage management with land-use planning is perhaps the single most important factor brought to light in the recent past. The number of countries moving in this direction reflects the validity of this principle. We can see the foundations laid during the colonial regime in this area. The key to land-use planning is the identification of different types of archaeological resources and mapping them. This was started in the mid-nineteenth century in Sri Lanka, when the Department of Survey prepared maps covering the entire country. All archaeological sites encountered by the field surveyors are marked in the maps. This set of records forms the primary source of knowledge on the archaeological landscape. It is interesting to note how the entire administrative machinery has supported each other's areas though there were different departments to handle different subjects.

Establishment of the archaeological reserves was one of the key functions under the *Antiquities Ordinance* of 1940, when the country was still under colonial rule. According to the Act, 'the Archaeological Commissioner may declare by notification published in the gazette, any specified area of that land (crown) to be an archaeological reserve'. Such declarations were done in consultation with the Land Commissioner of the country. Although there are many shortcomings in identification of large reserves, this process has helped to identify and maintain many archaeological reserves in the country. This in turn helps to understand large settlements and monastic complexes in their overall context.

The Town and Country Planning Act of 1920 is used extensively for planning and implementation of a programme known as Sacred Area Schemes (Deraniyagala 1996 b: 4). Under the scheme, an integrated development plan is prepared for the conservation and development of a large archaeological site. There are over 25 sacred area schemes in the country. The management plan for the World Heritage Site of Anuradhapura comes under this category.

Another important feature of the colonial legislation was the power it possessed to control the environment around a monument or a site. Four hundred yards of land area around any monument or sites are under the control of the Department of Archaeology. This is to protect the monument or site from any physical damage caused by construction, mining, blasting, and so on, as well as to prevent any damage to the aesthetic value of the monument or the site.

Public participation in connection with interventions to private monuments has been in place since the 1940s. The advisory board appointed for the purpose has a very wide participation. Most of the sites being living religious sites, the public had the opportunity to observe and criticise the interventions by the government authorities. Some restoration works of the ancient religious monuments were carried out by the societies established solely by the members of the public. Many sites being living religious places, pilgrims had the opportunity to comment and criticise the interventions through media. However, the top-down process of planning inherited by the colonial system had the fault of neglecting the opinion of the public.

Article 3: Legislation and Economy

Under this article, the charter recommends the provision of funds for heritage-management programmes and areas where legal provisos for the protection of the heritage are to be made. It recommends the provision of legislation 'appropriate to the needs, history, and traditions of each country and region, providing for *in situ* protection and research needs' without any form of bias. It recommends legislation to forbid destruction of monuments, sites and their surroundings by any means and to permit investigation and documentation when destruction is authorised. It recommends the provision of legislation required for all aspects of management such as conservation and maintenance. Punishments for violations are also to be included in legislation. It further recommends that the protection should extend to the unprotected and undiscovered parts of the heritage. Impact assessments and necessary steps in the case of development activities are recommended.

With regard to the legislative needs highlighted by the charter, it can be stated that all of them are incorporated into the *Antiquities Ordinance* of 1940, with a few additions in 1956 and 1998 (Wijesuriya 1996a). Protection is ensured for both identified and unidentified objects, monuments and sites irrespective of the social, geographical or any other types of divisions. Legislation applies to objects, monuments and sites located in both private and public properties. The protection of sites is not governed on the basis of race, religion or other such divisions. In a predominantly Buddhist country, monuments of diverse groups have been declared as protected monuments and even the colonial heritage has been raised to the World Heritage status among other indigenous sites (Wijesuriya 1996d).

The development of legislation for the protection of cultural heritage reflects some conflicts encountered by the colonial administration. The Heads of the Department during the colonial period fought hard against the restoration of the religious buildings by the local community. Legislation of 1940 was born mainly as a reaction of the authorities against these restorations. But the legislation itself contained procedures for restoration.

Article 4: Survey

This article highlights the importance of an inventory or a fuller knowledge of the archaeological resources of a given country for their proper management and protection and to develop strategies for the purpose. The importance of inventories as a primary resource database for scientific study and research is highlighted. Compilation of an inventory is regarded as a continuous and dynamic process.

The prime function of the Department of Archaeology as given in the *Antiquities Ordinance* of 1940 was the preparation of an inventory of ancient monuments. This is a continuous exercise and has been commenced from very early days. The department created a staff position in 1941 to handle this task alone. The inventory is prepared from the sources brought to notice of the Department by the public and systematic surveys carried out on selected geographical areas. Inventory items are supported by background information extracted from chronicles, inscriptions and other sources, and maintain a high scientific value (Schofield 2000: 79–91). The results are published annually.

Article 5: Investigation

Article 5 deals with the principles of investigation. It acknowledges the fact that archaeological knowledge is based 'principally on the scientific investigation of the archaeological heritage. Such investigation embraces the whole range of methods from non-destructive techniques through sampling to total excavation'. It recommends minimum destruction in the process of investigations. Non-destructive methods are advocated as against excavation. While emphasising the decision to excavate be taken only after careful assessment, it recommends excavation of sites threatened by various unavoidable means, excavation for the purpose of scientific research and for presentation. Attention is also drawn to UNESCO's 1956 recommendation on the excavation of archaeological sites.

The Department started in 1890 as a 'Survey', where it was expected to record archaeological ruins. This was fundamentally a non-destructive process, though certain buried monuments were exposed purely for the purpose of taking correct measurements for documentation in early days. Oertel (1903: 8) started criticising this in the 1890s. Ayrton took over the Department in 1912, with experience in excavation (including Egypt), but his untimely death prevented establishing a strong tradition in this activity. There was also a time when the excavations of monuments were carried out for the purpose of conservation and presentation. Although guided by a set of principles and procedures, both of these were unsatisfactory but were in keeping with the styles of the day. However, a strict set of measures was available in the *Antiquities Ordinance* of 1940 to prevent the destruction of the sites and to ensure that proper procedures are followed in excavation.

Publication of the annual reports of all the Departments was a statutory requirement, an opportunity used by the archaeologists to publish their work on a regular basis. The high standards of the publications during the colonial era can challenge even present-day archaeologists. In addition, it was also possible to publish them in a series called *Memoirs of the Archaeological Department*.

Article 6: Maintenance and Conservation

Recommendations connected with maintenance and conservation are given in Article 6. Conservation of monuments *in situ* and their regular maintenance are recommended. No excavation is to be carried out if proper maintenance and management cannot be guaranteed. Local participation for the conservation and maintenance of sites is recommended. Participation of indigenous people and their active management role is recommended. When selecting sites for protection it recommends 'the diversity of sites and monuments, based upon a scientific assessment of their significance and representative character, and not confined to the more notable and visually attractive monuments'.

In its one hundred years of work, the Department has given much emphasis to the maintenance and conservation of the country's heritage. At present,

80 per cent of its human and financial resources are allocated for these areas of heritage management. It is also in this context that we can demonstrate the management role of archaeology in protecting the heritage in this part of the world under the colonial rule.

Maintenance of sites and monuments possessed by the Department were carried out on a permanent basis with a regular staff employed for the purpose. A group of permanent masons were also employed as far back as the 1930s for regular weeding (Hettiaratchi 1990: 61). Weeds are common destructive forces of brick ruins in tropical conditions. There was also a mechanism to look after the isolated monuments with local participation. A person from the neighbouring village is appointed to an isolated monument as a paid guardian, whose responsibility is to look after the monument, clean the site on a regular basis and report to the Department of any major conservation needs. This proved to be a very successful system, which is still being used. With regard to the private monuments, it was the responsibility of the owner to maintain them but the *gramasevaka* or the village-based public servant was asked to visit the places monthly and report any conservation needs.

Contrary to the practice that prevailed in the West, *in situ* conservation was the only principle adopted by the Department. This was because the place value of religious sites was a main concern to the public, which underpins any conservation decision. The Western concept of moving buildings into different locations and making open-air museums was never in practice. However, a large number of site museums have been established for the storage and display of movable artefacts discovered from the sites and from neighbouring areas. One of the principles inserted in the *Ordinance* and of the standing orders of the Department is that no excavation to be carried out if no provisions are made for conservation. Hocart in the early 1920s had followed the principle that 'excavation is possible only if conservation is possible' (Hettiaratchi 1990: 60).

I have observed three distinct periods of conservation in Sri Lanka: the Exploratory (pre-1910); Consolidatory (1910–40); and Explanatory I (1940–60) and II (1960–90) periods (Wijesuriya 1993: 15–18). This has illustrated how the Department has progressed from mere documentation of monuments at the start, through consolidation of ruins, to the restoration of living religious monuments, while embracing international standards and nationally developed practices.

Conservation work has been carried out with a set of principles, procedures and techniques (known as standing orders of the Department). Marshall's conservation manual of the 1930s was in circulation. Principles to be followed in the preparation of restoration plans for privately owned monuments were included in the *Antiquities Ordinance* of 1940. All the modern principles, such as the documentation of every step of conservation and publication, were well respected from the beginning. Every aspect of academic and professional standards were maintained (Wijesuriya 1996b: 95–113).

Conservation management of living religious monuments needs elaboration, as it reflects the failure of the colonial rulers to impose the rules that were developing in Britain. Oertel (1903: 9) in 1890 states that 'as regards the general principles which should guide us in the task of conservation, I need hardly say that we should confine ourselves to preservation, and that restoration is only justified when the preservation of the rest of the structure demands it'. However, taking into consideration the religious needs of the people, he advocated the restoration of one of the *stupas* in Sri Lanka for which he prepared plans. Oertel was sent by the Royal Asiatic Society of Great Britain on request of the colonial government to prepare restoration of a major ruined *stupa* that dated to the second century BC. This was the time when Britain had embarked on a major campaign against the restoration of religious buildings (Wijesuriya 1993)!

This was also the time Sri Lankans were re-creating their lost identities by restoring their neglected heritage. Restoration was an inevitable need of the people whose monuments bear traditional cultural and religious significance other than their material values. These values have been illustrated during the colonial period itself:

> In controlling the restoration of ancient shrines by private bodies, the Department has undertaken a task bristling with many difficulties. It has to be carried out without hurting the religious susceptibilities of the propel; for this much work of an adductive nature has to be undertaken to convince the religious authorities that intervention by the Department does not affect their vested interests and traditional rights . . .
>
> (Paranavitana 1945: 43)

Restorations were carried out with a developed set of principles. What follows are some of the principles of restoration adopted by the Department during the colonial regime and, more importantly, 17 years before the Venice Charter was born (Wijesuriya 1996c).

> Moreover, it has to be kept in mind that the proper restoration of an ancient monument is a work of highly specialised nature, requiring in the person who carries it out a thorough knowledge of evolution of art, architecture and culture which produced it and a feeling therefore, often to be required by a lifetime devoted to it. Modern technical and scientific developments have also to be called into aid if such restoration is to be carried out efficiently, without endangering the ancient fabric.
>
> (Paranavitana 1947: 3)

Conservation becomes a true challenge when the complex needs of the users and owners are respected and accounted for. It is here that restoration is demanded and our challenge becomes greater. In this context, the experience of the Department over a century becomes useful in modern-day conservation efforts, where intangible values are being respected. The need for the restoration of monuments, which belonged to living religious traditions, was perhaps difficult to digest in Western society after the turbulent campaign led by people like Ruskin in the 1890s. This was what made the Western conservation professionals place their valuation of monuments on material remains and advocate the material authenticity (Jokilehto 1986: xxiii). However, the Asian experience discussed in Nara (Larsen 1995) has changed this view. Restoration of monuments is justifiable or inevitable as the particular cultures demand (Wijesuriya 2000a: 108). The spiritual values and functional needs of living religious monuments and the demand for restoration are aspects overlooked by the archaeologists in the past.

Article 7: Presentation, Information, Reconstruction

The presentation of sites is considered as the means to promote understanding of the past and the need for protection. Article 7 recommends that the information provided to the public should be revised as and when new knowledge is brought to light. Reconstruction is recommended for experimental research and interpretations. The need for precautions and to follow standard principles in reconstruction is highlighted. The presentation of sites was directly linked to conservation work and reflected in the annual programmes published by the government. The idea expanded from smaller monuments to large archaeological sites (Silva 1996; Wijesuriya forthcoming). Detailed descriptions of monuments, name-boards and footpaths were essential features of sites maintained by the Department. In fact, there were permanent positions in the Department for those involved in preparation of name boards, and so on. Guide maps, guide books and regular articles in the newspapers were conscious attempts in this direction (Fernando 1990: 82, 84). We believe that reconstruction not only serves experimental research and interpretation, but also the functional needs of different groups, an aspect always overlooked by the archaeologists. The Department possesses a wealth of knowledge in reconstruction work as it has been involved in many projects.

Article 8: Professional Qualifications

The need for high academic qualifications in relevant fields for the management of heritage, international co-operation in the process, standards of professional training and professional conduct are the highlights of this article. Shifts in academic training from conventional to new areas of *in situ* preservation, indigenous cultures, and so on, are recommended. Provisions for the professionals to update their knowledge and emphasis on heritage-management training are highlighted.

The existing administrative set-up allows a person to start his or her career in the department with any academic qualification and to advance towards being a sound archaeological heritage-management professional. Persons with primary university degrees in languages, chemistry, architecture and even a general arts degree (in addition to possessing skills on their own specialities) have become the Head of the Department of Archaeology by possessing required skills to manage the archaeological heritage of the country. This is not possible for the administrators or finance managers. The most important feature is that they had a gradual rise from the lower staff levels, which gave them sufficient time to acquire the wider knowledge required to be a better manager of the heritage.

In 1890, a colonial administrator was appointed as the Commissioner of Archaeology (the designation of the Head of the Department which was changed in 1990 to Director-General of Archaeology). The colonial rule then looked for professionals, which resulted in bringing in Ayrton, an archaeologist from England who had experience in Egypt. Since then, most of the appointees have been professional archaeologists. The first Sri Lankan to be appointed under the colonial rule was Paranavitana, who was appointed in 1940 and is considered to be the father of Sri Lankan archaeology. He obtained his PhD from Leiden University, The Netherlands, under distinguished oriental scholars in 1938. Since then all his successors have qualified with PhDs (from Oxford, Cambridge, Harvard, London, Leiden, etc.) before becoming Head of the Department. All of them started with primary degrees on subjects other than archaeology. Until the government took over the sole authority of appointing a Head of the Department by cabinet in the late 1980s, even the scheme of recruitment had specified higher qualifications for the position.

I argue strongly that it is only in this type of model that a manager envisaged by Cleere can be created. Cleere (1989: 16–17) explains his ideal heritage manager as follows:

> By definition they must have an extensive knowledge and understanding of the archaeological record and its interpretation, which bespeaks a primary training to university or equivalent level in the academic discipline of archaeology. This must include a solid practical grounding in the techniques of modern archaeology – survey and prospecting, excavation, the use of computers, and the like. In addition, archaeological heritage management acquire basic management skills such as financial control and budgeting, personal management, communication, project planning, human relation etc. It is important that they also receive training in the legislative framework of heritage protection, land use planning, health and safety etc. and understand the working of government at all levels, and of commerce and industry. Conservation must also be an integral element of training for heritage managers.

This speaks of more than one area of training that cannot be obtained only through university degrees. Such a vast knowledge can be gained through academic training combined with skill development programmes and experience of directly handling relevant activities over a period of time. The Department of Archaeology provides an opportunity for young graduates in archaeology or allied subjects to engage in professional development programmes and to gain experience over a period of time. The model is deliberately aimed at the training of a heritage manager. In addition, it is also aimed at the developing of an individual to act as the head of the antiquities department of the country. Cleere (1989: 17) has strong views on top-level management of heritage:

> All too often antiquities services are headed by specialist administrators, archaeologists being relegated to subordinate roles in management and decision making. Until the situation is reached when it is unthinkable that top-level management in any antiquities service should be in the hands of anyone other than a professional whose basic training was in archaeology, archaeological heritage management will not have reached maturity and heritage will remain at risk.

We can demonstrate that the antiquities services have been headed by professionals fulfilling Cleere's ideal for the last hundred years in Sri Lanka, until recently in India and in other neighbouring countries. Heads of the Department of Archaeology have been well respected in society, having authoritative views on relevant matters. However, archaeologists have been replaced by non-professional bureaucrats recently in many countries (Wijesuriya 2000b: 196). Apart from the attraction to the position by non-professionals, the managerial weaknesses of some archaeologists also contributed to this situation. This suggests that academic qualifications from archaeology should be combined with managerial skills, which can form a part of the archaeological education. An archaeologist with very little effort can become a manager but not vice versa (Wijesuriya 2000b: 196).

Article 9: International Co-operation

International co-operation, the sharing of information and the exchange of views, personnel and the new knowledge and methods for providing technical assistance are the recommendations of this final article. Internationalism at present-day levels is a recent phenomenon but a constant exchange of views among the colonial countries and the Western world has existed from the beginning.

CONCLUSION

The above discussion proves beyond doubt that archaeology itself was a subject taken seriously by the British during the colonial administration. It was built into the public administration system and considered a management discipline. It also reveals that the archaeological heritage management model which exists

in Sri Lanka, as well as in India, a vestige of the colonial legacy is, in fact, what
the Western world has tried to re-invent in the recent past. The model has
matured over a long period. It is a dynamic one with full potential to respond
to local needs and to grow and absorb any current ideals and practices and also
to adapt to new situations. It is a model that has undergone transition from
colonial domination to fully independent status in the countries concerned.
Even with such radical transitions its fundamentals have remained unchanged.
As mentioned previously, the world has acknowledged the existence of certain
aspects, but the valuable experiences that can be learned from the model have
been overlooked. Archaeology as an academic discipline is an essential management tool for the heritage protection in this part of the world. It has produced
a huge wealth of knowledge and, moreover, has protected substantial parts of
the archaeological heritage. Inquiry into these aspects will reveal both the
Britishness of the system and the elements of imperial power.

Today, however, there are obstacles to working as in the times of the 'sudda'.
Entire administrative machinery needs independence from bureaucracy,
politicisation, and archaic rules and regulations if the model of this nature is
to function properly. A simple example will illustrate this. In 1990, approval
was granted by the cabinet to recruit 64 new graduates to the Department
but the bureaucracy of the country has failed even by 2000 to recruit a single
graduate! This is in spite of the fact that the money was allocated every year
and there are over 10,000 graduates unemployed. There is no one accountable
for this type of serious mistake. While the archaeological heritage management
model that is being reinvented in Britain exists as a vestige of the imperial
power, we are now looking to the modern West for changes to the public
administration system. The President of Sri Lanka recently announced that
the government is in the process of revamping the public service, as has been
done in Australia, New Zealand, Malaysia, Canada and the UK. In this process,
we are not certain whether the archaeological heritage management system
discussed above will disappear or be apparent as a model for other countries
to follow.

REFERENCES

Antiquities Ordinance of Sri Lanka 1940, rev. 1956 and 1998. Enactment of the
    Government of Sri Lanka.
Bandaranayake, S. (1996) International recognition of the problems of conserving
    of cultural monuments together with ancient city centres – some personal observa-
    tions. In G. Wijesuriya (ed.), *Monuments and Sites – Sri Lanka*, 171–90. Colombo:
    ICOMOS Sri Lanka.
Cleere, H.F. (ed.) (1984) *Approaches to the Archaeological Heritage.* Cambridge: Cambridge
    University Press.
—— (ed.) (1989) *Archaeological Heritage Management in the Modern World.* London:
    Unwin Hyman.
Dagens, B. (tr.) (1985) *Mayamatha – an Indian Treatise on Housing, Architecture and
    Iconography.* New Delhi: Sitaram Bharatiya Institute of Scientific Research.

Deraniyagala, S.U. (1996) Monuments and sites – the archaeological heritage of Sri Lanka. In G. Wijesuriya (ed.), *Monuments and Sites – Sri Lanka*, 1–7. Colombo: ICOMOS Sri Lanka.

Fernando, M.B.W. (1990) History of the Department 1930–1950. In N. Wijesekera (ed.), *History of the Department of Archaeology*, 77–118. Colombo: Department of Archaeology.

Geiger, W. (tr.) (1960) *Mahavamsa or the Great Chronicle of Ceylon*. Colombo: Government Publication Bureau.

Hettiaratchi, S.B. (1990) History of the Department 1910–1930. In N. Wijesekera (ed.), *History of the Department of Archaeology*, 45–76. Colombo: Department of Archaeology.

ICOMOS (1993 and 1996) *Charter on Archaeological Heritage Management*. Sri Lanka: ICOMOS.

Jokilehto, J. (1986) A history of architectural conservation. Unpublished PhD thesis, York University.

Larsen, K.E. (ed.) (1995) *Nara Conference on Authenticity in Relation to the World Heritage Convention*. Paris: UNESCO.

McManamon, F.P. and Hatton, A. (eds), (2000) *Cultural Resources Management in Contemporary Society – Perspectives on Managing and Presenting the Past*. London: Routledge.

Oertel, F.O. (1903) *Report of the Restoration of Ancient Monuments at Anuradhapura*. Colombo: Ceylon Governmental Sessional Paper.

Paranavitana, S. (1945) *Administrative Report of the Department of Archaeology 1940–45*. Colombo: Government Publication Bureau.

—— (1947) *Protection of Ancient Monuments other than Those on Crown Land. A Pamphlet*. Colombo: Government Publication Bureau.

Rahula, W. (1960) *History of Buddhism in Ceylon*. Colombo: The Buddhist Cultural Centre.

Schofield, A.J. (2000) Now we know: the role of research in archaeological conservation practices in England. In F.P. McManamon and A. Hatton (eds), *Cultural Resources Management in Contemporary Society – Perspectives on Managing and Presenting the Past*, 76–92. London: Routledge.

Silva, R. (1996) A proposal for the layout of the ancient city of Anuradhapura – Ceylon. In G. Wijesuriya (ed.), *Monuments and Sites – Sri Lanka*, 147–50. Colombo: ICOMOS Sri Lanka.

Ucko, P.J. (1989) Foreword. In H.F. Cleere (ed.), *Archaeological Heritage Management in the Modern World*, ix–xiv. London: Unwin Hyman.

Wijesekera, N. (ed.) (1990) *History of the Department of Archaeology*. Colombo: Department of Archaeology.

Wijesuriya, G. (1993) *Restoration of Buddhist Monuments in Sri Lanka: The Case for an Archaeological Heritage Management Strategy*. Colombo: ICOMOS Sri Lanka.

—— (1996a) Legislation. In G. Wijesuriya (ed.), *Monuments and Sites – Sri Lanka*, 7–11. Colombo: ICOMOS Sri Lanka.

—— (1996b) Conservation and maintenance. In G. Wijesuriya (ed.), *Monuments and Sites – Sri Lanka*, 95–113. Colombo: ICOMOS Sri Lanka.

—— (1996c) Venice Charter, ICOMOS and other charters. In G. Wijesuriya (ed.), *Monuments and Sites – Sri Lanka*, 203–9. Colombo: ICOMOS Sri Lanka.

—— (ed.) (1996d) Special volume on European architecture and town planning outside Europe (Dutch Period). *Ancient Ceylon* 18. Colombo: Department of Archaeology.

—— (2000a) Conserving the Sacred Temple of the Tooth Relic (a World Heritage Site) in Sri Lanka. *Public Archaeology* 1(2): 99–108.

Wijesuriya, G. (2000b) Review of the book *Cultural Resources Management in Contemporary Society – Perspectives on Managing and Presenting the Past*, by (eds) F.P

McManamon and A Hatton. *Conservation and Management of Archaeological Sites*, 4(3): 194–6. London: James and James Science Publishers.

—— (forthcoming) Proposal for the presentation of Mirisaweti monastic complex. In *Annual Report of the Department of Archaeology 1993* Colombo: Department of Archaeology.

Concluding comments: Disruptive narratives? Multidimensional perspectives on 'Britishness'

MARY C. BEAUDRY

In one way or another, directly or otherwise, all of the chapters in this book explore the concept of 'Britishness' by problematising and unpacking what the term has been taken to mean by various people, at different times, both 'at home' in the British Isles and abroad in the many colonies that that were incorporated into what became known as the British Empire. This diverse set of case studies examines the shared material culture of Britain and its colonies as well as its regional differences through a broadly comparative framework that works to subvert the sweeping narrative of 'British imperialism' by working outward from specific contexts, prying into its gaps and omissions. Here we find an array of intriguing examples of historical archaeologists working at 'writing antitriumphalist histories that emphasize the role of social relations as well as individuals, the common people as well as the prominent, the struggles along class, color, and gender lines, and the emergent social and cultural diversity of a supposedly uniform nation-state' (Paynter 2000a: 23).

The trend towards a global historical archaeology was given impetus through the writings of scholars such as James Deetz (1991, 1993) and Charles Orser (1996), who shared the conviction that historical archaeology's contribution to an understanding of colonialism is best derived from a global, comparative approach that looks for and tries to explain universal patterns within European colonialism in the early modern and modern eras. Yet the authors of the chapters in the present volume do not find any great measure of satisfaction with the vaguely defined programme of decontextualised global comparison advocated by Orser and Deetz. This is because so-called global archaeology of this sort is a project that is bound to fail as it is based on an erroneous and incomplete understanding of colonial discourses and the culture(s) of colonialism. What is more, its underlying premises are directly contradictory to much of what is now understood about the consequences of colonialism (for correctives, see Funari et al. 1999; Hall 2000).

Chris Gosden (2001: 241) points out that all archaeology today is post-colonial, and that a growing number of archaeologists have been influenced by what is termed post-colonial theory, which critiques colonialism and the academic disciplines that have produced the scholars who write about colonialism, 'a series of discussions about the sorts of cultural forms and identities created through colonial encounters'. The primary thrust of this critique is that colonialism is best understood as a cultural process, not as a cultural system, that it cannot be understood as a global, transhistorical and logical imposition of power, that it generates and is generated out of a great variety of asymmetrical inter-social relationships (Thomas 1994: 2–3).

Post-colonial theory cross-cuts many disciplines, from literary theory to cultural studies and beyond, and its critique of the role of anthropology in constructing narratives of domination is part of the impetus for the emergence of a new brand of historical anthropology that takes local manifestations of the culture of colonialism as its main subject matter. It is also extremely relevant to the work of historical archaeologists and enriches the work of those who incorporate its concepts and perspectives into their work (cf. Hall 2000). While offering an outstretched umbrella of concepts and methodological approaches, it does not, however, readily accommodate any of the versions of a unified or unitary historical archaeology espoused of late by several major figures in the field (e.g. Orser 1996; Leone and Potter 1999; Paynter 2000b).

Even a cursory examination of the literature of post-colonial theory makes it 'increasingly clear that only localized theories and historically specific accounts can provide much insight into the varied articulations of colonizing and counter-colonial representations and practices' (Thomas 1994: ix). Nicholas Thomas (1994: x) notes that

> colonialism can only be traced through its plural and particularized expressions. The paramount irony of contemporary colonial studies must be that critics and scholars, who one presumes wish to expose the false universality and hegemony of imperial expansion and modernization, seem unwilling themselves to renounce the aspiration of theorizing globally on the basis of particular strands in European philosophy.

The present collection of essays moves cleanly away from the once-popular but misguided and wholly incorrect notion that colonialism 'was monolithic, uncontested, and efficacious' (Thomas 1994: 12), 'a homogeneous thing of the past' (ibid.: 13). Anthropologist Ann Stoler has suggested that the attention ethnographers have given to cultural complexity among the colonised has never been matched by interest or sensitivity to heterogeneity and tension among colonisers, noting the tendency to perceive 'colonialism and its European agents as an abstract force, as a *structure* imposed on local *practice*' (Stoler 1989: 135). The foregoing chapters offer the antidote of exploring localised manifestations of colonialism's culture in a variety of settings through closely contextualised case studies, turning the notion of British imperialism and its manifestation through colonialism in on itself, inspecting variation both within Britain and within its colonies. The exercise is as vast and complex as the former British Empire was far-flung; what we have thus far is no more than a series of fragments, of bits and pieces of the untold story. There is a great deal of work to be done before our understanding can constitute more than merely the comprehension of scattered images, glimpses, but the project is surely a worthy one. Only by exposing gaps and silences and questioning historical givens can we hope to liberate ourselves and others from the grasp of the mythic grand narrative and the false inevitabilities represented by history written in the dominant mode.

Researchers employing a diversity of theoretical and methodological approaches provide for a somewhat disparate and patchy look at British imperialism, but nevertheless the essays share themes. Funari, Jones, and Hall, in *Historical Archaeology: Back from the Edge* (1999:11), delineate as common to postcolonial historical archaeologies: identity; power; domination; resistance (or, as Lydon notes in this volume, in some cases, disregard); nationalism; ethnicity; and the interplay among these, especially the relationship between power and identity (see also Meskell 2001). In this more closely thematic volume we note the exploration of some additional themes, particularly an attention to finding ways of complicating and problematising 'Britishness' in the first place; some authors approach this through the examination of regionalism within Britain (see especially Green but also Klingelhofer and Leech). I argue that there is also room for further explorations of regionalism within English settler colonies, many of which – North America, for example – were anything but internally uniform, a point reinforced by Mytum in his overview of mortuary practices throughout Britain and its colonies.

It really is not appropriate for those of us who know better to talk or write about 'British culture' in totalising and universal terms. In this volume the chapters by Graves, Southern and Merrington provide clear examples of diversity within British culture and of shifting meanings of the concept of 'empire'. Johnson offers ideas about how to undo what he calls the 'muffling inclusiveness' that masks differences not just within the British Isles but within 'traditional English' culture that is referenced as the baseline against which 'Britishness' was and is measured throughout its former Empire. Symonds makes it clear that Irish and Scots people who themselves were 'colonised' by the English have distinct ethnic identities, and Brooks makes similar observations about the rural inhabitants of Wales. In each case study similar objects, often mass produced in heavily industrialised parts of the Empire, were assigned different meanings by marginalised groups, though in the end these different meanings seem always to be involved with the construction of distinctive identities that subverted the ethnic, social or racial definitions imposed on people by their colonisers.

It is just these sorts of subtle differences in the deployment of material culture that lend historical archaeology its own subversive power. Here the contextual approach first establishes a local framework for interpretation, standing in contrast to decontextualised comparisons that force the researcher to argue backwards towards context only after he or she perceives some seeming anomaly in the data (see Beaudry 1996). If we are aware of how the intersubjective space of cultural transactions can be constructed through deliberate manipulation of material culture, as in the case of the 'mangling' of symbols of

Victorianism in the American West (Praetzellis and Praetzellis 2001), we are prepared to interpret ubiquitous items such as ceramics not as universal reflections of monolithic 'total institutions' but as potentially multivalent props employed in colonial (and post-colonial) discourses. Perhaps shocking to some is the very notion that heritage management in and of itself is an outgrowth of colonialism and colonial discourse, but in this volume Wijesuriya demonstrates the extent to which it was British colonial rule in Sri Lanka that introduced the notion of heritage as something to be managed in the first place.

What the essays in this book provide us are multiple demonstrations of the richness of the 'historicised style of analysis' that Nicholas Thomas espouses, which he acknowledges has to be carried out 'in a way that must be partial and illustrative rather than exhaustive and extensive' (1994: x). I think it is important for us to ask, just what can historical archaeology contribute to our understanding of colonialism? To my way of thinking what we are uniquely equipped to do as historical archeologists, through our accumulation from diverse sources of insights and strategies that are recontextualised in our close critical readings of sites and of place (see, e.g., chapters by Lawrence, Seretis, Lydon, Malan and Klose, and Lafleur), is to provide historicised studies of local contexts that can lead to a more 'nuanced understanding of the plurality of colonizing endeavors and their continuing effects' (Thomas 1994: 20).

If, as Lyotard (1984: 37) has so aptly noted, 'The grand narrative has lost its credibility', we are still charged with the task of constructing stories – 'explanatory structures' (Morris 1998: 254–5) – the sorts of narratives that Hall refers to as 'colonial transcripts' (Hall 2000). The chapters in this book show just how much we stand to gain if we accept the challenge to push our interpretations beyond bland generalisations about 'colonial' or 'imperial' material culture and colonial interactions, to ply back and forth between our study of imperial power and settler colony to ferret out how in each instance material culture in all its manifestations, including archaeological commonplaces like ceramics, figured in colonial discourses as part of local knowledge in multifarious contexts and to examine the ways they were used in the construction of cultural meanings and cultural identities.

REFERENCES

Beaudry, M.C. (1996) Reinventing historical archaeology. In L.A. De Cunzo and B.L. Herman (eds), *Historical Archaeology and the Study of American Culture*, 473–97. Winterthur, DE: Henry Francis du Pont Winterthur Museum.

Deetz, J.F. (1991) Introduction: archaeological evidence of sixteenth- and seventeenth-century encounters. In L. Falk (ed.), *Historical Archaeology in Global Perspective*, 1–9. Washington, DC: Smithsonian Institution Press.

—— (1993) *Flowerdew Hundred: The Archaeology of a Virginia Plantation, 1619–1864.* Charlottesville, VA: University Press of Virginia.

Funari, P.P.A. (1999) Historical archaeology from a world perspective. In P.P.A Funari, M. Hall and S. Jones (eds), *Historical Archaeology: Back from the Edge*, 37–66. London: Routledge.

Funari, P.P.A., Jones, S. and Hall, M. (1999) Introduction: archaeology in history. In P.P.A Funari, M. Hall and S. Jones (eds), *Historical Archaeology: Back from the Edge*, 1–20. London: Routledge.

Gosden, C. (2001) Post-colonial archaeology: issues of culture, identity and knowledge. In I. Hodder (ed.), *Archaeological Theory Today*, 241–61. Cambridge: Polity Press.

Hall, M. (2000) *Archaeology and the Modern World: Colonial Transcripts in South Africa and the Chesapeake*. London: Routledge.

Leone, M.P. and Potter, P.B., Jr (eds) (1999) *Historical Archaeologies of Capitalism*. New York: Kluwer Academic/Plenum Publishers.

Lyotard, J.-F. (1984) *The Postmodern Condition*. Minneapolis, MN: University of Minnesota Press.

Meskell, L. (2001) Archaeologies of identity. In I. Hodder (ed.), *Archaeological Theory Today*, 187–213. Cambridge: Polity Press.

Morris, D. (1998) *Illness and Culture in the Postmodern Age*. Berkeley, CA: University of California Press.

Orser, C.E. (1996) *A Historical Archaeology of the Modern World*. New York: Plenum Press.

Paynter, R. (2000a) Historical and anthropological archaeology: forging alliances. *Journal of Archaeological Research* 8(1): 1–37.

Paynter, R. (2000b) Historical archaeology and the post-Columbian world of North America. *Journal of Archaeological Research* 8(3): 169–217.

Praetzellis, A. and Praetzellis, M. (2001) Mangling symbols of gentility in the Wild West: case studies in interpretive archaeology. *American Anthropologist* 103(3): 645–54.

Stoler, A.L. (1989) Rethinking colonial categories: European communities and the boundaries of rule. *Comparative Studies in Society and History* 31: 134–61.

Thomas, N. (1994) *Colonialism's Culture: Anthropology, Travel and Government*. Princeton, NJ: Princeton University

Index

CPSIA information can be obtained at www.ICGtesting.com
Printed in the USA
BVOW04s1614200713

326351BV00004B/41/P

9 780415 589055